Marilyn Tucker Quayle & Nancy Tucker Northcott

✦✦✦ THE ✦✦✦ CAMPAIGN

A NOVEL

ZondervanPublishingHouse

Grand Rapids, Michigan

A Division of HarperCollinsPublishers

The Campaign
Copyright © 1996 by Marilyn Tucker Quayle and Nancy Tucker Northcott

A hardcover edition was previously co-published by ZondervanPublishingHouse and HarperCollins*Publishers*

Requests for information should be addressed to:

ZondervanPublishingHouse
Grand Rapids, Michigan 49530

Library of Congress Cataloging-in-Publication Data

Quayle, Marilyn T.
    The campaign : a novel / Marilyn Tucker Quayle and Nancy Tucker Northcott.
        p.   c.m.
    ISBN 0–310–21653-2   (Softcover)
    I. Northcott, Nancy T.   II. Title.
    PS3567.U24C36   1996
    813'.54—dc20   96-3389
                                                                    CIP

This is a work of fiction. The events described here are imaginary; the settings and characters are fictitious and are not intended to represent specifice places or persons living or dead.

Photograph on page ten by Cleo Photography, St. Paul, Minnesota
Interior design by Sue Vandenberg Koppenol

Printed in the United States of America

97 98 99 00 01 02 / ❖ DH/ 10 9 8 7 6 5 4 3 2 1

*This book is dedicated with thanksgiving
to those Americans, Honest and Wise, whose sacrifices have
secured and preserved the blessings of liberty for us all.*

Acknowledgments

Without the help and inspiration of family and friends, we would have been unable to complete this book. Our deepest thanks to our understanding husbands, Tom and Dan, and to our children for their unfailing support and encouragement.

Special thanks are extended to our sister Sally Tucker; Nancy's children Melissa, Craig, and Amy; and to Elizabeth Bowling for pitching in and helping with computer editing. Our brother Jim Tucker kindly lent his firearms expertise to ensure accuracy. Sandra Soesbe did yeoman service for us as a specialty reader. Thank you all.

No book is published without the help of a good editor. We were pleased to have David Lambert of Zondervan as ours. He and his associate Lori Walburg were patient, helpful, and ever pleasant—even with last-minute changes.

Finally, thanks to the many friends who offered assistance and lifted our spirits. We are truly blessed with our family and friends.

Cast of Characters

Robert Hawkins Grant—United States Senator from Georgia
    Rachel Grant—His wife, an oncologist in Washington, D.C.
    India—Their elder daughter, a senior at Georgetown University
    Bailey—Their elder son, a junior at Georgetown University
    Olivia—Their younger daughter, a senior in high school
    Henry—Their younger son, an eighth grader
Tucker Grant—Bob Grant's older brother
    Melissa Grant—Tucker's wife
Curtis Grant—Bob Grant's younger brother

Cynthia Novitsky—Grant's administrative assistant
Mike Masterson—Grant's campaign manager
    Robby Hoge—Grant's driver during his Georgia campaign
Stephen Yao—Friend of Grant's
    Ramon Guiterrez—Employed by Yao
    Tommy Shipp—Employed by Yao
Matt Goldie—Friend of Grant's
Ginger Wright—Fulton County Republican Chairman
    John Wright—Her husband
Brandon Bascham—Oconee County Republican Chairman
Benjamin Dashev—Deputy Chief of Mission at the Israeli Embassy

The President of the United States—POTUS
    Estelle—The First Lady
M. Eugene Corforth—White House Chief of Staff
    Amy Corforth—His wife
Jonathan Hunter—Attorney General of the United States, Head of NIIA
    Joey Hunter—AG's son
    Rebecca Hunter—AG's wife
Chadwick Stevenson—National Security Advisor to the President
    Edmund Miller—National Security Council staff member
    Charles Kendall—National Security Council staff member
Phillip Loomis—Late United States Senator from New York
    Janet Loomis—His widow, former cancer patient of Rachel Grant

Peter Evans—Editor of the *Washington Herald*

Kirk Vinton—Investigative reporter for the *Washington Herald*

Russell P. Frederickson—Murdered reporter for the *Washington Herald*
    Corinne Frederickson—Reporter's widow

Jimmy Jenks—Sheriff of Oconee County, Georgia
    Martha Jenks—His sister-in-law, owner of Martha's Fabulous Diner

Hank Farrar—Chief deputy

Sally—Computer expert

Gus—Watkinsville hardware store owner

Captain Fleming—Washington, D.C., police officer

Sergeant Alvarez—New York City police officer

Derek Bender—NIIA chief investigator

Tobias Stewart Caruso—Candidate for Senator from Georgia

Maribeth Pariss—Former employee in Grant's Atlanta office
    George Beterman—Maribeth's boyfriend

Gayla Sergek—Former employee in Grant's Atlanta office

Shirley Spade—Former employee in Grant's Atlanta office

Hal Olexey—Convicted drug dealer

Frances Sandborne—Professor at Georgetown University

Cora Snyder—Professor at Georgetown University

Anne Peabody—Late stockbroker
    Julie—Peabody's secretary
    Craig C. Flannery—Peabody's lawyer

Scott Patterson—Young boy at Crazy Sam's

Sherrill Holmes—Bailey Grant's girlfriend

Milton Clark—Bailey Grant's best friend

Andrew Stoner—Friend of Bailey Grant

Larry "Bear" Baranowski—Friend of Bailey Grant

Reggie Dixon—Friend of Andrew Stoner
    Angel Soesbe—Dixon's girlfriend

Elaine Thomas—TV announcer

David Curry—TV announcer

Preserve me, O God, for in Thee do I put my trust.

THE HOLY BIBLE, PSALM 16:1
INSCRIPTION IN THE SENATE CHAPEL OF THE CAPITOL

Sunday, October 25:

Nine Days Before the Election

Russell Frederickson is dead."

Senator Bob Grant turned a startled face to Mike Masterson, his press secretary. Masterson leaned closer and raised his voice to be heard above the chant of "Grant! Grant! Grant!" echoing behind the high-school auditorium curtain. "Found dead in his motel room. Shot."

Grant's ruggedly handsome face softened with concern. "Robbery?" he asked.

"Who knows? He was found a few minutes ago. No details yet, but definitely not a suicide."

"Russell Frederickson murdered—hard to believe." Grant thought of the intense young reporter who'd been dogging him for over three weeks, visibly yearning to break a story that would cost Grant the election. Aggressive reporters like Frederickson must make plenty of enemies. But murder?

On the other side of the curtain the spirited chant slowly subsided. Chairs scraped, and feet shuffled. The murmur of voices throbbed both with anticipation and with the comfortable camaraderie of those secure in their shared values and beliefs.

Grant's pulse quickened as he awaited his cue. He loved these rallies. For him they embodied the strength and hope of the country—profoundly American celebrations of freedom. He felt an odd mixture of humility and pleasure at being the focus. That cheering crowds of diverse backgrounds and all races would work together to reelect him, a black man, United States Senator from Georgia proved that faith, family, and love of freedom were powerful unifiers.

Grant heard Brandon Bascham, Republican Party Chairman for Oconee County, Georgia, begin his introduction. Bascham's booming voice expounded on Grant's virtues, including an unabashedly partisan account of how the year before Grant had almost single-handedly rescued Cuba from the hands of yet another dictator, one even worse than the late, unlamented Fidel Castro. His remarks well-seasoned with the crowd's cheers, Bascham exulted that their Senator Bob Grant had the courage to fight for what was right and had even stood up to the President of the United States to insure that justice was done.

Grant smiled to himself at his friend's hyperbole. That *had* been a most satisfactory, though admittedly white-knuckle time, but definitely not to his credit alone.

"Find out about Frederickson's family," he said, his lips only inches from Masterson's ear to be heard above the roar of the crowd.

Bascham's voice rose as he reached the climax of his introduction. "I can't tell you how proud it makes me," he shouted, "to present the best senator the great state of Georgia has ever had. . ."

Grant looked toward the stage and squared his shoulders. He made an impressive figure. A tall man, more distinguished than handsome, he carried the few added pounds of middle age with a straight-backed equanimity indicative of both his military background and relaxed personality. "I want to write Frederickson's family a note," he said without turning.

Masterson nodded and jotted himself a reminder.

". . . and if the rest of the nation is as smart as we are here in Georgia," Bascham thundered in conclusion, "the next President of the United States, Robert Hawkins Grant!"

Masterson grinned and slapped Grant on the back. The Senator took the steps two at a time and strode onto the bunting-festooned stage. The crowd went crazy.

Every blemish of the tired motel room was revealed by the penetrating halogen lights of the murder scene investigation. Oconee County, Georgia, may have been primarily rural, but even here murder investigations had a set rhythm. The fingerprint expert, the ballistics expert, the coroner, all the professionals worked together with the precision of too-often repeated practice. The well-choreographed activity at this murder scene, revolving around the body of Russell P. Frederickson, recently robbed of life if not possessions, was different only in the particulars.

The phone on its side amidst the mess of papers littering the floor; the browning apple core sticking out from under one paper pile; the motel pen leaning against an overturned thick white ceramic mug, a drying blotch of coffee forming a halo around it; the white paper bag with a wrapped hamburger and cold fries tumbling from it; the black velvet painting of overripe bananas, grapes, and apples, hanging crookedly on the faded wall, fruit in no way tempting to the hairy black fly he heard buzzing louder, then more distant, as it circled near the bed—Jimmy

Jenks, sheriff of Oconee County, Georgia, for twenty-two years now, looked everywhere but in that direction.

He heard old Burt grunt with the weighty effort of exertion. He heard the metallic sag of the gurney. With slow dignity, he removed his brown round-brimmed sheriff's hat and held it over his heart. As if on a switch, the room turned quiet. Jenks's eyes narrowed and followed the now-full body bag on the gurney, staring after it even when the motel room door closed on the cool October sunlight outside.

Jenks always did that. Hank Farrar, his deputy, didn't quite understand, but he, too, stood hat in hand. Nowadays, Hank did most everything he did, Jenks thought to himself, part in good humor—he was a good-humored man—but part with a tired sigh. He could almost hear Hank's thoughts: The sheriff was getting old—fifty-seven, the sheriff snorted to himself—and who better to take over than his number-one deputy.

Maybe it *was* time to quit, Jenks thought. Murders were commonplace these days, even in this quiet countryside. Too much hatred, too many folks expecting something for nothing, demanding it, too little value placed on privacy, responsibility, even life.

But this murder was something else, Jenks was sure. It just didn't feel right. No glaring differences, but just not right all the same. He'd seen too much random violence over the years not to have a well-honed instinct about this one.

Jenks slowly circled the room, pausing every few steps to jot down information and impressions in the notebook he'd begun for this case. He surveyed the mess on the floor. The room's only wastebasket, military green and metal, was overturned. Crumpled papers, most covered with type, were strewn in an almost perfect circle around it. Might even have been deliberate, Jenks thought. He would read through those papers tomorrow. Could be someone expected him to, and no need to disappoint him. Lots of clues for a man to follow, an embarrassment of clues, seemed like. Made his skin positively prickle with suspicion.

He walked to the simulated-wood desk and thoughtfully examined the memo pad they'd found there, half covered by Ma Bell's well-worn book and an almost pristine Gideon Bible. "Fingerprints?" he asked.

"Room's been used a lot," Farrar told him. "Boys got a few good lifts—most probably his and the maid's, though could be any of the folks who stayed here before."

"Could be," Jenks agreed. "I'm going back to the office. Try calling this Evans." He tapped the pad in its protective plastic bag. The name Evans had been printed in caps at the top, followed by a phone number, area code 202—Washington, D.C., if Jenks recollected right. Maybe Evans, whoever he was, would know something about the murdered man.

"You finish up here," he told his men. "And take care. Don't miss a thing. This is one murder those reporters are going to be howling about—one of their own and covering a Senate campaign, too." He paused with his hand on the doorknob. "Don't you go telling those reporters anything. For that matter, don't tell anyone. Heads'll roll if there's any loose talk. I mean it. Wives, girlfriends, anyone. I'll do all the talking around here."

Sunlight streamed through the windows of the Oval Office, throwing blocks of white light onto the blue wing-backed chairs flanking the fireplace. The President straightened from the mantel where he'd been leaning and began pacing the room, a technique he'd used for years to avoid direct eye contact with those importuning or berating him and which now brought with it the comfort of habit.

"Grant's starting to develop a following," he said, stopping to stare at the two men in the room, his most valued advisors as well as closest friends: Attorney General Jonathan Hunter and White House Chief of Staff M. Eugene Corforth. "Grant's harangues against us are being mimicked by talk radio," he added with some bitterness. The object of his concern was Robert Hawkins Grant, junior senator from Georgia, running in the coming November off-year election.

"Grant has the gall to challenge my foreign-policy decisions," he groused, but without undue heat. Such opposition was annoying, but standard politics. If anything, he relished the challenge, confident he would find a winning angle. He always did, he and Hunter. The irritant the President found hard to tolerate came from Grant himself. Grant was beginning to develop a following outside Georgia. That took the issue beyond annoying. "Now Grant's hammering our drug interdiction policy," he added, letting his annoyance show.

"Voters like that kind of thing," Hunter reminded him. "The lone voice against 'crime and corruption.'" His tone added the quotation marks. "Give the self-righteous prig his due—Grant's good. He understands what voters want."

Hunter was a short man, barely five feet five inches, but no one ever thought of him as small in any sense. His unconscious air of confidence gave him stature. He deferred to no one. The few who had challenged him had long since been vanquished from the arena of power.

"Voter perception is everything," Corforth said, his naturally ruddy face growing even ruddier. "Grant appeals to the people right now. He's positioning himself perfectly for a run for the presidency. I was told *Time* is coming out with a piece on him right after the election. They may even give him the cover. Either way, it'll do wonders for his credibility nationally. He's looking good, really good."

Hunter, his chin resting on steepled fingers, gave him a speculative look. Corforth was a bit too positive toward Grant. Handicap your opponents, yes. But excessive compliments—that was a sign of something else.

Mentally storing away this newest sign of change—at times even of softness—that he thought he'd detected in Corforth, Hunter slid his gaze to the President.

"If Grant wins this election by a wide margin," Hunter told him, "and barring a miracle, it'll be a landslide—he'll be the front-runner for the Republicans for sure. He'll be tough to beat."

"I can see he would have appeal," the President countered, his face hardening into lines of displeasure, "the first black candidate of a major party. But tough for me to beat? Come on now, Hunt. For me?"

Hunter merely nodded.

The President frowned in annoyance and resumed pacing. He stopped to gaze out the window and then turned back toward the two men. "Then he mustn't win by a landslide," he said. His eyes bright with the thoughts his mind considered and rejected, he stared at the Presidential Seal woven at the center of the dark blue oval rug which covered all but the edges of the intricately patterned parquet floor. His voice when he continued was reflective. "It isn't too late for us to weigh in for his opponent. Can we do anything for Caruso?"

"He's definitely salable," Hunter replied, if possible sitting even straighter in his chair. "A Horatio Alger success story, and he's a good speaker—plenty of country humor. They seem to like that down there. We sure could do worse. But unless Grant makes a major blunder—and he won't, not on his own—Caruso could be a Kennedy, and he still wouldn't win. Grant's entrenched and knows it."

"Nothing we can do?" The President watched his friend closely, gauging the innuendoes in the answer by the degree of shrewdness in Hunter's eyes. The nuances of their conversational style had been honed over years of friendship and political association, most notably the latter, and offered the advantage of communication on two levels, one of them unknown and unknowable to all others. Even Corforth couldn't intercept it.

"Nothing that would enhance your stature, at least at this point," Hunter told him. "Caruso's the only one who thinks he has a chance of winning. By the way," he said, looking directly at the President and forcing him to hold that look, "I had John Smythe contacted yesterday."

John Smythe? Corforth wondered, glancing through shuttered eyes from Hunter to the President. Who was John Smythe? A vague uneasiness slowly seeped in to fill that void of unaccustomed ignorance. Knowledge was power in Washington. Being out of the loop meant being eased out of power. Corforth slipped his hand into his pocket and began working his worry beads, holdovers from his college days in the late sixties and a sure sign to others of his anxiety.

"John Smythe? Good." The President bestowed a reassuring smile on Corforth. His eyes, however, continued some inner calculation. "Smythe's a master at turning an election around."

"With the help of a timely misstep by your predecessor," Hunter noted sardonically, peering over his half glasses.

"Whatever," the President rejoined with a shrug. "We won, didn't we? See what you can come up with on this Grant problem. A strong challenge, we don't need."

Giving a dismissive wave, he turned his back.

Corforth and Hunter left.

Of the three, only Corforth's face showed lines of strain. Furtively, he unwrapped an antacid tablet and popped it into his mouth. Even he wasn't sure exactly what worried him, but his stomach was definitely sending signals.

Sheriff Jenks dialed the number written on the memo pad in Russell Frederickson's motel room. He leaned back in his oversized leather desk chair, contoured through years of service to envelop every curve of his massive body, and waited patiently to be put through to Evans. Turned out Peter Evans was editor of the *Washington Herald*, D.C.'s biggest paper and one of the most influential media outlets in the country.

Jenks liked placing these calls himself. It gave him a feel for the other's sense of self-importance. This time he was shuffled through four women before Evans deigned to speak himself.

"I've been expecting your call," Evans said peremptorily.

"You have?" Jenks asked, his words dripping with a pronounced southern drawl not usually so evident in his speech. "You were expectin' this ol' sheriff from clear down in Oconee County, Georgia, to be callin' you? I'm right surprised."

"You *are* calling about the Russell Frederickson murder, aren't you?" Evans asked, his pencil beating an impatient tattoo on his desk.

"That I am. That I am," Jenks said soothingly. "You mind if I tape this? Wouldn't want to forget anything important. The old memory ain't what it used to be."

"No, go ahead," Evans replied. "I'll tape it, too, just to keep you honest."

Jenks turned on the tape recorder. "I'm wonderin'," he said after a slight pause to roll Evans's "honest" jab around his mind, "how you knew 'bout this here murder so quick-like, Mr. Evans."

"Quick!" Evans exploded. "The body was discovered over two hours ago! The paper was called almost immediately."

"Mind tellin' me who called?"

"Of course not," Evans said, taking a steadying breath. "A stringer called in the story . . ." His voice trailed off in the face of the dead silence on the other end of the line. "Let me explain from the beginning," he said, forced patience resounding in his voice.

"I'd be right pleased if you would."

"All right, but I haven't much time." When the sheriff made no reply, Evans gave a much-put-upon sigh but began speaking. "Russell Frederickson was covering the Grant-Caruso campaign for us."

"You take a look-see at *all* Senate races?" Jenks interrupted. "That right?"

"No, no," Evans said. "Just those of special interest. Why don't you let me explain, and *then* you can ask your questions."

"Mighty fine idea, Mr. Evans," Jenks agreed, broadening his drawl even more and adding a touch of twang for good measure. "Mighty fine. You just say your piece. I got all the time a body could want."

"As I was saying," Evans continued with poorly disguised contempt, "Frederickson was covering the campaign and had been for several weeks. He called in two days ago. Asked to speak to me personally. Said he was on to something big, something damaging to Bob Grant. You do know who I mean, don't you? Robert Hawkins Grant, the Senator?"

"Now, Mr. Evans. Most everybody in Georgia knows Senator Grant. Cain't say I've ever met the man personal-like, but I know who you mean. Course I do. A fine-looking colored man," Jenks finished, hoping calling Grant "colored" wasn't a bit much even for the dumb redneck image he was cultivating so assiduously.

"Good, Sheriff," Evans said, apparently finding Jenks's words no more than he would expect from a small-town southern sheriff. Boss Hogg come to life, no doubt, Jenks thought with a ghost of a smile.

"Then you understand how vulnerable Grant is right now with the election only days away," Evans continued, his impatience in no way tempered. "Frederickson was excited when he called. Said he'd found something that would do 'irreparable damage to Grant both personally and politically.' That's a direct quote, Sheriff. When I was informed of Frederickson's death, of course I expected to hear from someone in authority. Find what Frederickson had on Grant, and you'll find the motive for the murder."

Jenks remained silent for a long moment. "Nothin' more to tell me, Mr. Evans?"

"Of course there's more," the editor retorted sarcastically. "But they're details. Irrelevant. I've been in this business a long time. Trust me—my instincts are always right, and my instincts say Grant's all you need to know."

"Well, now, I reckon you may be right, but let's start with some of them details. This here stringer for one. Just how'd he come to tell you 'bout this murder so quick-like?"

"A stringer," Evans said quickly, wanting to end the conversation since Jenks obviously was too slow to know anything useful, "is a reporter who doesn't work for one paper but sells his stories to any interested venue." Evans paused as if daring Jenks to ask what a *venue* was. Jenks didn't oblige. "This particular stringer had been covering the Grant campaign for several days, was staying at the same motel as Frederickson, knew we'd want to know, and called immediately. Simple as that."

"Mighty simple," Jenks agreed, drawling each word slowly. "Thank you, sir, for clearin' that up. Maybe you can clear up somethin' else: your name and phone number here on this pad in Mr. Frederickson's room. His handwritin', I'd reckon."

"I told you. Frederickson called about Grant several times, the last time from New York two days ago. A big story. Obviously, he wrote my name and number down."

"New York, you say." Jenks paused, the better to fan Evans's arrogance. "That's right interesting. Any idea how he came to be back in Oconee County?"

"How should *I* know?" Evans retorted bitingly. "Following a lead, I would have to assume. We don't baby-sit our reporters, Jenks, certainly not one of Frederickson's caliber."

"I don't expect you do, sir," Jenks said equitably. "This here big story—any ideas 'bout that?"

"Not really." Evans's voice became thoughtful, losing its impatient edge. "All Frederickson said was that it was big and damaging. Said he was keeping a copy of his notes in his briefcase and the original in his computer. He needed a few more facts and interviews before he was ready to go public. Said he had one especially interesting angle he'd just heard and wanted to check before committing himself. A real eye-opener, he called it. Frederickson was thorough, a sound reporter. But the story's there, at least enough to provide Grant's motive from what Frederickson told me. Have you gone through his briefcase? Brown leather, pretty beat up, with his initials in gold barely discernible under the handle."

"Mighty interestin' you'd ask, Mr. Evans. Cain't say that I've looked through no briefcase."

"You haven't even *looked* through it?" Evans bellowed, his annoyance in full bloom.

Jenks's eyes glittered at the other's obvious anger. Enough yet to cause some indiscretion?

"What are you waiting for, Jenks?" Evans demanded. "Read everything in it. Believe me, you'll find Grant's motive."

"Oh, I believe you, sure enough, Mr. Evans. Trouble is, there ain't no briefcase nowhere."

"No briefcase," Evans said, his voice suddenly speculative. "Someone must have taken it then. So Frederickson really *had* uncovered something important. The computer—have you checked the computer? Or has it disappeared, too?"

"No, sir, it's right here, but them newfangled machines—I just don't feel comfortable 'round 'em. But we've got a young'un hereabouts can right croon to them machines. Smart young'un, for sure. Real modern. If'n that li'l ol' machine's got somethin' on its mind, ol' Bubba'll find it. Bubba sure will. Yes, sir."

"Bubba!" Evans roared. "You do realize the importance of that 'li'l ol' machine,' don't you? If anything happens to it, I'll destroy you!"

"I'll keep that in mind, Mr. Evans. Sure will keep ever'thin' you said in mind."

"And you keep in mind Grant's part in all of this," Evans growled. "Senator Robert Hawkins Grant."

"Senator Grant?" Jenks said, with an especially exaggerated drawl. A puckish grin played at the corners of his mouth as he fed Evans's all-too-obvious antipathy for the Senator. "Always reckoned him a fine man, even if he is a colored."

"Your 'fine man' is smack in the middle of this murder," Evans shot back. "I guarantee it. Don't let Grant fool you, and don't let his supposed power keep you from doing your duty. I'll have people dogging you until you make an arrest. The *Washington Herald* looks after its own."

He slammed down the phone.

Chuckling, Jenks leaned farther back in his chair. His fingers drummed his notebook, covering, then uncovering, Evans's name. His conversation with Peter Evans had been most enlightening, he thought, wondering what to expect from Grant.

Senator Robert Hawkins Grant. Jenks had heard little but good about the Senator, at least what Jenks considered good. According to all reports, Grant was a commonsense man who liked the heavy hand of government as little as Jenks himself did. Grant was black, true, but no harm there. Couldn't help wondering what kind of friends he had though. This was politics, after all, and politics like everything else had its share of evil. How much was Grant willing to do to keep his job? Murder? Jenks shook his head as if to clear it. Too early for that kind of speculation, way too early.

"What was that all about, Sheriff?" Hank Farrar asked, coming into the office and handing him a report. "You sho' sounded like a jerkwater hayseed."

"Did I?" Jenks asked with a grin. "Glad to hear it. Been talking to a big-shot Washington newspaper editor, Peter Evans." He pointed to Evans's name on the pad. Farrar nodded. "Hope Mr. Evans decides to teach me a thing or two. I might just learn more than he bargained for. Pretty condescending was Mr. Evans."

Farrar laughed and shook his head.

"And pretty set against our Senator. Senator Grant, I mean. Insistent, too. Seems to think Grant's our murderer."

Farrar gaped at him, but some emotion, seemingly pleasant, sprang into his eyes.

Jenks gave Farrar the gist of the conversation. "I'll need to speak to the good Senator," he finished, banging his boots on the linoleum-covered floor as he sat up. "See if you can track him down. Tell him to come on by at his convenience. Just make sure he understands that means as soon as possible. I'll handle it if he calls complaining, but I will see him tonight."

Chief of Staff M. Eugene Corforth had come to hate the War Room.

Early on, Jonathan Hunter had commandeered the small annex off Corforth's White House office and dubbed it the War Room because the critical-care strategy sessions of the administration were held there. The reproduction Chippendale furniture and richly detailed oil paintings in their ornate gilt frames did little to obviate the utilitarian, sometimes base activities initiated in the room. A political adversary getting too much media play, an adverse rumor needing squelching, a potentially disastrous slip by an administration spokesperson who now needed to be eased out as quietly as possible, any spin doctoring, any scheming best kept within the inner circle—in short putting out the brush fires of the administration before they could become politically damaging infernos: These were the activities that consumed those who toiled in the War Room.

The windowless room was soundproof and microwave-proof. Each telephone had its own outside line, bypassing the switchboard and swept daily for bugs. No recording devices of any kind were allowed. The paper shredder in the corner had logged many hours.

Hunter, an unusual glint in his normally emotionless eyes, liked to say the room was his tribute to "two former Presidents, one who needed to know everything and the other who needed to erase daily blunders. I'll leave their identities to your imaginations." The last was always uttered with amused mockery.

Today, only Corforth and Hunter were involved, a high-stakes meeting for sure. Hunter was in charge. When Hunter attended, Hunter presided. No one else had his uncanny knack for grasping the essence of any situation; no one else had his single-minded ruthlessness to attack it head-on; and no one else had more control over this administration. Hunter now made all but the most critical decisions, and of late he seemed to be making the majority of those as well. Certainly, his stamp was on everything. In the past few months, he and POTUS had become almost interchangeable.

POTUS: So much easier to say than the President of the United States, Corforth thought. That full title stuck in his throat these days. Why was it that the little things bothered him so much lately? Maybe because he felt slightly more shut out each day. POTUS didn't rely on him as much. He was losing access.

"Anne Peabody is dead," Hunter announced. His voice held no more emotion than if he were quoting polling data. Anne Peabody was the Wall Street broker whose accusation two years before against the then-President had helped bring about his defeat. Peabody had discovered that he'd accepted a hefty sum of money from a Saudi sheik, unreported money which the media and his challenger, the current President, had declared a bribe. Peabody had also been a staunch supporter of this President, who'd come to power with that defeat.

Corforth's stomach churned. "A heart attack?" he asked. He knew he sounded hopeful, but he couldn't help it.

"Heart attack?" Hunter queried. "Why would you think that? Peabody wasn't much over forty. No, she was killed by a mugger. In Central Park, no less."

Relief flooded Corforth. A mugger. He wasn't sure what he'd expected, or even why he was so on edge, but if it were merely a mugging . . . "Any special response from us?"

"No," Hunter answered. "I doubt we'll even be asked about it. She had no relationship to us." He looked at Corforth over his half glasses, a look that Corforth had come to dread: speculation mixed with a growing hostility.

Surely Hunter trusts me, doesn't he? Corforth thought. He had no reason not to. The President's snacks? The thought popped into Corforth's head at almost the same moment that Hunter spoke. Second sight? Corforth wondered. At times, Hunter's prescience seemed malevolently inspired.

"The President's appetites are increasing," Hunter said, examining Corforth like some insect under glass. "If, God forbid, the media gets a whiff, we have to be prepared to squelch it."

"But—"

"Don't worry, Eugene," Hunter interrupted sarcastically. "You won't have to soil your hands. Just laugh at the absurdity of such an idea. Then move on."

Again, Corforth felt relief. He covered it with a laugh. "I may not like POTUS's penchant for anything in a skirt, but believe me, Hunt, I'm quite capable of handling the press."

"Sure," Hunter said dismissively, as if any assurance Corforth could give wouldn't be enough. "Just remember to limit press access to POTUS. Don't give the pack time to shout questions at him." He picked up his stack of papers. "Above all, make sure photo-ops are just that—picture-taking sessions—no questions."

"No problem," Corforth responded, "as long as POTUS cooperates."

"You keep your end moving," Hunter said as he walked toward the door. "I'll handle the big guy. And Eugene." He paused. Corforth tensed. He knew Hunter, and he knew Hunter's trick of dropping the bombshell, the real reason for the meeting, in this seemingly nonchalant manner. "Russell Frederickson, the *Herald* reporter, was murdered down in Georgia."

"You're kidding!" Corforth exclaimed. His look of surprise turned into a frown, but the ball of dread in his gut eased. "What does that have to do with us?"

"Nothing—except Bob Grant's been implicated in the murder," Hunter threw over his shoulder as he passed through the door. "The Georgia race has been blown wide open."

Bob Grant. Corforth reached into his pocket for his antacids. First, Hunter had brought up Anne Peabody, then Russell Frederickson, now Bob Grant. Was Hunter up to something or just being his usual secretive self? The more power Hunter got, the harder he was to figure. The man is a walking enigma, Corforth thought gloomily. He picked up his own stack of papers and with relief left the War Room.

It was a glorious day for a parade: A friendly late-afternoon sun, its rosy-gold rays shimmering against all they touched, warmed a cloudless blue sky and gave promise of a sunset in keeping with the occasion. Thousands of Georgians, residents of several rural counties, lined the parade route. Blankets and lawn chairs covered the curb. Latecomers stood on the sidewalk, ten or twelve deep. Vendors pushed carts laden with helium balloons, inflatable animals, cotton candy, and snow cones. A bright purple balloon floated lazily upward, its metallic shine caught by the sun. A child's anguished cry was followed by a promise to buy another.

Neighbor greeted neighbor, relishing the opportunity but bemoaning the infrequency of such meetings. In small towns, as everywhere, neighborly chats had been sacrificed to the demands of modern reality. This parade, evoking past memories and promising new pleasures, was a welcome excuse to slow down and savor simple blessings: perfect weather, long-time friends, childish excitement, patriotic fervor.

As one of their U.S. Senators, Bob Grant would be at the front of the parade behind the color guard, local high school band, parade queen, and fire engines and police cars with their sirens screaming and blue lights twirling. In ten minutes the parade would pull out and begin its two-mile jaunt down Main Street.

The staging area was alive with last-minute preparations: streamers added to cars, band uniforms straightened and brushed, baton routines practiced one last time, beauty queens positioned just so on the backs of convertibles, floats repaired, horses calmed, missing participants frantically summoned. Bob Grant, a smile on his face, watched the activity while shaking hands and exchanging pleasantries with a constant stream of supporters. Many wore white T-shirts emblazoned with bold red and blue letters announcing "BOB GRANT IS MY SENATOR."

"Senator!" Grant felt Mike Masterson's hand on his arm. "A message for you from a Sheriff Jimmy Jenks of Oconee County. Wants to talk to you, ASAP." Masterson's voice was low and conspiratorial, at odds with his smiling, cherubic face and boyishly rumpled hair, scant though it was.

He handed Grant a pink slip with the phone number. "A deputy called, but I said you'd only talk to the sheriff."

"Russell Frederickson?" Grant asked, disheartened that Masterson would pull rank with a deputy. Momentarily, some of the shine came off the day.

"Must be, but he didn't say." Masterson was impervious to the nuances of others, a trait Grant found inconvenient in a political operative. Surprising that Phillip Loomis, the Senate colleague who'd recommended Masterson, had been so high on him, Grant had thought more than once. Loomis had probably figured Masterson's intelligence and industry made up for his lack of sensibility, that and his truly comprehensive list of sources. Besides, Masterson was easy to be around, equally important in an aide who was at his side almost twenty-four hours a day.

Grant glanced at his watch, then at the cellular phone Masterson held. "Better see what he wants."

Masterson's momentary frown was wiped away by a conciliatory smile. "You'll need to hurry. The band will start up any minute."

Grant was already dialing. He was put through to Jenks immediately.

"Sure do thank you for getting in touch, Senator," Jenks said. "Be pleased if I could meet with you this evening."

"We can't discuss this over the phone?" Grant asked. He was puzzled. He'd expected some questions. After all, Frederickson had spent a fair portion of his last days following them around. But a formal interview? The sheriff must know how tight Grant's schedule was with the election little more than a week away. True, he was far ahead of Tobias Caruso in the polls, but that was today. Much could happen during the next week. Grant needed to attend every barbecue, every rally, every whistle-stop that he could. A political campaign couldn't be taken for granted, no matter the popularity of the incumbent, no matter the encouraging numbers in the polls.

"Sorry, Senator. I know you're busy," Jenks said as if reading Grant's mind, "but this is something we'll have to discuss in person."

"I see," Grant said slowly, wishing he did. He'd had no contact with Frederickson apart from the normal reportorial ones. "I'm about to walk in a parade," he continued, shouting now to be heard above the band's rousing rendition of "Stars and Stripes Forever," proclaiming the parade's imminent departure, "but I should be done here about nine. Sorry I can't be more exact."

Those near Grant straightened their ranks and began watching the Jaycee volunteer who would give them their signal to pull out.

"I reckon I understand your problems, Senator," Jenks said. Grant thought he detected an undertone of irony in the sheriff's deep voice. Odd, if so.

They made arrangements for that evening.

Grant, a preoccupied look on his face, handed the phone back to Masterson.

"Time to line up, Senator," Masterson said, his eyes darting along the route.

Grant stared at the pavement a moment longer, then responded to the pressure of Masterson's hand. "Oh, sure." He walked toward four teenagers, all wearing navy shorts with their Grant T-shirts. They carried a long banner which proclaimed "GEORGIA'S OWN SENATOR BOB GRANT" and which stretched from curbside to curbside.

Grant, dressed in a white shirt and navy sweater above tan chino slacks, had been supplied a convertible, but he much preferred to walk. The convertible, swathed with campaign banners, would follow behind, a repository for wrapped candy that T-shirted supporters would toss to the crowd. Several teenagers grabbed handfuls of Grant bumper stickers, ready to pass them out to the many in the crowd sure to be eager to have them.

"We love you, Bob!" someone shouted. "Keep up the good work!"

A grin lit Grant's face as he turned to wave.

"Have the car ready to take us to Madison as soon as we finish here," he told Masterson. They were booked into a Madison hotel that night to be near their first event early the next morning. "Sheriff Jenks is meeting us there."

It was Masterson's turn to look puzzled as he ran to the side of the road out of the way. The Fall Festival Parade had begun.

Peter Evans had called a late staff meeting at the *Washington Herald*. Such meetings weren't normal, but they weren't so unusual as to account for the almost palpable excitement of the assembled editors and reporters awaiting Evans's arrival. All those present had known Russell Frederickson and were shocked by his murder. Loud bursts of conversation were followed by periods of electric quiet. Ashtrays were already overflowing, but no admonitions had been raised by the nonsmokers, an unprecedented tolerance. The name Grant hung in the air, seeming to escalate the excitement with every speculation. These were news people, and they sensed a story. A big story.

The door opened and Evans strode into the room, a sheaf of papers in one hand. Except for the scrape of chairs and rustle of paper, the room was instantly quiet.

"I've just come from talking to Orlando Ivan," Evans said. Ivan was owner of the *Herald*. "He's pledged the paper's resources to uncovering the murderer of Russell Frederickson and to making public the circumstances surrounding that murder."

Several editors gave in-the-know looks. Several reporters leaned forward, hoping to be part of the investigative team sure to be named.

"We're going to dig until we uncover the truth," Evans said. "We have several lines of inquiry. First, an in-depth study of the last few weeks of Frederickson's life. I want to know what he ate for breakfast, where he ate it, and with whom. In short, an accounting of every second of his last days."

Evans paused. A look of grim satisfaction played on the corners of his mouth. "Frederickson's conversation with me two days ago," he continued into the expectant hush, "makes it clear he'd uncovered something mortally damaging to Senator Robert Grant."

An excited rush of words greeted this not unexpected announcement. Evans raised a hand for silence.

"'Irreparable damage to Grant both personally and politically' were Frederickson's exact words."

Kirk Vinton, a tall bony man with a kinky thatch of graying red hair, listened even more intently than those around him. Before the meeting he'd been tapped to head a yet-to-be-named team of reporters for the *Herald*. Vinton had already won one Pulitzer for his investigative journalism. An exposé of a Senator was good material for another, especially since that Senator was involved in the murder of a reporter and especially since he was the first black seriously touted as a Presidential candidate by a major party, the Republican Party at that. Vinton ran a hand over his mouth to cover his thin smile of satisfaction.

"We need to discover what Frederickson discovered," Evans continued. "We'll keep in close touch with the sheriff down there—Jimmy Jenks, a real rube." Evans's mouth pursed in a moue of distaste. "But even he might stumble onto something useful. We'll just have to recognize its importance because Jenks certainly won't."

Vinton chuckled softly to himself and settled more comfortably into his chair. He was used to dealing with lesser men. In fact, the more inept the sheriff, the more leeway Vinton would be given and the more credit he would garner when he finally broke the Senator. Vinton began jotting possible avenues of investigation on his pad. He would talk to some of Frederickson's associates here in D.C. before he left for Atlanta. He'd have two hours at least before he had to get to the airport.

"Frederickson had been in Georgia for the last three weeks," Evans continued, "except for one day in New York, reason unknown. But let's not get bogged down with New York. Remember, Grant is our focus, just as he was the focus of Frederickson's last weeks. Check into Grant's Atlanta office. Find disgruntled employees, former as well as current. Investigate every rumor, every hint, every innuendo, no matter how far-fetched. It's hard to tell what may have sparked Frederickson's interest. Check with all those who've interviewed Grant in the past and all his associates, especially those who've had run-ins with him. Don't forget his naval career. Discover the truth about Bob Grant. If he's tainted—and Frederickson obviously thought he was—we're going to nail him."

"Only a few of you will be assigned directly to this story," Evans said. His eyes rested on Vinton, then moved on. Again, Vinton covered his smug line-thin smile with his bony hand. "Don't let that stop the rest of you from using your own perspective and your own sources. We'll need all the input we can get. We have to work quickly."

With the advent of the satellite, news spread around the globe so quickly that a morning paper like the *Herald*—or, for that matter, an evening paper or newscast—could be at a disadvantage depending on the time of day a story broke. Therefore, the print as well as the electronic media often worked together, if only in the sense they made use of each other's information. Together, they controlled the news—their perception of the news—for the entire nation for the entire day.

Journalists tended to behave like members of a pack, finding safety in numbers, safety in conformity. Every journalist wanted to break a story first, but no journalist wanted to be so far out front that a misstep would bring all-too-public ridicule or mockery from colleagues. The tightrope between peer approval and censure was slippery, and too often a journalist felt more secure with the safety net of accepted viewpoint underneath, anything to avoid the public scorn of other journalists for not being "smart enough" to report the story "properly."

And so it was that day after day the same stories were reported similarly throughout the country. The public assumed each newspaper, each television show, each magazine conducted its own investigation and did its own research. The perception was that each had personally uncovered the same facts, and that, therefore, those facts must be true. Few guessed that almost all media received their news information from a mere handful of people. These men and women, few in number but mighty in power, determined the focus, content, and in essence the bias of much of the national news.

Peter Evans, a master at manipulating the news both to his professional advantage and to his personal viewpoint, was one of the most adroit and, therefore, most powerful of that handful. Evans was equally adept at heaping ridicule and censure on any reporter or editor who dared disagree. His newspaper set the standard others followed, and he was proud of it.

Evans continued, "If someone breaks a story first, we'll be sure to put the information in perspective in our follow-up."

He paused and stared around the room, capturing every reporter in his fiery gaze. "Frederickson was our reporter. This is the *Herald's* story!"

Evans's usually suave voice was tight with suppressed passion, but even in this moment of emotional intensity, his appearance remained unflawed and ever the same: dark suit, perfectly cut to his athletic body; stark white shirt with antique cuff links; distinctive but never flamboyant silk tie. He smoothed his tie now as if trying to smooth away his emotions. Then he continued, those emotions barely in check.

"I hope I've made myself clear. This isn't just another murder but an attack on a friend and colleague. Violence mustn't be allowed to reign free over the media! For Russell Frederickson, his family—and yes, for freedom of the press—his murder must be avenged."

Again, Evans smoothed his tie. "We'll not allow some backwoods sheriff to blow this investigation," he continued more moderately. "Grant is popular in Georgia, admittedly, but even his blindest supporters will have to face the truth when we hit them with it. Frederickson found that truth. I want it!"

The motel room where Russell Frederickson had been murdered was beset with shadows, the dark blotch on the carpet by the bed blending with the shadows cast by the setting sun. Jenks turned on the overhead light. The shadows disappeared, but the dark blotch remained.

"Anyone interested in the room?" he asked, turning to the deputy who'd been leaning back in a chair outside the door when they arrived.

"Naw. Someone snuck 'round back." He moved his toothpick to the other side of his mouth. "Reporter. Left when he saw Old Burt back there. Lotta rubbernecking out front."

Jenks nodded. He hadn't expected otherwise. No nervous first-time killer would have come back here. This had the feel of a professional hit in spite of the mess. Supposed to look like a search, Jenks reckoned, but didn't feel quite right. No, sir, something wasn't quite right. Clean wound straight through the head—maybe a .45 from the size of the exit hole—but funny thing: No slug anywhere. And why a .45? The uneaten hamburger and fries were a puzzle, too.

After a last speculative look, Jenks bent down and began picking up papers, numbering them as he did. "Well, Bubba?" he asked, looking up at the young woman, an attractive blond, who'd accompanied him from the police station.

She returned his look with a puzzled frown. "Bubba?"

Jenks grinned. The girl shook her head in amused resignation. She reached down toward the computer, now partially uncovered under the papers, but stopped and looked back questioningly toward Jenks.

"Sure. Go ahead. Just a few smudged prints on the keys. Frederickson's. Do whatever you need."

She squatted, opened the computer, and examined it for several minutes without touching it. "A nice laptop," she said. "Not the newest but plenty fast. An internal modem, looks like." She closed the case, then stood.

The sheriff frowned. "Aren't you going to turn it on?"

"I'd rather not, not here anyway." She smiled, the rather superior smile of the computer literate toward the obvious illiterate. Then she grinned. Her long blond hair swung beside her face as she bent to pick up the machine. "Okay, so I'm showing off or trying to. But I don't want to

31

take a chance of messing something up. The more times the machine is turned on and off, the greater the difficulty in recovering erased memory. I'm hopeful I can find something even if someone *has* messed with it."

The sheriff started to speak. Raising a silencing hand, she hurried on before he could. "Don't count on it. Everything may be gone."

"Oh, I doubt that," Jenks said, tucking the papers under one arm and taking the computer from her. They walked toward the door. "I doubt that very much. I've a feeling someone's counting on us finding something. Why else leave the computer? I'm right interested in what that something is."

"What do you expect?"

"That's a tough one, Sally." The sheriff shifted the computer to his other hand as he reached for the door. "This li'l machine's been pointed out to me once already, and . . . I can't rightly put it in words, but it just feels important. May be nothing more than an old man's wishful thinking, but I'm hoping you'll find something useful."

Sally's face was thoughtful as they left the motel room. Oconee County didn't have many big cases, but Sheriff Jenks was a good lawman, a painstaking worker with both an intuitive understanding of the frailties and strengths of man and an overriding sense of justice. More than once he'd bucked the county establishment, putting his job on the line because he'd disagreed with their quick and convenient solution to a case. He'd always been proved right and had his share of enemies, as well as staunch allies, to show for it. If the sheriff thought the computer was important, then it probably was.

The man outside the door saluted them with his toothpick, then leaned back in his chair and tilted his cap back over his eyes.

The movie theater at the White House is located on the first floor near the visitors' area. The room is relatively small, with several slightly raised tiers for seating. Each First Family determines the furnishings. LBJ liked beanbag chairs and cushy pillows distributed casually around the room. The Reagans preferred cushioned folding chairs for their guests with overstuffed chairs for themselves.

Only one constant remained through the years: Everyone wanted popcorn. This evening the air was redolent with the smell of popcorn, hot and buttered.

Like the Reagans, Estelle used folding chairs except for intimate gatherings like tonight when club chairs seemed more appropriate. In the darkness of the room with the light from the film throwing its constantly changing shadows, she vaguely wondered whether her guests were comfortable, but she couldn't really make herself care. Lately she didn't seem able to care about much of anything. Oh, she continued her duties as First Lady. Helping unwed mothers and increasing awareness of the dangers of environmental pollution were important causes. She was passionate in their support, but lately that passion was the only one she seemed capable of feeling, and even it had lost its urgency.

Memories of their first few months in the White House floated through her mind. How the twins had loved using this room for parties! They'd all been so happy then, even her husband. They'd seemed like a family. Estelle felt a sob seize her throat and fought for control. The scene on the screen dissolved and blurred through her tears, and she closed her eyes tight against their falling. She ached with the poignant pain of remembering.

The girls were away at college, and she was glad. At least they and their older brother and sister weren't here to witness the travesty that had once been their parents' marriage, a marriage born in love and nurtured in mutual caring.

Not that their marriage had been without its problems. He'd had two brief affairs over the years, painful and humiliating to be sure, but he'd been wonderfully repentant, and she'd known he loved her. She'd believed him and believed in him. But that had been before—before too many late nights, too many unexplained absences, too many whispers, too much neglect, too much pity in too many eyes.

He'd changed when he'd become President. She thought it was the siren song of ultimate power that had released in him a need to prove he could have anything he desired without the strictures of decency, honor, and plain good manners that bound lesser men.

The movie was almost over. Estelle could feel the heat of her husband sitting next to her though she was careful to keep any portion of her body from touching his. Even so, he reached over and squeezed her hand before he stood. He even threw a smile in her direction.

As the houselights came on, she could feel him tense. He was always "on" when he was in public even when, as tonight, public was only a few close friends.

"Inspiring movie, wasn't it, Hunt?" he asked Jonathan Hunter, who was on his other side. When they were together—and that had been the case since soon after law school—Hunter was always at her husband's side. The President and Hunter went back a long way. They'd both been elected to the House at the same time years before and had followed almost the same path to their present positions.

Hunter had, in fact, been the one who'd insisted her husband run for the presidency. As President, his first appointee had been Hunter, whose first act had been to push through Congress the National Investigation and Intelligence Agency (NIIA), an omnipotent bureau which combined the FBI, CIA, DEA, Federal Marshals, and Secret Service into one organization under the power of one man, Jonathan Hunter. All local law enforcement agencies were required to use the NIIA's computer system and urged to bow to the power and superior wisdom of those running the NIIA. The new federal agency could supplant local law enforcement at any time at the discretion of the administration—all in the name of combating the escalating crime problem.

Estelle wasn't thinking of Hunter in such grand terms. Instead, she thought of him disparagingly as her husband's chief procurer. She'd overheard them talking about "snacks" one day, and suddenly she'd understood what they meant, what voracious appetite of her husband's they were discussing so cavalierly. She'd felt sick, a nausea that continued to claw at her, day and night.

"You're looking lovely." Estelle heard the words, then realized they were addressed to her by Peter Evans, editor of the *Washington Herald*. She pulled her mind from its labyrinth of futile thoughts and gave a brittle smile—or tried to. Her lips wouldn't soften.

"You're much too kind," she answered. Even tonight she was aware of Evans's extraordinary good looks. Seeing the look in his eye, she knew that as always no one was more aware of those distinguished good looks than Evans himself. Estelle had never been comfortable around him, but tonight when she yearned for straightforward niceness, she could barely force herself to meet his eyes. She searched frantically for something to say and was saved by, of all people, her husband.

"Where's your young lady?" he asked Evans, looking around the room. He spied the woman in question talking to Hunter. The President smiled. Estelle's heart twisted at the frank admiration radiating from that smile.

"She is lovely, isn't she?" Evans said. A proprietary pleasure touched his lips as they watched her sensuous advance toward them. Since his divorce, Evans seldom dated the same woman twice, but they were always young, always beautiful.

Evans draped an arm around this beautiful young woman's shoulder. She smiled at them all but gave extra wattage to the one she bestowed on the President.

"Thanks for that tip about Frederickson," the President said, tearing his eyes from Evans's date and back to Evans. "Can't say I'm sad about Grant."

"Grant?" Estelle asked. "Are you talking about Bob Grant?"

"You haven't heard?" Evans glanced at the President before explaining. "Grant is the prime suspect in the murder of one of my reporters."

"Bob Grant?" Estelle's voice rose in disbelief. "No. There has to be a mistake. Not Bob Grant. He's one of the few decent men in Washington."

"Oh, Estelle." The President tried to sound pleasantly humoring, but a note of displeasure underlined his words. Throughout his political career, he'd always helped his friends and paid back his enemies. The name Bob Grant had simmered at the back of his mind for a long time. Grant: who'd behaved abominably toward him personally during the tense change of government in Cuba. Grant: who'd publicly challenged his—his!—policy toward Cuba. And on worldwide television! "You're an innocent," he told Estelle condescendingly. "Bob Grant takes pleasure in trying to embarrass me and my administration. If a murder investigation prematurely ends his career, I for one will be glad."

Little more than a year earlier, Cuban dictator Fidel Castro had died, throwing the island into chaos. The choice of a successor had come down to two men, General José Moya, quietly backed by the enslaved people of Cuba, and Caesar Valles, backed at the insistence of Evans by the President. Unfortunately, several anti-American factions had been grooming Valles for years for just such an opportunity. At the last moment, Grant had shown the President the folly of his choice. Moya had come to power amid the cheers of the Cuban people and was now slowly stabilizing his ravaged country.

The President had interpreted Grant's interference in Cuba as a blatant attempt to grab power and notoriety for himself at the expense of the administration. Now that Grant was mentioned as a presidential contender, the President felt vindicated in that assessment. A man who had succumbed to his own insatiable lust for power and who reveled in the seemingly unlimited gratification that came with it, he assumed Grant would feel the same obsession. The President was a man daily more consumed by images of his own creation.

"Russell Frederickson uncovered one of Grant's scams," Evans said quickly, trying to soften the President's words. The naked vulnerability in Estelle's eyes made him want to shelter her—an impulse he hadn't felt for more years than he cared to remember. With unexpected clarity, the equally haunting eyes of his ex-wife assaulted his mind. He'd thought he'd expunged her completely from his life, silly woman that she was. Angry now, Evans continued roughly, "Only a fool wouldn't understand that Grant is the worst type of politician, more interested in himself than in those he serves."

"Someone's a fool," Estelle replied, but she felt her interest dissipating. Apathy—her now habitual apathy—kicked in.

Jonathan Hunter approached and laid a hand on the President's arm. "Sir, I hate to be the bearer of bad news, but you have a meeting in—" He looked ostentatiously at his watch. "Fifteen minutes."

"Duty calls." The President reached out to shake Evans's hand.

Estelle watched the scene dispassionately, hearing herself saying the proper words but oblivious to them. A meeting. Time for a "snack" was what they meant. She looked at Jonathan Hunter and felt nothing but contempt. His poor wife, Rebecca, standing slightly behind him as always, might not have lost her husband to a woman—or women, Estelle amended with a wrench of her heart—but she'd lost him to at least as formidable an adversary, the seductive aphrodisiac of power.

Unlike herself, who'd taken to wearing reds, bright blues, and other powerful colors as protective camouflage, Rebecca had instead adopted the drab colors of dun and pewter to match her increasingly drab personality. Her cropped grayish-blond hair seldom looked more than hastily combed, and she never wore any makeup other than pale pink lipstick. She was in danger of fading away completely, Estelle thought with a stab of compassion. Only when Rebecca spoke of their only child, Joey, a freshman at Georgetown University, did her face light with animation and her voice regain some of its former lilt.

Estelle felt her husband leaning toward her and turned her head in time to avoid more than a grazing of her cheek by his lips. The skin that they fleetingly touched burned as if imprinted by fire. She kept her face rigid, hoping to hide her humiliation.

Finally alone, she made her way slowly toward the Family Quarters. Usually when she walked the long hall, hung with portraits of former First Ladies, she liked to imagine where her own would one day hang. Each First Lady rearranged the portraits, keeping her favorites conspicuously in view and virtually hiding ones she didn't like. Estelle had wanted to hang Jackie Kennedy's portrait in the most visible spot at the foot of the stairs but finally had decided against it, afraid the choice would be thought all too predictable. She'd considered Eleanor Roosevelt. For one thing, she liked the painting. Clever Eleanor had ringed her portrait with cameos of the real Eleanor at work, an effective device to remind viewers that outer beauty wasn't all-important. Estelle also admired Eleanor as a woman, especially now that their situations were so similar.

So similar. She began walking faster. At least Eugene Corforth hadn't been there tonight, she thought, her eyes lowered to the carpet. Lately, she realized, Eugene had been absent from several of their more intimate gatherings. She was glad. The compassion in his eyes was almost as painful to bear as the indifference in her husband's.

As she walked past the usher holding open the door to the family elevator, she wondered if any other First Lady had been as lonely and unhappy as she. If so, she'd been smart enough not to allow her portrait to reveal it.

For Janet Loomis, the past five months had been a suffocating, mindless torment. First, the policemen had arrived on her doorstep with their nightmarish news that her husband, Phillip Loomis, Senator from New York, was dead. A suicide! Then she'd endured the funeral and the friends and family with their many kindnesses only partially masking their pity. Finally had come the months of dragging despair when her mind was obsessed by one unanswerable but unremitting question: Why? Why had he chosen to leave her?

Tonight for the first time, she felt a stirring of her old tranquillity, a desire to return to the routine that had patterned her life in the past. She supposed to others she'd appeared to be coping all along. She had taken care of the boys, both their physical and emotional needs, helping them manage their devastating loss. She'd succeeded, she knew, thinking of the lighthearted camaraderie that had returned to their lives, marred only occasionally by a bleak darkness in their eyes.

For herself, however, such normalcy had seemed impossible—until this evening when she'd finally admitted that an answer wasn't to be found. She didn't understand why Phillip had felt it necessary to end their life together. She knew she never would, but she couldn't allow his momentary aberration—that was what it had to have been!—to maintain its stranglehold on her life.

Tonight, she was taking her first step to meet the future, choosing to do something that in the past had brought her unalloyed pleasure. Every year on each of her sons' birthdays, she took out his precious baby book and relived the joy of his life. This year, Chris's birthday had come too close to Phillip's death to make such a sentimental journey possible, but tonight she was going to rectify that omission. Tonight she was going to wallow in the pleasures of the past, banishing for as long as possible the devastating question mark of Phillip's death.

Her hand shaking only slightly, Janet opened the drawer and brought out the book. It felt wonderfully familiar under her hands, and she remained standing for a moment, eyes closed, drinking in the memories it evoked.

"I don't care what your death seems to mean," she whispered defiantly to the empty room. "I know our life together was good, and I'm not going to allow you to take that from me."

Sinking into a chair, she opened the book. The pages parted to the middle where a strange manila envelope had been inserted. Her eyes widened. Her breath caught. Her name was on the envelope in Phillip's writing!

Janet slammed the book shut, trying to regain control of her racing heart and spinning mind. Phillip had written no suicide note. He'd left no explanation. None. Was this it? Was this the explanation she'd hoped—dreaded—to find?

Slowly, she let the book fall open once again. Her name on the envelope stared up at her. She hadn't imagined it. Phillip knew she always looked in the boys' baby books on their birthdays. Was this his way of speaking to her, of explaining the unexplainable?

With unsteady hands, she picked it up, pushed the baby book aside, and slowly traced her name with her finger. Then taking a deep breath, she lifted the flap and poured out the contents. Her eyes narrowed, puzzled. Her lower lip began trembling, and she caught it with her teeth.

Newspaper articles! Why would Phillip have left her yellowing newspaper articles? She glanced at them only long enough to realize they described legislation Phillip had sponsored in the Senate.

Then she spotted the white envelope buried beneath them. Her breathing harsh and as unsteady as her hands, she picked it up.

As she read the words on it, her racing heart seemed to jolt to a stop. Her previous disbelief was nothing compared to the brutal shock she experienced now.

"Janet," she read, "please give this to Bob Grant unread if he seems to be in any kind of trouble." That was all. She turned the envelope over, but the back was blank.

A feeling of dread knifed through her, but she clenched her teeth and ripped the envelope open. Her face was haggard when she finished reading.

Conversation during the trip to the hotel in Madison was desultory. Both Grant and Masterson were tired from a long day of campaigning, following long months of too many similar days. Having to spend time with an unknown sheriff for what was a pro forma task didn't appeal to either of them.

When they stepped out of the car, Sheriff Jenks and his deputy moved out of the shadows by the hotel entrance and walked toward them.

Although over six feet himself, Grant felt dwarfed by the sheriff. Jenks was a mountain of a man, Grant thought. Must be at least six-five or six-six, with the bulk to go with it. Not an inch of it was fat, Grant was willing to bet.

Jenks was attired in a traditional sheriff's uniform: starched tan shirt tucked into dark brown slacks, the creases as sharp as any Grant had seen in the military. Then Grant noticed the sheriff's well-worn alligator-skin boots, polished to a mellow patina, and had to work to stifle a smile. The heels were stacked. The sheriff wasn't above augmenting even his prodigious stature, a fact Grant found rather comforting for some reason.

Maybe because it bespoke a lawman using every advantage to the fullest? Grant hoped so. He wanted to see this murder investigation pursued vigorously and the murderer punished suitably.

They greeted each other politely and entered the lobby, following an eager campaign volunteer to an already open and comfortably appointed suite.

"Coffee?" Grant asked. He poured some into a white ceramic mug and lifted it toward Jenks.

"Thanks," Jenks said, reaching for it and taking a sip. "Tastes mighty fine. This day's been longer than Effie Mae Freedown's engagement, and folks around here are bettin' she'll die before that marriage is consummated."

Grant grinned, figuring he'd been right in thinking the boots a bit of stage dressing, just like the exaggerated Georgia-cracker persona. "Deputy Farrar?"

Farrar scowled and shook his head. Short, wiry, consumed with restless energy, he seemed the antithesis of his hulking, easygoing boss.

"Mike Masterson is my press secretary," Grant said, gesturing toward Masterson, who had followed them into the room and was now seated on the couch opposite Jenks's chair. Farrar was seated behind, a notebook open on his lap. "Mike had more dealings with Russell Frederickson than I did."

Grant held a cup toward Masterson, who took it.

"Mind if I record this?" Masterson asked, indicating a tape recorder.

"Course not," Jenks said, settling into a somewhat dingy overstuffed chair and crossing a leg.

The Senator poured one more cup, seated himself, took a satisfyingly long drink of coffee, and waited for Jenks to begin.

Jenks's initial questions were friendly and predictable. Grant's answers were short and factual. He knew little other than that Frederickson had been tenacious, determined to break a story to Grant's detriment. After twelve years, Grant was used to such scrutiny. Because campaign coverage had been mainly local, the presence of Frederickson as a reporter for a Washington paper had been unusual.

"*Unusual* isn't the right word," Masterson amended, getting up to refill his coffee. He did the same for the others as he talked. "*Unexpected* is more like it. No one is paying much attention to this race, for sure nationally and really statewide as well, because no surprises are expected. Barring a catastrophe—which we certainly don't expect!—Bob will win hands down." Masterson dumped three heaping teaspoonfuls of sugar into his coffee and began stirring. "We had presumed Frederickson was here because Bob is being mentioned as a challenger to the President in two years. A black Republican presidential hopeful makes good copy."

"This murder is puzzling," Jenks said, his drawl becoming less pronounced the longer he talked to Grant. "Here's this reporter, who, according to you, was just doing what reporters covering you have been doing for the last twelve years. A necessary nuisance, nothin' more. But this reporter ends up dead. Shot through the head."

"It wasn't robbery?" Grant asked, shifting in his chair and regarding the sheriff curiously. "You've eliminated robbery as a motive?"

"Frederickson's wallet was just where you'd expect," Jenks said. "In his pocket. Some money, not much, and some credit cards were still in it. A right nice computer was left behind, too. Robber scared into runnin' 'fore he'd done much? Maybe, but no strange goings-on were reported, and Frederickson wasn't found till late morning, it being Sunday. Could be robbery, of course, but . . ."

"Do you have any leads?" Grant asked, still wondering why the sheriff had felt it necessary to see him personally. Jenks didn't seem the kind to enjoy using his power to prove that even a Senator had to do his bidding, nor did he seem the kind to like jerking black men around. But something odd was going on. The air fairly bristled with it. Unless the bristling was all on the deputy's part, Grant thought with a glance toward Farrar, whose scowl deepened with each passing minute.

"Lots of leads," Jenks said, taking a last swallow of coffee before lowering the empty mug onto the table beside him. "Whether any are worth more than roadkill, I can't rightly tell yet."

Grant smiled. Even so he noted the clear calculation in the sheriff's eyes. Jenks might cultivate a good-ol'-boy facade and do so with flair, but he was no fool.

"You fellers might like knowin' my intuition"—Jenks drawled the word out—"tells me this here murder is a mite peculiar. Brings to mind a professional hit. Mind you, we don't have many professionals around our parts. Tell truth," Jenks said, grinning broadly, "I don't reckon I've ever come across one, leastways so I knew what I was lookin' at. But we do have more than enough of the other kind, and this feels different. Hard to figure why a professional would have a mind to come to Oconee County though. A young reporter covering a 'benign' campaign, you said. You fellas have any ideas why a professional—if you figure my intuition's worth spit—might go after this Frederickson?"

"A professional killer?" Grant repeated dubiously, wondering what possible reasons the sheriff could have for such an unlikely idea. Was Jenks's intuition worth more than either spit or roadkill? Grant wondered, his twinge of amusement tinged with heightened caution. "That doesn't make sense. Frederickson wasn't covering anything potentially harmful to any-one, at least not if this campaign was his only story. I think even Tobias Caruso would admit that this campaign is about as controversy-free as a campaign can be. Any chance Frederickson was working on something else, something potentially dangerous?"

"Mighty busy man, Mr. Frederickson," Jenks said, "but seems like he had one thing on his mind. You, Senator. Just you and your campaign."

"You've definitely ruled out robbery?" Grant felt as if a noose had suddenly appeared above his head. That made no sense, he told himself. Why should he feel threatened? Even so his guard, fine-tuned from years in the military, was instantly on full alert.

"I haven't ruled out anything, Senator," Jenks said pleasantly. His tone dispelled some of Grant's misgivings, but far from all. "Doesn't seem smart to work that way, but I'd be a mite surprised if this murder had diddly-squat to do with robbery."

"I don't understand, Sheriff," Grant said. He watched the lawman closely, looking for clues to the uneasiness he felt. The more he watched, the more certain he was that Jenks was much deeper than he wanted to appear. "A campaign doesn't contain much in the way of danger. *Defeat* for someone—Caruso, I hope, in this case." Grant tried a smile. Jenks smiled back. Farrar continued to scowl. "But certainly not danger. Fred-erickson's death just can't have anything to do with the campaign, not directly anyway."

"What would you say," Jenks asked, slouching down in his chair, his hands clasped loosely on his stomach, "if I told you Frederickson claimed to have something on you?" Jenks's eyes were deceptively bland under heavy eyelids. Those familiar with him knew the signs: Jenks was preparing for the kill. "'Irreparable damage to Grant both personally and politically' were that poor boy's words."

Grant's vague misgivings could in no way have prepared him for the shock of Jenks's assertion. "Something damaging about me?" he asked incredulously. "With the potential of destroying me? I'd say you were wasting your time."

"The whole thing's outrageous!" Masterson exclaimed, bounding to his feet.

"Where'd you hear that?" Grant asked, never taking his eyes from the sheriff.

"Well, now, Senator," Jenks said, ignoring Masterson, who sat back into his chair but still looked angry. "I don't rightly know if I should . . ." He paused, then smiled. His smile was charming. One of his major weapons, Grant thought dispassionately, not a whit fooled. "I told the feller you seemed a good ol' boy. He took exception. No reason you shouldn't know. Feller named Evans. Russell Frederickson worked for his paper. This here Evans reckoned Frederickson was on to something mighty unsavory about you."

"Peter Evans," Grant said with a mirthless laugh. He relaxed somewhat back into his chair. "I might have known. Evans doesn't have much use for me. You could probably tell. He makes no secret of it, in print or out. I managed to embarrass not only Evans but his newspaper a year ago. I'm sure you remember the incident—the international disaster that was averted when José Moya came to power in Cuba."

Jenks nodded but remained silent.

"Evans has never forgiven me for exposing his feet of clay and hurting his relationship with the President," Grant continued, his face thoughtful, "but accusing me of being involved in a murder, especially with no evidence? Evans may be extraordinarily biased, but I can't believe he'd do that."

Grant shook his head in bemusement. "I thought I'd seen everything a campaign could dish out, but nothing could have prepared me for this. Nothing about it makes sense." He leaned forward, his expression earnest. "I know you wouldn't be doing your job if you took my word as truth, but believe me, Russell Frederickson couldn't have found anything damaging about me because it just doesn't exist. This is my third campaign for public office. The media hasn't been exactly friendly toward me in any of them.

By now all my dark secrets, such as they are, have been brought to light. I realize you'll have to follow up Evans's accusation, Sheriff, but I hope it won't be the only avenue you investigate. I had nothing whatsoever to do with his death."

"You needn't worry yourself, Senator," Jenks said, standing and picking up his hat by its broad brim from the chair beside him. "I've several avenues I'm fixin' to travel, and only one of them is Evans's dark secret about you." He walked toward the door. Farrar closed his notebook with a snap and followed. "We'd be right proud if you'd keep us posted on your whereabouts, Senator." He shook Grant's hand. "Pleasure to make your acquaintance. Yours, too, Mr. Masterson. We'll keep in touch."

Grant accepted his parting words as the statement of fact they were.

"Something damaging with the potential of destroying me," he murmured almost to himself as he closed the door behind the sheriff and his deputy. He looked up at Masterson. "Have you heard any rumors about me, Mike, something Frederickson might have latched on to?"

"Nothing," Masterson said. "This campaign is a no-brainer. You know that. Not even Caruso can think he has a prayer of winning."

"So why am I being linked with murder?" Grant shook his head in disbelief. "Murder!"

"I'll bet it's all Evans, wanting to sell papers."

"Maybe so, but I'm afraid there's something more here." Grant slowly lowered himself into a chair. "Jenks made it sound as if Evans was sure of his facts."

"Didn't Evans say something about revenge after you made him look a fool when you exposed his buddy in Cuba?"

"Sure, but it's a long way from words spoken in the heat of the moment to an accusation of murder." Masterson just looked at him. "And, no, I don't think he would've made up this story about Frederickson's last words."

"You're too trusting," Masterson replied, pouring himself another cup of coffee. He held up a mug to Grant, who shook his head. "At least the accusation won't stand for long." Again, Masterson dumped three heaping spoonfuls of sugar in the mug. "I can't think of anyone less likely than you to have a fatal secret or to commit murder."

Grant looked at Masterson thoughtfully. He appreciated the words of support, but how much, really, could anyone know about anyone else?

Could Masterson, for instance, feel confident he really knew Grant? They'd only met that spring when Phillip Loomis, his Senate colleague and Masterson's then employer, had recommended Masterson as Grant's press secretary.

Regardless of what Evans and his ilk reported in the media, Masterson wasn't likely to believe anything bad about him, but what about others? What about all those voters who didn't know him personally but relied on newspapers or TV to deliver the truth? Would they believe Grant, or would they believe the supposedly unbiased purveyors of news?

"What did you think of the sheriff?" he asked Masterson.

"Jenks? He *is* a Democrat, and he *is* white."

"And you think he'll hold my being both black and Republican against me?" Grant asked. He got up and poured himself a cup of coffee, deciding tepid was better than nothing. "Somehow I can't see Jenks letting politics enter into any investigation. He seems an independent cuss."

"Maybe," Masterson retorted, "but he's obviously a hick, maybe part of the Klan even. Hard to say how smart he is. I'd feel better if someone from Atlanta were handling the case. How often does a guy like Jenks get a chance for some media glory? He probably considers moonshine a major crime."

"Moonshine," Grant repeated. Feeling more relaxed, he even smiled. He, a serious suspect in a murder? Preposterous! Even so the vague disquiet continued to lurk at the back of his mind, a tiger who looked secure but whose cage door was slightly ajar. "Your Ivy League snobbery is getting the better of you," he quipped. "Jenks's good-ol'-boy pose seemed calculated to camouflage a sharp mind."

"Let's hope so," Masterson said, thumping his empty mug on the table. "We're going to have to do some fancy dancing to keep the media from crucifying you, evidence or no evidence. Having the sheriff solve the murder would certainly help. If I were you, though, I wouldn't trust Jenks too far until we know more about him." He rummaged through his briefcase and brought out a legal pad. "In terms of the campaign, how do we handle this?"

"Ignore it."

Masterson rolled his eyes in mock exasperation and slammed his pen down on the pad.

"Okay, okay," Grant said, inwardly sympathetic with his press secretary but wanting to prevent overreaction. "We don't have a problem, so let's not create one. I had nothing to do with Frederickson or his murder. That's bound to be obvious."

"Even if the murderer's not caught?"

"Not the optimum situation, admittedly, but Frederickson's murder had nothing to do with me. That's the truth."

"Being the truth won't make any difference," Masterson said, his pen again poised above the pad, "not if the publicity destroys your campaign and costs you the election."

"Why this attack of pessimism?" Grant asked, finishing the coffee. "In a few days no one will remember I was even questioned. The whole thing's absurd."

"Connecting you with a murder is absurd, but its implications for the campaign aren't."

Again, Grant felt a prickling of unease. Masterson's assessment, while overly pessimistic (a press secretary's usual stance), was too close to the truth to be comfortable. Reelection was never a sure thing, and this close to election day, even the hint of impropriety could change the outcome. For a moment the tiger of Grant's mind roamed free, increasing the feeling of danger with each step of its huge, deceptively soft paws. Grant groped for the source of the feeling but could find none. Nonetheless the feeling remained, coloring his thoughts.

"Why don't I book you into one of the big churches in Atlanta for next Sunday?" Masterson suggested. "Your saying something uplifting in that setting would offset any lingering taint from the murder."

"Come on, Mike," Grant said wearily, "we've been through this before. Make time for church on Sunday as usual but no publicity."

"But—"

"No," Grant interrupted. "I won't have worship trivialized by politics."

With a resigned shrug, Masterson walked over to the window, pulled back the curtain and looked out into the night. His portly body in its rumpled suit seemed comforting by its very ordinariness.

"Looks like the vultures have arrived," he said, nodding toward a huddle of people gathered outside the hotel. "Someone must have leaked the news."

Grant gave a tired sigh. Without looking, he knew "vultures" translated into media. "Wouldn't have been Evans. He'd want to keep it an exclusive for the *Herald*. You'd better go down and calm the waters. Call me if you learn anything."

Masterson left the suite and headed downstairs.

A reporter spotted him coming out of the hotel lobby. "Hey, Masterson," he yelled, "what about Grant's involvement in Russell Frederickson's murder?"

As if on cue, five news crews rushed toward Masterson. By tomorrow their ranks would swell—unless something more interesting replaced this story, Masterson reminded himself, or unless the murder was solved before then. A professional hit: Interesting that the sheriff had latched on to that. Masterson didn't like the idea, didn't like it one bit. A nasty premonition forced beads of sweat onto his brow. He patted them away with a handkerchief before addressing the reporters.

"The Senator was saddened to learn today of the death of Russell Frederickson," Masterson said with the ease of long practice at giving impromptu news conferences. "Mr. Frederickson was a fine journalist. Senator Grant extends his sincerest condolences to Mr. Frederickson's family and will help the authorities in every way to insure that the murderer is brought to justice."

"So the Senator's being questioned?"

"Sure," Masterson replied. "Everyone who was with Frederickson those last days will be." He grinned maliciously. "Including you guys."

Before they could send any more questions his way, Masterson slipped back through the door of the hotel. He pulled it shut, momentarily muffling the rising clamor for more information. As he hurried toward the elevator, the outside door opened. The barrage of questions intensified as reporters and photographers fought their way through, scrambling to catch up with the now profusely sweating Masterson.

Just in time the elevator doors swooshed shut, blocking out the reporters' questions and carrying Masterson safely back upstairs.

Peter Evans, surprised to be home so early and alone, loosened his tie and reached for the Baccarat snifter he'd just filled with one inch of Courvoisier. Somehow his date had vanished about the time of the President's departure. Evans grinned. Small price to pay for some points with the

President. His old friend had better be careful though, Evans thought, taking an appreciative sip from his glass. The young bucks in the newsroom had started raising questions. He couldn't hold them off forever.

Evans was just now getting back into POTUS's good graces after the fiasco of Cuba when his advice had caused the President so much grief. Blast Bob Grant anyway! Evans thought savagely. Grant had meddled in the affairs of Cuba and caused what should have been a routine change of power to turn bloody.

The man's very name had eaten at Evans for more than a year. Now was payback time. Grant had involved himself in a murder, and Evans would take brutal pleasure in twisting the knife that would destroy him. Grant would see what it felt like to be on the receiving end of disaster.

Evans opened the starkly modern cabinet that housed his elaborate audio setup. As the familiar timbre of Coleman Hawkins's saxophone filled the room, Evans turned and contemplated the two Picassos hanging in brilliant solitude on the white wall opposite. Jazz and Picasso: heaven. Or it would be if he weren't alone.

He took his drink and sank into the cushions of the custom leather sofa that faded perfectly into the whiteness of the room.

Bob Grant. At last, he'd gone one step too far. But murder? Evans couldn't imagine how Grant had expected to get away with it, but the accumulation of power had a perverse effect on some people.

Now, Evans considered, watching the dark amber liquid swirl languidly in his glass, how could he insure that the *Herald* led the journalistic pack on what was sure to become a major story? How could he insure that everyone understood the significance behind Grant's involvement? And finally how could he insure that Frederickson's murder, the murder of a crack journalist in pursuit of a story, was properly avenged?

As the music swelled and receded, soared and muted, Evans considered the questions. He would spend the next eight days thinking of little else.

Grant closed the door to his hotel room with a sense of relief. Privacy. The lines on his face eased even more as he caught sight of the attractive woman waiting for him on the bed. "Ah, Rach, I was hoping you'd be here."

Rachel Grant smiled and came to him.

Grant cupped her face in his hands, kissed her, then pulled her close, kissing her neck and momentarily resting his head there. Her perfume was light but distinctive and as dear to him as every facet of her being. He'd hoped to find her waiting but hadn't realized the intensity of his desire until he'd touched her. Stolen moments such as these served to heighten their passion for each other.

He didn't need to ask how she'd known he would want her there. Twenty-seven years of shared experiences had engendered between them an intuitive bond, unbreakable and sustaining. He didn't need to ask how she'd known where to find him either. The order of events was as predictable as was everything—everything until tonight's meeting with the sheriff—in this well-ordered campaign.

Rachel had taken a three-week leave of absence from her Washington oncology practice, the last three weeks before the election on November 2. As always during a campaign, she and Grant traveled separately so that they could personally cover as much of Georgia as possible. Because both of their schedules, down to the minute, were known to both of their staffs, finding him would have been easy. Rachel would have realized upon hearing the news of the murder and the innuendoes about her husband's involvement that their nightly phone call wouldn't suffice. As they'd done throughout their marriage, they would face this latest crisis together.

"They're playing rough," she said, touching his cheek. "How serious is it?"

"I'm not sure," Grant said slowly. He slipped his arm around her waist. She was a tall woman, perfectly rounded in his opinion, and perfectly beautiful, inside as well as out. "I keep telling myself it's no different than the usual crank threat, but something about this . . ." He paused, trying to put into words the niggling sense of danger he'd felt all evening. "It feels queer, slippery." He shook his head in frustration, unable to understand, much less articulate, his feeling of imminent peril.

She regarded him quizzically for a moment before sitting on the couch and tucking her feet under her terry-cloth robe. She was more relieved than ever that she'd insisted she come here for the night. He needed her to help focus his thoughts and then unwind before they began the inevitable planning needed to counter potential fallout from the Frederickson investigation. Their speeches, press releases, schedules—all would have to be considered and possibly reworked. Even more he needed her to help uncover the source of his disquiet. Bob didn't let outside pressures bother him. That he was aware of them now bespoke a serious problem.

After twenty years in the military and twelve in the Senate, his antennae were well attuned to potential danger.

"The story is certain to die down quickly, at least any speculation about me," Grant said, sitting close to her and taking one of her hands. His words were confident, but his tone was still tentative, as if he was hacking his way through an alien underbrush of thought. "Nothing else makes sense, but you're right. Our friends in the press are gathered below right now."

"You're not exactly a media darling, darling," Rachel said with a smile, eliciting an answering one from Grant. She helped him out of his jacket as she spoke. He loosened his tie and settled back into the cushions. "Now tell me everything," she said.

"A Sheriff Jimmy Jenks in Oconee County is in charge of the investigation," Grant told her. "I met him tonight. He cultivates the good-ol'-boy image, but I'd say he'd be hard to fool."

"Good. Then he knows any thought of linking you to murder is . . . is . . ." She sat up abruptly, sparks in her eyes. ". . . stupid! Totally stupid! Murder! How could *anyone* connect you with murder!"

"Peter Evans is convinced I'm involved."

Rachel regarded him with dawning enlightenment. "Now it's beginning to make sense," she said, settling back into the sofa. "Peter Evans is an egotistical fool."

Grant chuckled. Even so the gnawing concern remained, just below conscious thought, like a cancer that hadn't manifested itself but was wreaking its silent damage nonetheless.

"What has Evans been saying?"

Grant told her about Evans's accusations and about Sheriff Jenks's attitude. She considered it all for a moment.

"Is Jenks a bigot?" she asked.

"No, I don't think so. He seems fair-minded, though his deputy . . ." Grant shrugged, remembering Farrar's bristly attitude.

"As long as the sheriff's not affected."

"He doesn't seem to be."

"Good," Rachel said decisively. "Then he's bound to discount you as a suspect immediately. How will this affect the campaign?"

"Very little I'd guess after the initial excitement dies down. The whole thing's absurd. Me murdering someone because he'd discovered something about me? Lord knows I'm not perfect, but murder?" He took her hands and held them against his chest. "I'm only sorry this might touch you—hurt you."

She didn't let him continue. "Don't even think such a thing! A lie can't touch me or hurt me. Besides, this will be over in a few days. They'll catch the person responsible, and Evans will take his sensationalism elsewhere."

"Campaigns are a grind, aren't they?" Grant gave her hands a squeeze.

"And to think we've voluntarily put ourselves through three of them," she agreed, laughing wryly. The sensuous sound welled softly from deep in her throat. "We have to be crazy."

"No, just masochistic." He laughed with her. "Wouldn't the media love to have that quote?" He couldn't help wondering if just such an offhand remark had been the basis of Frederickson's condemnation of him— if Frederickson had, indeed, said anything. Evans was Evans, after all.

"We'd better call the kids," Rachel said, all humor wiped from her face. Being far from the children was always difficult. These circumstances made it doubly so. She stood and started toward the phone by the bed. "Do we tell them anything special?"

"To expect a few rough days, I suppose, but other than that . . ." Grant shrugged, reached for the phone on the end table, and began dialing.

"We're under reporter siege," Henry, their youngest, a thirteen-year-old live wire, announced with obvious relish as soon as he heard their voices.

"They bothering you?"

"Naw. I threw a few water balloons out the upstairs window. You should've seen them run. They're staying out by the street now." He sounded wistful. Rachel cocked an amused eyebrow at Grant.

"Is India there?" she asked.

"Sure. All of us are. Well, almost. Bailey's still out." "All" meant India, the oldest at twenty-two and a senior in premed at Georgetown University; Bailey, a twenty-one-year-old junior at Georgetown, who was taking the semester off to help in his dad's campaign; Olivia, a senior in high school; and Henry, the youngest, an eighth grader. Justice, a black Lab, rounded out the family.

"India, any problems?" Rachel asked when her daughter got on the phone.

"Not now. For once Henry did something right. Those reporters scattered just like the Three Stooges. What's going on? We heard about the murder of some reporter, but Dad involved? Now that's weird."

51

"Sounds like you know about what we do," Grant said. "Poor Frederickson was murdered, and since it's campaign silly season, you'd better be prepared. Any reporter who tries to corner you, just ignore him. Don't say a word. Everything will settle down in a few days. Now—"

"And if it hasn't?" India interrupted. She was a born pessimist, much to the despair of her naturally optimistic parents. They could only hope her pessimism this time was as unjustified as usual.

"We want you to stay with Cynthia, starting tomorrow." Grant looked a question at Rachel, and she smiled gratefully.

Cynthia Novitsky was Grant's administrative assistant. A widow with both sons recently on their own, she always welcomed overnights by the Grant kids. Rachel and India worked out the details, and after talking to Olivia, the Grants hung up.

"I wonder what Bailey's up to," Rachel said, her eyes thoughtful. She went to Grant's suitcase, opened it, and began unpacking.

Bailey lived at home while he attended Georgetown, as did his sister India. For this semester only, he'd taken time off and was learning the fundamentals of campaigning, at present helping Cynthia with commercials, speech writing, fact gathering, voter lists, the minutiae of a successful campaign. His real talent, however, lay in his genius with computers. Anything about computers Bailey understood. He'd been absorbed by them since his tenth birthday when he'd received the first of three. Presently, when he wasn't tied down with the campaign, he was working on getting Grant's office computer system up to speed and having great fun doing so, especially since his father was so in awe of his prowess.

"He probably found something to do with 'The Boys,'" Grant said, "though he mentioned a girl when he called this morning." Grant and Bailey held daily strategy conferences over the phone.

"A girl?" Rachel asked, turning from the closet where she was hanging Grant's clothes beside hers. "About time he thought of something besides his computers. I hope she's nice." She removed his shaving kit from the suitcase and started toward the bathroom. Grant dialed Cynthia's number.

"I'm glad you're sending the kids here," Cynthia told him. "You know how much I love having them. Besides, no need to take chances."

They both thought about riots, random attacks, emotional responses to improbable stimuli. Too many people enjoyed gratuitous violence, happy for any excuse to break the confines of authority. Political figures, like all highly visible personalities, were especially vulnerable. Even their children could become targets of mindless psychotic or amoral urges. Too many people accepted no responsibility for their actions. Too often, in a welter of psychiatric excuses, such irresponsibility, such depravity was excused and even condoned.

"I don't expect any problems," Grant reassured her, "but thanks for helping out." He recounted his conversation with Sheriff Jenks.

"Frederickson's supposed to have said *that?*" Cynthia exclaimed. "Strange. I'll see if anyone here remembers talking to him. I'll check with the Atlanta office, too. I'm surprised someone hasn't mentioned it though. Frederickson must have been real cagey—if any of this is even true." She sounded thoroughly puzzled. "Evans—do you think he made it up?"

"Mike suggested the same thing," Grant said, hesitantly, "but, no, I can't believe even Evans would do that. Something has to be there, with Evans, no doubt, adding his own touches. What are the tracking polls showing?"

"Tonight's remained steady. You're ahead by thirty-three, but that wouldn't reflect any fallout from Frederickson's murder. If the story dies out in a day or two, we shouldn't suffer much at all."

"It's bound to," Grant said, stifling a yawn, "in spite of Evans. The whole thing, to quote India, is too 'weird' to be believed."

Even knowing that to be true, he couldn't shake his feeling of foreboding.

Andrew Stoner's apartment was typical of college quarters everywhere. The room vibrated with the beat of the music coming from stereo speakers in opposite corners of the room. Pizza boxes littered tables and floor, vying for space with empty beer cans and dirty dishes. The furniture gave new meaning to the term *used*.

Bailey Grant leaned against a wall, wondering why he felt so uncomfortable. These were his closest friends, after all. He'd known them almost all his life. Then why did he wish he could be somewhere else? He couldn't figure out what had happened and why it seemed to have happened so quickly. Maybe it was the drinking, he thought, surveying the room. While he didn't mind a beer or two every now and then, his friends' main goal was to drink until they either passed out or puked, not a pretty sight either way. Or maybe it was the joints being passed from hand to hand.

The distinctive smells of marijuana and incense hung over the room, fighting the fog of cigarette smoke.

Bailey looked around the apartment and sighed. The music was good—Jane's Addiction—and at least Sherrill Holmes was with him.

He smiled at her, admiring her long, slender legs much in evidence under a provocatively short skirt. "You look great tonight," he told her.

She smiled, her dark gray eyes alight. "Thanks for noticing. You want another beer?"

"No, thanks." Probably the third or fourth time he'd said no. Maybe she was nervous and unsure how to please him, he thought, immediately buoyed by the idea she might care. He'd only known her since September, but he liked her. He liked her a lot. She was pretty, funny, and smart—a deadly combination, at least in his case, he was beginning to think. "Time to be going, I'd say," he told her, nodding toward the other side of the room.

Bear—Larry Baranowski—was about to pass out, judging by the signs. He wouldn't be leaving Andrew's apartment that night.

Nearby, Andrew was in whispered conversation with Reggie Dixon. If only Andrew hadn't started including Reggie in their group, Bailey thought. Reggie gave him the creeps, and Reggie was putting on a lot of pressure about heavy drugs, too much pressure.

Andrew had met Reggie somewhere and had insisted he join the group. Even Andrew wasn't sure just who Reggie was or where he came from. Reggie was fun; that was all that mattered.

Sherrill put her hand on Bailey's arm.

"Reggie wants you." She looked bored, but she smiled up at Bailey. He couldn't help smiling back. Just being with her—even here—made him feel good.

Sherrill was great company, and she was beautiful, no doubt about that. She reminded him of Cleopatra, or his idealized idea of her: glossy black hair; bronze skin; high cheek bones; slightly slanted deep gray eyes, wonderfully large and expressive; full sensuous lips. At the thought of those lips on his, Bailey's smile broke into a grin.

"Whatta you say we have a real party?" Reggie yelled. Several kids turned toward him. "Why don't you score us a couple of quarter bags and some coke, Bailey-boy?"

Andrew nodded eagerly. "Yeah, Bailey," he agreed. "You could do it."

"Come on, guys," Bailey said, his grin wiped away. He tried to keep his tone light, hard to do since he had to yell to be heard. The walls literally pulsed with the music. "You know that's crazy. Drugs'll make you stupid."

"I believe little Bailey-boy's chicken," Reggie sneered.

"Get off his back," Bear said, slurring his words. He lumbered over and draped an arm around Bailey. Bailey held his breath to keep from gagging. Bear's breath was a nauseating blend of booze and cigarettes. "Bailey here's my buddy."

"Buddy," Bailey said, tapping Bear on the arm with his fist, "help me convince them to forget this fool idea."

"Yeah, Bear," Milton Clark agreed, coming over to join them, "make 'em see sense."

"I don't know, guys," Bear said slowly. "We could use some excitement around here."

"Sure could," Andrew agreed. "We've turned into a bunch of wusses, never trying anything anymore."

"But not coke, guys," Bailey said. "It's stupid."

Sherrill stood quietly, listening to the byplay. Bailey could feel the tension in her arm where it touched his. He squeezed her hand.

"Maybe they're right, Bailey," said one of the girls sitting on the floor at their feet. "I like the idea of trying something different."

"We're talking drugs here, not some micro-brewery beer," Bailey retorted sarcastically.

"People die," Milton interjected, "even the first time."

"So," Andrew retorted. "People die in cars, too, and I don't see you walking." He spilled some beer down his chin as he took a swig. "You're no fun anymore."

Fun! Bailey thought with disgust. He took Sherrill's arm.

"We're gonna get out of here," he yelled over the music.

"Might as well," Andrew said, waving his beer for emphasis. "You're getting to be a real wimp, isn't he, doll, leaving just when the action's getting hot?" He leered at Sherrill. Then, weaving slightly, he began to turn away. Bailey grabbed his arm to steady him. Andrew brushed the hand off angrily. "Don't touch me, man. I can do just fine on my own." He walked unsteadily toward the bed in the corner and collapsed on it. The couple already there scooted over out of the way.

Milton, Bailey's closest friend, walked with Bailey and Sherrill toward their cars. "Thanks for coming by to help me keep an eye on things," he said.

Milton, Bear, Andrew, and Bailey were "The Boys," inseparable since grade school. Milton had called Bailey that afternoon, saying he thought Andrew and Bear might be considering doing hard drugs and would Bailey please come and help convince them otherwise. Since Sherrill had already said she wanted to come, Bailey had agreed.

"Andrew and Bear are looking bad," Milton said now. "Dead drunk most nights, skipping classes, the whole bit." He shook his head, his look half disgusted, half concerned.

"You really think we can do something to stop them?" Bailey asked, rummaging in a pocket for his car keys. He'd asked the same thing that afternoon. He still wasn't convinced they could help, but as Milton had said, friends were friends.

"Maybe not," Milton agreed glumly, "but the least we can do is stick by them. They got us out of some pretty hairy jams in the past."

"Yeah. The Big Drop."

Milton chuckled. "Weren't we something back then?"

They were barely twenty-one now, but that past predicated many of their present actions. The Big Drop had been only one of several classic exploits, a flamboyant excess of youthful exuberance. If Andrew and Bear hadn't done some quick talking, the police would've landed on their parents for sure.

"'The Big Drop?'" Sherrill asked. "What on earth was that?"

Both young men laughed. "Sorry, Sherrill," Bailey said. "That's one story you won't be hearing."

"I don't know about that," Milton retorted, grinning. "Remember when you—"

Bailey gave his friend a playful shove. "Open your mouth, and you're dead, old buddy."

"Now, you've *got* to tell me," Sherrill pleaded. "I can't imagine Bailey ever doing anything wrong." A surprising hint of exasperation colored her voice.

"He wasn't always the model citizen you see standing before you tonight," Milton said. "In fact—"

"Milton." Bailey's voice held a mock threat.

They both laughed. Sherrill joined in a little uncertainly.

"Seriously, though," Bailey said, "all this cocaine talk." He leaned against his car and looked suddenly immeasurably tired. "Reggie is really pushing it. Andrew's going to do it. Bear, too. I can feel it."

"Maybe it's not such a bad idea," Sherrill said, thrusting balled fists into her pockets.

Bailey was stunned. "Cocaine? Not bad?"

"Not for me," she said quickly. "But shouldn't they be able to do what they want?"

"Look, I gotta go," Milton said. "See ya tomorrow night. I'm counting on you, Bailey."

Bailey and Sherrill seemed not to have heard him.

With a shrug, Milton walked on down the street, his shoulders slumped.

Bailey unlocked the car door. "Get in," he told Sherrill. She'd barely settled on the seat when he slammed the door.

After he started the car, he sighed and leaned his head on the steering wheel.

"Look, Bailey. I'm sorry." Sherrill touched his arm tentatively. "Cocaine, I don't know . . . Sometimes I get confused, I guess."

"Confused!" Bailey swung around to look at her. "I don't get you, Sherrill. Most of the time you're just the kind of girl I've always hoped to meet." Sherrill dropped her eyes in confusion. When he continued, she looked up at him through her long black lashes. "But cocaine? How can you think coke could be good for anyone? And these are my friends! Milton just told you—they're my best friends!"

Sherrill didn't answer for a long time. Her voice was low when she did. Bailey leaned closer. "I'm sorry, Bailey," she whispered. "I know what you mean, but . . ." She stopped, then burst out. "I don't know what's right anymore! You're just so nice! I'm afraid I like you too much." When he started to respond, she spoke quickly. "Take me home, would you, please? Just take me home." She stared stonily out the windshield, ignoring him completely.

With an exasperated sigh, Bailey put the car into gear and edged it into traffic. Now he remembered why he'd been in no hurry to get serious about any girl. They were impossible to understand.

Monday, October 26:
Eight Days Before the Election

Grant let Masterson into the hotel room, pushing papers off the sofa to make room for him to sit. Rachel had left an hour earlier and would just now be arriving at her first campaign stop. She'd been upbeat when she kissed him good-bye, sure the Frederickson murder was of no more consequence than annoying static in a satisfyingly interference-free campaign. Grant, his antennae attuned to what he suspected was a more serious frequency, hoped she would prove him wrong.

He'd spent the last hour going over his schedule for the day, jotting down special mentions to make in each speech and reminding himself of people he would know at each stop. Even so, Jenks's questions and insinuations were never far from the front of his mind.

"Bad news, I'm afraid," Masterson said, indicating an article given prominent position on the front page of one of the papers he carried.

The *Washington Herald*, Grant noted. He skimmed the article, his brown eyes growing progressively harder. "They might as well have said I murdered Frederickson," he said, throwing the paper on the table in disgust.

"That statement from the Johns Hopkins law professor is the clincher: 'No one can be allowed to place himself above the law,'" Masterson quoted, taking a candy bar from his pocket. He held it toward Grant, who shook his head. "Of course, they don't say he was referring to you specifically, but the inference is obvious."

"Too obvious. Makes it sound as if Frederickson really had uncovered something unsavory about me."

"'Unsavory?'" Masterson questioned, his mouth full of candy. "Heinous is more on the mark. Details came in on the wire early this morning, courtesy of the *Herald*."

"Why am I not surprised? Has the Georgia media picked it up?"

"They're low-keying it, at least for now." He handed Grant several Georgia papers. "By tonight, who knows?"

Grant skimmed the pertinent articles, finding only peripheral mention of his name. "What's this about your saying I'm a logical murder suspect?" he asked, indicating a quote.

"Yeah, I saw that." Masterson wiped some chocolate from the corner of his mouth. "Crazy how reporters twist things. I told them they would be questioned, too. At least the rest's pretty straight, but who knows how long that'll last."

"Have you heard anything from Jenks?"

"Nothing. I called, but he wasn't in."

"Cynthia's checking to see who Frederickson contacted in our Washington office." With a last look at the *Herald*, Grant stacked the newspapers. "In Atlanta, too. Bailey will be doing Cynthia's legwork on Frederickson and will continue here if need be when he comes Friday. He can coordinate reports."

"Heaven help us if it hasn't died down by then," Masterson said, looking at his watch. "We'd better get going." He picked up Grant's suitcase and headed for the door.

"Right." Grant put his speech notes in his briefcase. "This is one time I for sure don't want to be late," he said as he shrugged his arms into his suit jacket. "The *Herald* would say I'd gone into hiding no doubt. And, Mike, call Jenks again if you haven't heard from him by noon. Be as cooperative as possible. We need to keep on top of this. That *Herald* article was vicious. Nothing about this feels right," he added with a bemused shake of his head. "Nothing."

His daily 7 A.M. senior staff briefing just completed, M. Eugene Corforth crossed the hall from the Roosevelt Room to his office, which was just a few steps from the Oval Office. He mentally scanned that day's schedule, wondering whether POTUS would spend more time in the Oval or in his inner sanctum, an office/den hidden beyond the Oval. Wrapped as he was in his thoughts, Corforth fairly collided with Edmund Miller and Charles Kendall, members of the National Security Council (NSC) staff.

"Anything traveling on the wires?" Corforth asked. The NSC staff kept up-to-the-minute on intelligence information from around the world.

"Nothing to speak of," Miller told him. "I've been out of the office the past few days so I've been at it awhile to see if I missed anything. Everything's been quiet." He cocked his head toward Corforth. "This mess with Bob Grant is something, though, isn't it?"

Corforth chuckled, as much at Miller's transparent attempt to learn the administration's attitude as at Grant's discomfort itself. Miller was a clever one, certain always to be in the middle of everything. "Sure hope Grant is squirming," Corforth said emphatically.

He, like the President, had suffered under Grant's hand in Cuba. Neither had forgotten the humiliation. Much to his bemusement, however, lately Corforth had found himself harkening back to that time all too often and feeling an uncomfortable sympathy with Grant and José Moya, the Senator's choice to lead Cuba. Gradually and reluctantly, Corforth had come to suspect that Grant might have been right.

Corforth stopped himself from shaking his head irritably at such absurd—and traitorous—thoughts. Instead, he pulled a fresh roll of antacids from his pocket, peeled back the silver lining carefully, and popped one into his mouth. His queasy stomach: That was of recent origin as well.

"Grant deserves anything that happens to him," Kendall said, pushing his glasses up on his nose, a gesture he repeated with annoying regularity. "He's a real problem for us."

"Unfortunately, an adept one," Corforth said. Again thoughts of Cuba. His hand rubbed the worry beads in his pocket. He let it remain there, unconsciously drawing comfort from the beads' cool familiarity.

"From what I've heard through contacts in Georgia," Miller said, smoothing back his hair, "none of us will have to suffer with Grant much longer. Apparently, things are turning decidedly sour for him, and Caruso could end up pulling this one out after all, against all conventional wisdom. Another interesting rumor—" Miller's eyes took on a malicious glint. The other two turned toward him expectantly. "Grant's old DEA file is supposed to be hot."

Corforth looked thoughtful but made no comment.

"With Grant gone," Miller continued, "the Republican presidential primary would be wide open, and we'd have a much easier time in two years. Not to mention being rid of Grant and his infernal Senate inquiries," he added. "Caruso's a good guy." He shifted the files he held. "He'd be a real asset. Is the President considering campaigning down there?"

"Could be," Corforth replied noncommittally, filing the idea away as a good one, that and Grant's DEA record. "Let me know anything you hear. This is important to POTUS."

Deputy Hank Farrar thumped a stack of reports down on the desk in front of the sheriff. With a resigned glance at his deputy, Jenks picked up the top one and began scanning it.

"Killed by a single shot through the head," Jenks read aloud.

"I could've told you that," Farrar said.

"No spent cartridge or slug."

"Could've told you that, too."

Jenks ignored his deputy, instead flipping methodically through the reports. Hank thought he could tell everyone plenty and wasn't bashful about saying so.

"No forced entry. No fingerprints other than Frederickson's and his wife's on any of his things. The maids were everywhere. Sixteen unidentified latents, about what we expected."

"The boys are checkin' the odd prints against the last folks to use the room. It'll take time." Hank wasn't bashful about stating the obvious either.

"They won't find anything useful," Jenks told him, not bothering to look up. "Our murderer wore gloves. Too smart not to. Anyone who watches TV's too smart. Says here Frederickson was killed between 9 and 12 Saturday night. Anybody hear anything?"

"Nope. Leastways not so far," Farrar said, sticking his thumbs into his waistband and rocking back and forth on his heels. "We're still huntin' for five folks who checked out afore the body was found."

"Must've used a silencer anyway. Only thing that makes sense. 9 and 12. What was the Senator doing then?"

"Plannin' to check this afternoon," Farrar said with a momentary pause in his rocking. "Other things to do first. I want plenty of ammo 'fore I see him."

"Just hold off a bit, would you? I want to do that interview myself." Farrar scowled. Ignoring his deputy's disappointment, Jenks asked, "You contact Frederickson's next of kin?"

"That'd be a wife, Corinne Frederickson. Couple of kids, too: boy, four, and girl, three. Police in Virginia got ahold of the wife yesterday. She's supposed to be at home this morning." Farrar handed Jenks a slip of paper with the phone number.

"Thanks." Jenks placed it neatly on top of the reports. "What about the hamburger Frederickson had? Anyone remember seeing him at Crazy Sam's?" Crazy Sam's Fast Food Emporium was the social center of Oconee County, at least for the under-twenty crowd.

"Yeah. Elizabeth Woodson was doin' the flippin' then. You know Lizbeth. Willie Warren Woodson's girl. She swears she recollects the guy. Came in around 9:45. Remembers 'cause they were hunkerin' down for a right good stampede after the movies."

Jenks raised an eyebrow in interest. "The time fits in with the autopsy report. Anyone with him?"

"Not 'cordin' to Lizbeth, least not so as she noticed. Cain't say whether he left by himself or not."

The sheriff leaned back in his chair, propped his boots on the desk, and laced his fingers on his stomach, his usual position for ruminating. "Frederickson bought the hamburger at around 9:45, according to Elizabeth. The coroner says he was dead at least by midnight. The hamburger was still in the sack wrapped. Stands to reason Frederickson died soon after he got back to the motel and soon after he bought it, unless he liked 'em cold. Question is: Did the murderer come back with him?" Jenks lifted one finger. "Did he follow him from Crazy Sam's and force his way in when Frederickson let himself in?" Two fingers. "Or did he somehow get Frederickson to open the door before he had a chance to even take that first bite of the hamburger?" Three fingers.

"How you gonna find out?"

"Find the killer and ask him, I reckon." Jenks sat up and reached for Corinne Frederickson's phone number. "Don't suppose anyone else can tell us. The boys keeping this tight?"

"Course, Sheriff . . . sir," Farrar said huffily. He bridled at the suggestion. "Ever'one's keepin' tighter'n a tick, just like you said."

"Good. Be sure it stays that way. Now send Sally in here, would you?" Jenks began dialing.

The Madison Rotary Club rose en masse at the conclusion of Grant's speech, bestowing on him the last of several noisy standing ovations. Matt Goldie, his hands raised in a victory clench above his head, stood out in the middle of the crowd. Grant grinned and waved. There was no one he liked better or respected more than Goldie.

Now retired and a flying fanatic who took any opportunity to crease the air with his private jet, Goldie had spent the last four years attending most of Grant's political events—social ones, too, for that matter. Goldie had been an unabashed Grant supporter from the beginning and had organized a group of influential white businessmen from throughout the state during Grant's first primary race twelve years before. Their support had in large measure secured Grant that first nomination and ultimately the election.

Grant, grinning broadly at the cheers of support, stepped off the stage and into the crowd. The faces around him were all smiles. The hands slapped his back and shook his hand. The voices spoke encouragement and appreciation.

Like Goldie, the people at this meeting were Grant's allies, kindred souls whose support of his philosophical positions had made his past victories possible. Many had spent as much time as he working for his reelection. Grant tried to give their words the attention they deserved, but his mind kept returning to his puzzling conversation with Sheriff Jenks the night before. Surely the sheriff wouldn't use the Frederickson murder to impede his campaign, Grant thought, shaking another hand. Even in the midst of these encouraging voices, he was nagged by a sense of something out of place, of something left undone or not quite right.

Slowly, he made his way to Goldie and gave him a bear hug. Side by side the two circulated through the room as Grant reassured his friends and supporters. Only after he'd visited with everyone did he move to the back of the room, where the media waited with their questions. The reporters, unlike the crowd, focused on Grant's possible guilt. He continually turned the questions into ones of innocence but was beginning to feel anger at the unremitting doubt inherent in them.

"Don't let them get to you," Goldie whispered in his ear.

Startled, Grant turned toward him. Goldie winked.

"Five more minutes," Grant said, smiling at the reporters and mentally blessing Goldie for cooling him down just in time. Goldie was a fire fighter in every sense of the word, he thought with amusement. "What do you say we concentrate on the campaign for a while? I have a Senate race to run, and you'd better believe I intend to win it."

Afterward, Goldie walked with Grant to the waiting car.

"You can't let this get you down," Goldie said, his hand on Grant's shoulder.

"Guess I've been spoiled lately, haven't I?" Grant climbed into the backseat. "I'd almost forgotten what a dogfight that first campaign was. Looks like the media's been sharpening its teeth ever since."

"Not surprising," Goldie agreed. "But most folks appreciate your making the tough decisions, the ones they'd make themselves if they had the chance. That's what the cheering was all about—thanking you for standing up for the truth." He closed the car door and leaned down so he could talk to Grant through the open window. "A lot's happened since that first campaign, Bob, most of it for the better, but that doesn't mean Caruso's not out there gunning for you. I've heard he's practically salivating for your job. Don't treat him lightly."

"After yesterday," Grant said with a wry smile, "you needn't worry. I'm not taking anything for granted. I've the oddest feeling about all this, Matt. Almost a sense of impending doom." He lifted an eyebrow in self-mockery. "Preelection jitters, you suppose?"

Masterson slammed his own door and fidgeted impatiently beside Grant. Both Grant and Goldie ignored him.

Goldie regarded Grant thoughtfully, then nodded, as if to affirm his belief in Grant's intuition. "I'll start poking around," he promised, "see if I sense anything. See how things are shaping up in different parts of the state, too."

"That would be a real help. Thanks."

"Keep in touch," Goldie said as he straightened and moved back.

Grant nodded to Robby, his driver, and the car pulled away.

"Five TV stations, one network show, maybe a dozen newspapers," Mike Masterson said, referring to coverage of the breakfast speech, "but you know that."

"Almost more media than public." As he spoke, Grant waved to smiling supporters lining the street. As always he especially enjoyed this spontaneous enthusiasm, Georgians hanging around after events for one last chance to show their support. Whenever time permitted, he stopped to shake hands.

Masterson didn't bother to look. "You had a good crowd," he said. "Supportive, too."

"That was a relief," Grant said, settling back against the seat after a wave and a smile for the last straggle of supporters. "I wasn't sure what to expect."

"The overnight tracking poll shows you with a commanding lead over Caruso, same as yesterday and every day before, for that matter. Almost no one's bought this murder garbage."

"Any word from Jenks?" Grant asked, reaching into the cooler on the floor for a bottle of water, always kept cold and ready.

"Nothing." Masterson got a cold can of pop and lifted the tab, releasing a tiny *fizz*. "Guess he doesn't know anything new."

"I expected to hear they'd found the killer by now. Or at least a motive more sensible than Evans's for me."

"Told you Jenks was dim. Too bad the media isn't giving you a break."

"They'll milk this for all it's worth, I suppose," Grant said with little interest. "Good for business."

"Their questions haven't been friendly, admittedly, especially Vinton's—he's a snake if there ever was one—but you handled them well. Grace under pressure. That's bound to look good to voters." Masterson opened his briefcase, took out the briefing paper for their next stop, and handed a copy to Grant.

"As long as they know I'm innocent," Grant said, glancing through it. "I keep remembering that old adage 'no smoke without fire.'"

"So will everyone else," Masterson said gloomily. "How many people will believe you have nothing to hide? After all, a man is dead, and his employer is saying you had a motive." He snapped the briefcase shut and stowed it under his feet. "Someone had to have a good and sufficient reason for killing him."

"Don't worry. The truth is bound to surface soon."

"Let's hope. Besides, voters won't ignore your years of public service."

"But the media will."

Masterson grunted his disgust. They were back in familiar territory.

"And what the media ignores," Grant continued, bringing the discussion full circle, "people tend to forget."

"Think we ought to cancel some events?"

Grant looked at him in surprise. "Cancel them? That's the last thing we should do. I don't want anyone to think I have something to hide."

"I just thought things might die down more quickly," Masterson said defensively, "if you weren't so much in the public eye."

"No. We change nothing," Grant said, making a notation in the margin of the briefing paper.

Masterson glanced at Grant's profile, firm and uncompromising, and made no further comment.

Looking at his watch, M. Eugene Corforth increased his pace. He didn't want to be late for the morning briefing with the President in the Oval Office. He'd spent more time reviewing staff requests than he'd planned. Leaving his office after a brief word with his secretary, he walked quickly down the hall, past the Caitlin oil paintings neatly spaced on the wall, and into the Oval.

National Security Advisor Chadwick Stevenson and Attorney General Jonathan Hunter were already seated. Even the Veep was there, not that he would contribute much of value. He seldom did. He wasn't out to impress his colleagues, who wouldn't have been fooled anyway, just to impress voters. Being visible in every photo-op was a cornerstone of that strategy. The President was popular; standing at his side enhanced the Veep's popularity and increased his perception as a world leader. Photo-ops and fronting for the President in no-win situations were his duties, that and raising money for the party. The media loved him—he'd grown up and gone to private schools with many of them—so he was gratifyingly successful at both.

The President was seated at his desk, flanked by the Stars and Stripes on his right and the flag bearing the Presidential Seal on his left. Armchairs were drawn up across the desk from him. He absently stared across the room at the roaring fire a Navy steward had lit in the white marble fireplace. Its warmth was more than welcome on this crisp fall day.

At Corforth's arrival, the others in the room murmured perfunctory greetings.

"Things are looking up in the Grant-Caruso race," Corforth told the President. "This murder investigation should keep Grant occupied."

"Bound to take time from campaigning," the President said, taking his eyes from the fire, "and that adultery charge!" He shook his head with bemused but obvious satisfaction.

The others smiled. Hunter even laughed. Only Corforth's face remained serious. Adultery? he wondered. What were they talking about? And why hadn't he been told? He wasn't about to ask, giving a clear admission that he'd been left out of the loop.

"Can you imagine?" POTUS continued. "Sanctimonious Grant involved in a sordid affair that leads right to a murder." He snorted contemptuously. "Gives all politicians a bad name."

"Peter Evans is on top of it," Hunter told him.

Corforth eyed Hunter speculatively, his interest, however, carefully concealed.

"He assures me," Hunter continued, "that he's just started digging and expects to find more, much more. Kirk Vinton's the lead reporter."

The President nodded, pleased at the choice. Vinton had a solid grasp of issues.

"I wouldn't have believed it a week ago," Hunter continued, "but we just might add Georgia to our side of the aisle."

"And get rid of Grant," the President said, his gratification obvious now. "Never have liked him. Any thoughts on how to help Caruso?"

"A trip to Georgia might be in order," Corforth said. His voice was steady. His thoughts, however, were chaotic. Why wasn't he in the know? Why was everyone else? He looked at Hunter and found the other's eyes on him. So Hunter *was* behind it, Corforth thought with a sinking heart. Hunter never allowed his victims to know they were being watched until he was ready. What power game was he playing this time? Corforth wondered, suddenly consumed with immeasurable weariness. The game of power politics had inexplicably lost its intrigue for him.

Corforth brought his mind back to the meeting. The President was speaking. "A Georgia trip is worth considering, certainly."

At least POTUS didn't seem cognizant of Hunter's plan, Corforth decided, trying to work his way through the conflicting messages in the room.

"If I could raise enough money to put Caruso in play," the President continued, "he would remember who got him elected."

He stood and began pacing, gazing into the Rose Garden as he usually did when thinking. He still felt a thrill knowing it was all his to use as he wished—and that he did, part of a calculated effort to always appear presidential. Being photographed greeting returning astronauts, the white columns of the walkway edging the Rose Garden providing a regal backdrop, was good for public relations. But what he, a diehard basketball fan, loved best was kidding around out there with both the professional and college champions each year as he honored their prowess.

"Grant loves to talk about getting tough on drugs," he mused. "Maybe we could use the Georgia rally to begin an in-depth comparison, Grant's blatant hypocrisy against our achievements through NIIA. Great sound bites."

"State and local police forces around the country have been reorganized using the guidelines of the NIIA," Hunter told them. The others in the room tried to show interest in information—dry information—they knew almost as well as he. "In the future all drug problems will be handled locally. We at the NIIA will merely oversee and insure competency. This change isn't new to you, I know," he said, fully aware their interest was feigned. "But remember, the realignment and its success have to be the focus of our news briefs. That'll stop Grant's anti-federal-government crusade. It'll help destroy the credibility of that whole philosophy and weaken the opposition in two years." He accepted the awe that now showed in their faces. No one was better at this game than he, Hunter knew. No one. "I've prepared an especially detailed report of those changes as they relate to Georgia. You've gotten that to Caruso, haven't you, Miller?"

"Yes, sir," Miller said. He looked up from his computer, which he used to record their meetings. "To emphasize it, I suggest we incorporate personalized anecdotes into the President's speech. First, random victims of drug attacks under the last administration, then others saved by our new policies."

The President looked interested.

"The people in the examples," Miller continued, consulting the appropriate file in his computer, "could be on stage with you, Mr. President. They would all be visually correct—a laborer, a teacher, even a migrant worker—thereby reinforcing your empathy with the working man."

"I'd want some street cops up there, too," the President told him, continuing his slow pacing, "'our warriors in the fight against drugs.' I don't want any question that we've sacrificed public security with our reforms."

Miller nodded. Again, he made a note in the palm-sized computer that seemed almost an appendage to the others since they seldom saw him without it. "We could develop commercials using footage from your speech, Mr. President," he added. "They could begin running almost immediately."

"Good. Winning this drug war is important to me."

"If the system works as well as we hope, this could be Nobel Peace Prize material," Corforth noted. "You should have won it with Cuba—would have if Grant hadn't interfered."

POTUS frowned at the memory, a memory distilled by time to his advantage. Corforth looked down at his notes, his face expressionless.

"A rally would be good," the President said decisively. He turned and resumed his pacing. "All benefit as far as we're concerned."

"As long as Grant loses," Hunter reminded him. He seemed preoccupied with polishing his glasses, a normal Hunter ruse.

"I'll have details tomorrow," Corforth promised, "but I won't commit until the last minute. We'll hold back on press releases, too."

"Of course," Hunter said. "I would hope you wouldn't commit us prematurely." He shifted in his seat so that his next words were directed toward the President—or more accurately toward the President's back. He was again contemplating the Rose Garden. "I've sent some NIIA agents down to Georgia to launch a thorough investigation into the murder. I'll be able to monitor the case and insure that justice is done, even if Grant is a United States Senator. If we need to point the sheriff in the right direction, we can do so."

As Attorney General and head of the year-old National Investigation and Intelligence Agency, Hunter might not have the legal right to interfere in a nonfederal case, at least at this early juncture, but no local sheriff yet had been willing to put his job on the line by refusing.

"Derek Bender, NIIA's chief investigator, is in charge," Hunter continued, putting his glasses back on and carefully folding his linen handkerchief into a perfect square before inserting it into his pocket. "Bender will report directly to me. He's aware of the need to handle everything properly. Media attention will be intense, which works to our advantage."

The President gave a nod of acknowledgment to Hunter. "I knew you'd be on top of it. The American people deserve our vigilance. No one is above the law." His face became thoughtful. "It's hard to believe Grant could have been so stupid. Convenient, though." He stared intently from one man to another. "Can't we apply some pressure from this end?"

"One of my aides says Grant's FBI and DEA files are worth a look," Stevenson told him.

"They have files on everyone, including us, probably," POTUS countered. "Any accusation, no matter how crackpot, is always investigated."

"But rumor has it these reports on Grant are hot."

"Have you heard anything about this?" the President asked Hunter.

"No," Hunter admitted with a slight frown, "but anything's possible. Maybe the last administration was able to keep the lid on them."

"Have them sent over," the President said finally. "Be careful though. Even if they have as little use for Grant as we do, black leaders can be touchy about investigations of one of their own. We need to keep them happy."

"Shouldn't be a problem," Hunter assured him. "I'll test the waters before we try anything, but they never support conservative blacks. Remember how they treated Clarence Thomas? They even tried to keep that Republican Gary Franks out of the Congressional Black Caucus. They'll be as glad to be rid of Grant as we are. He's an embarrassment."

The President looked out the window, blind to the wind-scattered leaves carpeting his putting green and to the gardeners working to remove them. "Getting rid of Grant is worth almost anything," he said quietly.

Bailey Grant hurried across the Georgetown campus toward The Cellar. He couldn't stop smiling. He felt good, really good. He was enjoying working for his dad's campaign even more than he'd expected, and that was a lot. He could kiss books good-bye for a few months longer and spend as much time as he wanted on computers without his parents complaining. It was his dad's office system he was working on, after all, and doing an awesome job at that. Even his dad seemed properly impressed. And his dad was blowing Caruso out of the water in the polls. No one was buying the murder garbage. Bailey's smile grew. To top it off, there was Sherrill. He couldn't help wondering—hoping, he admitted—that her remark last night about liking him—liking him too much!—had been serious.

He walked into the fusty dimness of The Cellar and scanned the tables. Sherrill was waiting for him, just as she'd promised.

"Anything look good?" he asked as he sat down beside her. Not an original opening, he thought, but she didn't seem to mind.

"You know you won't like what I ordered," she told him with a laugh. She was over her strange mood of the night before, Bailey was relieved to see.

"Yeah," he agreed. "A granola salad with roots on the side, I'll bet."

"Close, but without the roots. I'm dieting."

He laughed. Neither spoke for several minutes, content just being together. He reached over and took her hand. She gave his a gentle squeeze and let hers remain enclosed in his.

Though he wasn't enrolled at Georgetown that semester, Bailey tried to make it to the campus during his lunch hour. At first he'd sought out friends, Milton usually, but sometimes Andrew or Bear. Lately, however, his incentive had been different. Sherrill Holmes exerted a peculiar but far from unpleasant hold over him.

Their food arrived. Bailey gaped at the burger on her plate. "That's red meat!"

"For your information, sir," she said, arching a well-contoured eyebrow, "I have a most cosmopolitan taste in food. As in all things," she added for good measure. In spite of the humorous self-mockery, her eyes were troubled. Bailey would have liked to know why, but she seldom talked about herself. Sometimes he wondered whether something in her past caused her ambivalent feelings, as if she weren't quite sure what to believe or to do, or even how to feel about herself.

Their conversation made it around to Reggie Dixon, who'd been hanging out with Bear but especially with Andrew lately.

"A creep," Bailey opined succinctly.

"Agreed, but a funny thing," Sherrill told him, "I don't think he's even a student."

Bailey greeted this comment with interest.

"I mentioned McDonough Gym to him," Sherrill explained, nibbling her burger and not meeting his eye, "and he didn't have the foggiest. You tell me how he could've registered for classes without going there."

"In-ter-est-ing." Bailey drew out the word. "You make one fine detective. He's sure fooled Andrew."

"Andrew's so blasted most of the time," Sherrill retorted, "he wouldn't know Denzel Washington from Dolly Parton."

"Yeah," he agreed reluctantly, but he wished she hadn't said it. Andrew was his friend.

Bailey turned around as a huge hand clamped on his shoulder. The hand belonged to Bear, who pulled up a chair and began scarfing what was left of Bailey's fries. Milton joined them, too.

By the time they left, Bailey to hurry back to the Senate office and Sherrill and Milton to class—Bear wasn't sure where he would go but for sure wouldn't hurry—they'd agreed to meet at Andrew's apartment. With a backward wave, Bear ambled off.

"I can't make it tonight," Bailey said, watching Sherrill closely. She looked disappointed, he was pleased to see. "I've got some computer work that can't wait."

"I'll go," Milton said. "Try to talk some sense into them. Maybe I can keep them from doing anything too dumb."

Bailey felt a stab of guilt, but if anyone had ever taken on a losing cause he was afraid it was Milton. Even worse, these guys wouldn't appreciate his interference, at least not now they wouldn't.

Sherrill smiled beguilingly. "As long as we make it to Andrew's tomorrow night," she said to Bailey. "Promise?"

He looked doubtful, remembering all that needed to be done to help his dad.

"Really, Bailey," Sherrill said, a crease of exasperation marring her forehead, "all I'm asking is to go to Andrew's tomorrow night. Surely you can manage that, can't you?"

Bailey knew she was serious. He could see it in her eyes. He was surprised, considering what she'd said earlier about Andrew or, more accurately, the way she'd said it, but surely this stupidity about his dad and murder would be over by then, wouldn't it? Surely, he would have some free time.

"Yeah," Milton said, "if you could just hold down the fort till I get out of my night class . . ."

"Okay, okay," Bailey said good-naturedly. "Andrew's it is, tomorrow night."

Sherrill looked relieved, but she also looked sad, almost apprehensive. She touched Bailey's arm, then squeezed it.

"Bailey, I like you so much," she said in a rush. "I hadn't expected this to happen."

Bailey felt a surge of euphoria. He'd thought she cared for him, but now he was sure. Before he could think of the right response, she gave him a quick peck on the cheek and rushed out the door without so much as a backward glance.

Bailey stared after her, then let out a whoop of joy, totally oblivious to the laughs and pointed fingers of those around him.

As had been true at the Rotary breakfast, Grant's luncheon address was well attended and well received. Grant walked outside afterward feeling almost sanguine for the first time since he'd been suggested as a suspect in Russell Frederickson's murder. He was more than pleased to have his instinct about danger proven wrong.

As he and Masterson started down the weathered granite steps of the courthouse, several cars skidded to a stop in the street in front. Their doors flew open, and reporters and photographers jumped out and rushed toward them, clutching cameras, notebooks, and tape recorders as they ran.

"Something's up," Masterson said into Grant's ear. He'd gotten a heads up from Cynthia only minutes before. He grabbed Grant's elbow. "I don't know much about it. Don't say anything. Let's get out of here and find out what's happening."

"Senator!" The first reporter addressed him breathlessly as others ran up, hoisting equipment into place and jockeying for position. The clatter was loud in the quiet of the small-town street. "What's your reaction to Russell Frederickson's letter?"

Grant stopped, puzzled. Frederickson's letter?

"Senator!" another shouted. "Did you threaten to kill Frederickson as he alleges?"

"Kill Frederickson?" Grant repeated, his eyes growing hard. "Don't be absurd!"

"Are you saying—"

"The Senator has no comment at this time," Masterson interrupted. He took Grant by the arm and hustled him down the steps and into the car.

Recognizing that Grant was getting away, the reporters surged forward to bracket his car, which inched forward, then sped away.

"What do you suppose that was all about?" Masterson asked, smoothing his hair with one hand and reaching for his cellular with the other.

"Don't ever do that again," Grant said, steel in his voice.

Masterson looked at him in surprise.

"I have nothing to hide," Grant continued, his anger unmistakable. "I should have stood my ground. Now their only footage is of my backside as I'm being hustled into a car to run away like some mafioso." He leaned forward to address the driver. "Robby, find a pay phone."

"We'll be late for the next event," Masterson argued. Prickly after the rebuke, he thrust the phone toward Grant.

Grant ignored both the phone and Masterson.

"Find that phone, Robby," he said tightly. "From now on we treat this as a hostile campaign, and the first rule is to use ground phone lines whenever possible. I'm not about to have the press monitoring my calls. Yours either, Mike."

Cynthia Novitsky grabbed her phone on the first ring. "It's bad, Senator," she told Grant.

The fax machine in the corner chattered nonstop, as it had since the moment of the noon newscast. Around her, the staff worked with something close to desperation to find answers that would bring sanity to a rapidly deteriorating situation.

"Corinne Frederickson, Russell Frederickson's widow, just gave a live interview," Cynthia continued. "She swears her husband was afraid you would kill him."

"What!"

"I wish . . ." Cynthia began. She stopped, knowing such wishful thinking was not only foolish but a waste of time. "Frederickson sent a letter to their lawyer," she continued, all emotion erased from her voice, "to be opened in case of his death. Frederickson gave no specifics, nothing about why he was afraid of you or what he expected to happen. At least that's the impression his widow gave. She was suffering, and it was apparent she believed the letter. She ended by denouncing you as a murderer."

The silence stretched as Grant digested the information. He appeared to be studying the street around the pay phone, but his eyes saw nothing.

"Any proof Frederickson wrote the letter?" he finally asked.

"None mentioned, but—"

"Have someone transcribe the interview so we can study it, maybe pick up on some nuance. I'm calling the sheriff."

"Calling Jenks?" Cynthia asked, her frown reaching through the phone lines. "I'm not sure that's wise, not without having a lawyer present." A lawyer herself, she understood the implications of this latest revelation all too well.

"I'm not guilty," Grant said decisively. "I'm not going to behave as if I am. We have to get a copy of that letter as soon as possible. If Frederickson truly wrote it, then he was afraid of me. I have to know why."

"Don't go to Jenks just for that," Cynthia argued. "Let me check with some contacts in the media."

"That would take too long. I want answers *before* the media starts hounding me."

He hung up and called Jenks without giving Cynthia time to mount another argument. He knew she was probably right—he was bound to be a serious suspect in the eyes of the law, Sheriff Jenks included.

After a short delay, he was put through to Jenks. "What do you know about this letter from Frederickson?" he demanded.

"Hold on, Senator," Jenks chided. "You're the one who needs to be answering the questions."

"Then the letter is genuine?" Grant asked, reining in his impatience.

"It appears to be."

Genuine. How could that be? Grant leaned against the side of the phone booth, his mind finding, then rejecting all possibilities. Nothing about this made sense. His sense of foreboding rushed back, magnified tenfold.

"Printed on Frederickson's portable printer," Jenks continued. "Mailed before his death."

"Did anyone else have access to the computer?"

"Sure could have, Senator, but the signature appears genuine."

"I don't understand," Grant said slowly. "Why would Frederickson believe that? Afraid of me . . ." He took a deep breath.

"Senator, I've got to warn you to be careful what you say. You might want to think about a lawyer."

"I'm the prime suspect," Grant said flatly, putting into words what Cynthia had only hinted.

"Can't argue with that," Jenks agreed. "Hard to imagine evidence more convincing than the victim's own words."

"Did he say *why* I wanted him dead?" Grant had to shout to be heard over the roar of a garbage truck working its way slowly down the street in front of him. He faced the wall and cupped his hand around the receiver so his words wouldn't carry.

"Nothing specific," Jenks said. "Just that he'd discovered something that would destroy you personally and politically, just like that fellow Evans said. I'll fax you a copy of the letter if you'd like."

"Thank you, Sheriff." Grant was conscious of an expanding sense of unreality. "I was hoping you would. But—I almost hate to ask—why are you telling me so much?"

"Corinne Frederickson's lawyer sold the letter to the *Herald*. In the morning, everyone's going to know everything I've told you, and I'd guess a lot more besides."

Grant gave a short laugh. "The *Herald!*"

"Sorry I have to ask this, Senator, but where were you Saturday night between 10 and 12?"

Had they pinpointed the time of Frederickson's murder? Grant wondered, realizing with a sinking heart he had no alibi. He'd hoped an alibi would cut short any suspicion that he'd been involved. "In my hotel room, Sheriff, by myself. No alibi. No alibi at all."

"Talk to anyone?"

"No one came to the room, not even Masterson. Wait a minute—" Grant paused, wanting his account to be as accurate as possible. "I called Rachel at around 10, then Cynthia Novitsky, my administrative assistant, about 10:25 or 10:30."

"I know, Senator. We have the record of those calls. You were a mighty talkative fellow, on that phone from 9:53 until 11:16."

"And that establishes my innocence?" Grant asked.

"Not according to the official time of death, but to my way of thinking it gives grounds for doubt, especially since you've spent about the same amount of time on the phone every night the past few weeks."

"Thank you, Sheriff," Grant said, relieved at having his favorable estimation of Jenks affirmed. The more Jenks looked into his background, the better Grant would like it. He had nothing to hide.

"Anyone have what you might call a personal grudge against you?" Jenks asked.

"You mean someone killing Frederickson to get at me?" Grant turned and saw Masterson in the car, pointing with exaggeration at his watch. "That's almost as absurd as killing him myself."

"Well, then, what about someone taking advantage of the murder to frame you?"

"I have political enemies," Grant replied, turning his back to Masterson and the car and trying to assimilate the sheriff's bizarre suggestion. "I can't imagine they would use criminal means to get back at me. What gave you that idea?"

"I'm not rightly sure, but if you think it's unlikely . . ."

"I can't imagine anyone hating me that much or finding me that much of a threat," Grant said with finality.

"Maybe not, but you might give it some thought. Frederickson was investigating only you; all his information discredits you; every clue we have points to you." Jenks's voice was suddenly hard. "Right now you're our number-one suspect, Senator. To be honest, our only suspect. But you were on the phone. The question now has to be, if you didn't kill him yourself—and some around here reckon you could have cooked up some clever plot to do just that—but if you didn't, then did you go out and hire yourself someone to kill him for you? Think about that, would you? Then see if that enemy theory you laughed at doesn't sound a sight more likely. If I were you, I'd think about it plenty. Someone killed that young reporter, Senator. If you didn't, you'd better come up with some powerful good ideas about who might have and why. Right now we don't have diddly-squat but you."

Grant hung up the phone with infinite care. Slowly, he walked to the curb and climbed into the waiting car. He remained immersed in thought during the half-hour drive to the next stop. He didn't hear Masterson's questions, much less answer them.

Did someone have reason to frame him? That unlikely question bounced around his mind, looking for an answer and finding none. He wasn't about to leave it alone, however. The answer had to be somewhere. He hadn't killed Frederickson, but someone seemed intent on making it appear that way.

Grant was late for the rally, just as Masterson had prophesied, but the auditorium was packed nonetheless. The Frederickson murder was foremost on everyone's mind. Most didn't mention it, but he could see the speculative glances they cast in his direction and the way they looked quickly aside when they caught his eye. He couldn't blame them for wondering, Grant thought as he worked his way through the crowd, but he would have felt better had they assumed it was absurd. That they didn't was a sobering realization. How had politicians come to be held in such contempt that any allegation, no matter how extreme, would be immediately considered not just possible but probable?

The question for him was whether to face their unspoken doubts head-on and try to explain them away or to ignore them in hopes the murderer would be caught before any more damage could be inflicted.

Grant was still pondering that question late that afternoon as he dressed for a dinner speech. He bent down to tie his shoes and was staring at the carpet, weighing his options, when he realized the news had come on and his name was being mentioned. What now? he wondered as he turned up the sound.

"We take you now to Elaine Thomas in Atlanta," the announcer said.

"I have with me," Thomas said, "Tobias Caruso, Democratic opponent to Senator Robert Hawkins Grant. Mr. Caruso, can you assess the Grant situation for us?"

"I wouldn't like to make a judgment on that tragic situation at this time," Caruso said. His rich baritone exuded respectability and competence.

Big of him, Grant thought, frowning. Even so, he admired the man's political savvy. Free air time wasn't easy to come by, especially by a virtual unknown, as Grant himself had learned in that first campaign.

The phone rang.

"Caruso's on Four," Masterson told him.

"Thanks." Grant replaced the receiver.

A heavyset man with graying black hair and a swarthy complexion, Caruso looked at once both friendly and formidable. While not known for his political expertise—this was his first campaign—he was an entertaining speaker, stories of his stories preceding him as he campaigned around the state. Presumably, he'd entered the race for name recognition, targeting the next election as a more realistic shot, but now that the White House was hinting at an increased interest in his race, Caruso was even more eager to grab every opportunity for media exposure. For him, this race was looking more winnable by the hour, maybe by the minute.

"Bob Grant has enough problems without my adding to them," Caruso continued. "I'm confident the authorities will take proper action soon. However, while I make no accusations against Grant, I do feel, and feel strongly, that the people of Georgia deserve to know all the facts. They deserve the truth. This isn't just about a seat in the United States Senate. This is about justice."

Unable to stomach more, Grant flipped off the television, put on his suit jacket, and left the room. Masterson was just raising his hand to knock on the door.

Gilt-highlighted columns soared to the ceiling of the Mayflower Hotel ballroom, site of yet another political function. Many of the most posh of those events were held at this venerable Washington landmark.

Men dressed in custom-cut dark business suits were the perfect foil for well-coifed women, trim in their designer dresses, black, as always, the predominant color. The room was crowded with hundreds of such notables.

The buffet table with its artistically arranged trays of paper-thin salmon, caviar in red, black, and yellow, and other such tempting extravagances was barely touched. It was hard to eat and carry on a conversation. Alcohol, however, posed no such problems. Indeed, Eugene Corforth thought as he listened to the gabble of voices almost drowning out the piano, alcohol might even be considered a necessity.

"These affairs get to be a real bore, don't they?" Corforth said to Jonathan Hunter. They'd paused together as they mingled. This party, hosted by one of the nation's largest unions, was a must event for administration "names." The President wouldn't attend, but he would be conspicuously represented. At campaign contribution time, such show of force would be remembered.

Hunter looked at Corforth assessingly. Then he surveyed the people surrounding them, many of the most influential names in Washington. All held their drinks and stood their ground with the assurance of those comfortable in their power and confident of their influence. "I find that a strange remark, Eugene," Hunter said. "These affairs are where careers are made and broken." He nodded politely to Amy Corforth and moved away.

"Put you in your place, didn't he?" Amy said, nudging her husband with amusement.

"Obviously I don't have the right priorities," Corforth retorted. He felt his earlier suspicions heightening. Hunter was planning something, and that something would be at his expense, Corforth was sure.

Amy looked at her husband with surprise. Had she detected a note of bitterness in his voice?

"I think I'll go over and talk to Rebecca," she said, indicating Hunter's wife, standing by herself across the room. Maybe Rebecca would drop a hint about the goings-on at the White House—a long shot since the Hunters seemed to have little to say to each other, but worth a try.

"That would be nice," Corforth replied. "But let's leave as soon as is decent." He turned and joined the group behind him.

Eugene had seemed preoccupied lately, Amy thought as she threaded her way toward Rebecca. Was Jonathan Hunter part of the problem? Or something deeper? Though could it get much deeper than that?

Rebecca Hunter as usual seemed to blend into the background. Amy never saw her without feeling pity. Jonathan Hunter paid no more attention to his wife than he did to anything outside the halls of power. Thank goodness Eugene had more sense!

"An interesting group of people," Amy said when she reached Rebecca's side.

"Oh, hello, Amy." Rebecca's voice was as nondescript and vague as her clothes. "Interesting? Yes, I suppose so. Though they all seem alike to me."

Vague Rebecca might be, Amy thought, but her observations were on the mark surprisingly often.

"I don't suppose Jonathan would concur."

"No," Rebecca agreed, watching her husband as he shook hands and flattered yet another group. "I'm sure he wouldn't. He views people from a different perspective than I. I'm not much interested in making people useful, are you?"

"I suppose people like feeling useful," Amy said cautiously, unsure where the conversation was leading.

"But used? No better than a car or a fork or a tissue? To be put aside when no longer needed? Like markers in some high-stakes game with Jonathan as game master? Sometimes I wonder if he hasn't forgotten that life isn't a game and all men aren't eager to fall into his game strategy." Rebecca didn't wait for a response. She turned her gaze from her husband and looked at Amy. "But enough talk about Jonathan," she said with a sigh. "So boring. How are your children?"

Amy answered readily. She knew no topic was more likely to get Rebecca Hunter talking than her son, Joey. By the time Eugene returned, maybe a little sooner than was strictly decent, Amy had heard about Joey at Georgetown University, Joey at home, Joey in every possible circumstance. Unfortunately from Amy's viewpoint, the conversation had never made its way back to Hunter and the White House.

While Rebecca's comments had been glowing on the surface, Amy left with a feeling of disquiet. Something wasn't quite right. With Joey? With Rebecca? Or with Hunter himself? She wasn't sure. Maybe she could come up with some answers at Estelle's luncheon at the White House the next day.

Amy liked Rebecca, but Eugene was her main concern. If he were coming under fire from Hunter or even from one of Hunter's toadies, she wanted to be prepared. She'd lived in Washington for years, and she knew how to use the system, but she had to know the source of the threat in time to gather some ammunition. If Hunter was the source, she would need plenty.

Rachel sat beside Grant on the hotel room sofa. She felt cold in spite of his warmth and in spite of the terry robe she'd thrown over her clothes and tucked in around her.

Grant pulled her close. "I wish I could have spared you this." He kissed her forehead.

"Someone who hates you enough to kill someone else." She shivered. "Even the thought is sickening. At least the kids don't have to know about that part of it. Not yet anyway." As Grant opened his briefcase, she picked up the phone.

Henry answered on the first ring. "Hi, Mom. I hoped it would be you."

Rachel felt instantly better; his voice sounded normal. "You're all right?" she asked.

"Sure. A lot better than you, probably. That letter about Dad. What a stupid lie! He's all right, isn't he?" Henry was thirteen with all the pseudo-maturity of that age, but a catch in his voice betrayed his need for reassurance.

"Not only all right, but sitting here with me."

Grant put down the policy paper he'd been scanning and picked up the extension. "You hanging in there, son?" he asked.

"Gee, hi, Dad. You sound great." Henry sounded surprised.

"Of course I sound great. You can't let the talk upset you, Henry. It's campaign silly season, remember. I know this is worse than usual, but it will pass."

"I know that, Dad. It's just . . ."

"Some of the kids?" Grant prodded.

"Yes." The word hung between them.

"What have they been saying?"

Henry didn't answer.

"Something about my being a murderer?"

A reluctant "I can't tell you" followed a long pause.

Rachel stared sightlessly down at her robe. Her baby was suffering. She wanted to shield him. She knew she couldn't. Even more she knew she shouldn't. Maturity could be gained only through confronting and overcoming problems. To deny him the chance to develop those skills would only make him more vulnerable to the even greater pressures and problems that awaited him in life. Ultimately, success would come not through the enriching experiences but through the tough ones, through meeting the inevitable obstacles in life and overcoming them. The muscles of the soul had to be developed just as surely as those of the body. But that was hard to remember when it was her child being hurt.

"Much as I wish I could," Grant said, "I can't keep people from being cruel. Some people just are. But not all people."

"Even LaMont said something." Henry sounded aggrieved.

"Give him time," Grant counseled. "When emotions get involved, even the nicest, most sensible people can get caught up in the moment. That's what happens with a mob, and that's what's happening to us. People are believing what they're being told without wondering how it can be true. By tomorrow LaMont will probably be feeling thoroughly ashamed of himself."

"It's going to end soon, isn't it?" Henry asked. His words came quickly as if this were something he'd given much thought. "They're going to find the real murderer, aren't they?"

"I hope so," Grant told him. He wanted to be as reassuring as possible, but he'd never given his children false promises, and he wouldn't begin now. "Murderers aren't always caught."

"This is David time, isn't it?" Henry asked after a pause.

Grant could picture him, head cocked to the side, his lively eyes alight with thought. Grant's mouth softened into an affectionate smile. He would be glad when the campaign was over and they could get back to being a family.

"You know, Dad. David and Goliath." Henry sounded pleased that he might have one-upped his father. "You're always reminding us of what Grandmama Grant told you—to be like David and stand tall and face problems like he did. I like that idea. There he was, this puny runt of a guy—"

"But—"

"I know. He wasn't really a runt, but just picture it. This little dude," he continued, "up against this really big dude who's real nasty, too, and David's not afraid. Only a few stones against a humongous sword, but he's not afraid. Kind of like he was the only one wearing 3-D glasses—he could see God even when no one else could. Neat, huh?"

Grant looked at Rachel. She smiled, sharing his relief, and leaned back more comfortably. If their children could draw on faith to not only survive but triumph in this time of trial, then they were, indeed, safe.

"Anyway," Henry finished lamely, already somewhat regretting this parroting of his parent's words, "that's right, isn't it?"

"I couldn't have said it better myself," Grant assured him, smiling at the triumphant sound on the other end of the phone. "The Lord will take care of you no matter how impossible it seems. Don't let others determine how you act, Henry. You know what's right, and you're responsible to do it."

"I know, and stand tall."

"Especially when things are rough," Grant agreed. "Why don't you get India and Olivia if they're around? And, Henry, we're here for you when you need us."

"I know, Dad. Thanks. And we're here for you, too."

Could someone really be trying to destroy that love and trust? Grant wondered. His mind began its unending roller-coaster review of the "facts," trying to make sense of the senseless. "Facts" seemed a poor word choice for what little he knew, considering how divorced from the truth it was.

While Rachel spoke to the girls, her eyes were on her husband. Hard enough to live through all this but to feel somehow responsible—she'd never admired his strength more than now.

Rachel tore her eyes away and gave her attention to the girls. They were enduring the same injustices as Henry, but being older, they understood better. They didn't like it any better, but they'd learned not to predicate their actions on the actions of others and not to allow their emotions to be governed by others. At least they tried to remember what they knew to be true, though at times it proved impossible. People could be so stupid!

They assured their parents that while Bailey was out now, he was fine. They were all doing just fine, no need for concern whatsoever.

When they finished relating stories of ball games and aced tests (aced ones being the only ones they brought up voluntarily), Cynthia got on the phone and confirmed that the kids were hiding nothing from their parents. "They're hearing talk," she said, "but they know their dad, so it just makes them mad. Don't worry. They really are doing fine. They're nice kids. Tough, too."

"I'm glad you're there for them, Cynthia," Rachel said. "I feel so far away."

While Grant talked to Cynthia about the campaign, Rachel walked over to the blank television screen and faced it, deep in thought. Family was the center of their lives, and this campaign was pulling them from that center. Her children needed her, especially Bailey. She wasn't sure why she was so certain, maybe because he'd been staying out late. She knew that working on his father's campaign had been Bailey's dream. What she didn't know was why he wasn't devoting all his time to it as she would have expected and as he'd done until the last few weeks. Something wasn't quite right. She sensed it just as mothers for centuries have sensed the hurts and needs of their loved ones, often before they themselves were aware of that need.

"Tonight's speech went well," Grant told Cynthia, "better than I could have hoped."

"No hecklers?" she asked.

"Not in the audience, but Kirk Vinton—he's the *Herald*'s investigative team leader, would you believe!—was his usual obnoxious self."

"Was anyone buying it?"

"Not outwardly. Actually, some may have taken up for me because of it, but it's bound to have magnified any doubts. We'll continue our campaign appearances as we'd planned, but let's begin an information blitz to counteract those doubts. Mike's buying time for a repeat of those 'BOB GRANT—A GREAT SENATOR—A FINE MAN' commercials."

"Good," Cynthia said, making quick notes. "Bailey's come up with some good ideas on networking that theme quickly into radio ads. I'll have him call Mike first thing tomorrow." She checked her list of things to tell Grant. "Oh, before I forget, I've heard rumors the President may pay a visit to Georgia. Money as well as prestige."

"Makes sense. The vultures are circling."

"I'm going to a luncheon at the White House tomorrow. I'll see if I can pick up anything."

The First Lady had been Cynthia's roommate in college, and they'd continued their friendship over the years. Their political philosophies had gradually diverged, but their liking for each other as well as their common roots had remained. They made time for lunch together every month, or they had until two months earlier when Estelle had begged off. She'd done the same last month. The luncheon tomorrow wouldn't be private—another surprise—but Cynthia wasn't about to let that keep her from seeing her friend. Something was wrong. Cynthia wanted to know what.

"See what the White House is saying about Frederickson," Grant said. "I'd like to know if you feel any undercurrents."

"I can tell you that without asking," Cynthia shot back. "They're loving every minute. Anything to see you squirm."

"Without doubt," Grant agreed. "But see if you can feel out any specifics. Also, formulate our response to the President's visit, would you, and let's set a time for a debate, one that's to our benefit. As late as possible, I'd say, to give Jenks plenty of time to find the murderer."

"You'd consider a debate?" Cynthia made sure doubt was obvious in her voice.

"We have to," he assured her. "Let's start the negotiations. They can always fall apart."

Grant could hear her sigh of relief. Locking in a debate meant they were in serious trouble. Grant was adamantly opposed to them. They were media circuses with no real value, especially for the incumbent.

"Caruso should be an easy mark," she said. "He's only a token candidate."

"Maybe so, but he's smart and a good speaker. He has nothing to lose."

"But you . . . What a nightmare!"

"Only if the murderer isn't caught," Grant reminded her, hoping he was right. "Can you think of anyone who might be out to get me?"

"'Out to get you?'" Cynthia repeated, obviously puzzled. "What do you mean?"

"'A personal grudge' were Sheriff Jenks's words. He wondered if someone might have killed Frederickson, or maybe used his death, to get at me."

"Strange. Someone out to get you . . . I can think of people who don't like you, too many of them."

Grant felt a welcome glimmer of amusement at her indignant tone. He would have to keep a relaxed mental attitude if he hoped to think his way through this puzzle. Indignation, demoralization, fear, even this odd feeling of impending doom: They would defeat him. He hadn't the luxury of self-absorption. His glance went to Rachel. Too much depended on his ability to understand and analyze.

"But someone who hates you that much?" Cynthia continued. "I'll have to think about it."

"Do that, and, Cynthia, if that letter is legit—and from what the sheriff let fall, I'm afraid it is—Frederickson wrote it for a reason. I have a bad feeling about all this. Too much is happening, and all we're doing is playing catch-up. If I'm someone's target, we have to figure out who and why."

"And quickly," Cynthia added. "We're down to seven days. I'll pull in all our IOUs. Someone's bound to have heard something. If you're a target . . ." Her voice trailed off into bleak silence.

"I know. This could be just the beginning."

Gayla Sergek was an habitué of the Cottonball Bar and Grill. Her brittle good looks seemed suited to the dim light, glitzy but faded decor, hard beat of the jukebox, and malt- and smoke-scented air. She sat on a vinyl-covered bar stool, one of her elbows resting on the scarred counter. Smoke spiraled from the cigarette she held negligently between two pink taloned fingers. Her wandering glance regularly swept the mirror in front of her. So far no one interesting had come her way. Gayla defined interesting as any male older than eighteen and still breathing with money enough to spend some on her.

"Say, you're Gayla Sergek, aren't you?"

Gayla jumped at the voice. She hadn't noticed the man sit down on the stool beside her. She must be slipping, she thought. He was definitely worth a look. The dark beard was rather much, but the rest of him looked just fine.

"Sure, I'm Gayla. Do I know you?" she asked, feeling certain she would have remembered.

"We've met," he said. His voice was nice, educated. "In Senator Grant's office."

"The Senator's office! Why, I haven't worked there for two years!"

"Has it been that long?" he asked, obviously surprised. "All I know is you're hard to forget." He looked her up and down, his eyes registering lingering appreciation. "Can I buy you a beer?"

Reciprocal appreciation now filled Gayla's eyes.

When the beer arrived, foam dripping down the sides, the man made a show of presenting hers. He touched her hand longer than necessary. Her pulse quickened.

"What do you think about Grant being suspected of murder?" he asked.

She took a long drink of her beer. "Grant? I don't know. I was kind of surprised, I guess."

"He ever make passes at you?" he asked. At her frown, he smiled engagingly. "Don't look so shocked! He'd be blind not to."

She smiled at his obvious admiration and thought about saying *yes*. The *no* she finally forced out was reluctant.

"What about your friends?"

"Maribeth had a crush on him, Maribeth Pariss," Gayla said, enjoying the celebrity status that went with knowing Grant. "Not that it ever came to anything."

"Does this Maribeth still talk about him?"

"What difference does it make?" she asked, her face pert with curiosity. "You're asking as many questions as that reporter, the one who was murdered."

"The murdered guy talked to you?" The man's eyes were suddenly awake with interest.

Gayla nodded.

"Well, I'm no reporter," he said when the lengthening silence made it obvious she was waiting for his response. "I'm just interested, that's all." He smiled at her intimately and leaned closer. "Grant did it, didn't he?"

This time she shrugged.

"I've never known anyone who knew a murderer," the man said appreciatively. "A real turn-on." He leaned even closer. She giggled as he whispered in her ear. After several minutes he brought the conversation back to Grant.

"This friend of yours . . . Maribeth?" She nodded. "She have any good stuff on Grant?"

"Maribeth?" She giggled again. The beer was beginning to tell. "That's a good one. She's dead."

He looked shocked. "Dead? You've got to be kidding! What happened? Grant involved again?"

"No, silly." She kissed him lightly, enjoying the tickle of his beard on her face. "One day she took some pills and—poof!—no more Maribeth."

"Wow!" he exclaimed. "Why'd she do that?"

"She was preggers." Gayla licked beer from her fingers, provocatively she hoped.

"And she killed herself?" he asked incredulously. "Hadn't she heard of abortion?"

"That's what I said, but she just went on and on about how precious the baby was. And then she goes and kills them both. Go figure."

"What if Grant was the father?" he asked. At her look of disbelief, he leaned closer and continued. "Well, think about it. She didn't want an abortion because the baby was special—child of a Senator—but she couldn't face life without him. Makes you think, doesn't it?"

"I don't know," Gayla said dubiously.

"And that reporter dying," he continued, his voice persuasive. "Awfully convenient for Grant. Say!" He snapped his fingers as if at a brilliant idea. "I bet you could sell what you know to some newspaper or magazine, maybe even a TV show. Make a bundle, too. They're always looking for inside information like that."

Gayla sat up straight. "Someone would pay me to be on TV?"

"Wouldn't doubt it. With what you know and with all the publicity," he said with a faraway speculative look, "I'll bet you could pull down some real money."

Excitement suffused her face but was quickly replaced by dejection. "Sounds great, but how many TV types do you think I know?"

"Yeah." He looked downcast, too. Suddenly, he sat up and began spitting out words like a suddenly unjammed typewriter. "Wait a minute! I got an idea! A great idea! I just remembered. A guy I used to go to school with works at one of the networks. I bet he would come through."

"And all I gotta do is remember something that happened?"

He nodded. By the time they left the bar, Gayla had remembered all kinds of stories she knew would interest the television people. She even remembered some letters from Maribeth she thought might help.

They went to her apartment, and he was impressed when he saw the letters. He helped her pick out the parts that would bring her the most money. Then he suggested she sell some of her information to his TV friend but sell the rest, including an especially graphic letter she couldn't for the life of her even remember having, to the *Washington Herald*. That way she would get her picture in a major newspaper, too. Twice the money and twice the publicity!

Somehow he left before she even learned his name, but that didn't matter. He knew where to find her. Hadn't he found her this time?

He hadn't been gone much more than five minutes before her phone rang. Someone from the *Washington Herald!* It was too late to make the regular morning paper, they told her, but they would sure like the letter for the late morning edition.

The guy had been right, Gayla thought contentedly. It wasn't TV, not yet, but the *Herald* had been pleased, and they were paying.

You sure we got the right house?"

The night was dark, the street lights pooling brightness only to the edge of the lawns. The three young men, bravado hiding their strained nerves, crept through backyards. They jumped at each sound, at every bark of dogs safely penned inside houses. Each man tried to disguise his nervousness: a stifled cough by one, an angry kick of a stone or twig by another, a quick backward glance.

They'd skulked into one hedge-enclosed yard when the back door opened and light streamed out. The young men froze, looked around wildly, then flung themselves to the ground behind a row of shrubs. The ding of a rock against one of the metal gas cans they carried sounded frighteningly loud.

"Anyone out there, Dale?" a female voice quivered.

"Of course not," a male, presumably Dale, answered, bored and angry. "Blister, you be quiet. Mangy beast," he muttered. ". . . don't know why the wife wants . . ." The rest of his words were lost as the door closed. The hiding men could hear the lock turn and the chain slide into place.

"Think he'll call the cops?" one of them whispered as they picked themselves off the ground and started walking again, crouched over but moving fast. All three heads turned toward the street. They heard and saw nothing unusual.

"Naw. Didn't you hear him? He won't do nothing. He's mad at his dog."

"Come on. This is it."

They skirted the darkened row house and crept to the front.

"Here?" one of the young men asked, taking a trowel out of his pocket and kneeling down.

"Closer to the street," commanded another, the arrogant assurance in his voice marking him the leader. "Don't want anyone to miss it. And you," he added angrily to the other man-boy, "what you think this is? A tea party? You know what to do."

With a nervous glance first toward the street, then toward the leader, the other took a can of black spray paint from his pocket and ran to the house.

They worked quickly, continually shooting wary glances toward the cars passing on the street, then up at the house.

"Put some gas on the grass," hissed the leader. Slighter than the other two but with an angry emptiness in his eyes, he watched as the gasoline was poured. Light from the street reflected eerily on the golden liquid, on his shaved head as well. They were all bald, the shiny skin obscene above their immature faces. "No, stupid!" he growled. "In the shape of a cross. Geez." He grabbed the can and made the mark, saturating the wooden cross as well.

He threw a match, and without pause all three sprinted down the short lawn and along the sidewalk. Fire whooped through the grass and up the cross.

Less than three minutes to do it all, the leader thought, looking at his watch with a smirk. A new record. They were swaggering now, all danger behind them.

The leader paused a moment to look back. He laughed, excited as always by the flames. Their flickering reflection in the windows seemed to consume the house.

He'd return when the house was for sure empty, steal the gun and car, then leave them in the car park exactly as Bonfire had instructed.

Bonfire—the mere thought of the name brought with it a frigid tremor of fear even in this travesty of a man who found sport in mutilating helpless animals and in destroying the dreams of those weaker than he. He inhabited the fetid underworld of the depraved, and in that world the name Bonfire was both feared and revered. Bonfire, the unknown phantom whose altered voice might phone at any time of the day or night. He paid handsomely for exact adherence to his orders. He destroyed like the vermin they were any who deviated from his orders even in the smallest detail. None dared say *no* to his demands any more than they dared violate them. The bodies of those who'd failed, bodies viciously mutilated before being allowed the blessed release of death, made such denial unthinkable.

And so this amoral young man was visited by the cold shiver any thought of Bonfire always occasioned. He knew not why he'd been hired or the desired effect of his actions. He knew only that failure was inconceivable.

He gave no thought to the people of the cross. Even without Bonfire, their welfare, the rightness of his actions, would have stirred no flicker of doubt, and certainly none of remorse. With Bonfire giving the orders, such thoughts were unthinkable.

Conquering the shiver and mentally checking to be sure he'd accomplished every aspect of his orders, the leader caught up with the others. Sirens sounded in the distance. The three skinheads jumped in their car and roared down the street, leaving the burning cross, a monstrously grotesque symbol, shooting vivid tongues of flame into the black sky.

The phone by Grant's motel room bed rang. Three A.M. The children! Grant grabbed the phone. Were the children all right? He listened in silence, asked a few questions, then hung up and turned to face a worried Rachel.

"Not the kids, Rach." She sank back into her pillow in relief. "That was Cynthia. Someone burned a cross on our lawn and spray painted swastikas on the house."

"Oh, Bob!"

"I'm sorry." He pulled her into his arms, stroking her hair. "No one was home. No one was hurt. The children didn't see it."

"Thank God for that."

"Someone called the fire department—and the *Herald*. They were vague about who, just that the *Herald* got there first." His eyes were bright with anger. "No one saw anything. They'll get away with it." He got out of bed and stalked to the window.

"It makes me sick," Rachel said, shuddering. "How could they do it!" She pushed her body into the softness of the bed, comforted by the warmth and illusion of safety. That they were clean comforted her, too. She felt dirty just thinking about the incident.

Grant turned away from the darkened window and toward her. "This goes beyond dirty campaign tricks or hooligans up to no good."

Rachel's eyes reflected his thoughts. "Could Sheriff Jenks be right about a vendetta? Could this be part of it?"

Grant sat on the edge of the bed and took her hands into his. "Normally, I wouldn't think so, but reporters were there in time to get pictures while it was still burning. Reporters before the fire department! Someone involved had to have told them. You'd better believe I'm going to find out who."

Tuesday, October 27:
Seven Days Before the Election

Anything new?" Grant asked Cynthia as they began their morning telephone briefing. As usual Mike Masterson had come to Grant's motel room. He was sitting on a nearby couch, an extension phone held to his ear.

"A letter from a dead man declaring you're his murderer, a cross burned on your lawn, both stories plastered on the front page of one of the most influential papers in the country, not to mention who knows how many others, 326 angry e-mails from constituents—at least that's who they purport to be though they all sound suspiciously alike—271 angry phone calls and 56 angry faxes," Cynthia enumerated. "And you ask about anything new? Oh, and I forgot the ongoing TV melodrama with you as the star."

"I suppose that's the good news," Grant said dryly. He raised an eyebrow at Masterson.

Grant hadn't slept much, but his good humor had returned. He was more determined than ever to uncover the plot behind the cross burning, but he wasn't about to let it affect his prime focus of the moment, winning the Senate race. He couldn't help wondering, improbable as it seemed, if that Senate race were somehow behind what was happening. Was Tobias Caruso taking winning to the extreme? Politics was strewn with more than its share of conveniently dead bodies, but why Frederickson?

"Actually, things *are* looking better," Cynthia told him. Though in her fifties, her upbeat personality and blond good looks belied her age. Grant blessed the day, one of his first in Washington after his election twelve years before, when she'd agreed to head his staff. Her focused intellect made her an asset, but her common sense, intuitive kindness, and integrity made her a dear friend. "Strange, isn't it?" Cynthia asked. "You're now the underdog. Morale is higher than ever among campaign workers. They're mad at all the lies. This cross-burning will make them madder still. Hard to believe people can be so bigoted, isn't it? You've gotten almost as many letters and calls from people pledging their support."

"Keep those names close." Grant jotted a reminder on his pad. "We may need their help later."

"If we can just make it through today without any new revelations," Masterson interposed, "we should be all right. People have short memories, and we still have a week until the election."

"The overnight polls dropped eighteen points," Cynthia told them, "but seem to be holding steady now. We still have a cushion, not much, but some."

"What about this idea of Jenks's that someone has targeted me personally? Have you gotten any leads, Cynthia?"

"Not a whisper. No one can remember anyone with that kind of motivation. The usual wackos, of course, but no one that extreme or with the money to coordinate all this. With your work on drug interdiction—is that worth considering? Violence and money—can drug lords be far behind?"

Grant, a member of the Senate Armed Services Committee, had been holding hearings on using the military to combat drug smuggling. He felt interdiction, the prevention of drugs reaching the country, should be a major part of the drug war.

He was pushing for stronger punishments for those bringing drugs into the country as well as for more military participation in drug interdiction, including a closer, more coordinated association among the armed forces, the National Guard, the Coast Guard, the consolidated agencies of the NIIA, and state and local agencies. He wanted local authorities to have the final say, but he wanted them all to work together. Grant had made this restructuring of the war on drugs a major platform of his Senate reelection bid. He made sure to mention it in every interview about a possible run for the presidency.

In direct contrast the President through Attorney General Hunter had lobbied hard against drug interdiction, claiming that because of military cuts, local governments should be expected to police themselves and, further, that the United States shouldn't be involved in other countries' export practices—even illegal ones.

"Rachel wondered about drugs, too," Grant told Cynthia. "I agree that drugs bring out the worst in people, but why me? I haven't targeted any groups or individuals, and I sure haven't changed the administration's position. If drugs are at the bottom of all this, I haven't a clue why. Drug kingpins importing into the United States? Countries eager to develop new drug networks into the country? Could be almost anything."

"Or could be nothing," Masterson added tartly.

"Exactly," Grant agreed. "Keep digging, Cynthia, but don't limit yourself to drugs. We can't afford to ignore anything. That letter of Frederickson's seems more ominous the more I think about it. Either he genuinely thought he'd discovered something about me, or someone's trying to make it appear so. Either way, someone's gone to a lot of trouble to discredit me. I can't say that's a comfortable feeling."

A few minutes later as Grant and Masterson walked out of the hotel, they were ambushed by a group of screaming protesters, double the usual number and more than double the decibels.

"You're a murderer!"

"Jail's too good for the likes of you!"

"Orphan maker!"

"Murderer!"

Each shrill recrimination was as vile as the one before.

One cameraman rushed Grant and shoved the camera only inches from his face. Grant's scowl deepened. An up-the-nose camera angle was anything but flattering, and every cameraman knew it.

Grant finished his speech to the businessmen and opened the floor for questions.

"Maribeth Pariss," Kirk Vinton yelled from the back of the room where he'd just rushed in. Reporters and cameramen stood several rows deep in front of him. "Tell us about your affair with Maribeth Pariss."

Even as Grant ignored the question and motioned to another reporter, his mind raced. An affair? Who was Maribeth Pariss?

"Your affair, Senator!" Vinton repeated belligerently, his voice overriding all others. "Are you responsible for her suicide?"

By now, all eyes were moving from Vinton to Grant and back again. A wave of stunned disbelief swept through the crowd.

No one was more taken aback than Grant. He felt his face hardening into an angry frown and forced himself to relax. "I'm surprised you'd stoop to such a question," he said. "I've never had an affair and never will. Trust is essential to my marriage. Your question is insulting."

"Come on, Senator!" Vinton yelled. "You expect us to believe you never had a little on the side?"

"What an ugly insinuation! That's exactly what—"

Vinton interrupted. "So you're calling Maribeth Pariss a liar, are you, Senator?"

"Maribeth, Senator!" another reporter yelled. "Tell us about your affair with Maribeth!"

"Enough!" Grant's deep voice boomed out over the cacophony of questions from the reporters and the escalating murmurs of the crowd. The room quieted instantly. "You call yourselves journalists," he said, speaking directly to the reporters, several of whom, including Vinton, were trying to shove their way through the crowded tables to the front of the room, "but you do little more than feed on sensationalism."

Several of his supporters cheered. The sound petered out in the face of the hushed skepticism and naked curiosity that filled the room.

"I don't know what you're talking about," Grant finally said into the now oppressive silence, "but I do know that I'm not going to dignify such intolerable accusations by saying more."

Masterson reached the Senator's side and touched his elbow.

"As you know," Masterson told the clamoring media, "we're on a tight schedule, and the Senator must leave now. We'll have time later today to answer all questions."

He hurried Grant from the stage. The audience looked shell-shocked. The media looked excited, rushing now to be in position to question Grant outside.

Several supporters approached Grant as he was leaving, but after a few embarrassed comments, they, too, turned away, relief obvious in the haste of their retreat. The ovations given his speech were forgotten. Vinton's accusations weren't.

"What is going on?" Grant asked Masterson. "Who is this Maribeth? I've got to alert Rachel. Find me a phone!"

At that moment, Rachel Grant, a relaxed smile on her face, was walking into the Sunnyside Senior Citizens' Center, her mental armor in place. She ignored the catcalls of the group of protesters waiting for her outside. She ignored the badgering of the media.

The campaign was exhausting, both physically and emotionally. If she hadn't been totally convinced of Bob's innocence and equally convinced that he made a difference as a Senator, she would have suggested he drop out when the vile accusations had first surfaced. She believed with all her heart that her husband had a duty to his country to use his unique abilities to help preserve its freedoms. They had to stay and fight, or the last twelve years would have been meaningless. One thought kept reverberating through her mind—so little time remained, less than a week.

Rachel looked out over the assembled group. Their hearing aids were turned on, and their walkers and canes rested at hand beside their chairs as they patiently waited for her to bring a small bit of change to their routine. She smiled at them and received numerous smiles in return.

Dressed in a Chanel-style burnt orange suit, she appeared composed and cheerful. No one would have guessed her husband was being suggested as a possible murderer. No one in the audience was rude enough to mention it, and, other than a local reporter, the event had been closed to the press. The audience received her speech with intelligent questions and polite appreciation.

As she left the building afterward, the dazzling brightness of the early morning sun momentarily blinded her. Before her eyes could adjust, she was encircled by a mob of reporters and cameramen. They jostled against her, one errant microphone hitting her face. She reached up to rub her stinging cheek, just as a barrage of questions began. Disoriented, unsure what was happening, she listened.

"Your husband's affair, tell us about it!"

"The affair—"

"Pariss—"

"The murder—"

The words pounded her, bewildering, unbelievable. She stared at them, these reporters so serious about their duty and so bereft of empathy. An affair? A murder? What did they want from her? How far would they take their persecution? Suddenly, the bewilderment splintered into the clarity of white-hot anger.

"My husband have an affair?" Her voice was steely. Her eyes glinted black in the combined glare of sun and camera. "I pity you. You know nothing of honor or integrity. You sanctimoniously stand there slandering an honorable man, without thought of the consequences, without accepting responsibility for the results. Whoever has made these false accusations is intent on destroying my husband. That is the story you should be pursuing, instead of being taken in by lies."

There was a moment of silence. Then: "Doesn't it bother you that your husband caused a young woman to commit suicide?" a female voice yelled at her.

Three more reporters yelled questions almost in unison. After a deliberate and unflinching look at each of them, Rachel walked with head held high toward her waiting car. The reporters parted, but they followed her. Their questions continued, growing louder and more insistent the closer she came to escaping them.

What beasts! Rachel thought as she leaned down and got in. Her shaking knees gave way, and she sank gratefully into the upholstery of the front seat. Even so, she let nothing but determination show on her face, knowing cameras would be focused on her until she was out of sight. Her driver spoke to her, but she was oblivious.

Fiery thoughts raged through her. Sheriff Jenks was right. Someone was working systematically to destroy Bob. Of that, she was now certain. The affair story was ludicrous, just as she'd said, but it had to have come from somewhere. Who hated Bob that much, to spread such filth? What would they do next?

With heart-stopping certainty, Rachel knew this last question was the one that mattered. Murder and character assassination so far, but what next?

Over the years, she and Bob had reaped untold benefits in the service of their country. Had their country demanded too much of them this time? Stripped of his good name, his integrity forever tainted regardless of the outcome, was this a necessary adjunct to public service? Rachel thought of those who'd fallen on the sword of similar treatment. Phillip Loomis had even been driven to suicide by the demons of public office.

Her head sank forward onto her chest as the enormity of it all engulfed her. What was happening to them? Were the children safe? Was Bob?

As her thoughts dissolved into the blackness of despair, a prayer formed of its own volition. Slowly, the blackness gave way to hope.

She and Bob weren't going to allow themselves to be cowed into defeat by some faceless enemy! She would not let them, whoever they were, destroy her family! She would fight with everything she had before she would let that happen. Bad enough to have their years of public service denigrated and destroyed but then to be denied the opportunity to defend themselves and their record—that she couldn't tolerate. This was one fight they would win. They had to.

Straightening her back with resolve, she concentrated on remembering anyone or anything from the past which might give form to the amoral menace which threatened them. Methodically, she began outlining what they knew and comparing it with a list of unanswered questions. The second list grew disturbingly long.

Sheriff Jenks punched the button on his intercom.

"Tell Hank to get in here pronto."

Almost before he'd finished speaking, Farrar was in the office, drawing up a chair to the side of the desk. As was his custom when feeling especially full of himself, Farrar turned the chair backward, looped one leg over it, and sat down. His chin rested on his hands folded on the chair back.

"You wanted me, Sheriff?"

"What you got on Gayla Sergek?"

"Li'l ol' Gayla's 'in seclusion,' accordin' to her lawyer," Farrar told him. "We're workin' on her, though."

"Her job?"

"Receptionist, file clerk, that kinda thing in an insurance office. Lady there says she called in, claimin' to be sick. Said she wouldn't be back for more'n a week."

"What about family? They know anything?"

"Naw. Say she up and lit out soon as she turned seventeen. Hardly keeps in touch."

"Tell her lawyer we have to see her now," Jenks said. "If he plays smart, let me talk to him. The whole thing stinks."

"You don't believe her? Even with the letters?"

"About the affair?" Jenks asked with a shrug. "Who knows. Grant wouldn't be the first. Bothers me about the timing, though." He leaned back in his chair. "That and murdering to hide an affair. To win an election? Hard to believe. Too much of that almost paraded around at election time. Just another lifestyle choice. Doesn't make sense as a motive for murder."

"Even if the little wifey might get nasty? That and the election might be enough, specially for Grant."

Jenks cocked his head at Farrar, guessing what he would say.

"Being black, you know. Stands to reason."

Jenks said nothing.

"A lot to overcome," Farrar finished belligerently.

"Hank, I want you to listen to me and listen good," Jenks said, sitting up and leaning forward on the desk so he was looking eye-to-eye with his deputy. "You may be right. Grant may be guilty. But we don't know that. Matter of fact, several things just don't add up."

Farrar's look turned mulish.

"All that's beside the point," Jenks continued, his eyes never wavering from Farrar's. "You'll never see the truth, you'll never serve justice if you go into a case with blinders on."

Farrar's jaw tightened, and he raised his eyes to just above Jenks's head.

Jenks's voice became as hard as Farrar's face. "Now listen here, Hank. Most ways you're a good lawman, but you've got a blind spot big as a sinkhole and at least as dangerous." He moderated his tone, trying to make Farrar understand. "You've got to look at everyone full on, okay, but don't forget the sides and back. You've been at this long enough to know you can't judge a thoroughbred till you see him run. Lots of good lookers turn out to be nags."

Farrar, his expression thoughtful, finally looked Jenks in the eye. Hank was thinking, Jenks realized with relief.

"Grant's no worse than lots of folks we know and a heck of a lot better than some," Jenks continued.

The line of Farrar's mouth again hardened. Jenks's heart sank. Some prejudices were powerful hard to overcome, he was afraid. Suddenly, his sympathy was all with Grant. If Hank Farrar, who was supposed to balance justice in his hands, was this prejudiced against Grant, what else was the Senator enduring unfairly? And, Jenks wondered, what should he do as sheriff to shift the balance back to center where it belonged? Where did his duty lie? "I mean it, Hank. Long as I'm sheriff, we'll treat everyone equal and check every angle. Understood?"

"Yes, sir." Farrar spoke through gritted teeth. He started to say more, thought better of it, and just stared in seething silence at the same point above Jenks's head.

"Good." Jenks's tone put a period to the conversation. "Now," he continued, "have the boys poke around Sergek a mite deeper. Talk to her friends, specially from Grant's office. Could be her story's changed since then. Check, too, if she's come into some money. If so, I'd be mighty curious to know where it's coming from. Sergek was on Frederickson's 'Leads' list," he said, picking up a computer printout, one of two files that Sally, with the help of several "expert experts," as she called them, had found in Frederickson's computer.

The "Leads" file had been easy to find, Sally had told him. Jenks had felt a surge of satisfaction to have his suspicion that the computer had been left on purpose proved correct. The other file, which Frederickson himself had dubbed "Pulitzer," had been buried deep, Sally had said, a fact the sheriff found mighty interesting. They'd just happened to stumble on it, she'd said.

Jenks wondered whether Frederickson's murderer had realized it was there. He glanced through it again, though he knew it practically by heart, all three pages. Names, places, and just single words. Nothing to hang an investigation on. In fact, nothing that made any sense.

He sighed and laid the file down.

"I can't help wondering," he continued, "if someone counted on us digging Sergek up."

Farrar just stared at him, but his eyes were alive with thought. He'd never cottoned to the vendetta theory and had made his feelings clear to anyone who would listen.

"Anything on Maribeth Pariss?" the sheriff asked when Farrar didn't respond.

"We're askin' 'round. All we got nailed down now is she worked for Grant and she's dead. Ruled a suicide. Should know more directly."

"I'll need the autopsy report." Jenks put the "Pulitzer" file away and leaned back in his chair. "Check on her friends, too. See what they recollect about Grant. Ask about letters. If she wrote Sergek, I'd reckon she wrote others." Farrar nodded. "Call Grant. I want to see him today, ASAP." Farrar's face brightened. "Then tell the boys to take double shifts for a spell. We gotta tie this up, and quick, too. Those media boys are giving me a real headache."

"Thought you'd be proud having your kisser on the tube every time folks turn it on."

Jenks scowled as Farrar walked, laughing, out of the office.

The White House usher greeted Cynthia Novitsky with a smile and escorted her to the family elevator that would carry her to the private quarters of the White House. Several women were already gathered in the sitting room on the second floor, a lovely yellow room that repeated the oval shape of the Blue Room on the formal state floors below. Multipaned windows, framed by yellow damask draperies, overlooked the Truman balcony and the limestone brilliance of the Washington Monument beyond.

"Cynthia, how are you?" Estelle said brightly, giving her friend a quick peck on the cheek. Her eyes darted to some point over Cynthia's shoulder.

Cynthia eyed her quizzically for a moment but smiled and returned the greeting. Abruptly, with almost uncivil haste, Estelle turned to greet someone else. Cynthia was left standing alone, her mouth open in midsentence.

She'd been right in thinking something was wrong, Cynthia thought, walking slowly, with several troubled backward glances, to a spot where she could watch Estelle unobtrusively. A steward brought a cup of hot tea— English Breakfast, her favorite. She smiled her thanks at his thoughtfulness, but her eyes never left their watch of Estelle. Not only did her friend act distracted, Cynthia soon realized, but, always slender, she'd lost so much weight she now looked anorexic. Something was definitely wrong.

Within minutes lunch was announced by the majordomo.

The family dining room, a well-proportioned, high-ceilinged room on the second floor, was illuminated by a glittering, two-century-old chandelier. Jackie Kennedy had created the room so that her family could have a more cozy place to dine than the formal floors allowed. She'd covered the walls with an antique hand-painted paper depicting scenes from the American Revolution on a background based on engravings from the early nineteenth century. That blue-toned wallpaper, mellowed with age, had become as identified with this room as the blue, green, and red had with the rooms below.

Today, Estelle had chosen to set the Sheraton pedestal table with Lady Bird Johnson's china. Each setting was painted with a different state flower. Cynthia was touched to see the Indiana peony, her home state's flower, at her place. However, she found herself placed between Janet Loomis and Amy Corforth at the far end of the table from Estelle. Considering Estelle's earlier aloofness, Cynthia wasn't surprised, but she was disappointed. She wanted to talk to Estelle.

"I can't believe what's being said about Bob," Janet Loomis said.

Cynthia forced her mind from Estelle and looked at Janet. She'd had cancer two years before, had been close to death if rumor were correct, and her husband had committed suicide less than six months earlier. But Janet Loomis seemed to have met her trials and surmounted them. Cynthia admired her tremendously.

"I don't care what anyone says," Janet continued, a surprising vehemence in her voice. "Bob's not that kind of person."

"You're right," Cynthia agreed, realizing that Janet, too, had lost weight. Too much weight. Makeup failed to hide the dark crescents under her eyes. "We're convinced someone's trying to destroy him."

"And they murdered poor Russell Frederickson just so they could blame him?" Amy Corforth asked skeptically from the other side of Cynthia. "Don't you find that a bit farfetched?"

"No more so than accusing Bob Grant of murder," Janet retorted. "Do you know Bob?"

"We've met," Amy said without enthusiasm, "but I don't know him. I haven't heard much good about him, though."

"I knew it!" Janet exclaimed, again with unnecessary heat. "I knew you couldn't know him, or you'd never say that. I hate it when people are judged unfairly. Bob and Rachel Grant are two of the finest people in the world. I'm sorry you don't know them, and I'm sorry they're being treated so unfairly."

"I'm sure, my dear," Amy murmured. "Though from what I've heard, the majority don't share your sentiments." She turned and began talking to the women on her other side.

"I hate it!" Janet said angrily. Almost immediately, the anger was replaced by despondency. "How can this be happening? Bob and Rachel really are wonderful. They're close to finding the real murderer, aren't they?"

"I'm afraid not," Cynthia said. She reached out to touch Janet, who'd suddenly paled. "Are you all right?" she asked worriedly.

"I feel so alone, Cynthia," Janet said, a touch of pink reentering her cheeks. "If I could just talk to someone. No, if I could just talk to Phillip." The last words were forced from her with agonizing slowness, but her eyes when she looked at Cynthia were tearless. "I'm sorry. I shouldn't have said that, but at least you understand, understand a little anyway."

Cynthia did. She, too, was a widow, but her husband had been killed by a crazed drug addict. He hadn't killed himself as Phillip had. Cynthia didn't know how Janet could bear it. The death of a beloved spouse was devastating enough without having to wonder if you were somehow responsible. Feeling alone, yes, that she understood. What she didn't understand was this sudden change in Janet. Cynthia had thought Janet was coping, but now she wasn't sure.

"I'd like . . ." Janet began, then hesitated.

"Yes?" Cynthia prompted as she desperately sought the right words, words that might ameliorate some of Janet's obvious distress.

"If you think of it," Janet said, her voice now artificially bright, "you might tell Rachel I'd like to talk to her. Nothing important."

Nothing important? Before Cynthia could respond, she heard the scraping of chairs. The luncheon was over.

Over desultory good-byes, the women walked the length of the gallery, past the baby grand piano, and down the red carpeted stairs. Cynthia paused for a moment on the landing, surprised, then saddened to realize the portrait of President Reagan that had hung there for years had been replaced by one of Woodrow Wilson. Slowly, she continued to the state floors below. There she took leave of the others, giving Janet an impulsive hug. Janet returned it.

"Please call me if I can do anything for Bob," she said, her eyes not meeting Cynthia's. She turned and left, almost running. Feeling helpless, Cynthia watched her retreating back.

She'd learned nothing to help the Senator, Cynthia thought as she walked through the wrought iron gate outside the White House, and she'd been unable to talk to Estelle. In fact, a serious concern for Janet Loomis had wormed its way into her thoughts, and she knew it might be days before she could do anything to help her friend.

She had gone to the White House hoping for answers and left having found only more questions.

Bailey Grant was wrapped in thought as he walked down Prospect Street near the Georgetown campus. Again today he was meeting Sherrill for lunch, a quick bite before he resumed his computer search for any clue to the source of this smear campaign against his father. So far he'd come up empty. His father was counting on him, and despite his best efforts, he was letting him down. If only he could find something concrete, some thread that would unravel the whole. He hoped this lunch break would provide an inspiration.

Someone grabbed his arm.

"Hey, Bailey, why so gloomy?" Andrew Stoner asked, trying to steer him in the opposite direction. "You need a pick-me-up, couple of beers at The Cellar. Come on."

"Can't, Andrew. I'm meeting Sherrill." Bailey grinned as he saw her sauntering toward them. She really was something—a bit mixed-up, agreed, but under it all he was convinced she was one very nice girl. He was willing to wait for her to get her act together.

Andrew hadn't yet seen her. With a grimace of disgust, he let go of Bailey's arm. "What's gotten into you?" he asked. "No time even for a couple of beers? Geez, Bailey, you're turning into a regular nun—priest, whatever. Well, maybe not," he said, staring at Sherrill as she neared them. "How'd you ever get such a hot babe interested in you?"

Bailey wondered the same, though Sherrill's good looks weren't at the top of his list of reasons.

"You have real wild parties," Sherrill told Andrew with a laugh as she linked her arm through Bailey's.

Andrew looked gratified.

"You ain't seen nothing yet," he said with a suggestive leer. "Drop by tonight. We're going to fly. Reg really wants you there, Bailey. So do I. You, too, babe, especially you." He was practically salivating over Sherrill.

Then Bailey realized what Andrew had said. "Are you crazy?" he asked angrily.

"I knew you'd say that." A scowl distorted Andrew's face. "Reggie's got a supplier and swears it's a trip worth taking. What've we got to lose?"

"You believe that creep?" Bailey demanded. "What do you know about him anyway? Coke's bad enough, but who knows what Reggie might use to cut his?"

With a disgusted snort, Andrew turned and started to walk away. Bailey grabbed his arm and swung him around. They glared at each other angrily. "Don't be a fool, Andrew. People die, even on the first try."

"Bailey, please!" Sherrill's voice was pleading.

"Come tonight and really live. Or stay away," Andrew said, shrugging off Bailey's hand. "Suit yourself. Just don't try to run my life."

"Hey, Grant! Bailey Grant!" someone yelled from across the street. "Hear your old man's got a 'ho'."

Bailey spun around, his fists clenched.

"Yeah, nigger! A burning cross is too good for a mother-lover like you!"

With an oath, Bailey started toward them.

"Whoa, buddy." Andrew grabbed his arm and held him back. "Fighting won't cut it. Just put you in the headlines with your old man."

The obscene taunts continued, getting uglier as a crowd formed around the original tormentors. Bailey tried to shake off Andrew's hands. Andrew just gripped harder.

"Think, man," Andrew hissed in his ear. "Don't let them see they're getting to you."

Slowly, Andrew's words penetrated Bailey's anger. Slowly, Bailey's fists unclenched. With obvious effort, he reclaimed control, turning his back on the taunts—but not before he'd seen the sun glinting on a camera lens. A camera!

"Thanks, Andrew," he said, his voice unsteady. "I owe you. Those jerks! I'd like to smash their lying teeth down their lying throats. How can they say that! And about Dad! Lies! It's all lies!"

"Sure, Bailey," Andrew agreed. "Sure. They're trash." He sounded genuinely upset. For a change he sounded like Bailey's friend of old. "But even so, if you throw a punch, you're the one who'll be sorry. That's exactly what they want."

"You're right," Bailey said. "Thanks." His hands were trembling, he realized, shocked. "I'd have made a mess of things if you hadn't been here."

"And they'd have made a mess of the sidewalk with your worthless black carcass."

By now the taunts had diminished. With a quick glance over his shoulder, Bailey saw that the crowd was dispersing. Only the original two guys remained. The camera was gone—if it had actually been there. In the confusion, he might have been mistaken. The unease Bailey felt was lost in Andrew's next words.

"Look, Bailey," Andrew said, his eyes downcast in embarrassment, "I didn't know what to say before, but I've known you a long time. Right?" Bailey nodded. "And, well, your dad's a great guy. A straight arrow, but a great guy. I know what everyone's saying, and I know it can't be true. Not your parents. You can't let 'em get to you. The good guys always win. Remember that."

"I will, Andrew. And thanks."

During all this exchange, even during the taunting, Sherrill had stood motionless, a stunned look on her face. Now Bailey, concerned, squeezed her hand. "You don't have to look like you lost your last friend," he told her with a laugh, trying to bring a smile back to her eyes. "Nothing happened."

"Nothing happened?" Her voice was choked. "You call that nothing! Those cretins just stood there, waiting for you to ..." Her voice trailed off.

"But I didn't," Bailey reminded her. He gave Andrew a crooked smile. "Though, believe me, I wanted to. Politics isn't always nice, and I've had twelve years of this kind of thing."

"This kind of thing? Twelve years?" Her voice held disbelief.

"Not this bad, maybe," Bailey said with a shrug, "but intolerance, bigotry. And you know the funny thing? It's usually not because Dad's black, but because he's a conservative black. But you're right. Being accused of murder isn't your everyday campaigning."

"I didn't know, Bailey. It's horrible." Her eyes swam with tears. "I'm so sorry."

He put his arms around her. "Come on, now. You—"

"You don't understand," she whispered. She pushed his arms down and turned away. "You may be used to it, but I hate it. Hate it! How could they say those things to you?"

"I've got the perfect solution for you both," Andrew said. Bailey and Sherrill looked at him blindly. They'd forgotten he was there, had forgotten that anyone existed outside themselves. "You need something to help you forget this whole mess. Tonight's your chance. A little bliss and you'll forget all your problems."

Without waiting for their response, he sauntered away, heading toward The Cellar. "See you tonight in Wonderland, kiddos," he called over his shoulder, an impish grin on his face.

At the sound of the door opening, Sheriff Jenks looked up from his paperwork.

"Appreciate your dropping by, Miss Sergek," he said, walking toward her, hand outstretched.

He led Gayla Sergek to a chair facing his desk. The light from the window behind him streamed in, highlighting her frizzed blond hair. A tad too much makeup, Jenks thought, but good looking in a pinch-faced way. Her dress, a bright lime green that turned her skin sallow, looked new. He wondered what the boys were learning about her finances.

Her attorney sat beside her. Jenks hoped, probably in vain, that he would keep quiet. What had Shakespeare said? Something about killing all lawyers. Probably be considered self-defense, at least for this Atlanta specimen. He looked respectable, expensively respectable, but something about him . . .

"I want to do my duty," Miss Sergek said, primly crossing her legs at the ankles. Her jaws worked on a piece of gum. To help calm her nerves? Jenks wondered. Or merely habit? "I've always admired Senator Grant, but the truth is the truth. Besides, he treated poor Maribeth horribly." She smoothed her skirt a little closer to her knees and looked at him coyly from under thickly mascaraed eyelashes.

"Reckon we ought to begin with poor Maribeth," Jenks said. "You and she real thick, were you?"

"Why, we were best friends," Gayla explained earnestly. "Gosh, we hit it off right away. No wonder, bunch of old bi—I mean, ladies, working there."

"At Senator Grant's office? That where you met?"

"That's what I said, wasn't it?" She moved the gum around in her mouth. "I couldn't care less about politics, but I needed a job and the work was easy. I told them some stuff about loving the Senator and needing the work, and they hired me. Kind of surprised me, to tell you the truth. I sure didn't fit in. Found out later they were short-staffed right then and needed a secretary in a bad way. A lucky break for me. Anyway, when I left—I got a better job—Maribeth kept in touch. She wrote me, too, sometimes. Great one for writing, Maribeth. Even kept a diary, if you can imagine that at her age."

"I'm a mite confused," Jenks said, leaning casually back in his chair. "She wrote you letters?"

"When she went on vacations or I did," Gayla explained. The gum moved again. "That's what I meant. Actually, I think Maribeth hoped to change me." She raised a disbelieving eyebrow at Jenks. "If you can credit that. She was always begging me to 'believe in the Senator.' Her exact words. Like a religious experience. I think that's why she kept in touch—trying to convert me. Brother, was I glad to get out of that place!" She laughed, and her face was transformed. Jenks felt a reluctant liking for her. She might lack what his eighty-five-year-old mother called class, but she had no illusions about herself. She knew who she was and was comfortable with it. He could believe she could fool Grant's staff long enough to get hired. She had a gutsy charm. "I've got to admit they weren't exactly sad to see me go either."

"Still got those letters?" Jenks asked, letting his own smile develop.

Gayla looked at her attorney. A pop of gum accompanied the look.

"I regret to say," he said with lawyerly precision and inaccuracy, "that my client is unable to produce the letters at this time. She'll be glad to comply with your request in a matter of days."

So that was why she'd cozied up to the attorney, Jenks thought. Trying to sell the letters, no doubt, if she hadn't done so already. The tabloids would eat them up. "Don't rightly believe days will do," he said, keeping his voice bland. "I was thinking more toward this afternoon."

The attorney protested but finally agreed to the next morning. He continued to interrupt throughout the interview, but Gayla Sergek, much to Jenks's relief, was content to ignore him. Jenks couldn't help wondering how she happened to have hooked into such a smooth mouthpiece. That was something else for the boys to look into.

"Miss Pariss, now, she say much about her and the Senator in them letters?" He was gratified to notice that the dumber he sounded, the more bored the lawyer became.

"Like I told the reporters and like I told Russell Frederickson, Maribeth talked about Grant all the time."

"About Grant, you say. Any others?"

"Well, sure. She liked the guys—who doesn't—but the Senator, now. Boy, did she have a case for him. Wouldn't shut up about him. She was real starstruck."

"Miss Sergek," Jenks continued, feeling his way, "I ain't aiming to upset you or nothing, but you ever see your friend and the Senator, well, together?"

"Sure, I suppose so." She gave him a quizzical look. "I had to, didn't I, her working in his office?" Her face brightened. "Once I caught him sneaking out of her apartment, but he didn't see me."

"The Senator?"

She nodded.

"Now I find that mighty interesting. Mighty interesting indeed. Right certain you are about its being the Senator?"

"Said so, didn't I?" The gum bobbed around erratically. "I worked for him, didn't I? Of course, I'm sure it was the Senator." She crossed her legs and pulled the skirt down a few inches. It still left plenty of leg showing, a shapely leg as she well knew.

Her account of the occasion outside Pariss's apartment was sketchy. She contradicted herself several times. Sheriff Jenks's impassive but kindly face gave no indication of his thoughts.

The lawyer continued his sporadic interruptions. Gayla continued popping her gum and ignoring him.

"You say you met Russell Frederickson?" Jenks asked.

"The murdered guy? Sure. Gives me the creeps just thinking about it." She shuddered theatrically, her skirt inching up with each movement. "First Maribeth, then Frederickson. Lot of good his warning did him."

"His warning?"

"Yeah. He told me Senator Grant played rough and to be careful. So he ends up dead, and me, I end up on TV. Course he's on TV, too, but not quite the same way." She giggled and straightened her skirt, popping her gum again as she did.

Miss Sergek could add little more. Frederickson had said something about thugs calling to threaten him on Grant's behalf, but she hadn't paid much attention. No, Frederickson hadn't seemed scared. Pleased was more like it. Yes, she was surprised her friend Maribeth hadn't had an abortion and been done with it, but the father being a Senator made things difficult, she supposed. Maybe Maribeth just couldn't handle it all, poor thing, seeing as she'd really loved the Senator. He had a lot to answer for, did Senator Grant.

He would be watching out for his client's rights, the attorney murmured as they left the room.

Senator Grant falling for a girl who would be best friends with Gayla Sergek? Jenks wondered doubtfully as he watched her leave, her brittle blond hair a halo above her slim body swaying in its too tight, too short dress. Not that the Senator's taste in women mattered. Disproving the accusations against him would take more than a question of why he would choose such an unlikely sex partner.

The letters, though, were concrete. He would get a subpoena for those right now, Jenks decided. He wasn't about to trust that lawyer.

Gayla had mentioned a diary. Jenks wondered what had become of it. Something else for the boys to check.

The sky was a translucent wedgewood blue unmarred by even a trace of a cloud. A perfect Indian summer day, the President decided. His eyes traveled down to the small, partially enclosed area in front of him. Queer how few roses actually grew in the Rose Garden. Not for the first time, he wondered why such an inappropriate name had stuck.

Hands clasped behind his back, a slight smile on his handsome face, he was enjoying a brief interlude of solitude during the day's normally hectic pace. The sound of his office door opening ended his reverie. Reluctantly, he turned.

"How's the Georgia trip firming up, Hunt?" he asked his attorney general, who was walking into the room.

"Almost done. A rally Friday night in Atlanta followed by a thousand-dollar-a-head reception. All the usual heavy hitters, plus some new blood, too."

"That's good news."

"Yes, and just when Caruso can use it most. The latest poll shows him closing the gap, speedily I might add."

The President, a grin on his face, shook his head in amazement. "Remarkable, isn't it? Whether Grant wins or not, there's no way he'll be in a position to challenge me in two years."

"By Tuesday, Grant will be a nonplayer," Hunter agreed. "What am I saying?" he amended with feigned solemnity. "Nonplayer, nothing. He'll be facing a murder trial."

They both laughed.

"I told you Derek Bender would be going down to Georgia," Hunter continued.

The President nodded.

"I chose him specifically. He's the best the NIIA has, smart but with no illusions about who's boss and how to earn advancement. He'll make sure the Grant investigation is handled as comprehensively as possible—no concessions granted. Plus, he'll give the media just what they need."

"I assumed as much," the President said. "Maybe we can help things along. Call Bill Tarr." William C. Tarr, Democratic Senator from Michigan, was ranking member of the Senate Ethics Committee. "Suggest he begin making noises about an investigation into ethics violations by Grant. Sexual harassment of an employee demands full Senate hearings. He can hint that the Senate will be saved that embarrassment if Grant is defeated, but it'll still be a matter for the civil courts. Have Tarr make a major statement about Grant at least every other day until the election. I don't want anyone being deluded about just what Grant has done. Even if he's reelected and the Senate does their usual whitewash, voters will remember, at least those outside Georgia, and they're the ones that matter."

The President turned to stare out the window, his face thoughtful. "Morty Edgerton is having some problems in his campaign, isn't he?" Edgerton was the Vermont Senator whose recently exposed sexual proclivities were exciting some interest in his home state.

"Nothing that will keep him from winning," Hunter replied. "His coalition is well entrenched. They're rallying around his right to his sexual orientation, but he's probably our weakest candidate."

"Call him. A statement from him denouncing Grant would strengthen his hand in some quarters. Consensual sex among equals as opposed to intimidation of a young employee." He smiled cynically. "Confusing the issue never hurts. What Republican can we get to come out against Grant?"

"Kennard Wylie?" Hunter suggested.

"Sure," the President agreed as he walked behind the eagle-carved desk made famous by John-John Kennedy's playing hide and seek under it. "We'll take that military base in his district off the closure list. I'll call him myself tomorrow morning. That way his statement can make the evening news. Maybe that'll help force a wedge in that confounded Republican solidarity." His face clouded with thoughts of his ongoing battle with Congress. Then it cleared, and he chuckled. "Wouldn't you love to be there when Grant realizes he's finished? About time we had Georgia on our side. But, Hunt," he said, his eyes thoughtful, "Grant is slick. Let's keep our options for the Georgia rally open for a day or two longer. I don't want to back Caruso unless he's a sure winner."

Perception was everything in politics. The President was a winner, and he took care to surround himself with winners. Winners never trusted to luck. He was President; he could afford to wait. He couldn't afford to act prematurely.

Thanks for coming here, Sheriff," Grant said, opening his hotel suite door to Jenks and his deputy, Farrar.

The Senator looked weary, Jenks thought as he shook the proffered hand, and little wonder. The wonder was that it hadn't hit him harder sooner.

"Sorry I couldn't come to your office," Grant said, leading them into the room. "But I would hate to miss any campaign event. You can imagine what the media would make of that. I'd like you to meet my wife, Rachel." He motioned toward an attractive black woman rising from the couch.

Both Jenks and Farrar looked at her with barely concealed consternation before returning her handshake.

"I hope you don't mind if she sits in?" Grant asked, sensing their unease. Rachel had come to the hotel earlier that afternoon when her dinner speech had been canceled, no explanations given.

Jenks shook his head. "Although, Mrs. Grant—"

"Rachel, please," she told him with a smile.

"Rachel, then, thank you."

Rachel and Grant sat on the couch, Mike Masterson, Jenks, and Deputy Farrar in the chairs facing it. Grant had considered asking a lawyer to be present but had decided it smacked too much of a declaration of guilt.

"I don't mean to tell you what to do, ma'am," Jenks continued, "but you may find this conversation little to your liking. I hate that we might say something distressing for you."

"No, Sheriff," she said with the calm certainty Grant loved so much, "distressing only for you. You see, I know that everything being said about Bob is untrue, and I'm not about to sit by silently and let them get away with it."

"Good enough, ma'am," Jenks said with a slight nod.

Rachel thought he seemed pleased with her answer. Bob was right; the sheriff was a nice man. If only they could be sure he was capable of solving the murder!

Jenks leaned down and carefully placed his hat under his chair. "This story about Maribeth Pariss, Senator," he said, straightening and looking Grant in the eye. "You have anything to say about that?"

"I had nothing to do with the girl," Grant said easily. "In fact I'm embarrassed to admit I don't remember her at all. I can't prove that, of course. That's why this story of an affair is so devilishly clever."

"And so effective for that very reason," Rachel said softly. She was wearing a champagne-colored suit in a nubby wool. Her hair was pulled back in a neat but elegant French roll. Though her back was uncompromisingly straight, the expression on her face was serene, and her eyes radiated a gentle kindness.

Grant squeezed her hand, thankful as always to have her beside him.

"Miss Pariss worked in your Atlanta office. That right?" Jenks asked, determined to stick to facts.

"Yes," Grant said. "I checked as soon as I heard the story. She worked there for about six months. That was two years ago. I can give you the name of her next employer if that will help."

"No need, Senator. We've already contacted him."

"I'm sorry, Sheriff," Grant said, shaking his head. "Of course you would have." He mentally kicked himself, hoping he hadn't sounded too patronizing. Stupid to have suggested the sheriff might have neglected something so elementary.

"I can't quite get a handle on this," the sheriff continued unemotionally, "why you wouldn't have known Miss Pariss. Your office that big?"

"Ten people in Atlanta," Grant said. "I try to get to know all my employees, but Miss Pariss was only there for a short time, during most of which the Senate was in session and I was in Washington. Besides, I only work closely with two of the people in my Atlanta office."

"The Senator spends little time with anyone other than those in the field," Masterson explained, "and Miss Pariss never worked in the field, meaning she never accompanied him when he visited around the state."

"I accompany Bob when I can," Rachel added, "and I know Miss Pariss never went with us."

"But he wouldn't—" Farrar blurted, stopping abruptly at a look from the sheriff. Farrar bent back over his notebook, scribbling furiously.

But everyone knew what he'd been about to say. If Grant were having an affair, he would be careful to keep his wife from ever meeting his lover.

Rachel continued as if there had been no interruption, no moment of heightened tension. Her face had lost none of its serenity. "From what our Atlanta staff says—I gave a speech there this noon and talked to them afterwards—while Miss Pariss was a decent employee, she wasn't with us very long. No one can remember ever seeing her with Bob."

"And what about you?" Jenks asked Rachel and Masterson. "Either of you ever meet Miss Pariss?"

Rachel shook her head.

"No," Masterson said. "She was gone before I signed on to the Senator's campaign."

"Mike joined me early this spring," Grant explained.

Jenks nodded. "Gayla Sergek, Senator, you remember her?"

Grant ran a hand over his hair. "This gets embarrassing, but, no, I don't remember her either. We checked our records, and she was with us less than two months. We let her go. General incompetence."

"Was she fired or did she quit?"

"My understanding is she was given the option of being fired or quitting. She chose to be fired. Wanted unemployment compensation, apparently, then discovered Congress had exempted itself."

"So she might have been mad?" Jenks asked, a spark of interest in his eyes.

Grant shrugged.

"The Senator would have little contact with someone in her position," Masterson said, leaning forward to make his point, "especially someone who worked such a short time."

"You don't say, Mr. Masterson." Jenks's tone was dry. He turned back to Grant. "Miss Sergek mentioned something mighty interesting. Said Russell Frederickson warned her about you, Senator. Said she best be careful. Said you were dangerous and had hired thugs to do your dirty work."

Rachel gasped but said nothing.

Grant was silent for a long moment. "Hired thugs?" he finally asked, his voice brittle with disbelief. "Hired thugs," he repeated more moderately as if to convince himself his hearing hadn't deceived him. "So that's how they worked it." His dark eyes narrowed dangerously as the full implications sank in. "I couldn't imagine why Frederickson would be afraid of me, but now it makes sense. Easy enough for someone to call him pretending to be speaking in my behalf. Another mark against me, another one impossible to disprove.

"You know it's odd, Sheriff," Grant continued, his voice now thoughtful. "The last few days have been one outrage after another, but what you just said, that Russell Frederickson had reason to be frightened of me, that seems the worst of all. I'm beginning to think you're right about someone having made me his target. This has to have been planned long before Frederickson's death, with someone placing me in the role of murderer from the beginning. Each clue to my guilt falls into place too neatly."

"Don't rightly know if you'd call this help," Jenks said, "but a car was seen leaving Frederickson's motel about the right time for the murder and in a mighty hurry."

They all looked at him expectantly.

"Had a 'GRANT IS MY SENATOR' bumper sticker."

Grant looked stunned, but slowly a grin split his face. His laugh when it came was genuinely amused. "That's almost too much," he said, still laughing. "One of our bumper stickers. Never thought I'd be sorry to hear about a car with one of those."

Rachel returned his smile, but her lips trembled.

"I'm having trouble seeing the humor in any of this," Masterson groused. The tension returned. "Has the car been found?"

"Could be it has," Jenks said, watching each of them with deceptively mild eyes. "Just could be it has. Near the motel where you were staying that night, Senator. A stolen car. No fingerprints."

"Another neat little piece stacked against me," Grant said, leaning back now and once again appearing relaxed. "Are you still considering the vendetta theory?"

"I can't help wondering." Jenks stuck out his long legs, crossing them at the ankles. "Been a lawman a long time. Don't reckon I've ever come across anything so plumb one-sided. Neat, too, like you said. Besides, the timing's right suspicious, coming almost in election week like it does. No chance for you to mount much of a defense."

"The timing works two ways," Grant said measuredly. He was determined to put all his cards on the table, even the losers. "If Frederickson really did have something on me, I would want to silence him before the election."

"Nice of you to point that out, Senator," Jenks said mildly. "Deputy Farrar and I've been chewing that very possibility for a fair piece of the afternoon."

Farrar continued to write studiously in his notebook.

"Any ideas about someone who might want to nail your hide?"

"No," Grant replied. "No one I'd consider seriously. I've brought you a copy of every threatening letter I've received over the last two years." He handed Jenks the letters Cynthia had faxed him. "I don't expect you to find anything there. Every politician gets his share. You, too, I'd guess."

Jenks nodded, thinking of the stack he kept locked away in a drawer. Basically harmless, like the Senator said. Folks letting off steam.

"And here's a list of threatening calls," Grant continued. "The usual cranks. You'll find as many came in yesterday as in all the last six years."

"So no one stands out?"

Grant shook his head.

"You, ma'am?"

"No one." She returned his look with a level one of her own. "I've tried to consider every possibility. No angry neighbors. No jealous colleagues. We have many acquaintances, some who no doubt don't like us much, but no one I'd consider an enemy, no one unless you count Peter Evans."

Jenks raised an inquiring eyebrow.

"No, Sheriff, not really," she said with the trace of a smile. "Evans uses his newspaper for his assassinations. He doesn't need to dirty his hands with an actual murder."

Jenks regarded her reflectively for a moment, then turned back to Grant. "Anything at the Senate?" he asked.

"The only committee work that might have even a remote connection to the underworld would be the subcommittee on drug policy."

"Drugs? Now that's mighty interesting."

"The subcommittee deals with drug *policy*," Grant said. "Not drugs themselves." He explained about his committee work, admitting that he was the driving force behind the investigation into curtailed drug interdiction efforts and its correlation to increased drug trafficking and use in the United States.

"Might specific drug cartels be studied by the committee?" Jenks asked.

"Possibly, but I would have no influence on any investigation. The NIIA under the attorney general would handle that."

"The NIIA," Jenks repeated. Grant thought he detected a flicker of distaste, but the sheriff continued too quickly to be sure. "Let me see if I've got this right. Excepting for you, these hearings about drugs might be dropped?"

"Possibly," Grant said, "but more probably muted."

"Now's no time to be modest, Bob," Rachel interposed. She leaned forward, capturing Jenks's complete attention. "The truth is, if Bob wasn't chairing the subcommittee, the administration would be able to table all discussion. They would like nothing better. For some reason, they've made the proliferation of drug use in this country a nonissue. Bob's the one who's kept attention focused on it."

"But is that enough for someone to do all this?" Grant asked, his voice leaving no doubt he wished the answer could be *yes* but knew otherwise.

"Doesn't sound likely," Jenks admitted, "but I reckon I'd best take a look. Any way to get information?"

"I'll have Cynthia send you full transcripts of our hearings—deadly dull, most of it—and I'll put you in touch with my subcommittee staff."

"You own a handgun, Senator?" Jenks's eyes were again hooded but watchful.

"Yes," Grant replied. "Two, both registered. Any particular caliber?"

"Just a handgun, Senator. Any chance you could turn them in for ballistic checks?"

"Certainly," Grant agreed without hesitation. "They're in our D.C. house. I'll have Bailey go by and get them tomorrow. Who should he give them to?"

"I'll get you the name and number of a D.C. police officer," Jenks said, leaning down to retrieve his hat. "They can be turned in to him." He moved toward the door. "He'll get them to me. If you'd fax me the registrations, that would be mighty helpful."

"First thing tomorrow," Grant assured him. "Have you found any indication Frederickson was working on any story other than my campaign?" he asked as they reached the door.

"Bubba—that's my computer whiz," Jenks said, "Bubba found a file. Contains a few details, but mostly just a list of names, Gayla Sergek and Maribeth Pariss among them." Grant's eyes became thoughtful at this news. "We're following up on it now. Could be another file in the computer, Bubba reckons, but," Jenks shrugged, "guess we won't know for sure for a bit."

A firm believer in breasting his cards, Jenks was keeping the "Pulitzer" file under wraps a while longer. The "Leads" list was something else altogether. A tad too easy to find, almost as if it had been left on purpose. The more people who knew about it the better, he'd decided. Maybe smoke out a mole that way.

Jenks nodded to Farrar, who stowed his notebook in his breast pocket and stood.

Grant shook Jenks's hand. Farrar remained out of reach. With a mental shrug, Grant put his arm around Rachel's shoulder and turned back to the sheriff. "I know the evidence is stacked against me. I appreciate knowing you're checking into everything, not just the obvious."

"We'll keep in touch, Senator."

Farrar followed the sheriff out of the room, slamming the hotel room door behind them.

Less than an hour later, Grant walked into a Republican Bean Supper in East Atlanta, normally an area of strong voter support. He appeared confident; however, he'd steeled himself for the worst. The five o'clock newscasts had rehashed the Gayla Sergek story and had included interviews with several experts who'd been only too pleased to opine that a young pregnant woman under Miss Pariss's circumstances—in love with a married man who'd abandoned her—might, indeed, have resorted to suicide as her only recourse.

The newscasts had concluded with William Tarr, ranking member of the Senate Ethics Committee, censuring Grant and calling for an immediate postelection investigation by his committee into Grant's misconduct. Tarr intimated that Grant might well be expelled from the august body of the Senate were he by some miracle to win reelection. He challenged the Republicans to stand by their pledge to clean up government.

Grant knew the effect of these pronouncements, even on his most ardent supporters, was bound to be depressing. It was.

Ginger Wright, Fulton County Republican chairperson, was waiting for him in the holding room where he would remain until time to greet the crowd. At least he hoped there would be a crowd, a supportive crowd. Mike Masterson was checking it out now.

Ginger was an old friend. Her husband, John, had been chairman of the English department at Landsdowne College, a small liberal arts school in Atlanta, when Grant was college president. Together, the Wrights had been instrumental in getting Grant to run in that first Senate race and had helped swell the ranks of black Republicans in the Atlanta area since then.

"What's going on?" Ginger asked, not bothering with a greeting. "Folks are worried, saying these charges must mean something."

"Abandoning a sinking ship, are they? I'd hoped they would give me the benefit of the doubt, at least long enough for us to find the truth."

"You've been accused of murder, adultery, and Senate ethics violations—Tarr's a blithering idiot, isn't he?—so you can't expect too much blind understanding." Her tone was friendly, but she refused to meet Grant's eye. Her normally laughing round face was drawn with worry. "John had a meeting tonight, by the way, or he would be here, too. He didn't want you to think—well, you know."

Grant nodded, hoping Ginger was being truthful. If a strong supporter like John Wright was shying away, then his campaign was, to be succinct, down the tubes.

"Tell him I understand," Grant said. "It's all lies, Ginger."

She nodded but made no comment. Turning, she began fussing with some papers on a nearby table.

"I can understand people's concern," Grant continued. His eyes were sad as he looked at her slumped shoulders. "Our hope is that Frederickson's murderer will be identified soon so we can get on with the campaign."

"Don't forget little Miss Sergek." Ginger turned slowly, finally looking him in the eye. "Adultery could still stick even if the murderer *is* caught."

"We're working on it," Grant assured her, rubbing a hand wearily over his hair, "but it's like fighting in the dark. How can we prove that something didn't happen? If any of your people know anything about Maribeth Pariss or Gayla Sergek, we would appreciate hearing it. If they get wind of anything else, too."

"You think there could be more?" Ginger asked, looking, if possible, even more shaken.

"I'm prepared for it. What else can I think? Some pretty big guns seem to be trained on me. Murder, adultery—charges that would seem ridiculous, except they seem to have proof for it all. They won't give up until they're certain I'm destroyed."

"You mean you think you're the target of some conspiracy?" Her voice was disbelieving.

"I'm not sure," Grant admitted. "All I know is that every accusation against me is false."

"And all the evidence?"

"All too believable, isn't it?" His mouth twisted into a wry smile. "Someone's spent a lot of money and time setting me up. They even convinced Frederickson I'd hired thugs to keep him from making public my horrible secret—whatever it is."

"Hired thugs! That's ridiculous!" Ginger exclaimed, for the first time sounding as if she might be inclined to believe him. "You'd be as likely to hire thugs as I would." Her eyes narrowed angrily. "You really *are* being framed. It's racially motivated, isn't it? I'd hoped we'd moved beyond that. They still can't stand it when we succeed on their turf."

"I don't know, Ginger. I don't think race has anything to do with this."

"They're ready for you, Bob," Mike Masterson said, coming into the room and moving Grant toward the door. "An okay crowd. Lots of media."

Ginger took hold of Grant's arm and held him back. "Oh, Bob! I'm sorry." She seemed to come to a decision. "You're a good man, Bob Grant. We can't let this happen! Just let me know what I can do. John, too."

Grant patted her hand and smiled his thanks. Masterson motioned him to hurry.

"Bob!" Ginger called to his retreating back.

Grant turned.

"I'll get the word out," she said, her voice fired with determination. "I'll be sure everyone knows what's really been happening. And believes it," she added, her mouth set in an unwavering line.

Grant nodded. He started to leave but changed his mind and walked back to her.

"You'd better hurry," Masterson told him impatiently.

Grant ignored him. He took both of her hands into his.

"Thank you, Ginger," he said, his voice leaving no doubt as to his sincerity.

She nodded, then took his arm and urged him forward. "And I'll be on stage right next to you," she said.

"Ready to do battle, are you?" Grant asked with an affectionate smile.

"You'd better believe it. Anyone who attacks you will have me to deal with."

The high-school cafeteria, where the supper was being held and where a makeshift stage had been erected, became eerily quiet as soon as Grant, with a smiling Ginger Wright on his arm, appeared. Then a lone clap sounded sharply in the silence. Matt Goldie, Grant realized with a surge of gratitude.

Hesitantly at first, but with growing fervor, others joined in.

"We're behind you, Bob!" Goldie again.

"We believe you!"

More added their shouts of support. Grant felt both pleased and disturbed. The room was only half full at best, and his reception was as much embarrassed or only curious as genuinely supportive. Slumped shoulders and furtive glances spoke more loudly than the cheers.

Media lined the walls of the room, their cameras and microphones trained on him. Grant wondered if the cheering crowd would make the news. Probably not, he thought with resignation, just Gayla Sergek with her accusation. She and William Tarr. Poster children for journalism run amok. If only he could get the media to really dig into the story!

Grant abandoned the remarks of thanks and appreciation that normally preceded his speeches. Tonight he looked around the room, trying to make eye contact with as many as he could. He stood silent and tall, waiting until the audience, almost as one, leaned toward him in tense anticipation.

"I am innocent of every charge that has been brought against me." His voice was low, but forceful. "I did not kill Russell Frederickson. I had absolutely nothing to do with his death. Russell Frederickson *was* covering my campaign. That is true. I'm sure it's equally true that he'd been delving into my life in hopes of discovering a 'big story.' But he had not, I repeat, had *not*, uncovered anything damaging about me. That is the truth. I'm not perfect, but I've done nothing in either my public or private life which cannot withstand the light of public scrutiny."

No one applauded. But they were listening, Grant reminded himself. At least they were willing to listen. With Ginger beside him, conspicuous in her support, they were even more likely to give his words serious consideration.

"Twelve years ago," he continued, praying he would strike a responsive chord, "I was privileged to become your Senator. I knew that position would bring with it a tremendous responsibility, necessitating a tremendous amount of work. I also expected to be attacked, both personally and politically. Both of my expectations have been met. I *have* worked diligently for the people of Georgia, and while my efforts haven't always met with success, especially under the present administration, I feel I've made a genuine contribution to the defense of our country and its liberties. And as I expected, I *have* been attacked. But my attackers have always been visible: disgruntled constituents, members of the opposition party, the liberal media, anyone whose livelihood depends on the federal government.

"Today, however, my attackers are faceless. Their accusations are vicious and totally without foundation. Murder, adultery, lying: The crimes laid at my feet are barbarous. I have no idea why I've been attacked so viciously. Neither do I know who's behind these attacks. I assure you, however, that every one of the accusations is totally and completely false. I further assure you that I will not allow lies to defeat me.

"This faceless enemy cannot be permitted to destroy what I've spent a lifetime creating. My integrity and my honor are at stake. With your help, I will expose every lie. With your vote, I will continue to honorably serve the people of Georgia for six more years."

After a moment of throbbing silence, the crowd erupted into cheers. Grant watched them, his face unsmiling. He was a realist. He'd persuaded them to set aside their doubts for now. But another attack against him, even one that in a previous campaign would have been dismissed with a laugh, would now bring into full bloom the doubts that his speech had managed to allay.

While Masterson made some calls, Grant walked to the car. Normally, he would have remained, talking to supporters. Tonight, however, much more could be accomplished by Ginger alone.

The night was dark with only a few stars dusting the sky. The glow from streetlights formed dirty yellow blotches on the asphalt, doing little to soften the intervening darkness.

A hand closed around Grant's arm. He turned, heart racing. It was Matt Goldie.

"Sorry, Bob," Goldie said. "Didn't mean to startle you. I just wanted to talk to you alone." Keeping his hand on Grant's arm, Goldie continued earnestly. "I want you to know that I'm behind you 100 percent. These attacks make me fighting mad!"

Goldie was a short man of muscular build. Only on formal occasions did he wear other than the khaki slacks and light blue, button-down, oxford cloth shirt he wore now. His rough hands bespoke his years in the field, first as an oil fire fighter and then as the owner of one of the largest companies in the world. They had met when Goldie had been called in to fight a fire at a naval base where Grant was the commanding officer. They'd formed an immediate friendship that had continued through the years. Since his retirement, Goldie had begun raising beefalo, leaving his extensive farming operation to fight only the most difficult blazes.

Goldie recognized the emotion in Grant's eyes and squeezed his arm. "Just tell me what needs to be done," he said, his eyes glittering fiercely in the dark, "and I'll do it."

"I'm certainly finding out who my friends are," Grant said. "Thanks."

"Nothing like a bit of trouble to send folks packing," Goldie agreed, nodding. "Too many latch on for the benefits and couldn't care less about the principles of good government. Now, what needs to be done?"

Grant regarded Goldie thoughtfully. "You understand that things could get worse, probably much worse?"

Again, Goldie nodded. "Wondered if that might be the case."

"And being around me may be dangerous."

This time Goldie grinned. "Then count me in. Retirement's too dad-blamed boring."

The knot of tension Grant hadn't even realized existed began to dissolve. It was comforting to have a friend ready to fight shoulder to shoulder with him. He returned Goldie's grin. "Considering what's happened so far, I think I can guarantee boredom won't be on your dance card."

Rachel Grant sat on the hotel room bed staring at the TV, only vaguely aware of what was being said. Bob should be returning from the bean supper at any moment. Had he been treated decently? she wondered. Had they listened to him, really listened, and weighed his words and his character fairly? Had he opened any windows of doubt? Surely yes, but nothing made sense any more. Hired hit men! How could anyone believe that about Bob?

She felt a gnawing need to see him, to hold him, to have him hold her. The evil that was out there was frightening, its miasma pervading every moment of the day, every corner of their lives. She was tired, so very tired. The suspense of waiting for the next move in this all-too-real mystery was enervating.

As for so many others in perilous and terrifying times, faith gave her strength. Silent prayers were her weapon. Tired she might be, but defenseless she was not. She would face them all and show them that she had no doubts, absolutely none, about her husband or about his integrity.

The news came on the TV. The Frederickson murder was again the lead story.

Ever since the Menendez and Simpson murder trials had proven themselves sure ratings winners, television covered potentially titillating events from the beginning. Thus, the Frederickson murder was getting optimum air time, much of it live. Viewers were already looking forward to these breaks, their window into a real-life soap opera. A powerful politician, a black who was throwing his hat into the presidential sweepstakes, was being touted as an adulterer and murderer: What could Hollywood dish up to compare?

The face of the anchor, by now successfully associated with the "Grant Affair," as it had been dubbed tongue-in-cheek, filled the television screen.

"We take you now to Elaine Thomas in Atlanta."

Rachel turned up the sound.

"Thank you, David. Shirley Spade, a former employee of Senator Robert Grant, is with me in the studio. Ms. Spade will shed light on the allegedly illicit relationship between Grant and his young employee Maribeth Pariss, which even now rocks both Washington and Georgia."

Shirley Spade! Rachel stiffened in numb disbelief.

A pleasant, grandmotherly-looking woman appeared on the screen, smiling confidently into the camera. Rachel remembered her only too well. Spade had worked as a volunteer for a short time at the Atlanta office. She'd left after a bitter disagreement over accounts which had led to questions about missing petty cash and bogus expense accounts. Spade's benevolent facade hid a rapacious soul. Apparently, she targeted political and charity organizations for her scams, knowing they would avoid pressing charges to prevent adverse publicity.

Rachel leaned forward, her nails biting into the skin of her hands.

"I knew both the Senator and Maribeth," Spade said, smiling sweetly. "Such a nice young thing, Maribeth. Of course, I can't tell you what went on between them in private," she said with a sad sigh, "but I do know that Senator Grant was all Maribeth talked about. She thought he'd hung the moon. One day, all that changed. She was so sad, frightened, too. She said that the Senator had threatened to fire her if she didn't have . . . well, ahem, sex with him." Spade's delicate pink skin turned crimson with embarrassment. "Of course, that was Maribeth's side of the story," she continued with a knowing nod of the head, "but I always say, 'Where there's smoke, there's bound to be fire.' So unpleasant to think Senator Grant may have driven that poor child to suicide." Spade's kindly face, the picture of offended righteousness, faded from the screen.

Rachel could hardly believe what she knew she'd just seen. The *fraud!* she thought, outraged.

"In a further development," Elaine Thomas intoned, "Jess Werner, Miss Pariss's employer after she left Senator Grant's office, told this reporter that, although he never saw them together, Miss Pariss intimated that the Senator was a close personal friend. How close? With Miss Pariss dead, the Senator has many questions to answer."

Next Sheriff Jenks appeared, declaring that the murder was under investigation and that they hoped to make an arrest soon. No, he wasn't limiting his investigation to Senator Grant and had no intention of doing so. He asked anyone who had been at Crazy Sam's or Frederickson's motel on Saturday night between the hours of eight and one to please give his office a call.

Rachel heard the door open, but she kept her eyes on the screen. Bob was being shown leaving a school. Protesters were screaming at him. Kirk Vinton of the *Herald*, his face redder than his hair, stood at the front of the pack of reporters, yelling combative questions intended to goad Grant into an indiscretion, a pithy quotable one.

The bed creaked beside her, and Rachel felt her hand being gently caressed. She smiled up at Bob but looked quickly back at the screen.

"Wouldn't you rather listen to the real me?" the Bob beside her asked, an affectionate chide in his voice.

"Shhh," she told him, without looking. He'd been verbally assaulted far more than she, Rachel realized, listening to the catcalls and questions. Sad how some people seemed to lose their manners, even their decency, when they thought someone was vulnerable—or, almost worse, in the name of "investigative journalism" or "the right of the people to know."

"I categorically deny every allegation made in every news report," the Grant on TV said, "and I demand a full investigation into the source of these accusations. My name must be cleared, and the murderer of Russell Frederickson must be found."

"Good," Rachel murmured.

A clip of Tobias Caruso appeared on the screen. "I'm concerned that Georgia and our nation will be irreparably damaged in the eyes of the world by these events," Caruso intoned gravely, already looking every inch the concerned politician, "and I, like Mr. Grant, want to see any false accusations put to rest immediately. For these reasons I'm unbending in my demand for a debate with the Senator. If he continues to refuse, the people of Georgia will have no doubt about which candidate is afraid to face the truth."

Caruso was followed by a "political expert," one of those convenient hacks the media loves to trot out to buttress its own position. This supposedly "Republican" theorist opined that the once invulnerable Senator

Grant was on the brink of defeat. The equation of the Senate election had shifted dramatically, he said, and unless Grant could come up with strong proof of his innocence to all charges, emphasis on "all," he could be written out of the political picture entirely. Such proof of innocence would be difficult to find, he concluded.

"This evening at the conclusion of our normal newscast," Elaine Thomas said, "we'll bring you an exclusive one-hour in-depth report into the Grant Affair, including interviews with Democratic Senators William C. Tarr and Morty Edgerton, and Republican Senator Kennard Wylie. Several former associates of Senator Grant and Maribeth Pariss will give exclusive interviews. We'll attempt to find the link between Miss Pariss's death and that of murdered reporter Russell Frederickson. Peter Evans, renowned editor of the *Washington Herald* and employer of the late Mr. Frederickson, will share with us his paper's crusade to see that justice is done. We hope you'll stay tuned."

The news switched to the latest in a string of murders, ones that had nothing to do with politics or politicians.

Rachel clicked off the television but sat staring at the darkening screen. Grant waited.

"It's impossible," she finally said. "All these stories are totally false, and yet all that happens is lies and more lies are piled on top of the ones already there. And they all sounded so plausible!" she added, incensed. "This in-depth report is bound to be more of the same."

Her passionate defense of him brought crinkles of weary affection to the corners of Grant's eyes. "With Tarr, Edgerton, and Wylie, not to mention Peter Evans? It'll be bad."

Rachel finally looked at him. "No one even considers presenting your side. They're enjoying destroying you. Enjoying it!"

"Maybe so," Grant agreed. "But what matters is the end. One thing's certain, we can't rely on the much-touted 'investigative' skills of the media. It's time we began digging into this ourselves."

"Past time," Rachel said grimly.

Grant kissed her cheek, then walked to the window and stared out.

"You're right about Sheriff Jenks," Rachel said, going over to stand beside him. "He's being more than fair with us, but that deputy of his . . ." She shuddered.

"He's a sweetheart, isn't he? Not that it matters. Jenks calls the shots in that office."

"Why do you suppose Jenks is being so open? Why tell us so much?"

"We don't know how much he's holding back." Grant put his arm around her, and she leaned against him. "But I agree. He's being exceedingly forthcoming. I have to believe he's a conscientious lawman trying to make sure justice is done." He gave Rachel's shoulder a squeeze, then walked toward the closet, taking off his suit coat as he went. "Either that," he said, talking over his shoulder, "or he's decided I'm the killer, and he's giving me plenty of rope."

"I much prefer the conscientious lawman theory," Rachel said lightly. She saw fatigue etching its lines into his face and dropped her bantering tone. "Bob, who's behind it all? Not Sergek and Spade. They're not smart enough. A lot of money is involved, money and influence. If it's not drugs, then it has to be something equally serious."

Grant nodded. "The Frederickson murder is the key. It has to be." He lowered himself into a chair, then leaned forward, forearms resting on his knees. "Someone had to have fed Frederickson some damaging information about me. Was Frederickson then killed to make it look as if the information really was dangerous? And why was Frederickson frightened of me? Threatening calls would work only if he thought I had reason to silence him. Adultery doesn't seem enough, not today."

"So many questions," Rachel said with a sigh. "And not one answer."

"Here's another," Grant said, loosening his tie. "Were Sergek and Spade paid by my unknown enemy, or are they opportunists who saw their chance for money or media attention and came forward on their own?"

"That only makes sense if the affair letter was genuine," Rachel said, going to a nearby chair. "What I can't figure is why Maribeth would write it since it isn't true?"

"Warped psyche?" Grant asked rhetorically. "I'm hoping it's a forgery, and The Enemy figured no one would think to compare, at least not until after the election."

"The Enemy," Rachel repeated, her eyes thoughtful. "He's counting on our being too upset to fight back, isn't he? That would explain the crossburning, insignificant in itself, but something else to keep us off balance."

"And to keep us from examining the real issues."

"He certainly misjudged his prey." Rachel picked her briefcase from the floor beside the chair, took out the legal pad she'd used earlier, and rummaged for a pen. "Let's see," she said, turning to her lists. "We have Russell Frederickson and Gayla Sergek who definitely may be part of the plot. Right?"

"Right," Grant agreed. He took a long drink from the glass of cold sparkling water Rachel had left waiting for him by the chair.

"That letter," she said, after she'd put check marks by Frederickson's and Sergek's names, "the one that mentions an affair, it wasn't dated, was it?"

"No. We can't prove I was somewhere else."

"Too bad. That leaves Shirley Spade. You know," she said thoughtfully, resting the pen momentarily against her lower lip, "Spade just might give us a lead. She would be more than willing to do almost anything if the price were right. Remember the missing petty cash?"

"If we could prove she'd been paid to produce her story and then trace the money back . . ." Grant nodded. "Good idea. I'll have Bailey see if he can turn up something—financial transactions, phone bills, whatever—with that computer of his. Jenks needs to be told, too. And add Tarr, Edgerton, and Wylie to the list." Rachel cocked an eyebrow in surprise but began writing. "I want to know if they got any quid pro quo for speaking out and if so how much and from whom. Someone is trying hard to confuse the issues, maybe even hide something. We're the only ones who understand Washington well enough to figure out who and why. Jenks wouldn't have a clue, and the NIIA sure isn't going to give it a look.

"I'm going to talk to some friends in military intelligence," he continued. "Maybe they've heard something that would reveal a motive."

"Worth trying," Rachel agreed. "But they'll only know about international overtones."

"As you said, someone influential has to be financing this. With all the changes in power around the world, who knows who might see me as a threat. Now that the President has gutted our intelligence agencies, military intelligence may not know any more than we do, but I'm going to put out as many feelers as I can. Matt Goldie's helping with it."

"Matt's helping?" Rachel's face brightened. She got up and refilled Grant's glass. He nodded his thanks. Smiling, she handed him two chocolate-chip cookies on a napkin. "I passed a bakery and thought you might need them," she told him.

He took a bite, his expression leaving no doubt of his appreciation.

"I'm so glad about Matt," Rachel continued. "He has all kinds of sources—and different from ours. What about Benjamin Dashev? Do you think he might know something?" She referred to their old friend, ostensibly attached to the Israeli Embassy as the Deputy Chief of Mission but in reality an agent of Mossad, the Israeli intelligence arm. Dashev had provided much of the information that had helped Grant keep America's enemies from grabbing power in Cuba the year before.

"We certainly think alike," Grant told her. "I already have Cynthia tracking him down. Maybe she's heard something." He reached over and picked up the phone, dropping his napkin into the wastebasket as he did.

"While you're talking to her," Rachel said, gathering her notes, "I'm going to work on this some more."

"What's the story on Pariss and Sergek?" Grant asked Cynthia when she came on the line.

"I'm not sure. Everyone agrees Maribeth was a nice girl who happened to have a crush on you."

"Great," Grant groaned. "So that much is true?"

"Yes, but no one can remember her ever speaking to you. According to our records, you were only in the Atlanta office two times, three at the most, while she worked there, and she always got too nervous to say anything. In fact, between times, she continually bemoaned missing the chance to hear your voice speaking to her personally."

"At least that refutes Spade's story."

"It would, except now Spade claims you learned of Pariss's infatuation and started going to her apartment. 'Last-minute emergencies' are Spade's words. Only too plausible, given today's soap-opera mentality."

"And difficult to disprove," Grant said bitingly. "See if you can find someone who knew Spade when both she and Maribeth worked for us. They might notice something in her story we would miss. Also see if Spade has more money than usual."

"I'll have Bailey do some checking. His search for a motive came up empty, but it gave him a good feel for background."

"Matt Goldie can help, too," Grant told her. Her heartfelt "Matt?" brought a smile to his face. "He's pulling together some old buddies, including several who have intelligence-gathering experience. They'll be ready for assignments by early tomorrow. Have Bailey prepare fact sheets for them.

While he's at it, have him pull up a list of all countries whose governments are closely aligned with drug cartels, especially any new entries in the field, also any countries that might not like my stand on military preparedness."

"You've narrowed motive to those?" Cynthia asked. Grant could hear the scratch of her pencil as she took copious notes in her own illegible shorthand.

"No, actually that doesn't seem right to me, not personal enough. But it's a logical place to start. Bailey may come up with some link, maybe some person who appears on too many lists." He told her about some of the other ideas he and Rachel had discussed. "Back to Pariss. Why did she leave our office? Anything there?"

"Nothing. She said she'd found a better-paying job nearer her apartment. One possible break, though. Everyone in the Atlanta office agrees Maribeth was unusually moody during the last month she worked for us, one day exhilarated, the next day depressed. Rumor was she had a boyfriend, maybe a married one, and her moods reflected the state of their relationship."

"A boyfriend is out there somewhere," Grant said. "She really was pregnant. Sheriff Jenks confirmed that from the autopsy report."

"If we can find him, and prove he got her pregnant . . ."

"That'll be an interesting one to prove," Grant said dryly.

"You know what I mean," Cynthia retorted. "Find him, and your motive is gone. Although," she continued slowly, "I suppose some people will still assume you did it, just for some other reason."

"Probably so." For the first time, Grant's voice betrayed the depth of the concern he was beginning to feel. Rachel looked up sharply. He hid his disquiet behind a reassuring smile. "We'll have to trust Jenks on that one," he said.

"Maybe Frederickson was killed for some totally unrelated reason, and someone used you as a scapegoat."

"Won't work. Frederickson's letter indicates premeditation. The question is: Why me? And by whom?"

"We're looking into it here, and so is the Atlanta office."

"Tell everyone to be discreet," Grant cautioned. "We don't want to give the media any ideas. If things get worse, maybe then—"

"Worse?" Cynthia asked with a catch in her voice.

"Maybe they won't." The words came out slowly. "I can't imagine what else could happen, but . . ."

"But who would have believed Frederickson and Pariss, even the cross-burning," she finished for him. "The kids are waiting to talk to you, and, Bob, Bailey's doing a first-class job here, even if he seems rather pre-occupied with someone named Sherrill."

"So a girl has finally interested old Bailey, has she?" Grant asked, smiling in spite of himself. "She must be something special."

"To hear Bailey talk, she is. He'll be flying down to Georgia to hook up with you tomorrow night. You can hear for yourself then. Believe me, you won't have any trouble getting him to talk." A laugh bubbled in her voice, but she immediately became serious. No one was more aware than she that the election was less than a week away, and no one knew better than she the vagaries of voters. She'd been a denizen of Washington for almost twenty years. She'd thought she'd seen everything in that time, but a Senator seriously considered a murder suspect, especially a Senator of Grant's proven integrity? "Bailey's been working on accessing Frederickson's computer at the *Herald*," she continued, "and thinks he's close to breaking the code. He's hoping to have that list Jenks mentioned, maybe both of them."

"That was a good idea of Bailey's," Grant said. "Makes sense that Frederickson would modem files to his office computer. I'd have thought the *Herald* would've found and deleted them by now though."

"I said the same thing. Bailey assures me reporters are like everyone else who uses a computer but doesn't really understand it. Routine stuff they do fine, but hunting for a hidden file or trying to break into a file with a private password? They wouldn't know how and wouldn't like to admit it, and he's sure they would put off deleting files until they ran out of space."

"He may have a point," Grant agreed. "Hope so. He's certainly on target about not liking to admit ignorance."

"Well, we'll keep digging," Cynthia said. "Keep the faith. Here's Olivia."

Grant motioned to Rachel, and she picked up the extension. At the sound of her daughter's voice, her face softened.

Andrew Stoner's apartment was dark when Bailey Grant arrived, but the door was unlocked as usual. He looked around for a note, for some indication of where everyone was, but found nothing. Had they decided to blow this party, or were they out trying to score?

He started for the door. He had no business being here, even if it meant not seeing Sherrill. Drugs! His dad had warned him to be careful. Milton would just have to baby-sit the others alone tonight.

With his hand on the doorknob, Bailey saw the faded and curled snapshot Andrew had taped to his TV. Five boys grinned at the camera, the Potomac River shimmering in the background: Andrew, Bear, Milton, Sean—a friend who'd gone west to school, and himself, back in the days when they'd thought their friendship would last forever, back when their major concern had been finding fun that wouldn't bend their folks too out of shape if they heard. How he wished he could go back to that time! Life had been so simple then. "The Boys," his parents had dubbed them, and "The Boys" they'd been ever since.

After a long look at the snapshot, Bailey walked to a sagging chair in front of the TV and sat down to wait. Making no effort to stifle a face-obliterating yawn, he leaned his head back and propped his feet on the cluttered coffee table, tilting an empty pizza box precariously as he did. He had to stand by his friends. For old times' sake, he had to try his best to keep them out of trouble.

Half an hour later, the door to the apartment burst open, and a blast of cold night air rushed in.

"Hey, Bailey!" Andrew yelled when he saw his friend half-asleep in the easy chair. "So you decided to join us, did you, dude? Some party we're going to have!"

Andrew was wound tight, working himself up for something, Bailey realized. Andrew always got hyper before his more outrageous stunts. Bear shambled in behind him, already half-toasted. Andrew probably was, too, only he could hide it better, at least in the early stages. Reggie Dixon, shaking with silent laughter, stood framed in the doorway. Reggie was a jerk, Bailey thought, turning away to hide his frown.

"You got the stuff, didn't you?" he demanded of Andrew and Bear, knowing the answer but hoping he was wrong. He wished he'd left when he'd had the chance, but if he could keep them from doing anything, at least until Sherrill came ... Hopefully, Milton would be there by then, too.

"Only the best coke money can buy!" Bear shouted as he opened a bottle of beer and began guzzling. His words were slurred. "We're expanding our horizons, man." He grinned wolfishly.

"Plus a half bag," Andrew added, getting more cans out of the refrigerator and throwing them to the others. Bailey caught his and put it on the table beside him unopened.

Reggie picked it up and thrust it toward him. "Not afraid of a little brewskie, are you?"

"Stop doggin' him," Bear said, collapsing on the couch, his second beer already half gone. "Bailey's our designated driver."

They all laughed uproariously at this witticism. Andrew sorted through a stack of CDs, and turned the music up full blast. Several laughing girls came in, and Reggie tossed them cans. Soon the room was filled with young people. Apparently, word had gotten out.

When the room was really rocking, Reggie raised clasped hands over his head. "Let the good times roll!" he shouted. He reached down, pulled up a plastic bag, and presented it with a flourish to the admiring cluster.

Bailey argued with them. He even did some begging. They laughed at him, then got angry.

"You should be enjoying, not preaching," Andrew yelled. "Just leave, why don't you?"

"Don't do that, man," Reggie shouted, grabbing Bailey's arm. "Here, just for you."

Bailey stared at the powder being offered to him so enticingly. He felt revulsed but somehow tempted as well. Why not join his friends and forget his worries for a while? He certainly had enough of them. He reached out his hand, actually touching the paper, before he turned away in disgust.

Mad at himself, mad at his friends, maybe mad at an unjust world, he strode to a corner and leaned into it, his arms crossed.

Andrew, Bear, and Reggie all did a couple of lines of cocaine. Some others did, too, including several of the girls. Joints were continuously passed from hand to hand. Several kids used bhongs, holding the carb until the chamber filled with smoke too thick to see through. Letting up on the carb, they sucked in huge lungfuls, leaking the excess through their noses.

More kids arrived. Bailey thought one brought some hits of LSD, but he couldn't be sure. Whatever it was disappeared in minutes.

Then Sherrill walked through the door, her fuzzy pale green sweater bathing her in softness. Her smile faded as she surveyed the room. By the time her eyes found Bailey, she looked completely nonplussed.

"Here, babe," Reggie yelled, intercepting her as she started toward Bailey and offering her a line of coke.

She paused, her eyes uncertain. Then she raised them, and they locked with Bailey's. Something throbbed between them. "No," she told Reggie, shaking her head. She pushed his hand away. "No!" Her head-shake became almost defiant. With a final look at the white powder and at the unnatural state of those who had taken it, she rushed to Bailey's side.

"We've got to get out of here," she said, her eyes darting toward the door.

"I can't leave," he told her, puzzled by her vehemence. First she'd begged him to come, knowing about the drugs, and now she couldn't wait to get him out of there! "Someone needs to stay with these guys." He gestured around the room. "They sure can't take care of themselves."

"I don't care!" Sherrill shouted. Several faces turned in her direction, but their eyes registered only indifference. "We shouldn't be here!"

Bailey stared at her, peeved that he would have to explain. He didn't want to be here any more than she did, but Andrew and Bear were his friends, and friends didn't leave friends, not when they obviously needed help and not when no one else was around to give it. He opened his mouth, the explanation on his lips, when she gave him an angry shove, then turned and ran from the apartment.

Stunned, Bailey could only stare at her retreating back.

Oddly though, he felt relief. The feelings he had for her were overwhelming in their intensity. He was glad for an emotional respite. Enough problems with Andrew and Bear, not to mention his father, without adding Sherrill to the brew.

Bailey itched to get back to his computer. He'd accessed the *Herald*'s computer network easily. He'd gotten into one file immediately, and he just knew he was on the verge of cracking Frederickson's password for the next one. If he could do that, he might really help his dad. That seemed especially likely since the reporter had felt it necessary to use a sophisticated code to protect the second file. Not that he couldn't crack it, Bailey assured himself. It was just taking longer than he'd hoped.

He leaned back against the wall and ran the problem through his mind, much as he'd been doing almost every waking moment since he'd first begun working on it. Any second now, he knew the solution would fall into place like the tumblers on his old high-school locker.

Bailey watched as the kids in the room gradually became stoned out of their minds. At least Andrew and Bear were stoned; Reggie he wasn't so sure about. Reggie seemed tense, almost watchful, and the others certainly weren't. The whole atmosphere made Bailey nervous, jumpy.

Now as midnight approached, he was glad he'd stayed. They really did need a baby-sitter. Certainly, they couldn't take care of themselves. As if reading his thoughts, Bear rose unsteadily to his feet and started careening around the room. He bumped into the coffee table first, spilling magazines, old pizza boxes, overflowing ashtrays, and cups of spit and chew onto the floor. With a bellow of rage, he continued his bizarre dance, stepping in the mess and tracking it with him as he banged into a chair, then off the wall.

Bailey moved to intercept him. "Hang on, Bear," he said soothingly. He reached for Bear's arm but missed as Bear took a swaying turn back in the direction he'd just come. He stepped on a girl's hand where it lay turned up limply toward the ceiling. Neither the girl nor Bear seemed to notice.

"Come on, pal. Sit down for a moment, why don't you?" Bailey cajoled. He continued speaking, his tones soothing, but Bear wouldn't listen and couldn't understand.

Afraid of what Bear in his mindless rampage might do to himself or to one of those sprawled on the floor, Bailey sprang forward, nailing him with a flying tackle. They landed on a pile of filthy cushions and blankets against the wall. Bear wasn't hurt, not that he could have felt pain anyway, but the same couldn't be said for Bailey. Accompanied by a solid thunk, Bear's elbow had connected with Bailey's right eye.

Bear lay where he'd fallen, a sweet smile on his beefy face. Slowly, his muscles slackened, his eyes closed, and he began to snore.

Bailey got to his feet. His eye throbbed. He felt it gingerly, not surprised at the puffiness under his fingers.

What Cynthia would say when she saw his swollen eye, he couldn't imagine. He would have to come up with a good story, one that wouldn't alarm his parents. That was one explanation he wasn't interested in giving. Drugs! His parents figured he had sense enough to stay away from them, but then so did all their parents, he thought as he surveyed the wreck, both material and human, that cluttered the room.

Stepping over bodies, some almost comatose, others making agitated motions with hands commanded by some perverse force divorced from rational thought, he walked to the bathroom. He stopped just outside the door to soothe a frantic young woman who clutched and tugged at her flowing blond curls, all the while screeching a bizarre litany about love, spiders, and the color purple. With infinite patience, Bailey lessened the grip of her hands and convinced her to lean back against the wall. Though she eventually did as he suggested, he was certain none of his words had meaning for her.

With a backward glance full of bewilderment and concern, he stepped into the bathroom and looked in the mirror. His eye was bloodshot, the skin around it even puffier than he'd imagined. It would be a beaut. Would it be gone by the time he saw his parents? He slapped his palm against his forehead in frustration. Tomorrow night! He was supposed to meet his parents in Atlanta tomorrow night! Fat chance even the swelling would be gone by then.

He walked slowly back into the cluttered room, his face set in determined lines. Only a few more hours, and these bozos he called friends should be sober enough for him to leave. This was it, the last time, he thought. Friends or no friends, his baby-sitting days were over. Not even Milton could take him on this guilt trip again.

He went to a now-vacant chair, folded his arms across his chest, and leaned back to wait.

Less than an hour later, Bailey jumped up from his chair and looked around wildly. He must have dozed off, he thought groggily. It was Andrew's screams—seemingly of exuberance rather than anger, fear, or pain—which must have awakened him. He looked at his watch. Almost one o'clock.

He started to sit back down but jerked around as a girl's voice joined Andrew's, the baritone and soprano mixing in strident pseudo-harmony. While the two inebriates weren't getting physical like Bear, their alternating screams and mutters were pretty horrible in themselves. Their voices finally trailed off, lost behind the music that still blared, and they stared beatifically around the room.

With increasing uneasiness, Bailey's gaze returned to one of the guys on the couch. Bailey didn't know him but thought he'd heard someone call him Joey. Joey, if that was his name, had been hitting the bhong heavily throughout the night while doing an occasional line of coke. He now stared straight ahead, barely blinking, as if he'd become one with the couch. A motionless hand clutched a glass partially full of a clear liquid, vodka probably. As Bailey watched, Joey convulsed, tilted sideways, and collapsed into a heap on the floor. The glass fell from his limp hand and hit the grimy carpet with a dull thud.

Bailey ran to him. His foot kicked the glass, sending it clattering against a table leg. The carpet was soggy under his shoes.

Suddenly, he froze, his hand motionless where he'd stretched it out to check the boy's pulse. Someone was shaking and turning the doorknob, trying to get in! Bailey had locked the door when Bear began his strange dance, both to keep Bear in and anyone else out. This was one party he didn't want busted.

Mesmerized, Bailey stared at the doorknob.

The shaking stopped, and whoever it was began pounding on the door, the force intensifying with each blow.

After a despairing look at the motionless boy, Bailey crept to the door. At the next knock, he cautiously brought his eye to the peephole. Milton!

Bailey flung open the door, barely restraining himself from throwing his arms around his friend.

"Sorry I'm so late," Milton said. Then he saw Bailey's eye. He looked at Bear stretched out on the floor, awake now, his fingers pulling at imaginary threads in the air, at Andrew and Lisa, staring into space and occasionally muttering or swinging their arms, at Reggie who seemed to be coming out of it, at the others strewn in grotesque positions around the room. One girl, oblivious to everyone, was even doing another line of coke! Where she'd gotten it, Bailey couldn't imagine. He'd wadded up the bag long before.

"They did it, didn't they?" Milton asked. Bailey nodded. "Fools! They all right?"

"I think so." Bailey looked over at Joey. "What am I saying? I don't know. What's all right with all this stuff? Look at that guy. He collapsed just before you got here."

They walked over to the limp body. Only the slightly fluttering eyelids and struggling chest gave sign of life.

"That's Joey Hunter," Milton said. "His old man's the attorney general."

"You've got to be kidding!" Bailey exclaimed, staring down at the blue-tinged, strangely empty face. "The A.G.! That's just what we need now!"

"Joey'd go ballistic if word got out," Milton said. "I think he's scared of his old man. What's that sound?" He placed his hand tentatively on the boy's moist forehead. "Geez, it's him, isn't it?"

"Yeah," Bailey agreed. His eyes brimmed with worry. Leaning down, he straightened Joey out on the floor and reached for a ragged blanket wadded on the end of the couch. "Shouldn't we keep him warm? Shock or something?" he asked as he spread the blanket over the motionless boy, then tucked it in.

"What we should do is get him to a hospital," Milton retorted.

"Believe me, I know that! Think we should call 911?"

"Get serious! They'd see all this." Milton motioned around the room.

Joey began moaning, his body moving restlessly under the blanket. Desperate to do something, Bailey ran to the bathroom and came back with a wet washcloth. He began wiping Joey's forehead as Bailey's mother had always done when he was sick. Milton knelt on one knee on the other side of Joey, looking as helpless as Bailey felt.

Suddenly, Joey's eyes opened. He stared straight at Bailey.

"Feel awful," he whispered hoarsely. "Can't breathe."

"I know," Bailey soothed, leaning close to hear over the raucous music that pulsed around them. "We're going to take you to a hospital."

"No!" Joey began thrashing around, tangling himself in the blanket.

"Agree with him," Milton hissed. "He'll kill himself!" He ran over and turned off the music. The mutters and groans of others in the room jumped out from the silence.

"Okay, okay," Bailey soothed, gently forcing Joey's shoulders back onto the floor. "Just relax. Everything'll be all right."

"No hospital—no!" Joey's hand grabbed at Bailey's shirt. "Promise!"

"Sure, sure." Bailey watched Joey's agitation with mounting fear. He would have promised anything to calm him. He took the boy's cool hand in his own and held it comfortingly. "Don't worry. We'll take care of you. No one will know."

"Father . . ." The word was barely audible. His eyelids fluttered as he tried to keep them open. "Mustn't find . . ." He was motionless once again.

"Maybe we'd better get a doctor," Milton whispered, his voice high and frightened.

Both boys turned as Reggie Dixon staggered noisily to his feet. He stooped and began rooting around on the floor. Then he stumbled toward the door.

"Where you going?" Milton demanded.

"I'm outta here," Reggie said. He slurred the words.

Bailey reached out to steady him. "You can't go anywhere, the shape you're in."

Reggie threw off Bailey's hand. "Keep your filthy hands to yourself," he growled.

Bailey recoiled, almost stepping on Joey's upturned hand.

Reggie glared at him through venomous eyes, then looked around the room, studying each sprawled body in turn. His eyes returned to Joey, and his lips curled in disgust. Then he continued toward the door and opened it. "So long, Daddy's Boy," he said, speaking directly to Bailey, all slur wiped from his voice. "You're even more a fool than I expected." With a backward sneer, he slammed the door.

"What a jerk!" Milton said, unconsciously rubbing his palms on his pants.

They turned back to Joey.

When Sherrill Holmes left Andrew's apartment, she felt sick with despair. She hadn't wanted to leave Bailey, but she'd known she couldn't stay. She walked and walked, hoping exhaustion would empty her mind. Nevertheless, thoughts kept struggling through her defenses, frightening thoughts that repudiated long-cherished ideals. She finally found herself back at her apartment where she fell fully clothed onto her bed. She lay there in numbed exhaustion, tears seeping from under her closed eyelids.

Still, the thoughts kept intruding. She'd destroyed her life. She knew she had, and all because she'd tried to do something worthwhile, her small but valuable contribution to saving the world. She'd wanted to make her father proud, to make him notice her. She'd done just what she'd set out to do, Sherrill thought, so why did she feel so miserable?

Bailey. Her thoughts always returned to Bailey. He was so nice, so different than she'd expected. He even wanted her to meet his parents! She so enjoyed being with him she often forgot her mission.

Tuesday, October 27. She scrunched her eyes shut, trying to blot out the monstrous clock that ticked incessantly in her mind. Tonight! She scrunched her eyes tighter. Tonight! Tonight!

Unable to withstand its frightening urgency any longer, she jumped off the bed, grabbed her coat, and ran from the room. Regardless of any danger to herself, she had to know.

A short time later, she was crouching behind a tree, freezing, staring at the closed door of Andrew's apartment. It was past one, but nothing had happened. Not quite nothing. Milton had shown up just after she'd arrived, and she'd caught a glimpse of Bailey as he'd opened the door. A pain had shot through her, so searing she'd slid to the ground, hugging her knees and rocking back and forth. The pain had gone but a dull ache remained, filling her heart with dread. What should she do? How could she warn Bailey if it meant abandoning her beliefs and with them the chance of pleasing her father? But how could she not warn him? He was Bailey!

Suddenly, the apartment door opened again. A bright glare of light painted a rectangle of gold on the ground outside, stopping just short of her feet. She jerked her legs closer, her breath coming in sharp gasps.

Reggie was leaving! His departing words were loud in the cool late October air. ". . . Daddy's Boy. You're even more a fool than I expected."

Bailey was framed in the doorway beyond, surprise and revulsion mingled on his face. Then the door clicked shut, and she heard Reggie move away.

She also heard him chuckle.

She hugged her knees tighter, her eyes wide with despair. She hadn't known it was possible to feel so desolate.

A towering fear blazed through her. Reggie *was* the one!

W e've got to do something," Bailey said, wiping a cold hand over his sweating forehead. He wanted to take Joey to a hospital; but Joey's pleas combined with his own fear of publicity—no, a hospital was out, he decided, at least until he was sure that was what Joey really needed. Joey might not be nearly as sick as he looked, but how could they know? "I'm calling Mom," he told Milton with quick decision. "She'll know what to do." Drugs or not, he had to have help.

He threw himself into a nearby chair, picked up the phone, and dialed. When he finally got through to his parents' hotel room, the line was busy.

"Call again," Milton urged, leaning over his shoulder. "Maybe they tried the wrong room."

Again, the busy signal sounded hollowly down the miles of phone line.

Jabbing the phone buttons once again, Bailey asked the hotel operator to connect him with Mike Masterson. This time the phone rang and was answered. Bailey gave Milton a thumbs up.

"Mike, this is Bailey, Bailey Grant."

"Why, Bailey, late for a call, isn't it?" Masterson asked. "Cynthia need something?"

"Not Cynthia, I do." Bailey explained about the busy signal. "If you could just tell Mom I need to talk to her right away, I'd appreciate it."

"Sure thing. They're right next door. Anything I can do to help?"

"No, but thanks. If you'd just tell Mom." He gave Masterson Andrew's phone number. "And have her call as soon as possible. It's urgent."

"I'll take care of it right away."

Bailey hung up and turned to Milton. "Mom should be calling any minute. Mike Masterson is Dad's press secretary. His room is always next to theirs."

"I sure hope she calls soon."

They both looked at Joey. He continued to draw in frighteningly shallow sips of air.

"Any beer left?" Milton asked. His voice trembled only slightly.

"Maybe. Check the fridge."

The others in the room paid no attention to this exchange. They paid none to the swooshing of the beer can opening.

Reggie Dixon went straight from Andrew's apartment to the nearest pay phone. He may have been swaggering, but even so his pulse throbbed to some wild tune. He was calling Bonfire, and his heart knew it.

"What do you mean, we may have trouble?" Bonfire asked. His voice was quiet, but the undertone was deadly, the menace amplified by the voice-altering equipment he always used.

Reggie felt sweat pop onto his brow. He thought of the money he was getting, but even that pleasant thought couldn't silence the demons of fear. Bonfire inspired that fear in everyone, even the most callous, and Reggie was too self-absorbed to merit that description. "Not trouble maybe," he hedged. "I planted the drugs on Grant, like you said." He would never mention that the drugs weren't actually on Bailey Grant, just nearby. He'd gotten Bailey's fingerprints on the paper, hadn't he? That would be enough—as long as Bonfire never learned the truth. Reggie rubbed his jacket sleeve distractedly over his forehead. The denim fabric came away damp. "And I just hung up from calling the cops. I told them exactly what you said."

"So what's the problem?" Bonfire demanded.

"Well, like, this dude was there, too."

"This dude?" Bonfire repeated sarcastically. "Come on, Dixon. Just tell me the problem. You don't want to become part of it, do you?"

"Yeah, gotcha," Reggie said, his tongue darting out to touch his lips nervously. "Well, it's like this. One of the guys at the party, he came late, see. Turns out the attorney general's his old man. The cops could make a real stink, and not just about little Bailey."

Bonfire remained silent.

Reggie hurried on. "I just thought I'd better tell you. Thought it might be worth something to you."

"So that's your game, is it, Dixon?" Bonfire asked with deadly quiet. "More money?"

Suddenly, Reggie was shaking with fear. This phone booth, did Bonfire know he was here? The phone number Bonfire'd given him could be for a phone anywhere, even a cellular phone. With one movement, Reggie covered his hand with his jacket and smashed the light above him. The enveloping blackness brought only a sliver of relief. He had to get away, somewhere Bonfire couldn't reach him. "No, no," he said wildly. "I don't want no—"

"I hate slime like you." Bonfire's words cut through Reggie's panicked reassurances. "No, Dixon," he said, each slow word like a white-hot nail in Reggie's now fright-numbed mind, "you'll get no more money, but if you're lucky, I will let you live. How does that sound, Dixon? Do you think you'd like to live?"

A strangled moan was the only answer Reggie could manage.

"What was that?" Bonfire asked, remorselessly. "Did you say you'd like that, Dixon?"

"Yes, yes," Reggie croaked. The glass on the phone booth floor crunched under the agitated movement of his scuffed boots. "Just tell me what you want. I'll do it. I'll do anything."

"I want you to disappear, Dixon. That's what I want you to do. And, Dixon, how's your memory?"

"I don't remember nothing." Reggie was whimpering now. "I promise. Nothing."

"That's what I hoped you would say. But just in case, I'll be watching you. Wherever you go, I'll be watching. Remember that, won't you, Dixon?"

Reggie moaned a *yes,* but the phone was already dead.

Bailey crouched over Joey Hunter, looking in vain for a trace of normal color in the chalky cheeks. He checked his watch again. Ten minutes! Why hadn't his mom called? He couldn't wait any longer. He reached for the phone.

Someone knocked on the door, a soft but insistent knock.

Bailey's hand remained poised above the numbers he'd been punching. He and Milton exchanged frightened glances. Who could it be at this hour? If it were a friend, why hadn't he tried the door? It was always unlocked. A vision of blue uniformed policemen flashed into Bailey's mind. Soundlessly, he replaced the receiver.

The knock came again, this time louder. Bailey tiptoed toward the door.

"Bailey! It's me! Sherrill. Let me in."

Bailey reached the door in two strides and threw it open.

"Sherrill!" He pulled her inside and turned the lock. "What are you doing here?"

She shook off his hands, talking urgently. "Bailey, you've got to get out of here!" At his blank look, she grabbed his arms, thrusting her face almost into his. "You've got to leave. Now!" Her words came out in panicked gasps, punctuated by darting glances toward the door.

"What are you talking about?" Bailey asked. Lingering fear made his voice brittle. "Don't be crazy. I can't leave! Believe me, there's nothing I'd like better, but I can't. Just look at them!" He indicated the mostly motionless bodies in the room. Several were moaning groggily, their heads in their hands, but most still rested in drug-induced stupors. "This guy especially," he said, stepping toward Joey. "Someone's got to be here with him. I can't leave!"

"You've got to!" She tried to pull him toward the door. "Milton," she pleaded, "please, make him see sense." He took a step toward them. "He has to leave!" Sherrill said again. She was close to tears.

"I . . . can't . . . go," Bailey said. Each word came out harshly, like a verbal slap. "I can't just leave everyone."

"You're a fool, Bailey Grant!" Sherrill yelled, throwing down his arms. "If you won't leave, at least you can get rid of the stuff."

She began rushing around the room. Having no idea what to do with the scattered paraphernalia, she picked up several resinated roaches and threw them into an overflowing ashtray. Then she grabbed the bag the drugs had come in from beside the sofa where Bailey had wadded it and ran with it all to the bathroom. Bailey and Milton heard paper tear and the toilet flush.

She ran back into the room, grabbing the bathroom door frame to steady herself as she skidded around the corner. Her movements jerky with haste, she lit an incense stick, waved it around the room, and then stuck it, still smoking, into the now-empty ashtray.

"Don't just stand there!" Her voice cracked with urgency. A sheen of tears made her eyes large and vulnerable. "If you won't leave, then at least get rid of the evidence!" She looked at her watch, then frantically wiped up some powder with a piece of toilet paper she'd brought from the bathroom.

Bailey grabbed her shoulders and held her. She thrashed out, trying to get away. "Let go of me!" she yelled. "We've got to get rid of everything. Don't you understand?" The last came out in a sob.

"No, Sherrill, I don't." Bailey tried to keep his voice calm but felt panic seeping through. He had no idea what she meant, but a desperate foreboding seized him. The vague disquiet he'd felt all night, had really felt every time he'd come to Andrew's apartment for the last few weeks, coalesced into a palpable, evil presence. "Talk, Sherrill," he demanded, tightening his grip on her shoulders. "What do you mean by 'evidence'? For heaven sakes, tell us what's going on."

"I don't know." Sherrill hiccuped a sob, trying to control her voice. Bailey released her, but the anger in his eyes compelled a rush of words from her. "I really don't, but I'm so scared. You've got to get out of here. Call someone when you're safe—a hospital, a doctor, anyone," she pleaded, her fingers pressing into his arm, "but leave now before it's too late!"

Her urgency infected Milton. He grabbed his jacket. "She's right, Bailey. We can call from the 7–11."

Bailey looked from Milton's troubled face to Sherrill's panicked one. He reached for the door. Sherrill sobbed in relief and clutched his other hand. Just as he started to release the lock, a fist pounded against the other side.

"Police! Open up!"

That's all I know," Masterson told the Grants, handing the Senator a slip of paper with the phone number Bailey had given him. "Bailey couldn't get through to your room so he called me."

"Did he say what he wanted?" Grant asked. He pulled the phone closer and lifted the receiver.

"Only that he needed to talk to you. He didn't sound upset, just mad that he couldn't get through."

Rachel shrugged her shoulders at Grant's look of inquiry. "He wouldn't have called unless it was important," she said, echoing his own thought. "At least not this late."

Grant dialed and listened to the phone ring. Each ring escalated his feeling of urgency. Too much odd had been happening. Had Bailey somehow become ensnared in it?

"No one's answering." He started to hang up.

"Let it keep ringing," Rachel urged. "He'll answer."

"I'll leave you to it," Masterson said, opening the door. Neither of the Grants noticed his going. For them at that moment, all life existed at the end of the phone.

For almost two minutes, Bob Grant listened to the phone ring. Then he depressed the button, got a dial tone, and redialed. Again no answer.

"Why would Bailey ask us to call and then not answer?" Rachel asked. "Do you recognize the number?"

"No," Grant said, trying to keep the mounting concern out of his voice. "I'll try Cynthia. Maybe she's heard from him."

"Just a minute," Cynthia said when he reached her. "He left a number where he could be reached. I know it's here some—aha!" It was the same number Masterson had given them. "That's Andrew Stoner's apartment," she said. "Bailey said he would be there all evening."

"Senator, wait," she hurriedly added. "Just so you know, the alarm at your house was tripped a short while ago. According to the alarm company's security force, nothing seemed disturbed. They reset the system. I'll check it on my way into work tomorrow if that's all right."

"Thanks, Cynthia," Grant replied and hung up. Bailey's problem seemed much more pressing than the alarm, which had probably been caused by a power surge or a garbage-can-rummaging animal anyway.

"Maybe I misdialed," he told Rachel. "I'll try again."

Bailey, Milton, and Sherrill stood motionless. The word "police" throbbed around them.

"Don't let them in!" Sherrill hissed. She turned and raced through the room, frantically hunting for any signs of drugs. She wiped up some scattered granules spilled on a low table and ran toward the bathroom.

The phone began ringing, its insistence as mesmerizing as the continued pounding at the door.

Bailey reached for the phone, only to pull his hand back. Sherrill's panic infected him.

Reggie. What was it about Reggie . . . ?Bailey ran over to the place where Reggie had been lying and flung the debris around. He didn't know what he expected to find, but with mounting fear he knew something would be there. It was. His breathing became ragged and audible at the sight of a piece of paper with a pile of white powder on it lying protected under an empty pizza box. The same stuff Reggie had offered him? Bailey remembered the feel of the stiff paper under his fingers. Fingerprints! He scooped up the paper with its incriminating evidence. Milton watched with dawning comprehension and alarm.

"Open the door or we'll break it down!"

Bailey glanced toward the apartment door, then ran toward the bathroom. Without warning, Bear lurched to his feet in front of him. Bailey swerved to one side, trying desperately to avoid Bear's flailing arm. Just as he thought he was safely past, Bear gave him a staggering blow to his back. Bailey's breath caught in a gasp. He fought for balance, the piece of paper tipping precariously in his hand. His whole body shook with the effort to regain control.

"Hold on, would you?" Milton yelled toward the door. With frightened eyes, he watched the powder dance on the paper in Bailey's hand. He tried to force words past his shaking lips, failed, took a deep breath, then tried again. "I'm coming," he croaked. "I'm coming!" He yelled the words this time. "Can't a guy even take a leak without the cops checking on it?"

Bailey took a final step, pirouetted, and sank to the floor. Miraculously, the paper was still in his hand. Nothing had spilled—at least Bailey hoped nothing had. In a single movement, he stood and stepped into the bathroom.

Sherrill looked from Bailey into the toilet, which was still swirling, but with diminishing force too weak to dispose of Reggie's ominous cache of drugs. Bailey dropped them in anyway, the paper and the powder. He reached for the bathtub faucets and turned them on full force, putting his hands under the rushing water and forcing Sherrill's under as well. Would this be enough to destroy any trace of drugs? He didn't know. But at that moment he knew without doubt that he'd been set up. By Reggie, of course. But what about Sherrill? How had she known the police would come? The suspicion, so devastating, vanished as he heard the lock turn in the apartment door.

The toilet stopped running. He flushed it again.

The phone stopped ringing. A rush of heavy feet filled the silence.

"Hey! What do you think you're doing!" A policeman grabbed Bailey and flung him against the wall. Then he plunged his uniformed arm into the toilet, retrieving a soggy corner of the white paper. Bailey stood motionless, his heart racing. Would that fragment reveal enough under a microscope to convict him of drug use? He had no idea. Never before had he considered the legal implications of drugs. Never had he expected to need such knowledge.

Uniformed policemen filled the apartment, so many, all professional and competent.

A man in a worn tan trench coat followed them. "Search everywhere," he said. "Look for any traces of drugs. And call for some ambulances and a paddy wagon."

Sherrill was huddled in a corner of the bathroom, sobbing. Bailey looked down at her, then moved toward the man in the trench coat, who seemed to be in charge.

"Not so fast, buddy," the uniformed policeman said, reaching out to stop him. His push, though not as forceful this time, was far from gentle. "Where do you think you're going?"

"Joey needs help," Bailey said, motioning toward the living room. "He looks bad. I was trying to get a doctor when you came."

"I could tell," the policeman said sarcastically, looking pointedly at the now silent toilet.

The phone rang. A policeman answered it.

Just as sincerely as he'd prayed minutes earlier for her to call, now Bailey prayed it wouldn't be his mother on the other end of the line.

Rachel sat on the edge of the sofa, her feet tucked under her robe and her hands clasped tightly around her knees. Her eyes never left her husband's face.

This time when Grant dialed, the phone was answered on the second ring.

"Hello."

Grant didn't recognize the voice. "Could I please speak with Bailey Grant?" he asked. He could hear voices in the background, odd words he didn't associate with a college gathering. Before he could clarify his thoughts, the voice was responding.

"Could I tell him who's calling?" the stranger asked.

"This is his father. Who is this?"

Grant's question remained unanswered. Instead, a hand must have been placed over the receiver because all noise was muffled. Grant looked at Rachel, his eyebrows contracted in thought. Only moments before, no one had answered the persistent ringing of the phone. Yet now the room was obviously filled with people. What was happening? Too much noise to hear the phone? Grant knew that was logical, but something about the background noises increased his uneasiness. No music was playing, he realized. A college apartment and no loud music? Never had he expected to be sorry not to hear it.

"What's happening?" Rachel asked.

Grant held his hand up, listening intently to discern sounds behind the hand muffling the other receiver. He could tell nothing.

"Senator Grant." A different voice, obviously an adult male comfortable with authority, was on the phone. "Your son can't come to the phone now. If you'll give me a message, I'll be sure he gets it."

"Who is this?" Grant asked again. Again the receiver at the other end was covered. Grant rubbed his neck and tried to relax his tense shoulders.

"Senator Grant, this is Captain Fleming, of the D.C. Police Department."

"Bailey's all right, isn't he?" Grant's voice was steady, but his heart had plummeted at Fleming's words. At the sight of his tense face, Rachel squeezed her knees tighter.

"Yes, sir. Your son is fine."

Grant closed his eyes in momentary relief. He leaned over and squeezed Rachel's hand, mouthing, "He's fine."

"Then why are you there, Captain Fleming?" he asked.

"I'm not able to answer that now, sir, but we're taking your son to police headquarters. We'll answer as many of your questions as we can then."

"You're arresting him? What charges?"

"We're not arresting him, sir," the policeman said patiently, "just taking him in for questioning, a routine procedure in a situation involving drugs."

"Drugs?" Grant repeated dumbly. "Bailey?" With that thought, Grant's mind started working feverishly. Bailey wouldn't use drugs, of that he was certain, as certain as any parent could ever be. But drugs were involved, obviously, and so was a police captain. A captain at a routine college drug bust? And a captain who knew to call him Senator? "Routine, did you say, Captain?" Grant asked skeptically. Fleming didn't respond. "I would like to speak to Bailey," Grant repeated, this time as a demand rather than a question.

"I'm afraid not, sir, but you have my word that nothing is wrong with him physically." The emphasis on the word "physically" hung in the air between them. "Now," Captain Fleming continued, "if you'd just give me your address and phone number so we can contact you if need be . . ."

Grant did so, giving him Cynthia's as well. He hung up and turned to Rachel.

"The police have Bailey," he told her. "Drugs."

"Oh, no." Two small words but filled with a mother's anguish.

Grant's response, uttered so often by parents over the centuries, was more to the point. "How could he have been so stupid!"

Then he called a Washington friend, a criminal attorney.

Bailey listened to the policeman's end of the phone conversation with mounting tension. Even as he listened, he frantically tried to decide what he should do. He'd been set up. That was certain. If possible he had to keep the setup from succeeding. But how?

"Captain Fleming?" he asked when the man in the tan overcoat put down the phone.

"Yes, son?" Fleming was about forty, Bailey guessed, but his eyes were tired. Deep seams bracketed his mouth like parentheses. His chin was covered with a slight stubble, as if he'd been at work too long. He walked over to Bailey, who, realizing he was clutching the door frame, let go and straightened his back. "Do you mind if I call you Bailey?" the police captain asked.

Bailey nodded then hastily amended, "No, no, sir. That would be fine." He held on to the captain's kind tone as to a lifeline. Even so, he realized the kindness stopped short of the man's eyes. He would have to be aware of danger, even here in a man he wanted so desperately to trust. "Sir, I'm glad you're here. We needed help. Joey's going to be all right, isn't he?"

"Joey's the boy over there?" Captain Fleming asked, nodding toward the motionless body being placed on a stretcher. Men in blue jackets crowded around, juggling IV bags while they worked with quick efficiency. Other uniformed figures stooped and examined the bodies ranged in splayed confusion around the room, receiving listlessness or defiance from them in response.

"Yes," Bailey said miserably.

"He doesn't look good, son. You can help him if you'll tell me what he was taking."

"I want to help," Bailey said. "This has been a nightmare." His voice cracked, and he cleared it. "I saw Joey take a few lines of cocaine and smoke some weed. And he was drinking something, vodka probably. That's his glass," he said, pointing to the tumbler still on its side on the floor. "Someone brought something else, maybe LSD. I'm not sure. I don't know if Joey got any."

"Cocaine mixed with alcohol and marijuana," the captain told the men as they wheeled the stretcher out of the room. "Could even be some LSD."

The men acknowledged his words with weary acceptance. Cocaine. Crack. Marijuana. LSD. Ecstasy. Heroin. Night after night. The drugs varied; the results didn't. Death, destruction, the total annihilation of future: all in the name of a few hours of forgetfulness.

"He'll be all right, won't he?" Bailey asked again.

"I don't know, son. My guess is he'll be lucky to live through the night."

"No! Oh, no!" The words were torn in a despairing wail from Sherrill, who had been listening intently from where she still sat huddled on the floor of the bathroom. She sprang to her feet, ran into the living room, and flung herself at Fleming, clinging to his coat lapels. "He can't die! It wasn't supposed to be this way! Tell me he's not going to die! Tell me!"

Slowly, Fleming undid her fingers, but he continued to hold her hands. "I'm sorry, miss. I wish I could tell you that everything will be all right, but any drug is dangerous. And cocaine . . ." He shook his head. "It's one of the worst, especially now when so much of it's been laced with something else. I'd say a prayer if I were you. He's going to need it. Is this young man a special friend of yours?"

Sherrill didn't answer. She probably didn't hear his question. With a moan, she dropped to the floor at his feet and buried her head in her hands.

"Get a policewoman over here," Fleming shouted across the room. Then he turned back to Bailey.

"Bailey."

Bailey tore his eyes away from Sherrill and looked at the captain with bleak eyes.

"Bailey, we need to know your friend's name and how to contact his parents."

"Joey Hunter," Bailey said. "I'd never seen him before tonight, but I think he's Joey Hunter. His father is the attorney general. Milton knows him."

Captain Fleming, the lines on his face embedding themselves even deeper, turned to Milton. "Is that right, Milton? The boy we just took out of here is Attorney General Hunter's son?"

Milton nodded. "Yes, sir. I know he is. I met Joey at the beginning of the semester, and he made sure everyone knew about his father."

Captain Fleming gave the boys an appraising look. Then he picked up the phone and dialed.

"We've got a problem here," he said, "a bigger one than we expected."

Jonathan Hunter had been on the phone for several minutes, doing little but listening. As he listened, his body seemed to harden, then shrink in on itself.

"I understand," he said finally. "I'll be there as soon as possible."

With gentle deliberation, he replaced the receiver.

"What is it, Jonathan?" Rebecca Hunter asked. She rested on her pillows, far to one side of their king-sized bed. Her husband's frequent late-night calls seldom penetrated her sleep, but something about this one, maybe something about the tension in his voice, pulled her out of sleep and into frightened wakefulness.

Hunter remained motionless, his body outlined by the eerie red glow of the clock and White House phone gadgetry on the table beside him. He didn't answer her.

"Jonathan," Rebecca repeated, her voice rising shrilly, "this isn't one of your games! Tell me what's going on!"

He stood and with stiff limbs began dressing. His movements were mechanical, totally unlike his usual authoritative precision. He kept his back to his wife, who now sat upright, blankets clutched under her chin.

Finally dressed, Hunter picked up the phone and punched the line which would connect him to the NIIA agents who waited outside his house. "Have the car ready. I'm leaving immediately."

Turning to face his wife, but keeping his eyes averted, he finally answered her. "It's Joey," he said. His voice was unsteady. He could feel her fright, but he continued to avoid her face and to stare down at the blankets. "He's been hurt."

Rebecca scrambled out of bed, throwing off her nightgown and frantically hunting for clothes. "I'm going with you." She stopped and faced him, her white-knuckled fingers clutching a pair of pants against her nakedness. "He's all right, isn't he?" Her words were an anguished plea. "He's not . . ." She couldn't say the word.

Hunter ignored her questions. He continued to avoid her eyes. "I'm not going to the hospital, not yet."

"Not . . . going . . . to . . . the . . . hospital!" She spat out each word. "Let me guess. You're going to the White House, aren't you? The precious White House!" He didn't respond. She grabbed his arm and swung him around to face her. Even then he remained mute.

"Tell me, Jonathan!" she screamed. "Tell me about my baby!"

With fastidious care, he disengaged each of her fingers. "He OD'd. Drugs. He's been taken to G. W. Hospital. I can't do anything there now, but I can help him if I go to the White House. You may not like it, but that's the truth. I care about my son's good name even if you don't."

He stopped at the door and turned. "I'll have a car ready for you in five minutes," he said. "They'll take you straight to the hospital. Don't worry. I'm sure he'll be fine."

He left.

With a sob, Rebecca Hunter sank onto the bed. Then slowly, she wiped her eyes, stood, and continued dressing.

Wednesday, October 28:

Six Days Before the Election

The President enfolded Hunter in a hug, giving his back a sympathetic pat. "I'm devastated about Joey," he said, leading the smaller man to a large leather chair.

Edmund Miller and Charles Kendall, senior members of the NSC staff, were already seated as was Chief of Staff M. Eugene Corforth. All were used to middle-of-the-night meetings, but none except Miller had mastered the knack of looking fresh and alert no matter the hour. His hair was slicked back smoothly. His clothes, from his Windsor knotted tie to his polished shoes, were flawless.

"We'll do everything we can," the President continued. He seated himself beside Hunter, patting his friend's hand compassionately. "The White House physician is at the hospital now. He called just moments ago to report that Joey is holding his own."

"Holding his own." Hunter knew only too well those were words given when no hope could be. He removed his half glasses and began polishing them.

"How's Rebecca?" the President asked.

"She was on her way to the hospital when I left."

The President nodded. "Let's get this meeting over as quickly as possible so you can be with her." He looked at Corforth.

"Yes, Mr. President," Corforth said. "We want to help in every possible way, Jonathan. We've already taken steps to eliminate any mention of the nature of your son's illness." He nodded toward Kendall.

"Notes are even now being inserted into his medical record," Kendall explained. "They'll verify that his medical problems are due solely to a preexisting heart condition."

Hunter's face was rigid. His eyes never left Kendall's face. His hands never ceased their rhythmic polishing of the glasses.

"Further," Kendall continued, "the head of cardiac research at the NIH is en route to the hospital to supervise your son's care. After examination, I'm sure he will confirm the nature of the heart problem as congenital. We're committed not only to Joey's physical well-being but also to protecting him from the stigma of drug abuse."

"By a curious turn," Edmund Miller said, "Bob Grant's son was at the same party as Joey. We have reason to believe he may have procured the drugs."

Corforth looked at Miller in surprise. Then all eyes were drawn to Hunter, who surged to his feet, overturning his chair.

"Grant's son?" Hunter whispered, the glasses dangling forgotten from his hand. Flames of color rushed up his neck and into his cheeks. "You think Bob Grant's son may have . . ." He swallowed convulsively, then continued through clenched teeth. ". . . may have forced my son to consume cocaine?" His anger was painful to watch.

Surreptitiously, Corforth slipped an antacid tablet from his pocket and into his mouth. Then he leaned over and uprighted Hunter's chair.

"We can't be sure, sir," Miller said, his fingers poised motionless above his computer. "Grant's son is in custody and is being held for questioning."

"He can't be allowed to get away with it," Hunter said quietly, his sudden control as awful as his previous anger. "No one can do this to me."

"I understand that, Hunt," the President soothed. "I feel your pain. That's why I'm relieved you're here. You know the people who can apply appropriate pressure. I don't want Grant to pull strings and get his son off. If he procured the drugs, he deserves to be punished."

"He deserves to be hung!" Hunter sank into his chair, jammed his glasses on his nose, and turned to Corforth. "You did get reporters to the police station, didn't you?" He moved to the edge of his seat. "Pictures. We need pictures plastered on the front page of every paper in the country and on every major news broadcast."

"Miller called Peter Evans as soon as we heard," Corforth assured him. "Peter's taking care of all that. Even he doesn't know about your son. No one outside this room knows."

"Good," Hunter said. His face was set in lines of crafty implacability, a normal Hunter expression. "This is just what we needed to finish Grant. No one can seriously consider backing him for President now." He glanced around the room, but his mind was focused on some inner thought. Slowly, a satisfied smile curved his lips.

Everyone watched him with fascination, unsure how to respond. Finally, the President stood, went to him, and put an arm around his shoulder. Hunter didn't respond to his touch. "Perhaps you'd better go to the hospital?" the President suggested tentatively.

Hunter blinked, looked at his friend, and shook his head. His back straightened. "No, no. Too much remains to be done." Suddenly, he sounded and looked like the Hunter of old. Gratefully, everyone began to relax. Hunter was under tremendous stress, they realized, but he could handle it. Power was his nourishment. "We need to get down to business," he said decisively, "and make sure everything falls into place as it should."

When Hunter left fifteen minutes later, their plans were made. Joey Hunter's name would remain unblemished. The same couldn't be said for Bailey Grant's. Grant's bid for a third Senate term had just taken one more step into oblivion, dragging his presidential aspirations down with it.

Sherrill Holmes sat on one of three wooden benches which lined the dingy cinderblock walls of the jail's female holding room. Her knees were drawn up close to her body as if to touch as little wood as possible. Otherwise, she seemed unaware of her surroundings, even of the shouts, curses, and moans of the women incarcerated with her.

Joey's ashen face haunted her. If she'd had any part in causing that . . . She shivered and forced his image out of her mind only to have it replaced by that of Bailey. Bailey. She choked back tears. She needed to think, but constructive thought seemed impossible.

As a young child, Sherrill had created a carefully compartmentalized life for herself. Stepfathers changed; schools changed; so did homes. She had filed each episode of her life neatly away as it ended, moving on to conquer the newest challenge her mother placed before her. All of that self-imposed protection, previously impervious to chaos, was now falling apart. Never before had she allowed her life to career out of control. Never before had she felt so helpless or so confused.

Bailey: He was like a rock, she told herself, latching onto the image. Like a rock, strong and indestructible. He would be all right. He wouldn't suffer because of her. Surely not, surely . . . Her head sagged to her chest, burdened by an overwhelming sense of failure.

Rock of Ages. The old hymn hummed its way into her mind, its long-forgotten words and melody as familiar as if she'd sung it only yesterday. She'd been seven or eight, she supposed, when Abner, stepfather number two—no, number three, Mohammed had been number two—had introduced her to church. He'd told her he'd gone to church every Sunday for as long as he could remember and he wasn't going to stop just because her mother thought him a fool. For that entire year he'd taken Sherrill with him.

A Sunday school teacher at Abner's church—Miss Eleanor had been her name—had had kind eyes, Bailey's eyes, when she'd leaned down to talk to Sherrill, the prickly little girl so afraid to trust the kindness of someone who might at any moment disappear into the night like so many others before. By that time Sherrill seldom saw her father, and stepfather number two had vanished, never to reappear.

Two prisoners started fighting over a cigarette. Startled, Sherrill jerked upright, then leaned away in disgust. The two women looked like animals, and those crowded around, avaricious for blood, were no better. Their lips were drawn back, exposing chipped yellow teeth. Their hair, dredlocked from lack of washing, stood out from lined faces. Sherrill squeezed her eyes shut, trying to blot out their string of curses and her wretched surroundings. How had she let this happen? How?

She forced her mind back to Abner and one of the few pleasant periods she could remember. How she wished she could go back to that innocent time! Anything to forget what was happening to her now. Anything to blot out Joey's ashen face, and the welter of emotions that assaulted her with every thought of Bailey.

Miss Eleanor with her grizzled gray hair and wire-rimmed glasses had been so understanding. It was she who had suggested that Sherrill could talk to God and he would listen. Sherrill supposed God had become an invisible friend to her, one who wouldn't vanish some night, never to be seen again. She'd continued her silent dialogues with God even after Mother had shed Abner and moved to New Orleans for stepfather number four. On the playground at the predominantly white school where she'd initially been the target of cruel jokes, in her strange new bedroom where she'd shed so many tears: So many times she'd turned her thoughts inward, talking to God as Miss Eleanor had suggested, unburdening her childish heart and finding comfort in so doing.

Now, far removed from those days and those childish needs, Sherrill felt the sting of guilt. How could she be thinking in religious terms! Hadn't she agreed with her father and her professor that religion was the crutch of the weak and superstitious? Even so, she found herself searching for the peace she'd found in those long-ago conversations with God. Hesitantly at first, she began exposing her heart and finding comfort, just as that child had so many years before.

For a blessed few minutes she was transported from the squalor of the jail cell to an Eden of inner peace.

The Grants were finally allowed to talk to Bailey if only over the phone. Reggie, the drugs, the timely arrival of the police, the even more interesting presence of the media first at Andrew's apartment and then at the jail—his parents listened to Bailey's account with mounting helplessness. The implications were ominous. In the murky background of it all, their faceless enemy lurked, like a shadowy vampire, slowly sucking the lifeblood from Grant and his family.

Cynthia, a lawyer herself, worked with the Grants' criminal attorney, trying to secure release for Bailey and Sherrill, who didn't have legal counsel of her own. Both lawyers reported foot-dragging, unusual in an all-too-ordinary drug bust. Bailey couldn't be held much longer, they assured the Grants, not without charging him, and charges were impossible without grounds. Nevertheless, the foot-dragging continued.

And so Bailey and Sherrill would remain in jail for what little remained of the night. No one seemed able to prevent it—that despite the negative results of the blood, urine, and Breathalyzer tests Bailey had demanded they be given; that despite the absence of drugs or any illegal drug paraphernalia at the scene.

Unable to help Bailey, Cynthia went straight from the police station to Grant's Senate office, where she called an emergency meeting of senior staff. Matt Goldie was brought in via a conference call. Media control was immediately put in place to try to minimize adverse publicity for Bailey. Then every aspect of Bailey's curious tale was examined. His surmises about the events at Andrew's were being correlated with the information already gathered about the earlier attacks on the Senator.

This staff of political professionals, many of whom had worked with Bob Grant throughout his twelve years as Senator and all of whom had grown to admire and respect him both as a Senator and as a man, were determined to find the link that connected the so disparate but oddly coincidental events. Too, they were determined to find the link between Bailey's incarceration and the administration. Rumor had it someone in the inner circle of the White House had put his fingerprints on the case. The White House wouldn't have intervened without sufficient cause. Joey Hunter's presence at the party might be enough, but Grant's staff would continue questioning and probing until they were certain something else wasn't involved, something related to this campaign to discredit and destroy the Senator.

So many tenuous leads to follow and so many closed doors to open: They'd never faced a greater challenge, and the stakes had never been higher. Suddenly, destruction of reputation, imprisonment, even death loomed as real possibilities. A campaign for reelection had become one for survival.

Rachel was booked on the next flight from Atlanta to Washington. Grant, however, would remain in Georgia.

"You're right to stay here," Rachel told him. "Bailey's arrest has to be connected with Russell Frederickson's murder."

"As soon as you see Bailey," Grant said, "have him go over everything again, every detail. Record it all. Have Milton and that girl Sherrill do the same. Andrew, Bear, anyone who was there. Give a copy to Cynthia. I'll give one to Jenks. Logic says all this is related, but, Rachel"—pain filled his face—"what kind of monster would ruin a child to get at the parent?"

Rachel could do no more than look at him. Such a question had no answer.

Grant held her away from him, wanting to see her eyes. Longing stretched between them, a longing for the simplicity of the past as much as a longing for each other. Never before had Grant felt so vulnerable because never before had his family been targeted for attack.

"Rachel, we have to trust Sheriff Jenks."

"But—" she began, doubt large in her eyes.

"I know," he interrupted gently. "Jenks may take everything I tell him and use it against us, but we have to go by instinct now. Only Jenks knows everything about Frederickson's murder. We can't make sense of any of this unless we know what he knows." Grant's eyes softened, and he stroked her cheek. "I can't take chances with Bailey, with any of you."

Rachel caressed his fingers where they rested on her face. "But will he tell you anything," she asked, "even if you trust him? Aren't you taking an awful risk?"

"It's a risk, yes, but I'm convinced a necessary one. All my contacts agree that Jenks is intelligent and plays fair. Matt's checked him out and agrees."

She nodded. "His questions were tough but thoughtful. I don't like trusting your life to someone we don't really know, but . . ." She paused, searching his face.

"If the answer involves politics," he said, pulling her close, "we're the only ones who can put it all together. The secret agendas of Washington would make no sense to an outsider like Jenks."

Someone knocked at the door.

"My ride to the airport," Rachel said, starting to pull away.

Grant held her tighter, then kissed her, all his being concentrated on giving her the added strength of his love.

The time was right, Edmund Miller thought, to call Peter Evans again. Evans needed to know that the White House was more interested than ever in seeing Grant brought to justice.

Years before, Miller, through his position at that time on the staff of the Senate Foreign Relations Committee, had provided the classified, not necessarily accurate, information that Evans had used in his Pulitzer Prize-winning exposé of the CIA. That highly acclaimed exposé had subsequently led to Evans's present position as editor of the *Washington Herald* as well as to the emasculation of the CIA. Miller had proven two things: the power of the media in influencing the country's agenda and his own ability to manipulate that media. He continued to wield his power skillfully, his eye always on his personal advancement. His part in the exposé had never been revealed.

Evans welcomed calls from Miller, who continued to be a source of profitable tips.

"This mess of Grant's," Miller began, a chuckle in his voice, "it's choice, isn't it?"

"Certainly serves him right, the self-righteous prig." Evans was recently divorced. His many liaisons were daily fodder for gossip columns and a source of great personal pride. "You hear something new?"

"Just that Grant's DEA/NIIA file would be worth a look. Scuttlebutt has it that his contains more than just routine investigations of wild rumors. Too bad if someone else gets there first."

"DEA," Evans murmured. "Yes, you may have something. Wouldn't want to lose that story, especially since someone may have gotten into Frederickson's computer here."

"What are you talking about?" Miller demanded sharply.

"Apparently," Evans said, "when one of my reporters tried to open the file Frederickson was working on when he died, someone was already using it, someone from outside. We don't know who or even how long they'd been at it. We've beefed up our security, and it doesn't appear the file contained anything of interest, but . . ."

"Yes," Miller agreed, "but . . . have you considered trying to find out who's hacking into your system?"

"What do you mean?"

"I have a friend," Miller told him, "who specializes in tracking down unauthorized log-ons to computer networks. Interested?"

"Hmm," Evans said thoughtfully, wondering if a story might be in the making. "Not a bad idea. Send him over."

Jonathan Hunter entered G. W. Hospital by means of an unobtrusive back entrance. No media, he noted, acknowledging the evidence that his plans were already in motion.

The NIIA's protective detail hurried Hunter into a service elevator, which lumbered up to the intensive care unit, where he was met by a cadre of somber physicians. The White House physician stepped forward and introduced Hunter to the physician heading Joey Hunter's team of experts. He in turn explained the precarious nature of Joey's condition. The physicians standing behind him murmured their agreement.

"Are you telling me you can do nothing for my son?" Hunter demanded when the physician finished.

"You misunderstood me," the physician said. "We are doing everything humanly possible for your son. He could receive no better care than he's receiving here. We have all-too-much experience in caring for drug-related problems such as his. However, the drugs he ingested have done considerable damage to his system, most particularly to his heart. Until he's stabilized, we can't even assess the extent of the damage."

Hunter looked at the doctor, this man who dared to hint that his son might not recover. A challenge lit Hunter's eyes. "He's my son. He will live."

The doctor met his challenge, unblinking. "I pray you are right, sir."

Hunter looked away, stunned by the pity in the doctor's eyes. "He will live," he declared. "He's my son."

The doctor gave no assurances. Instead, he put his hand on Hunter's elbow. "Let me take you to him, sir."

He led Hunter to a large corner room at the end of the hall. The other white-clad figures fell in behind, mixing with Hunter's protective detail.

The motionless mound on the bed was almost invisible behind the machines that flanked it, their blips and hums giving them a lifelike quality in the cloying hush of the room. Tubes and cords crisscrossed above the white expanse of bed and body. Two nurses stood at the head of the bed, their backs to the doorway where Hunter had stopped. Their starched uniforms rustled reassuringly as they bent over the bed, one on either side. Hunter stared at them, mesmerized by their precise movements, by the gentle curve of their backs.

Unaware of the rasp of his own breathing, he turned his eyes away from the paraphernalia, away from the people sustaining his son's life, and brought them to his son's face.

Ashen, gaunt, it was Joey, his son, who lay on the bed, but a bloodless Joey, almost without life. Hunter's mind slipped for a moment from its rigid control.

Not without life! This was his Joey—his son, his only child! He would be all right!

He, Jonathan Hunter, was the attorney general of the United States, one of the two most powerful men in the most powerful country in the world. He'd always been able to get what he wanted, hadn't he? Why should this be any different?

Hunter turned and strode from the room, his back as ramrod straight as the line of his mouth. He never noticed his wife, sitting beside the bed, holding their son's hand. He never touched his son.

"I want a phone!" he demanded of no one in particular as soon as he reached the corridor. "And I want the best specialists in the country—in the world if need be!—to examine my son today. Get them here! Now!"

Leaning against the wall, one ankle crossed over the other, Kirk Vinton unfolded that morning's *Herald*. He'd bought it as soon as he'd landed at Washington National Airport. The name *Grant* leapt at him from the headlines. Wonderful, Vinton exulted. Evans had given his Pariss piece top billing, even better than he'd promised.

As he began reading, his smile dissolved into rage. Not his piece at all! Something about Grant's son being arrested for drugs. A three-column picture showed the Grant boy, handcuffs much in evidence, being led into police headquarters.

Vinton scanned the rest of the front page. Nothing! He tore through the paper, finally finding his article buried on page A–10 next to the continuation of the main article. A–10! His byline, true, and a picture of Pariss to draw attention to the article, but nothing like front-page prominence.

Leaning against a wall, oblivious to hurrying passengers pulling suitcases behind them, Vinton read the lead news story, a condemnation of both Grant and his son. Evans was right, he finally admitted. It deserved to be the lead. Still, he couldn't help feeling cheated. Crumpling the paper and tossing it into a trash can, he strode to an airport pay phone and called the editor.

"Sure, I promised you the front page," Evans said impatiently, "but yours was old news. Bring me something new on Grant, something related to this drug business, and then we'll see. Here's an angle that might tie in. Grant's DEA/NIIA file. Check it out. Just be sure you don't cut Grant any slack. If the story plays, we'll headline it Thursday."

"Sure thing," Vinton said, trying to mask his bitterness, "as soon as I have the Sergek piece covered."

"Contact Kathy Rowe at the DEA arm of NIIA," Evans continued. "She's been helpful in the past."

At least Evans's sources usually panned out, Vinton thought as he rang off. Something new on Grant. Drugs. Okay, if that was what it took, that was what Evans would get.

Vinton dialed Kathy Rowe.

"I was told you had information about Bob Grant," he said when she came on the line.

"Just a name," Rowe replied.

Her tone was cautious. He wondered if she feared being overheard. He didn't care. He despised all informants, especially government ones who betrayed the public trust. That they betrayed it for his benefit was convenient but made them no less weak and contemptible in his eyes. He used them, sure. If he didn't, someone else would.

"A name is all I need," Vinton told her. His voice gave no hint of his distaste. "I'll take it from there."

"Hal Olexey, O-L-E-X-E-Y, an inmate at Lorton."

"An inmate?"

"Just arrange to see him," she said. "It'll be worth your time."

Sheriff Jenks sat at his desk, his gleaming alligator boots firmly planted on top. That morning's copy of the *Washington Herald* rested on his lap. He'd ordered the bulldog edition expressed to him daily as soon as he'd learned of Frederickson's connection with it. Today's edition proved the wisdom of that decision.

Jenks stared at Bailey Grant's picture, sighing at the blatant exposure of the handcuffs. Compassion mixed with uneasiness knotted his stomach. Was he capable of untangling the web of evil with Grant at its center?

Jenks chuckled thinly. Derek Bender, the head NIIA honcho, had been at him already that morning, threatening him again if he didn't leave the Senator to them. They seemed too all-fired intent on hanging everything on the Senator for Jenks's peace of mind. Impartiality: Now that was something they were in an almighty hurry to forget.

Strange what Bender had let drop about the time of Frederickson's death, Jenks brooded. How had Bender known he'd narrowed down the time? He certainly hadn't let that tidbit drop! Darned if he was telling them anything they didn't absolutely need to know, leastways till they shoved some legal papers his way. No doubt that would be happening any day now, he thought gloomily, soon as they got their legal ducks in a row.

The intercom squawked. "Senator Grant's on line one, Sheriff."

Speak of the devil. Or maybe the devil's victim? Jenks thought he knew, but that impartiality he'd just been considering—he'd better hang on to that a tad longer before he committed himself. "Senator Grant," he said, "I was grieved to read about that boy of yours. Sounds bad."

"It is," Grant agreed tersely. "Can we meet? I'm getting paranoid about everything, phone lines among them, and I have some things to discuss with you."

"Things you'd rather didn't find their way to the feds?"

"You're a smart man, Sheriff."

"Well, Senator," Jenks drawled, "those NIIA boys are hankering to free up my time. Might as well oblige them. I'll tell them I'm going fishing. They'll believe it." And wouldn't be far from wrong, Jenks thought as he replaced the receiver.

Putting his hat on, he left the office. This case had more twists than Bugscuffle Road, he thought as he passed by the gimlet eyes of the NIIA agents, who hoped to commandeer the building. Give him a homegrown murder anytime. He narrowed his eyes and gave the NIIA men a taste of a real man's stare. Sad day when murders were so commonplace, they could be ranked. Sad day, too, when he felt more comfortable with the accused than with those on the side of the law.

His usual good spirits were restored by the time he walked outside and paused in the sunlight on the top step. He'd outstared every one of the miserable excuses for lawmen trying to horn in on his investigation.

The President signaled the start of the briefing by standing and beginning his habitual pacing in front of the long multipaned windows that overlooked the Rose Garden. The Vice President, Chief of Staff M. Eugene Corforth, and Attorney General Jonathan Hunter, looking his normal controlled self, sat near the fireplace. National Security Advisor Chadwick Stevenson sat with them, but since the NIIA had usurped most of his turf, Stevenson's inclusion was more courtesy than necessity. Edmund Miller and Charles Kendall from the National Security Staff sat slightly behind. Kendall fingered Grant's NIIA drug file, which he held along with several others in his lap. He'd been surprised to find it included in his packet but couldn't help feeling smugly appreciative. It was potent stuff.

"Jonathan," the President began, "you know we're grateful to have you here but don't feel you have to stay."

"Thank you," Hunter said, "but everything is under control. Experts are being flown in now. We're doing fine."

The significance of the need for more experts wasn't lost on those in the room.

"Air transport for them was expedited, I hope?" the President asked. He stared at the Presidential Seal woven with intricate precision into the carpet. He frequently did, but today his look was purposeful. Anything to keep from meeting Hunter's eyes. Hunter's composure was unnerving. It seemed unnatural. It *was* unnatural! Joey was his son, and, barring a miracle, Joey was dying.

"Yes, the planes should begin arriving within thirty minutes."

"Then all that remains," the President said with awkward optimism, "is for those experts to get here and get Joey back in shape."

"And for Grant to be brought to justice. He's at the center of everything." Hunter had already phoned Derek Bender to make sure the Grant drug connection would be part of the Frederickson murder investigation. Bender would have NIIA operatives working on it now.

Kendall opened his mouth to tell them about Grant's DEA/NIIA file, but Corforth, his fingers playing with the worry beads in his pocket, had already begun speaking.

"The Georgia trip should help." Corforth used his business-as-usual mien to dissipate some of the tension. POTUS reacted poorly to any emotional situation. Just being around Hunter, an eerily too-normal Hunter, was enough to make anyone uncomfortable. "You're set to arrive in Atlanta this Friday afternoon, Mr. President. That will allow us time to build proper momentum. If the Grant scandal has started to die down—though that's hard to imagine—it will give us an opportunity to fan the flames. Peter Evans has promised front-page coverage of any new information. That means most of the media will follow suit."

"The more inflammatory voices will come from outside the administration, I assume," the President said. "We can't be too careful."

"Evans understands," Corforth assured him.

"How much can we expect to raise for Caruso?" Stevenson asked. His question was far from idle. He intended to make a run for the Senate in the next election. The President's coattails should be helpful, given his uncanny knack for reading voter moods—uncanny knack combined with daily pollings of voter sentiment. Stevenson studied all aspects of current campaigns with clinical interest. He, like the President, intended to remain a winner.

"At $1,000 a person," Corforth told him, referring to the reception/photo-op format they often used for fund-raisers, "at least $400,000. The tickets are selling fast."

"Enough to buy some crucial air time," the President said, nodding appreciatively, "especially this late in the game."

"Caruso had already booked it."

"Already?" POTUS asked, surprised.

Corforth nodded.

"Cocky, isn't he? Wonder where he got the money."

"Dead relative?" Miller asked sarcastically.

They all laughed, all but Hunter. The laughter died abruptly.

"Actually," Corforth said quickly, "Caruso has several darn good ideas in the works. Miller's our point man and will be coordinating it all." He looked toward Miller, who nodded.

"Bob Grant." The President spit the words. "That's one name I'll be glad to hear the last of. And to think he brought it all down on himself! Amazing how things seem to fall into place at the right time."

"Sir," Charles Kendall said, "I have some information that indicates Grant may be even more compromised than we realize." He handed the President Grant's DEA/NIIA file and began to summarize its contents.

Unconsciously, Hunter moved to the edge of his chair. As he listened, the gleam of the predator grew in his eyes. He was beginning to get the outline of an idea, one that would destroy Grant forever. Unlike the President, he wasn't amazed by events. He'd never trusted anyone else to guide his destiny, and he wasn't about to do so now.

When she pulled up to the curb in front of her house, Rachel sat for a moment, her stomach twisting at the sight of the charred wood now lying on blackened grass. With shaking hands, she opened the car door and slowly crossed the sidewalk.

Her pace quickened as she neared the house. She averted her eyes from the hate defiling it. It wasn't that she couldn't bear facing it; more that she couldn't bear facing it knowing she didn't have time to do something about it. Were there cleaning services that took care of this kind of desecration? she wondered as she fitted her key into the lock. With a heavy heart, she realized there just might be—capitalism at work, erasing evidence of America's threatening moral bankruptcy.

At least the inside of the house was unchanged, she noted with relief, closing and locking the door. Maybe a little messier than usual because the kids had left so hastily, but normal. Even so it felt empty, like a sail without the wind to give it meaning. She switched off the security alarm and reactivated it.

Bob kept his guns in their bedroom, easy to get in an emergency but out of sight. Her movements were quick as she hurried upstairs. She was anxious to get the handguns, take them to the police station, and then get to Cynthia's in time to be there when Bailey arrived. They hadn't allowed her to see him in jail, but just let them try to stop her once he was out!

She walked into the bedroom closet, removed a concealing strip of wood, and reached into the space Bob had created to store the weapons. All color drained from her face. The space was empty! The handguns were gone, both of them.

She stared at the empty space, not wanting to believe. Desperate to find an explanation other than the one that shivered through her body, she ran back into the bedroom and yanked open the drawer where she stored her jewelry. Nothing was missing. She slammed the drawer shut, then raced to another room. Her steps slowed as she went from room to room.

Nothing was missing but the handguns, and as far as she could tell, they weren't anywhere else in the house. The shiver of dread became the cold pulse of reality. Someone had taken Bob's guns, guns which were sure to bear his fingerprints. Had one been used to murder Russell Frederickson? Would it now materialize, the final piece in the case against her husband?

With a backward glance at her home, violated now by their enemy, she closed and locked the door. She wouldn't tell Bailey or the other children, she decided. No need to alarm them prematurely, although she feared that only too soon everyone would know.

Anxious now to see Bailey and assure herself he was all right, she started the car and eased into traffic. A mile down the street, she pulled into a Wendy's and used the pay phone there to call Bob. His reaction reinforced her own cold certainty. The guns—one or both—would soon rematerialize.

During his seventeen years as a reporter, Kirk Vinton had interviewed several people at Lorton Prison—inmates, administrators, guards—so he was familiar with the routine. Familiar he might be, but he hated the place. The air seemed to get heavier and the light darker the farther he walked into the innards of the building. Even the walls seemed to close inexorably on him.

He followed uniform-clad backs down endless corridors. Feeling somehow emasculated, he nonetheless emptied his pockets at the command of a female attendant. He walked through the metal detector and retrieved his now carefully examined tape recorder, leaving the rest of his belongings to be reclaimed on his way out. Another door clanged shut behind him.

A uniformed guard on either side, he finally reached the visitors' room where he was to meet Hal Olexey. Vinton gritted his teeth as that door closed behind him. The grate of the turning key added the final period to his escalating depression. At least windows high in the north wall let sunlight into the room, he noted, but even the sunlight was cold and depressing. Bars diffused it, and the outside *was* outside.

Vinton sat at the scarred counter to wait. Carefully, he moved his chair to a square of sunlight before taking out his notes on Olexey. The *Herald's* library had come up with plenty: petty crime convictions starting in his late teens; suspected murders along the way but no convictions, several thrown out on technicalities; presently serving time for drug dealing.

He looked up at the sound of the door opening. The man walking toward him had to be Olexey, the orange prison garb said so, but he looked so ordinary: pale blue eyes in a pleasant face, lank blondish hair falling on his forehead, medium height, medium build. Physically fit: He obviously didn't use any of the drugs he sold. A nice ordinary-looking man. Suspected murderer? Vinton found that hard to believe.

"Thought someone would be in to see me 'bout now," Olexey said, obviously intent on dominating the conversation from the outset.

He took a crumpled pack of cigarettes from his pocket and shook one out. Vinton hesitated, then took out his own.

"Why were you expecting someone?" Vinton asked as they each lit up.

"Been hearing about Grant. Figured someone would remember I sold to him."

"You sold him drugs? The Senator?" Vinton's tone left no doubt he would take a lot of convincing.

"That's what I said," Olexey retorted belligerently, the well-contoured muscles of his arms tightening threateningly. "'Course I did. Told 'em all about it so they'd take a load off my sentence. Lot of good it did me."

"Who'd you tell?"

"What does it matter?" Olexey asked, bored now. He flicked an ash onto the floor. "Okay," he finally said grudgingly. "First the local pigs, then some NIIA jane."

Vinton leaned forward, the cigarette forgotten in his hand. "Tell me about the Senator. I'll make it worth your while."

Olexey's eyes glittered. "You bet you will," he said. When Vinton didn't reply, he resumed speaking, watching the smoke curl from his cigarette as he did. "I was in D.C., six months back about, sometime in the summer anyway. I was dealing a little. Grant was a customer. Liked coke, grass sometimes, too. Always bought plenty. Maybe he didn't use all of it himself, but you better believe he bought it."

"You mean to tell me he actually bought drugs from you?" Vinton demanded. "You sold to him in person?"

"Weren't you listening?" Olexey demanded, flexing the muscles again. He took a long drag on his cigarette, exhaled through his nose, and continued speaking. "I didn't sell to him personally at first. He's not dumb.

Someone else always bought it, least that's what I figure. When he finally showed up, he sure knew what he wanted. Knew what I could get for him, too." Olexey's stubby fingers tapped the table, the cigarette bouncing up and down with each movement. "Anyhow, there was Grant. Maybe his friend couldn't make it, and he had to have some. 'Course I didn't know it was Grant then. Didn't know till I saw his picture in the paper. It was the Senator all right. I could tell you plenty. I sold to a lot of suits." His eyes darted about, then bore in on the reporter with avaricious intensity.

Vinton, wondering how he could have thought the man ordinary, had trouble hiding his repugnance. "He bought enough for others?" he asked after taking a last deep drag on his cigarette.

"Sure, sure," Olexey replied impatiently. "He bought plenty."

With careful deliberation, Vinton ground out his cigarette in the cheap tin Department of Corrections ashtray. When he lifted his eyes, they were narrowed speculatively. "Can you prove you sold to Grant?" he asked.

"Prove?" Olexey laughed harshly, his cruel eyes raking Vinton, their derision unmistakable. "You think I have customers pay by credit card maybe? Got a picture, though, in a safe place." He looked around slyly, then lowered his head. "Cost you, but it'll be worth it."

"How much? And how can I be sure it's worth it?"

"Ten thousand big ones."

Vinton frowned.

Olexey watched him, his small-pupiled eyes never blinking. He knew he couldn't chance blowing this deal, not over a few lousy thousand, not with so much more at stake, and certainly not with Bonfire certain to snuff him if he did. Bonfire was one mean dude, Olexey thought, his mouth hardening unpleasantly. "Nine thousand then," he told Vinton. "You won't be sorry. Picture shows Grant and me together. No, Mr. Hot Shot Reporter, you won't be sorry."

Fields bare of crops, the remaining stubble browned by winter's first frosts, rolled past the car's windows. Grant didn't see them. He was late for his first event, but there wouldn't be much of a crowd anyway. Unless they'd come to gawk at a probable murderer whose son was a drug user, he amended with unusual asperity. His jaw hardened. Bailey would be exonerated. No matter what else happened, Grant would make sure of that.

"Let's see what we can do to salvage this campaign," he told Masterson as the car pulled up in front of the VFW hall, site of his next speech. "And, Mike," he said, as he straightened his suit coat, "keep in touch with Cynthia. I want to know exactly what's happening with Bailey."

The usual handful of protesters outside the event had more than tripled. They thrust signs into the air—

Grant = Murder + Adultery

Father and Son Fry Together!

Nigger Go Home!

And the sickest: *Grant: Abortion NO! Murder YES!*

Their desultory chants turned to malignant screams as they caught sight of Grant in the car.

"What scum!" Masterson said. He surveyed the crowd more closely. "Looks like most of our old friends," he said, referring to those pickets who followed them everywhere, "with a bunch of *their* friends thrown in. Not a spontaneous protest. That's encouraging."

"I'll try to remember that," Grant replied shortly. He paused for a moment with his hand resting on the door handle, a prayer for courage and patience in his mind. Then he opened the door.

Faces loomed toward him, mouths wide with obscenities. Screams of "murderer" shrilled toward him. Television cameras caught it all.

The rally was as disappointing as Grant had expected. More media than constituents filled the room, and the intensity of the media probe overpowered the tentative interest of the others.

Now, Grant was alone. He'd asked the building superintendent for an office isolated from media scrutiny, one other than the holding room he'd originally been assigned, one with a phone line not integrated with the one in the original room. Grant was taking no chances.

He called Cynthia. Benjamin Dashev, his friend at Mossad, would be standing by and would be patched through. In that way the phone log, if anyone checked it, would reveal no more than a predictable call to his own office.

"Sorry to be so mysterious, Benjamin," Grant said.

"You have every right to be cautious, my friend," Dashev replied. Though his voice held no trace of an accent, his precise diction hinted that English might not be his native tongue. "One under attack should never underestimate the enemy."

"Then you have reason to believe I've become someone's target?"

"If you mean, do I have proof of such," Dashev said, "then the answer is no. But do I feel coincidence has stretched too far? Then, yes, of course. The stakes must be high if even your son is being drawn in." His voice became grave. "Protect your family, Bob. Your enemy is ruthless and not to be trusted. He lacks what might be called the code of the civilized. The world of sane men is threatened by too many such barbarians. If I can help you incise and remove some of that barbarism, be assured I will do so."

"Thank you, Benjamin," Grant said gratefully. That Dashev believed his innocence without question and that he considered a conspiracy against Grant probable was a welcome change after the doubt and rejection he'd encountered from others.

Dashev had his hand on the underbelly of the world. No megalomaniac grasping for power missed his purview. No exchange of money, weapons, or drugs was too insignificant for him to question. His agents were almost as adept as he at reading the nuances of power and greed, for these are the engines that drive the enemies of freedom and dignity. If Grant posed a threat to someone with the means and ingenuity to mount this complex plot, then Dashev and his compatriots at Israel's extraordinary intelligence unit might well have an idea of who that somebody might be.

Quickly and concisely, Grant recounted every event of the last three days, beginning with Frederickson's death and ending with the arrest of Bailey. Dashev listened in silence. Grant could hear the scratching of a pencil. He knew Dashev would be taping the conversation as well.

"The net around you is, indeed, being drawn close, is it not?" Dashev asked when Grant had finished. "Your death is not the object, or they would already have succeeded; therefore, the destruction of your career and your credibility must be. The plan is well conceived and well executed. Your enemy has taken existing situations and distorted them; then he has created additional situations to further his ends. He has not caviled at the cost, either to himself or to others."

"Even the obviously innocent," Grant said, thinking of Bailey.

Someone tapped on the door. Probably Masterson, Grant decided. He disregarded it, concentrating instead on extracting as much help from Dashev as possible.

"As I said, whoever is after you is a barbarian," Dashev continued. "I have heard of no plot specifically directed at you, but I have several ideas that may pertain. You permit that I look into this for you and get back with you tomorrow, maybe the next day?"

"I would be most appreciative, Benjamin. Call Cynthia and she'll contact me immediately."

"You permit a piece of advice?"

Grant couldn't help but laugh. At this point he would have permitted Dashev almost anything. "I need all the advice you can give me."

"Just so," Dashev said with a hint of satisfaction. "Keep a detailed record of anything unusual that you see, hear, or do, no matter how insignificant. We'll need much information if we're to uncover your enemy." He paused a moment, then spoke with gravity. "I hesitate to belabor the point, but I must repeat: Be careful, Bob. Too many in our world have forsaken righteousness. They will scruple at nothing to achieve their end."

"The end justifies the means."

"A most dangerous American aphorism," Dashev said as he soundlessly replaced the phone.

A preoccupied Grant unlocked the door just as Masterson resumed knocking.

Within minutes, they were in their car being driven to the next campaign stop, this one in a small town fifteen miles away. As usual they used travel time to discuss the campaign. Grant hadn't told either Mike or Robby, the driver, that he was meeting Sheriff Jenks after the speech. But truth was, he was having trouble concentrating on anything but that meeting. So much depended on enlisting Jenks's cooperation. If the sheriff proved closed-minded . . . That was one limb Grant didn't relish being out on. But as he'd told Rachel, what better option did he have? He couldn't gamble with Bailey's future, not when Jenks might know something that would help.

"Any rough questions?" Masterson asked. He'd been watching the noon broadcasts on a Watchman while Grant gave his after-lunch speech. This needing to be in two places at once was taking its toll. He unwrapped a candy bar. His face mellowed with the first taste of chocolate.

"The usual," Grant said. He took a swig of water, leaned back against the seat, and closed his eyes. "Vinton wasn't there, so no surprises."

"Wonder what he's up to."

"Read tomorrow's *Herald*," Grant told him without opening his eyes.

"Yeah." Masterson sounded glum. He took another bite of candy and spoke as he chewed. "The noon news was no big surprise either, just a reprise of the Frederickson murder and Pariss story. Bailey was alluded to, but not by name. They're showing some decency on that at least. Only real downer, they brought on the national president of FOW." He referred to the Federal Organization for Women.

Grant's "Figures" was uttered mildly.

Masterson continued. "She lamented the naiveté of young women who work for politicians. Something about having their trust abused by the very people who should be above reproach."

"I have to agree with them on that one," Grant said.

"Sure, but they showed clips of politicians who've been involved in sex scandals in recent years." Masterson opened a can of pop and took a long drink. "Amazing how many there've been."

"Sad's more like it."

"Yeah," Masterson agreed. "Then they used the most boorish clips they could find of you to hint you were just another depraved womanizer."

Grant sat up at this news. "We've got to stop the hemorrhage."

"In less than a week?" Masterson finished the candy bar, wadded the wrapper, and dropped it on the floor. "To find not only a murderer, but also the truth about Maribeth Pariss *and* about Bailey? Not to mention getting the information to the voters before the election? I don't know, Bob. Sounds impossible to me, especially if they're just random events and not related."

"Still hung up on that, are you, Mike?" Grant gave Masterson a pat on the shoulder. "Have faith. The Lord takes care of all impossible situations."

The car rolled to a stop in front of City Hall. The pickets were in place. So was the media.

"Now don't look so glum," Grant said. "We have not yet begun to fight."

He smiled as Masterson rolled his eyes.

Bailey Grant and Sherrill Holmes didn't speak in the cab from the police station to Andrew's apartment, where they picked up Bailey's car. They didn't speak in his car as they drove to her apartment. By the time they were seated in her living room, the silence was a hammering oppression.

"I appreciate your lawyers getting me out of jail," Sherrill said. She stared at the tissue she was twisting into small tails in her hands. "I really do. But my dad would have taken care of everything. He's a lawyer, you know."

"No, I don't know," Bailey said. His voice was bitter. "But there's a lot about you I don't know, isn't there?"

"Maybe," she said listlessly, "and maybe we'd better just leave it at that." She still hadn't looked at him. "I really think you should go now."

"Oh, you do, do you? Just leave and forget what's happened," Bailey said, his voice rising. "Is that what you mean? Is that what you're hoping for? Look at me, Sherrill!" By now shouting, he stood and loomed over her. "Look at me! I'm at least entitled to that, aren't I?" He reached out to grab her but drew back sharply at the feel of her flesh under his fingers. He closed his eyes and took a deep, unsteady breath. "Why did you come back to Andrew's, Sherrill? Why did you say we had to leave? What did you know?"

With a gesture of finality, she tore the tissue in two, then slowly looked up at him. "Oh, Bailey, I'm so afraid." Her voice became a hoarse whisper. "I didn't mean for things to turn out like they did!"

She was beyond crying. Her tormented eyes, huge in her taut face, stared at him, seeming to plead for something. Understanding, help, comfort, penance? Bailey wasn't sure. He just knew he couldn't stand seeing such naked pain. With arms outstretched, he pulled her to her feet and held her close. She stood rigid in his arms, turning her head from his soothing words. He continued talking, stroking her hair, her back, her arms. His murmured words finally broke through her despair. Slowly, she leaned against him, feeling his warmth and strength. She lifted her head to look at him.

"I don't deserve this," she murmured. "I'm not the kind of girl you think I am."

"What kind of girl are you, Sherrill?" He let go of her and sat on the couch.

She sat down beside him, careful to keep her body from touching his. She felt contaminated, as if by touching her, he, too, might suffer her shame. She couldn't bear that thought.

"What kind of girl would set me up for a drug bust?"

Sherrill jerked upright and swung around to face him. He was leaning back against the couch now, looking at her with almost clinical interest.

"You mean you knew that?" she asked, her voice disbelieving. "You knew and you didn't leave me to rot in jail?"

"I can't say I knew for sure," Bailey admitted, "but I suspected, especially when you came back to the apartment. At first I figured you must hate me for some reason."

"Oh, no," she blurted. "No, I could never hate *you*."

"It was Dad, wasn't it?" he said, leaning forward intently. "You're part of the conspiracy to destroy him, aren't you?"

Sherrill bit her lip and struggled to control the tears that hung on her lower lashes. "Part of a conspiracy to destroy," she whispered. "How horrible that sounds, but I suppose you're right. That's what I wanted to do—get rid of your father. That's why I met you in the first place." She faced him defiantly. "There. I've said it. So why don't you just get out of here."

"I think you know why." All softness left his face. "You can't try to destroy a good man—and my dad *is* a good man—and then just walk away. You have to try to put things right."

"But everyone knows he's one of the main reasons the world is such a mess. Everyone!" she retorted. Her lovely face was transformed by the single-mindedness of the zealot. "He's an uncaring Neanderthal who's destroying everything that's good. He is, even if you won't admit it because he's your father."

Bailey looked at her, contempt raging in his eyes. "I get so tired of people who can't think for themselves."

"Can't think for themselves!" Sherrill shrieked, a frightened undertone in her voice. All her doubts of the night before came roaring back.

"Sure," Bailey said. "Someone tells you that Dad hates the poor because he doesn't believe in welfare programs. Right?"

"So?"

"Did you ever stop to wonder how anyone can learn to take care of himself if he always has Big Brother there to do it for him? And this bull about Dad loving war. That one makes me madder than anything. Dad spent his life in the military trying to protect his country. *Your* country! Do you honestly believe anyone who has seen his friends die on the battlefield could feel anything but repulsion for war?"

"Then why does he always ask for more money for the military?" Sherrill demanded. "Answer me that."

"Does the bully ever attack the strong?" He tried to keep his voice nonjudgmental and calm, but he hated explaining the obvious. "Of course Dad believes in having a strong military, but that's because as long as we're strong no one will be dumb enough to attack us. Surely you've heard of World War II, haven't you? Why do you think Hitler knew he could take Europe? You want to talk about dying, look at what happened then. And all because they weren't prepared. The way to stop war is to be so strong the enemy is afraid to attack. You do believe in an enemy, don't you? Other than Dad," he added, a thunderous scowl denting his forehead.

Sherrill stared at him. What he said made too much sense, and the word *enemy!* The way he said it sounded like an assault on her personally.

"You really think this is all part of a conspiracy against your father, don't you?" she asked hurriedly to hide her confusion. She couldn't keep the disbelief from her voice. Conspiracies were for right-wing nuts. But wasn't that just what Bailey and his father were? Not Bailey, she thought, examining his face, so hard now but with incipient laugh lines around his eyes and mouth. Surely not Bailey. He'd never been anything but kind to her, and while he'd seemed attracted to her, really attracted, he'd been a gentleman, treating her with respect. She'd been wrong in her blanket condemnation of him; she knew she had, and if she'd been wrong about Bailey, could she have been wrong about his father as well? The thought was like a spinning boomerang, coming back and back again, bringing its painful logic with it. She felt her eyes filling with tears and fought against them.

"Weird, isn't it, to be talking about a conspiracy?" Bailey asked. He watched her closely, wondering if the tears were a sign of remorse, hoping they were. "That deal with Maribeth Pariss was a put-up job for sure. Dad just wouldn't do something like that. Not Dad." When Sherrill looked up, her face filled with skepticism, he hastened to explain. "I know being faithful isn't the thing right now, but you've got to believe me. Mom and Dad are different. They say that marriage doesn't depend on finding the right spouse but on being the right one. They've pounded it into our heads that marriage vows are sacred. When you promise to 'love, honor, and cherish, forsaking all others,' you'd better be sure you mean it. They made that commitment to each other, and that's just the way it is."

Sherrill's heart was racing. Bailey was describing a marriage she'd thought possible only in dreams. To know her husband could be trusted to be faithful, that his vows were for eternity and not until someone younger or better came along, maybe that was real love. But was it reality? she wondered. Her parents were divorced and remarried, her mother four times, maybe five or even six by now. Sherrill had trouble keeping count or caring.

Bailey thought he saw a momentary chink in Sherrill's defenses. He began working to increase it. "And that charge that Dad murdered a reporter," he continued. "I've never heard anything dumber in my life. Do you think I could murder someone? I don't mean in self-defense," he added at her look, "but someone innocent?"

Sherrill stared at him appraisingly, then slowly shook her head. She didn't honestly think he could. The guy who'd taunted him on campus and insulted his father—Bailey'd had every reason to tear into him, but he'd controlled himself. No, Bailey couldn't cold-bloodedly murder anyone. Of that, she was sure.

"Dad would no more have murdered Russell Frederickson than I would." Bailey leaned forward earnestly, praying for the right words. "Look, Sherrill, I know you think Dad's Satan incarnate, but don't you think even he should have a fair hearing? What do you have to lose by telling us everything you know? If Dad's guilty, you've done what you wanted anyway." He took her hands in his and forced her to look into his eyes. "But what if he's innocent, Sherrill? What if you're wrong about him and something horrible happens and you could have prevented it?"

Her eyes widened, but he wouldn't let her look away.

"What about it? Do you have the courage to find the truth?"

Tension stretched between them. For each this was a defining moment.

"But everything's such a mess," Sherrill finally said, putting off the decision a moment longer.

"Sure, it's a mess," he agreed. "But 'all things work together for good.' I say that to myself all the time, especially when I screw up."

"As if you'd ever do anything wrong," she retorted before she could stop herself.

"Yeah, right. My folks would laugh if they heard that." His young face became bleak. "I've got to admit it," he said, lowering his eyes so he wouldn't have to meet hers. "I was even stupider than you. You thought what you were doing was right. I knew I shouldn't be at Andrew's." He lifted his eyes, and her heart ached at the pain in them. "I knew about the drugs, and I went anyway. Sherrill, can't you see? I've got to do something. I let Dad down." He stopped, embarrassed at having betrayed so much of himself. "All things do work together for good," he repeated softly, more for himself than for her.

Hating herself for doing it, Sherrill disengaged her hands from his. A look of disappointment flashed in his eyes before a protective shutter of indifference covered them. She wanted to cry out in protest, to tell him that she understood what he was feeling, but her own feelings were too intense. She had to think, and she couldn't when her hands burned with his touch.

"The drug charges they're threatening against all of us?" she asked, her voice low and her eyes averted. "Surely you can't think that's good?"

"That's what I've been trying to say," he retorted with more impatience than he intended. Probably reaction to his soul baring, he thought. Being wrong was a bummer. Having to admit it was even worse. Maybe, too, reaction to her rejection of him, that on top of all he was beginning to suspect. He pushed his hurt away. Too much depended on gaining her help. "Of course they aren't good," he continued, "but I keep thinking you may know something important. You were part of it after all," he added angrily, her betrayal suddenly hitting with all its implications. He looked at her, his affection battling with the duplicity he was only beginning to understand. He *had* to get her to help his dad, he reminded himself. After she'd revealed everything, then he could examine his own feelings. The thought made him cold. He took a steadying breath and continued, his voice vibrating with effort for control. "Won't you help us, Sherrill? All you have to do is tell what you know."

"All!" Sherrill retorted scathingly. It might not seem like much to Bailey, but he wasn't the one being asked to prove himself a fool. "Maybe I can tell you *some*—"

"That's my girl," he interrupted, acting as if she'd just committed herself body and soul. He wasn't about to give her time to talk herself out of it.

Sherrill wished her heart would stop rolling over every time he looked at her that way. After what she'd done to him, he was one person she'd best forget. Suddenly overwhelmed with sorrow, she wondered if it wasn't already too late. Could she ever forget him?

"I'm betting you know a lot more than you think," Bailey said, too intent on keeping her committed to notice anything odd in her silence. He stood and grabbed her hand, pulling her to her feet. "Mom wants to hear everything."

"Your mother?" Sherrill repeated, appalled. "I can't talk to your mother! She'll hate me!"

"Naw," Bailey said, coaxing her toward the door. "Mom's nice. Here's your coat." He picked it up from a chair by the door. "If you can remember something that'll help Dad, she'll think you're great." He followed her out the door and closed it behind them. "She always thinks the best of everyone."

Sherrill found herself in the car before she could protest more. Then they'd pulled away from the curb, and she was too nervous to speak.

Kirk Vinton hurried to a phone as soon as he was released from Lorton Prison. That's what it felt like, being released, even though he'd been inside for little more than an hour.

Evans was elated about Olexey's claim to have sold drugs to Bob Grant.

"The picture may not be worth much," Vinton cautioned. "I haven't seen it."

"As long as it shows Grant with Olexey, that's all that matters," Evans said with almost lip-smacking satisfaction. "They wouldn't be together if it didn't mean something. Let the reader draw his own conclusion."

"Yeah, yeah," Vinton said. He leaned against the wall, tapping his foot impatiently. "So we pay Olexey."

"Not yet. For now we dig. Follow the leads he's given us, especially this idea that Grant bought more than he needed for himself. Try to pin down what he did with the rest. Was Grant the source of the drugs at the party where his son was arrested? That's one angle I want explored in depth. You thought Olexey was holding something back?"

"Seemed that way," Vinton replied. "Maybe I can find some leverage to use against him."

"At least give it a try. When do you want to go with this?"

"Friday," Vinton answered quickly, surprised Evans had bothered to ask. "By then I should know everything. I'm going to start by getting a copy of Grant's DEA/NIIA file."

"I can help you there." Evans gave Vinton a name and number, one of Edmund Miller's sources. "He'll give you a copy. I'll hold Friday's front page for you," Evans concluded, "but, Vinton, I want that picture. Grant and a convicted drug dealer together: What could be more newsworthy than that, especially in light of everything else we're uncovering?"

When Grant arrived at the storage room in the back of Martha's Fabulous Diner, a small but successful eatery owned by the sheriff's sister-in-law, Jenks was already there, firmly ensconced at a small table. A platter piled high with fried chicken sat in front of him, with a platter of biscuits on one side and a bowl of green beans cooked with jowl on the other. Martha's food truly was fabulous, and Jenks was determined to make time for one meal that day. This murder was playing havoc with his eating schedule. And every other schedule, for that matter.

Grant sat down across from him and began nursing a cup of black coffee. The two men were alone in the room. Masterson and Farrar had wanted to be included; neither had been.

"I appreciate your meeting with me, Sheriff," Grant said.

Jenks nodded as he bit into a chicken leg. The golden crust crunched enticingly. A piece stuck to his lower lip, and he licked it off with a smack of appreciation.

"I was hesitant at first to approach you," Grant continued, oblivious to the food. He was focused on his problem to the exclusion of all else, even the insistent growling in his stomach. He attended plenty of breakfasts, lunches, and dinners during a campaign but seldom had a chance for more than a few bites. Too much schmoozing to do. He couldn't remember the last time he'd eaten a real meal—or what it had been. "I wasn't sure of the protocol in a murder investigation, but Rachel and I decided to trust you with everything we know—against several lawyers' advice, I might add."

"Try some of this chicken, Senator." Jenks pushed the platter in his direction. When Grant, obviously impatient, started to shake his head, the sheriff interrupted. "You've been under a heap of stress lately, but I reckon it's nothing compared to what'll be coming your way over the next few days. You'll need lots of help, and Martha's chicken is a fine way to start. Besides, Martha's a voter, and her feelings will be plumb hurt if you don't at least try it."

Grant smiled tiredly and reached for a piece. He took a bite, seemed to awaken to the taste, and nodded appreciation at Jenks.

"You're smart to lay your cards on the table," the sheriff said, watching with satisfaction as Grant dug into the food, "though I got to warn you your lawyers may be right."

"I'll take my chances," Grant said. "I'm innocent."

The sheriff eyed him thoughtfully, like a poker player trying to smell out a bluff. "I didn't like the feel of this case from the get-go," he continued, "and it stinks worse'n skunk roadkill now. I'm being pressured to turn you over to the prosecutor's office, Murder One, but I don't much take to being told how to run my office."

"Who's doing the pressuring?" Grant asked, reaching for another piece of chicken. "If you don't mind telling me," he added. He was reminded of one of his dicta for campaigns, one he would be wise to follow now: Never pass up food or a bathroom. You could never be sure when you might have another chance. Did Jenks follow the same rule, Grant wondered, and did that explain using Martha's for their meeting? Grant's eyes were thoughtful as he regarded the huge, deceptively simple man sitting across from him. Or was food another part of Jenks's southern persona strategy? Martha's chicken was certainly tasty enough to break down plenty of defenses!

"Nothing secret about the pressure," Jenks said, well aware of Grant's scrutiny. He was doing a right smart bit of his own. "The NIIA has several agents here trying to horn in on the case, with Derek Bender calling the shots. Then local Democrats, those who fancy themselves power brokers, are saying maybe they should run someone in the primary against me. Fools!" he said, grinning at Grant. "They should know by now they're just rilin' me."

"Politics is a gentleman's game, isn't it?" Grant said, returning the grin. Already he felt better—from the food, of course, but much more from the feeling he was getting from Jenks. "Sorry you're taking so much heat."

"Oh, they won't get rid of me all that easily. Lady Justice and I go back a long way, and I'm not about to abandon her because of a little arm-twisting. You needn't worry I'll let anyone railroad you."

"What made you decide I didn't kill Frederickson?" Grant asked.

"Don't get me wrong, Senator," Jenks replied, wiping some grease off his mouth with a huge paper napkin. "I'm still working you as a suspect; you're just pretty much at the bottom of the list. What sticks in my craw, 'sides the time of the killing and a for-real motive, is all this piled-on pressure. If you're really guilty, then why is everyone so dadburn eager to tie my hands? Lady Justice keeps whispering in my ear, and she's never failed me yet. I sure don't intend to fail her now. Why don't you just put those facts you mentioned on the table, and then we can see where we stand?"

For the next twenty minutes, between bites of tender chicken, steaming green beans, and biscuits dripping with butter, Grant outlined the attacks, beginning with the murder of Frederickson and ending with Bailey's arrest. Jenks listened, jotting down an occasional note. Soon a pile of bare chicken bones had replaced Martha's golden pieces. As if on cue, the door to the kitchen opened, and Martha herself, the only one who knew of Grant's presence, brought each of them a man-sized piece of rhubarb pie, a scoop of vanilla ice cream melting over it. She smiled at Grant's thanks but left without saying a word.

"I'm beginning to think Martha's will become a permanent stop on any trip I make through the state," Grant said, taking a bite of pie, "even if she is a Democrat."

"I think you'll find that a lot of us old Southern Democrats can think for ourselves. Wouldn't be surprised if her X found its way beside your name more than once in the past."

"That's what I'm counting on this time," Grant said, "that people will look at all the facts and not be intimidated by the media condemnation. Winning the election doesn't mean much to me at this point, but clearing my name and that of my son certainly does. Winning will be an indication that I've succeeded."

Jenks finished his last bite of pie, sighed contentedly, and leaned back in his chair. "Mighty glad you decided to trust me, Senator. Gives me a few ideas. Think I'll go back to the office and do a little pondering. I'll give you a call if I come up with anything."

"You might want to ponder this." Grant's eyes glinted an angry fire. "My handguns have disappeared, both of them, including an army issue Colt .45."

Even Jenks, pro that he was, couldn't hide his surprise. Couldn't hide his doubt either, Grant noted grimly as he related what little Rachel had been able to tell him. "They must have been taken last night when the alarm was triggered," he concluded.

"Let me know if they turn up" was Jenks's only comment.

Grant nodded, fighting the urge to protest his innocence.

Jenks stood. He regarded Grant thoughtfully for several seconds, then stuck out his hand. Grant shook it, feeling profoundly grateful as he did. Jenks was a proud man. He didn't offer his hand lightly, and unless Grant was mistaken, he wasn't offering just his hand.

As soon as the car stopped in Cynthia's drive, Bailey jumped out, loped around to the other side, and opened Sherrill's door. She sat there, staring straight ahead.

"Come on, Sherrill," he said, grabbing her hand and urging her out. "We don't have much time. Mom's waiting."

Hiding her shudder at his words, Sherrill reluctantly let him lead her to the back door.

At the sound of the door opening, Rachel looked up from the notes she was studying. Her face lit with pleasure. "Bailey!" she exclaimed, hurrying around the kitchen table, her arms spread wide in welcome. He grinned and grabbed her in a hug that lifted her from the ground.

"Your son, the jailbird, in person," he said, the grin bigger than ever.

Rachel frowned in mock anger. "And after all we've tried to pound into your head!" she said. Then her face became serious. "What happened, Bailey? What really happened?"

Bailey turned to Sherrill, who was standing partially concealed behind him. "This is Sherrill, Mom, Sherrill Holmes," he said, moving so Sherrill was completely revealed. "She's going to tell us everything."

Rachel took a step toward the obviously nervous young woman and extended her hand. "We're so pleased you would help us," she said with a warm smile. "Why don't you fix us some lemonade, Bailey? We can sit in here where we won't be disturbed."

Sherrill, her eyes wide with strain and fear, sat at the kitchen table where Rachel indicated. Her back was straight, her hands clasped tightly in her lap. Even so Rachel was struck by her understated beauty, a kind of self-contained calm she wasn't surprised had appealed to Bailey. What, she wondered, could have caused this lovely young woman to behave in such an unlovely manner?

Ice cubes clinked into glasses.

"I'm sure this is difficult for you," Rachel said, trying to defuse some of the tension. "When will your parents be arriving?"

A defiant stillness dropped over Sherrill's face. "They won't."

"Oh," Rachel said inadequately, her face registering confusion. "If you would like to use the phone . . ." She indicated the one sitting on the counter behind her.

Sherrill shook her head. "Wouldn't do any good." She lifted her eyes to Rachel's for a second, and anger flashed from them, anger with an underpinning of fear.

"But they would want to be here, I'm sure," Rachel told her. "You shouldn't be alone now."

"They don't care!" Sherrill retorted. "Can't you understand that? I've taken care of myself for as long as I can remember. Why should this be different?" She glared at Rachel as if defying her to disagree.

"But what will you do?" Rachel asked, cautiously feeling her way. "The drug charges could be serious. I hope not," she added quickly, at the look of despair that flooded the girl's eyes. "But you need someone to advise you. Tell me what I can do to help."

Bailey set glasses in front of them, then sat at the end of the table, his mother on one side, Sherrill on the other. Neither woman seemed to notice. Rachel kept her eyes on Sherrill's bent head.

Finally, Sherrill raised it. "I'm sorry," she whispered. "I seem to be saying that a lot lately, don't I?" She smiled weakly at Bailey. He didn't respond. "My family's not like yours," she continued softly. "My parents were divorced almost before I was born. My mom is somewhere in Europe right now, probably working on husband number six or seven, for all I know."

"But your father, Sherrill," Rachel urged gently, "surely he can be contacted."

Sherrill gave a bitter laugh. "He's a high-powered attorney. I'm just his daughter, not a millionaire client. I left a message with his secretary, and she said he would call me right back. That doesn't mean today, I can assure you."

"Then you're going to stay here with us until one of them can be reached," Rachel told her decisively. Both Sherrill and Bailey looked at her in surprise. "You don't expect me to let you stay by yourself, do you?" Rachel asked, patting Sherrill's hand. "I would be worried sick."

"I told you she was nice." Bailey's voice was full of satisfaction. Even so, he didn't smile.

"Thank you, Dr. Grant," Sherrill said. "But you've forgotten why I'm here." Again, her face burned with defiance. "Once you've heard everything, you'll change your mind. I won't hold you to it."

Rachel smiled, a mother's smile. "We all make mistakes, Sherrill. I want to hear everything, but the invitation stands regardless." She directed her attention to her son. "Why don't you begin, Bailey? Then Sherrill can fill in the details."

"Sure," he agreed. Rachel pushed the record button on the tape player she'd left ready in the center of the table.

As Bailey described the last few weeks and especially the night before, Rachel asked occasional questions. Eventually, Sherrill raised her eyes and watched him, too.

"Why did you try to get Bailey to leave the apartment?" Rachel asked Sherrill when he'd finished. Bailey turned to her, his eyes shuttered as if to deny what he was afraid he would hear.

"Because I knew the police would arrive soon after Reggie left," Sherrill answered, her voice again defiant.

"I knew it!" Bailey exclaimed.

"Hush!" his mother commanded, without looking in his direction. "Reggie was part of the plan?"

Sherrill nodded. "Cora didn't tell me it was Reggie, just that someone would help be sure Bailey was there last night. Since Reggie kept after Bailey to take drugs, I figured he was the one. Besides, Reggie was new to the group. I tried to warn you," she said, turning to Bailey. "I told you I didn't think he was a student."

"Some warning!" Bailey didn't look at her.

Sherrill continued quietly, seeming to address the half-empty glass of lemonade she held in her hands. "Last night was the target time all along. October 27." She raised her eyes to Rachel's. "I think I'd better start at the beginning. It won't make sense otherwise."

"Thank you." Again, Rachel touched her hand reassuringly.

Sherrill wanted to smile but couldn't. She took a deep breath, fighting tears, then stole a look at Bailey. He was staring at the wall in front of him, a strange, closed expression on his face. She looked back down at her hands.

"I told you my family is different from yours," she said, making herself look up into Rachel's eyes. "I spent a week with my dad during the summer, the first time I'd seen him in five-and-a-half years. All he could talk about was Senator Grant and how bad he was." She looked back at her hands, embarrassed. "An Uncle Tom," she whispered. "I told him I thought the Senator's son attended Georgetown. My father didn't say anything, but I knew he hoped I would do something. I thought it would be a way to make him proud of me," she said, her eyes beseeching. After a short silence and another drink, she continued. "Anyway, when Dr. Sandborne, my poli-sci professor, said the same things Dad had been saying, I decided to attend an FOW—Federation of Women—meeting. Dr. Sandborne is the sponsor."

"Is Dr. Sandborne the one who told you what to do?" Rachel prodded.

"Yes, but not really," Sherrill said slowly. She took another sip, then hurried into speech, like a platform diver who'd made the decision to jump, knowing she had no place to go but down. "Dr. Sandborne introduced me to her lifemate, Dr. Snyder, Cora Snyder. Cora—that's what she likes us to call her—gave me articles to read, ones that explained how ..." She gulped, the next words shooting out fast and overloud. "How Senator Grant is rich and hates the poor and takes food from their mouths, to feed his war machine. It made sense. Really it did," she finished plaintively.

Rachel patted her hand. "It's not always easy to recognize lies, especially when people you should be able to trust are saying them."

Sherrill studied Rachel's face and seemed satisfied by what she saw. "I did trust them," she agreed, nodding. "When Cora told me I could rid the world of Senator Grant by getting his son to do something that would embarrass the Senator, something criminal with drugs, I agreed. It sounded right, like the right thing to do. It almost seemed like a mission, something important only I could do."

She turned to Bailey, who met her eyes, then looked quickly away.

"I figured if you were dumb enough to take drugs, you deserved to be set up." She swallowed and continued, her voice lifeless. "Anyway, I got to know Bailey like she said, and then she told me to make sure he would be at Andrew's apartment last night." She glanced miserably at Bailey, wanting to tell him how her "mission" had quickly turned into a genuine liking for him, maybe even something more. He stared straight ahead, ignoring her.

"Did she mention the police?" Rachel asked.

"Not directly," Sherrill whispered. "Just that having his son caught with drugs would be the worst thing that could happen to Senator Grant since he's made the control of drugs into such an issue."

"That was Reggie's job," Bailey said bitterly, "making sure Andrew and Bear wanted to use drugs and that I stayed put. No wonder Reggie left when he did. He probably went straight to a phone and called the cops."

Or the enemy, Rachel thought. Maybe both. Gently, she elicited details, disappointingly few, from Sherrill.

When they were finished, she asked Bailey to make copies of the tape and offered to take Sherrill up to the bedroom she would share with India and Olivia until Sherrill's parents could be reached.

"When you've seen the room," Bailey told Sherrill with obvious effort, "I'll take you to your apartment to get what you need."

She nodded but kept her eyes focused on the floor.

A real break," Masterson told Grant, taking him aside. On any swing through the state, Grant paid courtesy calls on Republican officeholders and their staffs. Today, he was visiting those who worked in Jackson City Hall. Their reception had been tepid to say the least. The county clerk with whom Grant was now speaking, a comfortable-looking woman who looked decidedly uncomfortable at the moment, had trouble hiding her relief at his summons. Grant gave her a sympathetic smile. She didn't return it.

"Cynthia's found Pariss's boyfriend," Masterson said when they were out of earshot. "A volunteer who used to work in the Atlanta office knew something."

"Thank God. Is he willing to talk to the sheriff?"

"That's the catch. He's married and was when all this happened. He says going public would wreck his marriage."

"Will he talk if he's assured his name won't be mentioned?"

"They're working on that now."

"Arrange a meeting with him and call Jenks," Grant said, thinking quickly. "Make it someplace the media won't bother us, maybe Martha's Diner. We should be able to handle this quietly since nothing criminal has been done. A married man." He shook his head. "Poor Maribeth."

"At least you should be cleared," Masterson said. He hurried off to find a phone.

Of adultery, maybe, Grant thought, but not of murder. He left the building, deciding not to subject himself or his former allies to any further visitation.

A gray stillness hung over the white sterility of Joey Hunter's hospital room. For what seemed the first time in that interminable but all-too-brief day, Rebecca Hunter was alone with her son. Just as her mind had previously failed to register the presence of the nurses, doctors, and technicians, so now she hardly noticed their momentary absence.

Her entire being was concentrated on willing her son to live. Her hand cradled his hand. Punctured with IVs whose tubes extended into a labyrinth of bottles and sacks above his head, his hand lay flaccid and frighteningly cool in hers. Flaccid: She'd heard that word, even used it once or twice, but never had she understood its meaning as she did now—flat and unresponsive.

Now flaccid had been replaced by dead. She knew even before she heard the straight-line wail of the heart monitor. She knew before the room was overrun with frantic but orderly phantoms in white coats, who gently but firmly pushed her aside.

She'd felt his spirit leaving, a momentary rift between body and soul. She'd felt the almost imperceptible lessening of life and weight in his hand. She knew he was dead and felt a moment's relief that at least the wait had ended for them both. Then she felt nothing, nothing but the empty throb of despair.

Now back in a corner of the room, separate from the impassioned yet calm action, she sank into a state of lifelessness of her own. She heard the shouted orders and the sounds of the defibrillator. She saw the monstrous syringe being filled and felt profound relief when a broad white back blocked her view of its insertion into his heart.

She wanted to stop them, to tell them to leave her baby alone, that their efforts were destined to fail, but her voice was buried in the deep void that her body had become. She stood by passively, seeing but not seeing, until another gentle hand led her to a chair in another room. She wanted to protest that she needed to stay with her Joey, but that protest, too, died in the black void. Her Joey was beyond her help. Her Joey had left her even before he'd reached the hospital.

Her Joey was alone just as she was alone.

When M. Eugene Corforth heard POTUS's voice over the phone, he knew he was in for a bad time. POTUS was passing on a difficult task and feeling guilty for doing so. If the President was still capable of such an emotion as guilt, Corforth thought. So much lying and manipulation, had they blunted his conscience to the exclusion even of guilt? The facile ease with which he could concoct a cover-up tale, often under public scrutiny, made such a question legitimate. How much of his posturing on foreign and domestic policy was equally bogus? Corforth wondered. He seemed to be doing a disturbing amount of wondering lately. Sometime soon he was going to have to do something more than just wonder. But what? That was the question that always stopped him.

"You need to speak to Hunt," the President said now.

Corforth pictured him turned in his high-backed leather desk chair so he could stare out at the Rose Garden. The President's voice sounded as bleak as the Garden must look under the graying October sky.

"Joey?" Corforth asked, forcing the name through stiff lips.

"Yes," POTUS affirmed, "he passed away just minutes ago. Hunt's busy at Justice and wasn't at the hospital. I thought the sad news would come better from us."

Corforth remained silent, stubbornly refusing to make the conversation easy for this man, who purported to be Hunter's closest friend.

"I'm busy," the President finally said. "Just take care of it. And take care of the press releases. Heart disease. So sad."

Corforth felt as if he were suffocating. So sad? A young man, the son of his dearest friend, had died and all the President could say was "so sad"!

"Another thing," POTUS continued, "that sheriff in Georgia doesn't seem in any hurry to charge Grant. With the funeral and everything, Hunt may not be able to apply appropriate pressure. Be sure that ball isn't dropped."

Bob Grant and Sheriff Jenks arrived at the alley door of Martha's Fabulous Diner at the same time. The media was already camped out in front.

"Who leaked this?" Jenks demanded.

Grant merely shook his head and held the door open. His mind was racing furiously. How *had* the media learned not only that they were meeting, but the time and place as well? A leak to the media directly? Or a leak to The Enemy who had then contacted the media? The latter possibility had disturbing implications. It meant either he or Jenks, maybe even both, had a mole planted in his office.

In Martha's back room, Grant and Jenks found Maribeth Pariss's boyfriend already waiting. George Beterman was nice looking in a homely sort of way. He stood up nervously when they walked into the room, started to stick out his hand, decided maybe that wasn't the thing to do, and held it self-consciously at his side. Grant walked over to him and put out his own hand. After a moment's hesitation, Beterman grasped it.

"Wasn't sure you'd want to," he muttered. He gave a reflexive smile, then darted his eyes back to the floor. "I know I should've said something earlier when all this about Maribeth and the baby first came up, but . . ." His voice trailed off, a weak man who wished he weren't.

"We understand the pressure you're under," Grant told him. "A marriage is difficult at the best of times." Beterman nodded eagerly as Grant silently apologized to Rachel for this blatant untruth. "This is Sheriff Jenks, Mr. Beterman," Grant continued as he indicated a chair for Beterman, and they all sat. "The sheriff is investigating Russell Frederickson's death. If you could just tell him what you told my people."

"Uh, sure thing. It's like this, Sheriff . . . Jenks, is it?" Jenks nodded. "Maribeth and I, well, we were 'friendly.' She was nice, but she knew I was married." He licked his lips. "She told me about the baby, and I, well, I told her she knew I was married, didn't she? She couldn't expect me to just up and leave my wife. I have children." He looked from Grant to Jenks before his eyes again darted to the floor. "I know that sounds bad," he muttered, pressing his hands nervously down his pants legs. He was wearing a dark blue suit. It looked new and Beterman looked uncomfortable in it. "How could I know she was going to kill herself? Girls don't do that these days. Not with abortions, they don't."

Grant felt a welling of pity for poor Maribeth Pariss, to have linked her future to this weak soul and to have realized her mistake when it was too late. Was suicide her attempt at atonement, Grant wondered, an attempt as ill-founded as her ruinous relationship outside the sanctity of marriage?

"You suggested you had proof that Maribeth had no improper relationship with me," Grant prompted.

"Oh, uh, the letters. Well, I couldn't have her keep calling me, could I? She finally gave up doin' that, but she started writin' these fool letters. Sent 'em to 'Charlie's,' where I work." He held out a soiled bundle of seven letters, some with envelopes, most without. "Don't know why I kept 'em. She was a nice girl, I guess." When neither Grant nor Jenks responded, he muttered truculently, "Don't know why she had to go and kill herself. She had no cause for doin' that."

Jenks placed the letters on the table and began looking through them, careful to touch only the corners so as not to disturb any fingerprints. When he finished, he turned to Grant. "They establish that she thought George here was the father. Nothing to show you didn't have a relationship with her though."

Grant stared at Beterman, unable to hide his disappointment.

Beterman cleared his throat. He looked highly uncomfortable. His eyes darted from one man to the other, but he didn't speak.

"You have something else to tell us, Mr. Beterman?" Grant prompted.

"Well, I guess you might find what you need in this diary of Maribeth's." He pulled a red vinyl book from his suit-coat pocket, the kind of simple-lock diary a young girl might use.

"I was hoping that would turn up," Jenks said with satisfaction. He took it from Beterman. "How'd you happen by it, Mr. Beterman?"

"Oh, that was Maribeth," he said. "She sent it to me. Must have mailed it the day she died. I . . . I only read part of it." He looked bewildered. "I couldn't finish it. She really loved me, but I was married, wasn't I? What did she expect me to do? I didn't want her to die, not for the world, but what did she think I'd do? I couldn't leave my kids. Why'd she have to go and kill herself anyway?"

Grant and Jenks again had no answer.

"Thanks for coming forward, Mr. Beterman," Jenks said with no trace of censure. "I'll do my darndest to keep your name quiet, leastways in public. If this really is Maribeth's writing, then you have nothing to worry about." Beterman brought hopeful eyes up to Jenks's face. "We'll have to tell folks about the letters and diary though. Can't help that."

"Long as my name's out of it," Beterman said, wiping his brow, and rising, "you can do whatever you want with the whole lot. Anyway, can I go now?" He looked from one man to the other as he edged toward the door.

"Yes, Mr. Beterman, you may go," Jenks said. "One of my deputies will be in touch about signing a statement. Call my office if you've a mind to leave Georgia."

Beterman bobbed his head once and was gone. A plainclothes officer in the front room would get him safely through the gauntlet of reporters. With any luck they wouldn't realize he'd been anything but a customer.

"Not a strong character," Jenks said as the door clicked shut. "Wonder if he'll sell his story to one of the tabloids."

"Or a TV gossip show?" Grant asked. He leaned on the table and stared down at Maribeth's treasures. They looked so innocuous: a fat, shiny vinyl book and dimestore stationery covered in a sprawling rounded script. So innocuous, but with the power to give him back a portion of his dignity.

"People pay good money for that trash." Jenks looked mildly amazed. "Hard to figure." He gingerly lifted the letters and put them in a plastic bag. He dropped the diary in another. "Soon as we know these are in Maribeth's handwriting, I'll hold a press conference. That'll be one monkey off your back."

"Thank you, Sheriff," Grant said, watching the bags disappear into Jenks's satchel. "Any lightening of the load is appreciated. Curious how Gayla Sergek and Shirley Spade were so sure about Maribeth and me, isn't it?"

"Curious, indeed," Jenks agreed. His eyes narrowed as he regarded Grant. Possibly a shade more sympathetically? Grant wondered.

"And that letter supposedly from Maribeth," Grant continued. "If her diary supports what Beterman just told us, how is it she wrote such a sexually graphic letter about me?"

"That very question had crossed my mind," Jenks said. "I believe I'll have another little talk with the Misses Spade and Sergek. I can't see Miss Spade backing down—that woman bears a pile of spite for you, Senator, probably for the whole world—but Miss Sergek, now she just might forget herself and let something interesting slip."

"Any ideas what?" Grant asked.

"Not precisely, but I keep thinking that story of hers was a tad pat for her to have concocted it all on her own. And that letter—if it's a forgery, mentioning pulling down time just might do wonders for her memory." Jenks put his hat squarely on his head and picked up his satchel. "Think I'll go have a talk with those media fellows. Give 'em a hint of things to come. Maybe you can sneak out while I keep 'em occupied."

"Thanks," Grant said, hoping Jenks was right but all too familiar with the media's tenacity. Jenks still hadn't let go of any information, Grant thought as he slipped out the back way. Had he been wrong to confide in the sheriff?

Your mother didn't seem too upset with me," Sherrill said tentatively as she and Bailey drove to Andrew's apartment after their meeting with Rachel Grant. Sherrill felt worse—and more confused—than ever. Dr. Grant had been kindness itself. Bailey was nice, too, or had been, she amended with a sad sidelong glance in his direction. Could the Senator be so different?

"Yeah, but Mom's like that," Bailey said, staring straight ahead. "Nice. So's Dad," he added pointedly.

Neither spoke for several minutes. Finally, Bailey broke the silence. "Dad talks about his Grandmama Grant a lot," he said, still without taking his eyes from the road. "According to him, she was at peace with herself always, even when she was a slave."

"When she was a slave! But—"

"She said something important," Bailey interrupted. He slammed the brakes as the light turned yellow. Both he and Sherrill lurched forward against their seat belts. Still, he didn't look at Sherrill. He didn't apologize. "It'll explain why I'm having a hard time with what you . . ." His hands tightened on the steering wheel. He floored the car as the light turned green, throwing them back against their seats. "Anyway, Grandmama Grant and integrity are like watchwords in our family. We're supposed to do what's right because if Grandmama could do it throughout her hard life, then we certainly have no excuse. Ignorance is no excuse. It just means we haven't been paying attention."

Sherrill watched him, wondering if she understood and afraid she did. "You mean I have no excuse," she whispered when the silence between them had stretched almost unendurably.

"That's kind of rough," Bailey said slowly, "but, yeah, I guess that's it. I'm trying to understand how you could pretend to like me," he said in a rush, "when all the time you planned to hurt me. And don't tell me you didn't really know what you were doing. That won't wash. You did it, and that's all that matters."

Sherrill wanted to ask if Grandmama Grant had said anything about forgiveness, but she knew she would sound as bitter as she felt. She'd never met this Grandmama Grant and never would, but Sherrill was sure she would have been an uncomfortable acquaintance.

"I liked you, and I trusted you," Bailey said quietly. He had the car under control now, no more abrupt stops, no more quick getaways. "Integrity means being at peace with yourself and with God. That's all I wanted to say."

A rationalization on her lips, Sherrill stole another glance at Bailey. As she watched, his clenched jaw slowly began to relax. Even his lips softened. The words of excuse she'd been planning died. With heart-shattering insight, she knew that Bailey was done with her. He would be polite because he really believed what he'd just said, but anything more was impossible.

She wanted to say something, maybe to beg for forgiveness, but even as she started to reach out, she knew she couldn't. He was right. She'd taken his greatest gift, his trust, maybe even his love, and trampled it. Why would he believe her now when she'd been so clever at deceiving him before?

Remorse consumed her. The issue had never been political or philosophical as she had tried to convince herself, as Dr. Sandborne and Cora had tried to tell her, as even her father would have insisted had he known. Bailey was right about that, too. Integrity had been the issue. Miss Eleanor's face floated into her mind along with words from a Sunday-school lesson about Esau selling his birthright for a mess of potage. Sherrill hadn't understood at the time, but now she knew. Her integrity had been her price, she realized. She'd knowingly compromised her honor to gain something she only now realized was worthless. No, she amended with painful honesty. Not worthless. Evil.

She heard the car door slam. They'd stopped. Her heart heavy, she followed Bailey up the walk to Andrew's apartment. His broad shoulders and straight back went before her, now forever beyond her reach.

So be it, she decided. The past was over and best forgotten. The future, however, was hers to redeem. Integrity, Bailey had said. Live life with integrity. Pay attention to learn the truth. That was what she would do, that and do her best to atone for her betrayal. Senator Grant wasn't the issue. He never had been. Her treatment of Bailey was. Ironically, to atone for that she had to help his father.

Bailey held the apartment door open for her. She smiled at him. He smiled but his eyes were closed to her. Her smile faltered. No, she told herself. She wouldn't let it bother her. Head held high, she walked past him and into the apartment.

Bailey began questioning Andrew but almost immediately realized that if Andrew had ever known anything, he was in no shape to remember it.

"Reggie isn't a student here?" Bailey asked one last time.

"Nope," Andrew repeated. "How many times I gotta tell you?" He cradled his aching head in his arms.

Bailey ignored his friend's plaintive plea. "He approached you?"

Andrew nodded, then groaned.

"And you have no idea how he knew you or how he knew we were friends?" Bailey continued remorselessly.

"Nope."

"Come on, Andrew," Bailey pleaded. "This is important. Think. We've got to find him."

"My head is splitting, I spent the night in jail, and you want me to think? Brother!" Andrew sat in sullen silence, his head in his hands. He clasped his hands over his ears and moaned as the front door crashed open, then slammed shut.

"Hey, guys! What's happenin'?" Bear strode in, seemingly none the worse for his night.

"Hold it down, you idiot!" Andrew seethed through clenched teeth.

"What's wrong with him?" Bear asked, gesturing toward Andrew hunched in his chair.

"You mean you feel fine after last night?" Bailey asked, remembering Bear's wild dance. He felt his eye gingerly. At least jail had been good for something; his mom had pretty much ignored the eye. She'd asked, heard his explanation, and gone on to more urgent considerations.

"Sure, why not?" Bear asked. "I'm ready to try it again." At Bailey's shocked expression, he continued. "Well, maybe not jail, but the dust . . . Wow! What a trip!"

Andrew moaned.

"You heard about Joey?" Bailey asked. "Joey Hunter?"

Bear's smile vanished. "Yeah," he said. His eyes clouded. "Tough."

"That's all you can say?" Sherrill demanded. Every mention of Joey flooded her mind with guilt and filled her eyes with tears. Stinging from Bailey's censure and the picture of herself she'd been forced to accept, she lashed out at Bear. "Joey's dead, Bear. Dead! He took the same coke you did, he drank the same liquor, and now he's dead. Dead! That's a one-way trip!"

"Well, yeah," Bear said, regarding her warily. Then he turned and walked into the kitchen. "Didn't really know him, but he seemed nice enough. Anyway, he had heart trouble. Could've died anywhere, anytime," he said over his shoulder as he opened the refrigerator. "I heard some guys talking about it. Didn't have anything to do with drugs. Tough, but it won't happen to me. Heart's like a rock," he said, pounding the pertinent area. "Anyone want a beer?"

No one answered. He shrugged, took one out for himself, popped the top, and hoisted it. Immediately, he looked more relaxed. "Of course, I feel sorry about Joey," he continued, licking foam from his lips, "but I'm not about to let his bad heart keep me from tripping out. I tell you, it was awesome!"

"You don't remember this?" Bailey asked, pointing to his swollen eye.

"Sure is a beaut," Bear said, taking a step closer to admire it. When Bailey just stared at him without responding, he looked puzzled. "Say, what's going on? You act like I had something to do with it."

"If you call your elbow you, then you did," Bailey said sarcastically.

"I elbowed you? You got to be kidding, man. Why would I do that?"

Suddenly, Bailey didn't feel mad or sarcastic, only frightened that Bear might not realize the danger of what he was doing. "You may not remember, but you went crazy last night."

"Naw, man, I never did." Bear shook his head and walked back toward the refrigerator, pitching his empty can toward the overflowing wastebasket. The can hit, then bounced off and clattered on the floor.

"Pipe down, can't you?" Andrew demanded weakly between pitiful moans. They ignored him.

"And when I tried to keep you from hurting yourself or anyone else," Bailey continued, "your elbow connected with my eye." Bear looked mildly amazed. "I was scared, let me tell you. You're one big dude."

Bear grinned, then fingered his sore chin. "You?" he asked.

"Yeah," Bailey admitted. "Sorry, but I had to tackle you. What else could I do? Just remember my eye and your chin if you get the urge to trip again."

Bear didn't look convinced.

"And remember Joey," Sherrill added quietly.

A look of tragic mortality flicked into Bear's eyes, but he shook his head as if to clear it, took another drink, and the look was gone.

"Dad's in big trouble," Bailey said. "I guess you know that. Reggie set me up so I would be arrested and Dad would look bad." He carefully omitted Sherrill's part, though his eyes went to her and slid quickly away. "He didn't care who got hurt."

"Reggie?" Bear asked. "Man, that's heavy."

"I've told you and told you I don't know nothing," Andrew complained. "Get off my back, already!"

"What about you, Bear?" Bailey asked. "Can't you think of something that might help us find Reggie? You like Dad, don't you?" Bear nodded. "Then think of something."

Bear cleared a chair by tipping it and letting the clutter slide onto the floor. Then he righted it and collapsed onto it. "I'd help if I could . . ."

He stared at his beer. "Hey, Andrew." Bear sat up and looked at his friend. "Remember that time we came up on Reggie at a pay phone?"

"Yeah. So what?"

"I don't know if this means anything, but we heard him talking, and he went ballistic when he saw us."

"That's all?" Bailey asked, his face falling.

"I guess that doesn't help," Bear said at Bailey's look of disappointment. "The phone was over on Prospect," he added helpfully. "Once I saw him go into an apartment near there."

"Where exactly?" Bailey asked, hope returning to his face.

"I was kinda blasted," Bear admitted sheepishly, "but it was on the same side of the street as the phone. I remember that." Bailey waited for more. Bear squinted his eyes in concentration. "It had steps. Reggie went down under them!" he finished with a note of triumph.

"When he was on the phone," Bailey asked, "can you remember what he said?"

Bear looked surprised that Bailey had asked. "Me? Remember something?" Then his face brightened. "Hey, Andrew, Reggie said something about a fire, didn't he? Weird. Ninety degrees and he's talking fire. Remember?"

"Yeah," Andrew said, not bothering to raise his head. "A bonfire."

"A bonfire?" Bailey asked, looking both puzzled and disappointed.

"Yeah, a bonfire," Bear said, taking a last swallow of the beer and looking around as if expecting another to materialize. "Told you it was weird."

"Reggie's apartment," Bailey prodded, hoping for something more useful than a fragment from a conversation that these two had probably gotten wrong anyway. For the first time he looked at his longtime friends, not through the forgiving eyes of shared elementary- and high-school experiences, but in the harsh light of reality: their unshaven faces, bloodshot eyes, disheveled clothing. He didn't know them anymore, he realized with a pain he didn't yet recognize as the onset of maturity. He would feel other moments of regret as the comfortable and comforting familiarity of childhood gave way to the reality of adulthood. Eventually, he would come to appreciate the need for such change, but for now he felt only a vague sadness. "Do you think you can find Reggie's apartment building?" he asked, stifling a sigh he didn't understand.

"Maybe," Bear said doubtfully. "I don't know. I told you I was blasted."

With that reluctant admission, Bailey piled them all into his car and headed out to find Reggie's pay phone. They did find it, but after several drives up and down the street, Bear admitted he wasn't sure exactly which place had been Reggie's. The best he could do was narrow it down to five possibles.

Better than nothing, Bailey thought as he took them back to Andrew's. Then he and Sherrill went to find Milton. They found him, but he could tell them nothing. He didn't like Reggie, never had. Maybe that was why he'd made no effort to get to know him. Despite Milton's desire to help, they'd reached a dead end.

They went by Sherrill's apartment. Bailey waited in the car while Sherrill ran in for her things. Then they returned to Cynthia's, knowing little more than they had when they left.

In Atlanta, Grant stood at a pay phone, trying to curb his impatience. Rachel in Washington was going to another pay phone to return his call. All these precautions were necessary, he was certain, but they ate up time, time they couldn't afford to lose.

The phone rang. Rachel.

"Bailey was deliberately set up, Bob."

"No doubt about it?"

"No doubt at all."

Set up. Before, Grant had been content to learn the truth and make it public; now he was determined to uncover the evil and destroy it. No one could be allowed to abuse innocents with impunity.

"Some FOW fanatic," Rachel continued, "a poli-sci professor, convinced Sherrill you should be destroyed no matter the cost. Bailey's arrest on drug charges was the goal. They even gave her the day. Yesterday." Silence greeted this alarming news. Rachel's next words came slowly. "It had been planned at least from the beginning of the semester. That means for more than two months someone's been working to destroy you. Two months!" She went on to explain about Reggie, giving every detail of the night before at Andrew's apartment and the events leading to it.

"Bailey and Sherrill are out now talking to Andrew and some of the others, hoping to get a lead to Reggie."

"I wish they'd leave it alone," Grant told her. Masterson signaled him from the car. Grant waved to him dismissively, then turned to face the blank brick wall beside him. "It may not be safe. If our enemy planned to use the children all along, if they're that kind of people ... using Bailey to get at me puts this into another level, a dangerous one. Try to make him understand."

"I will," Rachel said, "but I've already told him much the same thing. You'll love his crowning argument." Even with the emotional stress they were under, her voice was highlighted with affectionate amusement. "He's 'taking responsibility for his own actions.' A direct quote."

"Nice to know he's been listening to us, but he has to appreciate the risks. Have him call me if he sounds at all flippant."

"I will," she promised. "We may have another problem. I'm not sure it's part of this, but according to a friend at G.W. Hospital, while there's no doubt Joey Hunter died of a drug overdose, the death is being attributed to heart problems. All drug-related notes have been removed from Joey's medical records, and a history of preexisting heart disease has been put in its place."

"Someone has been busy."

"But who?" Rachel asked. "If they're covering up Joey's presence at Andrew's and that he died of a drug overdose, at least they can't try to connect his death to Bailey."

"Maybe, but so far logic hasn't played much of a part in what's happened."

Rachel sighed.

"Thank Cynthia for all her work in tracking down Maribeth Pariss's boyfriend," Grant said, stuffing his notes into his pocket. "I just met with him and Jenks." He told her about the meeting. "The boyfriend can prove I couldn't have been involved with Maribeth. In fact, he had her diary," he concluded.

"That's wonderful! Without a motive, connecting you with the murder is ludicrous."

"I'm not expecting our enemy to give up that easily," Grant warned. "Why don't you see if you can track down Joey's family physician, an attending resident, or the EMTs who brought him to the hospital and get proof of that heart disease story one way or the other? I'll need all the ammunition I can get if this ever comes to a showdown. I'll get in touch with you after my meeting, probably close to midnight."

He replaced the phone just as Masterson, a scowl on his face, climbed out of the car to come get him. Normally, Grant appreciated his press secretary's single-minded adherence to their schedule, but for now the campaign was far from his number-one consideration.

As soon as Mike Masterson was safely in his room for the night, Grant eased out of his room next door and hurried down the hotel's back stairway to the parking lot below. A black sedan with an Auburn University bumper sticker was parked in front of a "Do not litter" sign, an ignition key under the back floor mat. Grant drove to a motel near the Atlanta airport. The door to Room 134 was unlocked. He entered. Stephen Yao was waiting inside.

When Yao had phoned earlier that day offering his help, Grant had viewed it as the answer to prayer. They'd met years before when Yao was a naval intelligence officer under Grant's command. Mutual respect had become friendship. Now retired from the military, Yao owned a security firm based in New York. He'd set up this meeting.

"You don't look too bad," he said, shaking Grant's hand enthusiastically, "not for a dangerous desperado."

"You either," Grant replied, laughing. Yao handed him a bottle of sparkling water and a glass with ice. "I see your memory's as good as ever." Grant indicated the drink.

Yao shrugged modestly, but his eyes flashed with satisfaction. Nothing much got by him. He possessed the intellectual keenness and physical agility of his Asian heritage. His mother's Caucasian genes had somewhat blunted the Chinese cast of his features, but his father's contribution was obvious nonetheless in his perfectly straight, still-black hair, wiry build, and dark eyes.

"So someone's tagged you for a little rough play, have they?" Yao asked.

"Sure seems that way," Grant agreed, settling back into his chair.

"Any idea who?"

"Afraid not."

There was a tap at the door, a pause, then two more taps. In three strides Yao was at the peephole, glancing through it. He opened the door wide enough for entrance.

"Matt Goldie, I presume," he said, his eyes twinkling.

"None other," Goldie agreed, shaking his hand and nodding to Grant, who'd risen to greet him. Then Goldie turned his attention back to Yao. The two men regarded each other gravely. The inspection lasted only seconds, but years of experience were packed into them. Finished, they turned to Grant.

"Satisfied?" he asked, a shade tartly.

Yao laughed, and the tension was broken. "Remind you of two male predators, checking each other out?" he asked. He handed Goldie a beer.

Goldie eyed the somewhat rare German brew with appreciation. "Not to worry," he told Grant, taking a long sip, "any man with Yao's good taste in lager will do just fine."

"If I'm not mistaken," Grant said, "Stephen didn't just chance to have that particular brand."

"Makes it even better," Goldie said, raising the beer in salute to Yao. "To a short but successful campaign."

"Amen."

Again, a knock sounded. This time Yao looked through the peep-hole and opened the door immediately.

"Cynthia," he said, pulling her in and giving her a delighted hug. "It's been too long."

"Agreed." Her face warmed with pleasure. "You couldn't have picked a better time to resurface. Things are certainly heating up."

"So it seems," Yao agreed, helping her off with her coat and placing it on the bed. Goldie gave her a hug and seated her in the chair next to his.

Yao poured a cup of coffee. "Time to relax," he said. "I've booked a room for you next door, and I'll have you back in D.C. by eight tomorrow morning. Promise."

She took a sip and smiled. "Tastes good."

"Now I understand how George Patton must have felt," Grant said, looking at each of his friends in turn, "going into battle knowing he had the best officers in the war standing at his side. I must say it's comforting." He looked down at his hands momentarily, then up at his friends, his feelings naked in his eyes. "Thanks for knowing the risks and still coming on board."

"Can't wait to lay my hands on the yellow-bellied cowards taking these swipes at you," Goldie said, rubbing a clenched fist in his open palm.

Yao chuckled. "I knew we would hit it off just right, Goldie. My fingers are itching for action, too. Leave the reconnaisance to us, Bob," he said, turning to Grant. "The strategy's your baby."

Cynthia remained quiet, but her eyes, as darkly determined as theirs, missed nothing.

Grant filled Yao in on everything that had happened, with Cynthia and Goldie adding amplification.

"First thing to do," Yao said when they'd finished, "is to put your family under protection, Bob." He looked at Cynthia. "I want someone with you at all times, too, Cynthia."

Grant nodded, his face grim. "Again, I thank you."

"I hope it's not needed," Yao said, "but from what you've said, I sure don't want to take chances. I have some friends on standby." He reached for the phone and began dialing. "I'll put them on it right away."

Grant listened to Yao's end of the conversation and felt immense gratitude and relief, the same feelings he'd had in the military when protective air cover had been ordered for those under his command.

Yao finished his instructions and hung up. "Okay," he said, "that takes care of our defensive measures for the moment. Let's see what kind of offense we can mount."

"Operation Integrity," Cynthia said quietly.

"Exactly," Goldie agreed.

Yao nodded.

"Then Operation Integrity it is," Grant said. "And beginning none too soon. We have a lot of ground to make up, judging by what's happened so far."

He outlined his plan, merely a skeleton at this point. As Yao had suggested, information gathering was the first priority. "Know thine enemy" took on added urgency when the enemy was no more recognizable than the shadow of a ghost, impossible to identify, much less defeat, without the bones and marrow of knowledge.

Yao would concentrate on New York, especially the financial community since the scope of the attacks suggested that considerable money was involved. Cynthia would work on the Washington connection, looking for political overtones and motivations. Goldie, with his familiarity with Georgia, would key on the Frederickson murder as well as any Georgia-Washington connections. After lengthy discussion, they decided to rely on Benjamin Dashev for insights into international ramifications. Rachel would act as a clearinghouse for them all, coordinating their information—with the help of Bailey and his computer—and getting it to Grant.

The burden of correctly interpreting that information and then formulating a plan of attack would fall on Grant. The ultimate success of the operation rested squarely on his shoulders, a responsibility he welcomed.

He thought of the words Rachel had stitched in petit point for him. Framed, it hung in his Senate office directly across from his desk:

PRESSURE IS INEVITABLE. STRESS IS OPTIONAL.
FEAR SEES THE PROBLEM. FAITH SEES THE SOLUTION.

Many times, he'd raised his eyes to the words, and his entire mental outlook had shifted gears—from frustration, anger, sometimes even depression into optimism and renewed commitment. He would need to brand their truth on the front of his mind if he hoped to reason his way through the pressures that now afflicted him and come to the solutions that would bring total vindication, not only to himself, but to Bailey as well.

When Grant left Room 134 an hour later, Yao kept him well in sight. Goldie left five minutes later after making sure Cynthia was locked safely in her room.

Operation Integrity had begun.

It was almost midnight before Attorney General Jonathan Hunter finally entered his home. As he walked through the door, he felt a mantle of fatigue and emptiness enshroud him. The emptiness came from the vast cavity of his darkened house. Never again would his son Joey fill the house with promise.

Hunter walked from room to room, stopping to touch some of the many pictures of Joey that Rebecca had positioned on almost every surface. Joey as a baby, chubby and smiling; Joey as a gap-toothed youngster; then Joey as an unsmiling, rather wistful preteen; and finally Joey as he'd been before his death: a sullen, defiant teenager. He seemed almost a stranger in those last pictures, a confused man-child, perpetually unhappy.

Hunter felt a stab of anger. They might not have seen much of each other over the years, but that would have changed when Joey became an adult and could share his father's weighty concerns. But not now. Not ever. Never would Joey carry forward the legacy of power and influence that Hunter had so painstakingly, year after year, triumph after triumph, prepared for him. Joey was gone.

Hunter leaned on the dining-room table. His nostrils were assailed by the sickening aroma of food. Cakes, pies, salads soggy with dressing, meat globbed with hardened fat: all untouched. Nausea twisted his stomach. Who would have brought it? Not his associates. They would know food was immaterial now.

Seized by a wild anger, Hunter raised his hand and swept a towering chocolate cake on its footed pedestal off the table. The cake plate flew through the air, dumping globs of cake and spatters of frosting onto the parquet. The plate bounced and fragmented into chunks and slivers of leaded glass.

Before the crash finished reverberating through the empty room, Hunter wheeled and mounted the stairs. His steps faltered, and he stopped at the door to his bedroom. A shudder racked his body. He couldn't get in that bed, not yet. He couldn't lie in the dark waiting for the grotesque images of that boy in the hospital to assail his mind, that lifeless creature who couldn't be his son. Consumed with raging fury at his son's betrayal, at his own unaccustomed impotence, at the sense of unjustified guilt that continually pierced his mind with its outrageous taunts, he slammed his fist into the wall. His bellow of outrage echoed through the empty spaces and finally dwindled into nothingness.

How long he stood there, eyes squeezed tight, forehead pressed against the cool wall, hands hanging clenched at his side, he couldn't say. But slowly he came back to himself, ready to face the emptiness, then attack and defeat it. He'd lost his son. That segment of his life was closed. His own repute and dedication would now be his sole legacy.

He turned and strode to Joey's bedroom. In spite of his resolve to dominate the past, his hand hesitated before pushing open the door. The room was dark, but as his eyes adjusted, he could make out the rounded shoulders of a figure on the bed. Rebecca.

He flipped on the light.

"It's morbid to be sitting here in the dark," he told her, his voice contemptuous.

Rebecca ignored him. Instead, she continued staring blindly at the ratty two-tone blue raccoon she was stroking with rhythmic intensity. "Coonie" and young Joey had been inseparable. Even as late as last summer, she'd seen her son take the animal from the shelf and hold it. His look had been puzzled and wistful, almost sad, as if he couldn't quite understand where those years had gone. She'd wondered at the time if something could be troubling him. If only she'd ... She clutched Coonie to her breast, fighting breakdown.

Hunter remained where he was, his hand still on the door. At his wife's silence, he felt gorge rise in his throat. How dare she act as if her loss was more profound than his?

She spoke before he could translate his rage into words. "You wouldn't even let me donate his organs." Her voice was eerily disembodied.

"What are you ranting about?" he demanded. Her strangeness grated on his already raw nerves.

"I wanted Joey to go on living," she explained patiently in her odd, other-world voice. She still hadn't looked at him. She still hadn't stopped stroking the silly animal. "No one will ever see through his eyes. No one will ever feel his heart beat. No one will ever—"

"Stop, I tell you!" Hunter commanded. "Stop!" With two long strides, he went to her. His hands gripped her shoulders. His fingers dug deep into her flesh. "No one was going to defile my son's body! Can't you understand that? Not my son! No one!" He shook her and shook her, unable to stop himself. Her unresisting body flopped limply back and forth in his hands. She seemed to welcome the pain.

"He's dead, you know," she said. "Dead, dead, dead."

He threw her down on the bed. His cold hands pressed her body into the mattress. His words came out in gasps. "Why did he have to take drugs? Why drugs?"

She stared up at him. Pity filled her eyes and stretched her mouth into a grimace. "Is that all you care about? Drugs?" Her voice took on the caustic contempt that now tinted her face a mottled pink. "You ignored him his whole life, and now you ask why he would take drugs?"

Hunter backed away from her. "You're a fool! I gave him everything! I thought of everything!"

He rushed from the room, slamming the door, but he couldn't shut out the feeling of her eyes following him down the hall.

Hurrying through the dark bedroom and into the bathroom, he stripped off his clothes and stepped into the shower, turning the cold on full blast. Tomorrow, he would formulate a plan to insulate the Presidency against attack by Grant or anyone else, he thought as icy bits of water pricked his body and brought his raging heart under control. When those plans were firmly in place, inviolate, he would have time to mourn in the worthy manner only he was capable of attaining.

At Yao's suggestion, Grant checked into a new room on a different floor of the hotel. No one knew of the change. One of Yao's operatives had made the reservation in his own name. He'd even promised to bring a copy of the *Washington Herald* articles to Grant's room as soon as the bull-dog edition was faxed to him.

Yao had friends in Washington who even now would be giving Rachel the new room number and the name it was registered under, but it would take time for her to reach a safe pay phone and call.

Grant threw his jacket on the bed and settled into the only slightly comfortable-looking chair in the room. The day had been grueling, beginning with his first speech in eastern Georgia and ending with this room change in Atlanta. He felt the weight of every catcall, of every hostile question from reporters, of every nervous glance from confused supporters. More intensely he felt the pressure of the drug charges hanging over Bailey. Joey Hunter was dead. Would Bailey now be accused as an accessory to homicide?

Grant took a deep breath, thankful that he needn't travel that dark valley alone. As he promised, the Lord would guide him. Stephen Yao, Matt Goldie, and Cynthia were proof of God's continuing care.

Operation Integrity. Grant smiled.

His Grandmama Grant would have liked that, he thought. She'd had her share of trials: one daughter sold and never seen again, one son dead of the drink he'd adopted in self-pity, her beloved husband killed in a barn fire before their small farm had become productive.

Her voice husky with age and experience, she'd woven vivid tales for Grant. She'd made him feel the tears and sweat, the mosquito bites and infected sores, the sting of the whip and strain of the mules, the blazing sun and bitter cold. But her voice itself was what Grant remembered most: the hope that underlined every word about slavery and the joy that burst forth as she recounted the years of freedom.

Big as he was, she would pull him onto her lap, and with the squeak of the rocker keeping time with her words, she would gaze out over the land she'd conquered, the land she owned, and fill him with stories and hope. She always ended with the same admonition. "Your life is what you make it, boy. Don't ever let no man tell you different. Slave or free your happiness is what's right here." She would tap her bony bosom then and give him a lavender-scented hug and soft kiss. "You do your best, no matter what; you 'fess up to the Almighty when you do wrong and do whatever needs be to make it right; you put the good Lord first in everything, giving him the glory; and you'll feel good about yourself. That's integrity, boy, being true to yourself and to God Almighty. Some'll try, but ain't no one can take that from you."

She'd died when Grant was eleven. He'd been appalled at the celebration accompanying her death: more food than he'd seen in his life, rollicking hymns sung with gusto, laughter at recounting her life, many of the stories anything but humorous.

His father, recognizing Grant's desolation, had taken him aside. "This is what your grandmama would have wanted," his father had said, his hand heavy on Grant's shoulder. "She's with her lost children now and with your grandpapa. I can remember when he died." His father's eyes had gotten a faraway look. "I felt like you, like a black hole had opened at my feet. She'd been crying, but she was laughin' and smilin', too. I couldn't understand, and that made me mad. I sure didn't feel like laughin', I can tell you!"

Grant sure hadn't felt like laughing either. He remembered looking at his father then and seeing him as a real person for the first time.

"Your grandmama took me aside like I'm doin' with you, and she said, 'Son.'" His voice had sounded oddly like hers, and Grant had felt the sting of tears against his eyes. "'Son,' she said, 'I loved your father more than life itself, almost more than it's decent for one person to love another, but God's a sight smarter than me, and he knew it was time for that good man to go home. Won't be but a winking of the eye, and I'll be taking that fiery chariot ride myself. You, too. That's what you got to remember, son. Life's short, and you got to make every minute count. Your papa was a good man, a mighty fine man, and he loved his Lord even more than he loved me or you, and that's a powerful lot. He's up there right now, sitting at his Savior's feet, enjoying the rewards for his good heart here on earth. He's just waitin' for us to join him. We got to be sure we can make a good accountin' when our time comes. That good accountin'—that's integrity, son. You don't want to feel no shame when you meet your Maker. You want to be able to stand tall and have peace in your heart.'"

His father had smiled then, a confidential, man-to-man smile. "I'm willing to bet, son," he'd said, "that you know just what I'm talking about. I'm willing to bet she made sure you knew about that fiery chariot ride and about how good your grandpapa was and about integrity."

Grant had nodded.

"Then you know why we're celebrating. Your grandmama saw more than her share of evil and heartache, but she stood tall. She had a powerful peace in her heart. Her life is worth celebrating here on earth 'cause you'd better believe the angels are having one amazing jubilation right now, with your grandpapa leading the hosannas. She's gone to the mansion her Savior's been savin' for her. She's gone home."

Grant had looked around the room. Suddenly, the singing and laughter had sounded right, and he'd joined in, singing louder and laughing longer than anyone. He'd been celebrating her life ever since, every time he remembered her words and stood tall with peace in his heart.

Yes, Grant thought, grown now and facing his own trials, Grandmama Grant would have approved of Operation Integrity.

The phone rang. He picked it up on the first ring and leaned back, his eyes closed, the better to savor Rachel's voice. He'd been blessed by the women who loved him, he thought, strong women grounded in truth, women of integrity.

"Stephen was concerned for you and the kids," Grant told her after their greetings. His eyes darkened as he remembered Yao's warning, a repeat of the one given earlier by Dashev. "From now on you'll all have protection. Cynthia, too. Agents handpicked by Stephen. They should be at Cynthia's when you return. Listen to them, Rach, and be sure the kids do, too. They're professionals. They can anticipate problems."

Using general terms and no names, he told her about his meeting. Cynthia would fill in the details the next morning when easily compromised phone lines wouldn't be necessary. "I honestly believe we can lick this," he concluded. "We couldn't have better allies, and as Henry reminded me, David slew his Goliath."

"Oh, Bob," Rachel said tremulously, "what would we do without the children? I can't bear the thought, not after Joey." Not wanting to add to his burden of concerns, she hurried on. "David and Goliath. A comforting thought, and we do have five days, don't we? And we are forewarned."

"Cynthia named it Operation Integrity," Grant told her gently. "I find that comforting."

She understood instantly. "Grandmama Grant." He had recounted the stories often, not only to her, but more importantly to the children. "Comforting, indeed. Soon we'll all be together," she ended softly, aching to feel his arms around her.

"A lot can happen in five days," Grant agreed.

He would just have to make sure it was to their benefit. He thought of his Grandmama Grant and was filled with a quiet resolve that carried its own inner peace.

Thursday, October 29:

Five Days Before the Election

Grant held the *Washington Herald* as he might a puppy's befouled training paper. Today's story turned his stomach. He was still being touted as the only possible suspect in the murder of Russell Frederickson, but that was to be expected. This was the *Herald,* after all. However, today's edition was positively vitriolic, even by the *Herald's* standards.

It all but accused Sheriff Jenks of capitulating before Grant's power as Senator. As proof, it cited the sheriff's clandestine meetings with Grant at Martha's Fabulous Diner. Each word wove another lie into the noose of Grant's guilt. Each word was a condemnation of Sheriff Jenks, his integrity, and his handling of the case.

Grant picked up the phone and dialed Jenks's home number.

"Have you seen today's *Washington Herald*?" Grant asked, his jaw clenched.

"Can't say I have," Jenks replied, "but a friend in Washington called before sunup to give me a ribbing about it."

"I'm sorry to have dragged you into Evans's vendetta against me."

"No need to get in a bother about that, Senator. As a matter of fact," the sheriff said with a chuckle, "my friend was right impressed to find my name in such a prestigious big-city publication. By the by, Martha's rung up this morning, too. Said to give you a big kiss—which I'm not about to do, mind. Fit to be tied, Martha is. All that publicity and in a Washington, D.C., paper to boot. What sticks in my craw is who let on about Martha's."

"I don't suppose we'll ever know," Grant said philosophically, relaxing under Jenks's gentle humor. "The media's like kudzu—invasive as all get out. How they know where to be to cause the most trouble is one of the unsolved mysteries of politics. That and the way they selectively decide what to report."

"Maybe so," Jenks grunted, "but I'd still like to know. Might tell us a lot."

"Did Martha mention seeing anyone hanging around out front earlier?" Grant asked.

"Nope. Only the regulars. 'Course she bit off my head for thinking she had time to keep an eye on the sidewalk. If anyone was out there, no one remembers him."

"The *Herald* didn't mention Beterman, even by inference," Grant said. "That's an odd oversight, unless they somehow discovered he could corroborate my innocence."

"They'll cut you no slack," Jenks said. "That's for sure. You mentioned Evans and a vendetta earlier, Senator. What about it? You think Evans might be behind this whole Frederickson business?"

Only days before Grant would have answered immediately with a resounding no, but that was before Frederickson, before Sergek and Pariss, before the cross burning, before Bailey and Sherrill and Reggie, before his life had assumed its present nightmarish guise, and so he carefully considered the sheriff's suggestion. Evans hated him. That was a fact. Before their confrontation in Cuba, that hatred hadn't been personal, more of a knee-jerk antipathy for any philosophy other than his own. But in Cuba, Grant had committed the unforgivable: He'd made Evans look foolish. Even Evans's access to the President had been jeopardized. That Evans's hatred was now personal was beyond doubt. Evans used every opportunity to attack him in print and in public, his goal apparently not just to discredit him but to achieve revenge by making him appear the fool. But murder? Setting up Bailey?

Grant shook his head. "It's tempting to say yes," he told the sheriff. Again he considered, and again he shook his head. "But, no. No, I can't imagine Peter Evans mounting this attack. Being used to further it, maybe. My guess is he's arrogant enough to be easily manipulated, but the mastermind? No, I don't think so."

"Not enough hatred?" the sheriff asked, trying to understand. Until he could associate Evans's mental quirks with those of people in his own periphery, the workings of Evans's mind would remain beyond his understanding. One thing Jenks knew for sure; people were the same everywhere. The key was in sifting through their pretensions to the base motives driving them. All men were prey to lust—lust for power, attention, money, possessions, fame, sex, affection, whatever. Whether a graduate of Harvard or of public housing, the lusts were the same. Only the camouflage deemed necessary in the various strata of society was different. Slowly, Jenks was gaining an understanding of the mental workings of those populating Grant's world. Frederickson's world as well, though Jenks felt more and more certain that Frederickson was an innocent who had happened to stumble into the wrong place at the wrong time. Whether he'd arrived in that wrong place through his journalistic investigations, Jenks still needed to determine. "Or does Evans have the wrong kind of hatred?" he asked.

"Probably a little of both," Grant said thoughtfully. "I think Rachel was right when she said Evans would never pull the trigger, since he could achieve the same end through his paper. To Evans, prestige is more important than life. If he can destroy my reputation, he'll feel he's achieved more than he could if he killed me outright."

"And you think that takes him out of the running," Jenks asked, "because he would hate losing face worse than dying and figures you feel the same?"

"Well put." Grant was once again struck by the strange dichotomy represented by this man. Seemingly a simple country sheriff, Jenks, in fact, had much deeper insight into the workings of man than the outwardly sophisticated Peter Evans, a possibility which Evans would have found ludicrous were he ever to entertain it.

"Poor guy," Jenks said with a sigh audible over the phone lines. "We got our share of those same kind of folks. Too good for the likes of most of us and so unhappy. Unhappy people can prove downright dangerous. Can't figure out how to get happiness for themselves and despise anyone who seems to have it. They make dangerous enemies, Senator. You'd best be careful."

"Believe me; that thought has crossed my mind," Grant said. But he didn't tell Jenks about Yao and the bodyguards. About Goldie or Dashev either. He wasn't telling anyone.

"I appreciate your calling like you did," Jenks said. Somehow he wasn't surprised at Grant's concern for his reputation. Grant viewed the world through the eyes of others. Empathy: a fine trait to have and one Evans and his cronies would never understand. "But you needn't worry," he continued. "This old Georgia cracker grew up wrestling alligators. I'm not about to give up the good fight because of a few words in some high-falutin' newspaper. I figure I must be doing something right or they'd leave me alone."

Wrestling alligators, Grant thought as he replaced the receiver. Had Jenks meant it literally? Was that the significance behind the alligator boots with their mirror-gloss polish and two-inch heels?

The phone rang.

"Do you believe the nerve of that Peter Evans?" Rachel demanded immediately. She'd been angry when she'd read the paper, but not so angry that she'd neglected to use a pay phone, a different one this time, and not so angry she'd left without taking her bodyguard. "Evans has judged and condemned you already. Sheriff Jenks, too."

"I just spoke to the sheriff," Grant told her. He recounted their conversation.

"Thank goodness he's hanging tough." Her relief sang across the wires. "If the murderer isn't caught, you've lost the election. You have to win, Bob. You need the power of the Senate to expose the truth."

"Have you heard from our Cuban friend?" Rachel would know he meant Benjamin Dashev. That was one name better left unsaid, even with the precautions they'd taken.

"No message yet. I'll get word to you as soon as I hear. Bailey thinks he's getting closer to finding Reggie, and Sherrill is hopeful of figuring out who set her up. I can't stop them hunting, but at least they've agreed to the bodyguards as long as they don't 'bug them.' So many trails to follow, Bob. Whoever's behind this has buried himself deep. Speaking of which, Cynthia and I spent last evening going over Frederickson's computer lists."

"Bailey found the second one?"

"Gosh, yes," Rachel said apologetically. "Late last night. I presumed Mike had told you. I'll fax it to Matt right away." Goldie would be sure the list reached Grant and only Grant. "Bailey said it was a real bear to break. Frederickson called it 'Pulitzer,' if you can believe it. Bailey's been working on cracking another file, the last one Frederickson entered before his death."

"Sounds promising." The last one Frederickson had used . . . The more Grant thought about it, the more interested he became.

"That's what Bailey thought," Rachel continued. "But he said not to expect too much. He's afraid someone may have caught on to him. The main access codes have been changed, so he'll have to start over from the beginning. The file may not be there anymore."

Grant's heart began hammering. "Tell Bailey to stop immediately," he said urgently, "at least until we're sure no one at the *Herald* can trace him." If the *Herald* could figure out from their end who was breaking into the computer—perhaps by tracing a phone number—Bailey might already have problems. Yao needed to be warned immediately of potential trouble, Grant decided.

"I'll tell Bailey," Rachel promised, "but he was concerned enough to get out of there right away himself. He wanted to do some research on modems and 'compute the chances of capture,' as he called it. Until he's sure it's safe, he's working on tracing Reggie."

"First thing I'm going to do when this is over," Grant told her, "is have Bailey teach me about computers. Stupid not to have done so already. Tell him to leave the *Herald* alone unless he hears from me."

"I will. Cynthia and I have been concentrating on the 'Pulitzer' list he found."

"Learn anything?" Grant asked, forcing his mind away from hidden files and changed codes.

"We may have. You know how the 'Leads' file was basically information and people negative to you?"

"Sure. Jenks hinted it might have been left deliberately by the murderer."

"'Pulitzer's' not like that at all," Rachel said. "It's full of obscure references. Bailey says the computer date indicates Frederickson was working on it the day he died, or at least that someone opened it to read that day. Apparently, there's no easy way of telling what was added when. Anyway, Cynthia and I divided everything into two lists: people or events we could positively identify—there are surprisingly few if Frederickson was using it for notes about your campaign—and those that are total unknowns. Then we tried figuring out some of the unknowns. Does A. Peabody mean anything to you?"

"Peabody," Grant said slowly. "That name . . ."

"What about *Anne* Peabody?"

"Of course!" Grant exclaimed, sitting upright, his eyes alive with speculation. "The woman who brought down our President."

During the height of the last presidential campaign, Anne Peabody, a senior vice president at a large New York investment firm, had been directed by a Saudi sheik to move a substantial sum of money from his personal account into another, an account she inadvertently learned belonged to the incumbent President's blind trust. The proper authorities had been notified. Since the President hadn't reported the cash as a gift, it had been declared a bribe. The President, swearing no knowledge of any money, much less a bribe, lost the election nonetheless, largely because his character had been clouded by the accusation. Almost immediately after his inauguration, the newly elected President declared in a national television address that, regardless of personal consequences, he was going to pardon his predecessor. The nation, he'd pronounced gravely, must be saved from the devastating impact of a trial.

The whole sequence of events, including the fortuitous discovery of the money so close to the election, had bothered Grant at the time. Without a trial, the former President would forever be perceived as the man who had sold his country for a few pieces of silver. He'd died a short time later, a death attributed by many, including the majority of the media, to a guilty conscience.

"Anne Peabody's dead," Rachel said, "killed the day before Frederickson."

"What!"

"A mugging in Central Park."

"Talk about coincidence!"

"It gets even better. Cynthia talked to Anne Peabody's secretary. Frederickson called her the day she died. They were supposed to have met the next morning."

"This could be the break we've been looking for," Grant said. "I've got to talk to her coworkers today, before someone else gets to them. There has to be some vital connection between Frederickson and Peabody, maybe even the motive for Frederickson's murder."

They made plans. Grant would contact Matt Goldie and leave for New York as soon as a plane could be readied.

"Oh," Rachel said as Grant was ready to hang up, "I almost forgot. Cynthia wants you to turn on the TV and do some debate prep. Caruso is making the rounds of the morning news shows. The national ones, would you believe."

"And I'm rotten while Caruso is the savior of Georgia, I'll bet."

"You got it."

"Tell Cynthia thanks, but I think I'll pass."

"That's what I bet her you'd say," Rachel said with a laugh as she hung up.

I still don't understand all this secrecy," Mike Masterson told Grant fretfully. Masterson was mad. First, Grant had shown up early at his room for their morning briefing, not waited in his own for Masterson, as was customary. Then he'd dropped a complete change of schedule in Masterson's lap without so much as a question about his opinion. That on top of everything yesterday! "First you meet with that hick sheriff—"

"He's not a 'hick sheriff,'" Grant interrupted. "You would be wise to remember that."

"Maybe not," Masterson said, not sounding much mollified, "but I don't like relying on him when your future is at stake, and not just your political future either. You've canceled today's events, and now here you are sneaking off to who-knows-where when your campaign is crumbling around you."

"You think anyone would have attended those events, anyone but the media?" Grant asked, wondering what Masterson's blood pressure would have done had he known about the room change last night. "And *they* sure wouldn't be looking for a favorable story."

Masterson made no response to this obvious truth.

"Would you feel better if you knew my plans?" Grant asked.

Masterson glared at him. "I'm your press secretary, aren't I?" He grabbed a bag of potato chips and ripped it open. That and a can of pop were his usual breakfast. "How can I cover for you if I don't know anything?"

"Do you remember the scandal about the former President?" Grant asked. Masterson's icy belligerence slowly melted as Grant gave a sketchy explanation, carefully avoiding specifics, even about the city.

"But surely you don't think Frederickson and that bribery are connected?" Masterson exclaimed. "The bribery's ancient history! Besides, Justice checked into it thoroughly. You can't play detective and still expect to salvage your campaign." He crumpled the empty chip bag and threw it into the corner. "We only have five days. The overnight tracking polls are a disaster. Who can you see who'll have enough impact on the campaign to justify the time?"

"While I'm gone," Grant said, ignoring his question, "I want you to set up a meeting in Atlanta with as many of these supporters as you can." He handed Masterson a handwritten list of thirty-five names. "Make it for first thing tomorrow morning, the moment I return. Caution them to keep the meeting quiet. I don't want any media nosing around."

Masterson was taking a last swallow of pop as Grant left the room. Grant heard the can thud against the carpet by the door only moments after he closed it.

Everything was beginning to get to Masterson, Grant thought as he took the stairs up to his room. Scandals and low poll figures tended to have that effect on press secretaries.

Jenks fingered the memo neatly centered on his desk. The federal jack-asses, under the signature of Attorney General Jonathan Hunter, no less, demanded that all files on the Grant investigation be turned over no later than 5 P.M. that day. At that time Jenks's participation would be terminated.

The Grant investigation! Jenks fumed. Had they forgotten that Frederickson was the murdered man?

He stood and strode into the hall, sending off thunderbolts of anger with every step of his alligator boots.

"Where's Bender?" he demanded of the first NIIA agent he encountered.

The man jerked his thumb toward the main conference room. Jenks stormed into the room unannounced.

Bender's head jerked up from the papers he was studying. "What do you mean barging in—"

"Planning to horn in on my investigation, are you?" Jenks demanded, throwing the memo down on the table. "I got news for you. It's not going to happen."

Bender surged to his feet, as angry as Jenks. "You try to interfere with a federal investigation, and I'll see you in jail!"

"Just try!" Jenks looked like a brown-clad mountain ready to erupt. Deliberately stretching to his full height, he towered over Bender, who'd never before felt physically inferior to anyone. "I checked the NIIA statutes, Bender. All you can do is offer your help. You can't supplant me. No federal laws have been broken."

Bender regarded him from under hooded eyes. His face was flushed an ugly red. "All laws are federal in nature now, Jenks." He tapped the memo. "This says 5 P.M. I'd be ready if I were you. Jonathan Hunter signed it, and you'd better believe he'll get just what he wants."

It was Jenks's turn to regard the other man thoughtfully. "Right interesting concept of justice" was all he said as he left the room.

Jenks grinned to himself as he remembered Bender's apoplectic reaction to his declaration of independence and wondered what their next move would be. Certainly, there would be one. He sat down behind his desk to wait.

As he'd done every morning since Frederickson's murder, he leaned back in his chair and perused the *Washington Herald.* The story was just as bad as Bob Grant had intimated. Jenks's jaw hardened. He hated any aspersions on his integrity. A man's integrity took years to develop but could be destroyed overnight, its fragile fabric violated by even the whisper of misconduct. The *Washington Herald* believed in integrity-shattering screams.

He'd barely finished the article—and his fuming—when the NIIA fired its next shot. Judge Josiah Jackson—how the judge loved that alliteration at election time!—was on the line. Apparently, the good ol' boys, or some variation, had gotten to the judge.

"Hear you're hanging on to the Grant investigation," Judge Jackson began, his voice chummy. "Never knew you to be a media hound, Sheriff. Have to say I'm surprised, unpleasantly surprised at that."

Jenks made no response. He'd gotten one goat that day with Bender. Might as well try for another.

"This is a federal case, Sheriff, involving a United States Senator," Jackson continued, every bit of friendliness dried up and blown away. "It is my considered legal opinion that the NIIA has every right to take charge of this case. Surely you can see that."

"What I can see," Jenks said with drawn-out deliberation, "is that you've sold yourself and your opinion. Makes me right sad, unpleasantly sad at that."

Jackson didn't answer immediately, and when he did, anger seethed in every word. "You're a stubborn jackass, Jimmy Jenks. Whether you like it or not, the NIIA will take over the case. You might as well make it easy on everyone and give them your full cooperation. No one can buck the feds."

"Fine sentiment, Judge, mighty fine," Jenks said softly. "Cain't help wondering just what it cost them to get it."

He replaced the receiver soundlessly. Integrity was fragile, Jenks thought sadly. The judge must figure reelection was, too, or maybe he hankered for a ticket to a higher court and figured the NIIA could take him to that dance.

Regardless of what anyone ordered, Jenks decided, they'd have to haul him to jail kicking and screaming before he'd allow a man, any man, to be railroaded. He might be forced to work with the NIIA, but he sure enough wouldn't bow down to them.

His direct line rang. It was Bob Grant.

"Give me your number and a couple of minutes," Jenks said, reaching for his hat and jacket, "and I'll get right back to you." He took time to stuff duplicate files on the Frederickson case, as well as his working notes, into a grocery sack and to put the whole bundle into a bag he used for church league basketball. He was a referee. No one disputed his calls.

Jenks had made the duplicate files the night before, hoping he was wasting time but knowing he had no choice. He wasn't about to do anything illegal or unethical—he enforced even those laws he found incomprehensible—but that was one advantage he had: The NIIA was so new that its statutes were vague and untested. Better to err on the side of broad interpretation than to genuflect to their whims. No wonder the Founding Fathers had been so set against a national police force, he thought as he zipped the bag. The sound carried a feeling of finality.

"Be back in a minute," he told his secretary.

Bypassing the pay phones in the corridor as well as the nearest ones on the street, he turned instead into an old red-brick hardware store around the corner and down one block.

"Got a place you can keep this?" he asked the owner, taking out the grocery sack.

With a quizzical look, the wizened old man, a family friend of Jenks's father, slipped the bag under the counter.

"You might consider some place a tad less accessible," Jenks suggested.

"Like that, is it?" his friend asked with a wheezy chuckle. He picked up the bag. With a backward look out his cluttered front window to be sure he was unobserved, he headed for the storage room. "Won't interest anybody much if I put it in a box behind some supplies."

"Thanks, Gus. Mind if I use your phone?"

"Really up to no good, aren't you?" Gus said, grinning broadly and inclining his head toward the back office. Affection beamed from behind his wire-rimmed trifocals.

Grant picked up on the first ring.

Jenks told him about the NIIA's interest in the case. He didn't tell him about the duplicate files.

"Can you hold them off until you find the murderer?" Grant asked.

"Can't decide if that's the way to go or not," Jenks told him. He eyed the battered desk, wondering if he dared put his feet on it. Hard to think with them on the ground. "I might just give them their head to see which way they go." With an inward shrug Jenks swung his legs up. A contented smile curved his lips as he leaned back and eyed the intricate if brown-tinged pattern in the pressed tin ceiling. "Might give me an idea of why they're so almighty concerned with hanging you. Could it be that speech you gave last year, blasting the formation of the NIIA? You pulled no punches about the threat of a national police force. Almost convinced Congress, too. Think that's why the NIIA's so all-fired against you?"

"The NIIA?" Grant asked, considering. "Probably not. They weren't even around then. But Hunter? Maybe. I'm beginning to think his involvement is much too personal for comfort."

"Not much we can do about that, is there?" Jenks asked. "Might even say he's my boss," he added with a chuckle. "Sure seems to think he is anyhow. Anything new I should know?"

"Mainly, I'm calling to ask a favor. Several, actually."

"Fire away, Senator. Then we'll see."

"First, I'm hoping you can get your hands on some information. How did the police know about the drugs at Andrew Stoner's? Why was a police captain—his name is Fleming—sent to investigate a routine college party, a police captain who knew I was a Senator without being told? Coincidentally, how did the media know immediately that my son was involved? Why was Bailey taken to jail and kept there even though charges have yet to be brought against him?"

Jenks raised an eyebrow. His right boot tapped against his left in the rhythm of his thinking. Sending a captain? Held but no charges? Whole thing sounded downright strange. *If* Grant had gotten it right, he reminded himself. His foot stilled as the Senator continued.

"Also," Grant said, his voice in the cataloging mode of someone reading from a list, "why did the police keep the attorney general's son out of the reports? Was it purely political? If so, we can eliminate that loose end. If not . . ." He shrugged. "I'm betting it was at least partially political. Cover-up would be a reflex response. Public perception is important to them. To be fair, I would have done the same to keep Bailey's name out of it."

"Change medical records?" Jenks asked, sounding interested if surprised.

"No," Grant admitted, "not that. But keep his name away from the media? You'd better believe it! I tried my best to do just that."

"That's natural, Senator. The other isn't. Not legal either." All deaths caused by illegal drug use were required to be reported to the public health service and the federal marshal.

The old desk chair creaked as Jenks looked down at the notes he'd been taking. Already he was running names through his mind, considering who could best supply the information. "I'll see what I can do."

"Another thing," Grant said. "Bailey was able to tap into Frederickson's computer at the *Herald.*"

Jenks frowned. He slapped the notepad against his leg in frustration. He should have thought of that himself. Dang newfangled machines! *Learn about computers,* he wrote on his list. He bracketed the words with stars for emphasis.

"Bailey found one file easily," Grant continued. "Frederickson called it 'Leads.' That the one you found?"

"Sure is," Jenks agreed. He didn't expand.

"Bailey also found a file Frederickson called 'Pulitzer.'" Grant paused but continued when he realized Jenks wasn't planning to respond. "Said Frederickson had it well protected. Bailey thinks there may be another file as well, entered the day Frederickson died. I told him to back off—apparently the *Herald* realized someone was hacking into their system. Anyway, Rachel and Cynthia went over the 'Pulitzer' printout last evening. They noticed the name A. Peabody on it. Mean anything to you?"

"Can't say it does," Jenks said thoughtfully. He wrote *A. PEABODY* in caps on the pad, right under *PULITZER.* "Should it?"

"I can't be sure, but an Anne Peabody was the Wall Street account executive who accused our former President of accepting a bribe."

"And caused his defeat, according to more than a few folks," Jenks said, his pencil tapping the paper. "You just might have something there."

"Anne Peabody was murdered the day before Frederickson, a random mugging supposedly."

"Jumping Jehosophat!" Jenks exclaimed, underlining *PEABODY* with two broad strokes. "Any proof she's the one Frederickson meant?"

"Cynthia talked to Peabody's secretary. Frederickson called Peabody the day she died and made an appointment to meet with her the next morning. I'd like to go to New York to interview her coworkers, if you'll agree to it."

Jenks was quiet. Grant leaving the state—Bender would be madder than a hornet. Jenks grinned. The chair creaked its protest as he leaned back farther, the better to savor the image. "Sounds reasonable to me, as long as you fill me in down to the dust on Peabody's desk. Soon as you get back, too."

"Certainly," Grant agreed. "Every speck."

"This bit of information might make your flight a tad more pleasant," Jenks told him, having decided today was right for imparting a bit of quid pro quo. "The Pariss letter is a forgery. A good one, but a for-sure forgery."

Jenks smiled at Grant's loud "Had to be."

"And the diary?" Grant asked.

"No time yet for a full workup, but they're nigh onto positive the handwriting was hers and written over a long period of time. Almost five years, they're figuring. I should hear for certain this afternoon. That and what I'm expectin' li'l Miss Sergek to let loose should make for one fine press conference this evening. Maybe give us both a little breathing room."

"Maybe," Grant said, "but given the last few days, the only change I expect is in the direction of the attack." Jenks heard an airplane engine start up in the background. "Got to go," Grant said. "I'll be in touch."

Jenks folded his hands on his stomach and stared at the ceiling, enjoying the anonymity of his friend's cramped, dark office. He considered Grant's conversation. Slowly, a smile crinkled his eyes. If the Senator's enemies expected him to take their assaults without a whimper, they were in for a surprise. So was ol' Bender.

Only four days since he'd met the Senator, a man whose career he'd followed with a respect only slightly tinged with the skepticism of one politician for another. He couldn't recall many folks who had Grant's gumption. Four days wasn't long, but long enough to get the measure of a man.

More important than those four days were the five left until the election. Jenks lifted his boots from the desk, slammed the front legs of the chair down on the floor, and reached for the phone. Time to hook into the Bubba network again. He would call a D.C. friend he'd shared more than a few cups of coffee with at a law enforcement conference a few years back—see what he knew about this Captain Fleming who believed in personal appearances at college parties. Maybe his friend would know someone hooked into the Peabody murder as well.

Another murder, Jenks thought, his mouth tightening. A darn sight too many murders to his way of thinking.

Sherrill Holmes and Bailey Grant were discovering one of the more frustrating sides of detective work, the elimination of possibilities. They were canvassing old apartment buildings in the vicinity where Bear thought he'd seen Reggie Dixon. "In the vicinity" were the operative words because the first four buildings Bear had pinpointed had turned up zilch. No one admitted to ever having seen Reggie Dixon or anyone resembling him.

The night before, Sherrill had cajoled an art student friend into sketching a portrait of Reggie. The likeness was good. Bailey felt confident they were getting honest responses.

"I'm beginning to wonder if we'd even know if someone were lying," Sherrill said as they trudged up the sloping limestone steps of the last of Bear's old apartment buildings.

"That's where my little gray cells come in," Bailey said in an exaggerated parody of Hercules Poirot. He twirled his imaginary mustache with panache. "Stick with me, my little chickadee, and we'll unmask the villain, n'est-ce pas?" His eyebrow lifted above a devilish smirk.

"Hercules Poirot and W. C. Fields?" Sherrill said, raising her own eyebrow.

"Brains and humor: What more could you want?"

He burst into laughter at her look of mock derision, amazed as always at how good it felt to be with her. Then he remembered her betrayal, and his high spirits evaporated as if under a sudden cold shower. Would he ever be able to forget? His eyes clouded as he looked across the street at the dark blue sedan carrying their shadows. Ramon was a good guy with a great sense of humor. Tommy was even cooler. They tried to keep in the background, but as reminders of Sherrill's part in it all, they couldn't be more obvious.

Without another word, Bailey opened the heavy oak door to the brownstone. Sherrill followed, her eyes on the floor. She couldn't bear seeing the slump of his shoulders, knowing she was the cause. Resolutely, she straightened her back and forced a smile onto her lips. It wasn't easy, heaven knew, but she was determined to make amends.

As in the other buildings, they finished their questioning quickly. Most people were at work or in class.

They were about to admit defeat when a bearded young man, khaki book bag slung over his shoulder, came in from outside. Bailey showed him the sketch.

"Don't know him," he said after a cursory glance, "but you might try one of those buildings the next street down, second or third one in. Seems like I saw him hanging out around there."

His suggestion proved more helpful than Bear's. According to the scrawled name above a mailbox, Reggie Dixon did indeed live there in apartment 3C. No one answered their buzz. Bailey started to turn away. Instead, realizing the vestibule was empty and feeling infinitely foolish, he took out a credit card, inserted it above the lock, and pulled it carefully down, a trick he'd seen on TV.

His mouth dropped in disbelief as the door swung open. "It worked!" he exclaimed, pushing Sherrill inside and soundlessly closing the door behind them. Eyes flashing with excitement, he surveyed the hallway, then raced up the stairs to the third floor.

Reggie had left and in a hurry, they found when they pushed open the unlocked door. Except for the predictable litter, the room was empty.

"Well, so much for this great idea," Sherrill said despondently.

Bailey stooped to retrieve a wad of papers from under the dresser. He smoothed them and nodded in satisfaction. "Some bills and"—he turned a piece over—"even some writing on the back. Pick up whatever you can. Anything with writing on it. Maybe we'll get lucky. Then let's get out of here."

Sherrill was filling her pockets before he finished speaking. Four minutes later they were out on the sidewalk, grinning and giving each other a high five which Ramon and Tommy couldn't fail to see.

A man in the apartment building across the street saw it as well.

Jonathan Hunter walked into the morning briefing in the Oval Office a few minutes late. That wasn't unusual. He was a busy man. But today, for the first time in memory, he'd overslept. After a night of sleeplessness filled with plans for the White House, Hunter had finally fallen into a tossing sea of sweating gray nothingness.

He'd awakened disoriented and empty. His head throbbed, a blow that was repeated and repeated, as if a bizarre metronome of pain had been implanted in his brain. Struggling against it, he'd dressed and left, never looking for his wife. He'd consigned her and her wicked tongue to the same purgatory he'd prescribed for the son who had betrayed him.

Now, here in the Oval Office, Hunter felt as if he'd come home. Only vaguely aware of his colleagues' murmured condolences, he looked around the room. His eyes moved hungrily from the massive mahogany desk to the ceiling-high doors leading to the Rose Garden, from the inaugural portrait of the President resting in a gilt frame on the mantel to the crackling fire beneath it. They stopped at a collection of photographs on the far wall. A picture of himself with the President held a place of honor.

Hunter felt the tension of the last day slowly recede. This was where he belonged. Here his power was absolute.

"I appreciate your concern," he said finally, pulling himself back to the present. "I'm fine. Really," he added, seeing Corforth's look. Skepticism and pain. What was Corforth up to now?

"The funeral," the President said, his brow furrowed with concern. "Can we do anything?"

"No. Rebecca has set it for tomorrow at 4:00. A private service with calling tonight. You're still going to Georgia tomorrow, aren't you?" he asked, staring at the President. "Grant must be destroyed. He killed my son. He wants to take the presidency from us."

All eyes regarded him warily. No one was certain how to react to these statements, delivered as they were in tones devoid of emotion.

"My only concern," said the President, his voice tentative, "is that I won't be able to attend Joey's funeral if it's held in the afternoon."

Hunter looked thoughtful. "You must attend both, of course." He seemed in all ways the same decisive figure so feared by those around him. "I'll tell Rebecca the funeral will be at 11:00, the only possible solution. Now what do you need to insure the success of the Georgia trip?"

The discussion was productive. Edmund Miller, who was overseeing the rally, had it well organized. Hunter, however, made several perceptive suggestions. Hunter held the reins of power firmly in hand. Even his son's death had been unable to lessen their pull.

Bob Grant didn't get to New York often, but the city never failed to fascinate him. How so many people could thrive in an environment of wall-to-wall bodies, ground-to-sky sun-blocking buildings, throngs of beggars, outrageous taxes, and bizarre laws was a mystery to him. The city was invigorating with its understated excitement and single-minded purpose, but he would be relieved to return to the calm familiarity of his own world.

Calm familiarity! Grant threw back his head and laughed aloud at the absurdity of the thought, but no one seemed to notice. Maybe they were too intent on their own business, too self-absorbed. Or maybe it was merely the physical need to elude as quickly as possible the sharp wind bringing with it bites of winter unsure whether to become snow or sleet. Whichever, they ignored everything. Rachel had been right; he didn't need a disguise. Here he was one of the anonymous many.

Grant left the cavern of skyscrapers which was Wall Street for the sterile modernity of Anne Peabody's office building. Her secretary, setting large-framed red glasses atop her nose, read the Senate Ethics Committee form which Cynthia had prepared. It asked for complete cooperation in any matter concerning Miss Peabody or her dealings as they concerned the President's account, the sheik's account, or Russell Frederickson.

"Well, you're none too soon," the secretary—Julie, according to her nameplate—told Grant. She removed her glasses and regarded him with open curiosity. She refrained from asking questions, however. "Tomorrow Miss Peabody's accounts will be given to someone else. The only question is who. Why don't you come with me?" She led the way into the inner office. Before she closed the door, she glanced over her shoulder, frowning at a figure receding in the distance.

The modern and obviously expensive furnishings of Anne Peabody's office were overshadowed by the magnificent view of New York harbor, which shimmered through the wall of windows behind the desk.

"Pretty spectacular, isn't it?" Julie asked rhetorically, an enraptured smile lighting her dark features. "Miss Peabody was moved up here over a year ago because she had important friends in Washington. At least that was the rumor."

"Is that so?" Grant asked, grateful for this entrée to what had to be a touchy topic. "Like the President, you mean?"

"She wanted everyone to believe she was his right-hand confidante," Julie agreed, "though I never knew her to talk to him. I did place a call to

Attorney General Hunter the day she died, and he accepted it right away. She knew some of the right people, but not nearly as well as she let on. She went to college with Attorney General Hunter's sister or brother or something."

"Do you know why she called him?" Grant asked, his mind racing as he considered this highly interesting piece of information.

"No," she admitted, moving from the window to the desk, "but she had me call her lawyer, Craig C. Flannery, right afterward; and when she finished talking to him, she had me call Russell Frederickson, the reporter who died, you know." She stopped abruptly, embarrassed as she realized that Grant might know all too well. "Anyway," she hurried on, "Miss Peabody had me make an appointment with Mr. Frederickson for the next day. He came, but she wasn't here. That was a weird morning, let me tell you. We'd just heard about Miss Peabody's death when Mr. Frederickson arrived—two hours early, of all things."

"Did he say what he wanted?"

The young woman hesitated.

"Too many questions?" Grant asked with a rueful smile.

She didn't respond, but Grant thought he detected an amused glint in her eye. "You've been most kind to answer my questions so far," he said. "You must know I'm the number-one suspect in Russell Frederickson's murder."

She nodded, her face expressionless but her curiosity obvious. He was dressed in a well-cut navy suit which hung on his tall frame with comfortable familiarity. His tie was conservative stripes; his shirt, white Egyptian cotton; his plain leather shoes, polished to a brilliant black shine. His face, always attractive, had acquired the lines and shadows of experience.

"I didn't kill him, Julie," Grant said. His eyes as they held hers were weary but filled with a quiet confidence. "But my family is being destroyed by that accusation and all the others being leveled against me. I don't know if Miss Peabody's murder has anything to do with the rest, but the Senate committee asked me to check. If I can find just one clue . . ." He let the rest of the sentence hang, counting on her inquisitiveness if nothing else to make her receptive.

"I suppose I shouldn't even have let you in the office," Julie said, tucking a strand of black hair behind her ear as she continued eyeing him, "even if you do have that paper. They'd kick you out if they knew you were here." Her glance slid away from him and toward the closed door. "'This

233

firm avoids all unpleasant publicity.'" This last was an obvious parody, humorously accurate if Grant were to guess. "You can imagine how much they liked having a senior member murdered, even if it was a mugging." She raised her eyes to his. "It was a mugging, wasn't it?"

"I don't know," Grant said. He regarded her with increased respect. "I'm beginning to wonder."

"That makes things even worse. I didn't like Miss Peabody and hated myself for feeling that way, but she didn't deserve to be murdered." She continued to scrutinize Grant, as if trying to read in his face the chapter entitled "The Truth." "I don't know exactly why I'm trying to help you except I've never liked to see people being kicked when they're down. According to the news, you and your family have done nothing but suffer for the last few days. I can't help wondering if that much bad could happen to one family in such a short time without some outside help. Besides," she said, grinning, "wait till my boyfriend hears. He says your voting record is one of the best in the Senate."

"Tell him thanks," Grant said, blessing her curious soul, skeptical mind, and politically attuned boyfriend. Her inspection was at an end, and judging by the hint of compassion in her eyes, he had passed. "I don't want you to break any confidences," he said, "but I would certainly appreciate your help. We think Russell Frederickson's murder might have something to do with Miss Peabody."

"You mean that business with the former President and the bribe?"

Grant's heart started racing. "Any particular reason for mentioning the bribe?"

"Just that Miss Peabody was studying all the records on the sheik's account that day. I saw them on her desk."

"Before or after her call to the attorney general?"

"After the call from the reporter, but before she talked to Attorney General Hunter. Here," she said taking a key from her pocket, "I'll take a look at the file."

She unlocked the lower right drawer, took out a file, and put it on the desk. With practiced skill, she flipped through the pages. "That's odd," she said, a crease forming between her brows. "I thought the file was thicker." She flipped to the front. Her eyes got big. "The index is missing!"

"But you're pretty sure some of the file's missing?" Grant asked, leaning closer. He watched as she slowly went back through it.

"Without the index, I can't be sure," she admitted, "but I thought there was more. I'm sorry I can't let you look at the file—company policy, you know." She shrugged.

"I understand," he told her, his deep voice heavy with gratitude. "You've been extraordinarily kind as it is. Did Frederickson seem interested in the file?"

"That was the first thing he asked about," Julie told him. "What had been done with it. When I—"

Without warning, the door to the office flew open and hit the wall.

Three men, their faces hard and unsmiling, strode in. The man in the lead stopped at the desk, put his fists on it, and leaned toward them. He was a powerful man used to getting his way.

"What do you think you're doing, Grant?" he demanded.

Grant returned his look but didn't answer.

"Who are you?" Julie asked. She looked confused but far from intimidated.

The man ignored her. "Get away from that desk, both of you, and you—get out of here." He looked at Julie, jerking his thumb toward the door.

"But—"

"Now!"

With a backward glance at Grant, she left the room.

"Now, Grant," the man continued, "why don't you tell me what you're up to?"

Instead of answering, Grant walked toward the door. "You can't cover up murder," he said.

"Not so fast!" The man grabbed Grant's arm. "You're not leaving until I know you're not taking anything."

"Don't touch me," Grant growled through clenched teeth. He threw off the restraining hand. "I'm leaving."

"I have probable cause to believe you're removing evidence from this office," the man said mechanically as he flashed an NIIA badge and identification.

Derek Bender, a top gun in the NIIA, Grant saw. Well, well, well. And Bender'd been in Georgia a short time before, according to Jenks.

"I can search you here or at headquarters," Bender said. "It's your call."

"Forget that, Bender," Grant retorted, moving toward the door. "I'm a United States Senator on official business. I have immunity."

Bender started to speak, but Grant wouldn't let him.

"How is it, Bender, that you're even here? You have no open investigation into Anne Peabody's murder. It's a mugging, remember?"

With this parting shot, he walked from the room.

"We're watching you, Grant," Bender snapped before the door closed.

Join the club, Grant thought with grim humor. Even so he knew he'd made an enemy of the NIIA investigator.

Out of the corner of his eye, Grant saw two men pull quickly into a doorway. His shadows? He'd have to shake them and any other surveillance before he made his next call.

Julie was standing in the hall in conversation with several other women. They stopped talking and silently watched as Grant entered the elevator. As the doors closed, blocking them from view, Julie winked.

He'd learned little he hadn't already surmised, but now he was convinced Anne Peabody had been deliberately murdered and that her murder was connected to the accusations against him. He also had a disturbing feeling that the White House was involved. Why else would Anne Peabody have called Hunter? Was the administration the source of the power and money being used against him? The thought was chilling.

A more immediate question: How had the NIIA known he would be there? He'd told no one but Rachel, Cynthia, Jenks, and Yao. Mike knew generalities but no details. Was the NIIA's arrival mere coincidence, having to do with Anne Peabody rather than himself? If so, had the NIIA stripped Peabody's file of any damaging information—assuming Julie was right about its diminished size? But that didn't explain Bender, so recently in Georgia. The stakes must be high if the NIIA was involved. High, too, to bring Derek Bender out in person.

Remembering Julie's conspiratorial wink, Grant had a feeling he'd be hearing more from that young woman. He hoped so. Maybe Frederickson's questions of her would explain the motive for the murder. Grant was more convinced than ever that the reporter had discovered what he himself needed to discover. Little more than four days remained to do it, he thought, his step unconsciously quickening. Yao fell in behind, but at an unobtrusive distance.

Grant had been right about the NIIA tails. They, too, fell into place.

Jonathan Hunter was consumed by thoughts of the presidency. For the past two years, he'd spent every waking hour similarly occupied. Some unkind wags suggested that even his sleep wasn't immune. Hunter wouldn't allow the mere inconvenience of something as mundane as sleep to interfere with his profound thoughts, they were wont to say.

Hunter himself might have agreed. Amassing power and more power was the nectar that nourished the soul. Few men recognized its necessity. Fewer still had inhaled the intoxication of its fragrance. He alone sipped it at will. Waking or sleeping, no more tempting satiation could be afforded any man. No one could be allowed to wrest that pleasure from him.

When Bender called, Hunter listened. His eyes became thoughtful. "Grant was in Anne Peabody's office?" he asked, slowly sinking into his chair. "What did he want?"

Hunter sat motionless. Only his dark eyes moved, darting in their black-smudged sockets, like feral animals unwillingly caged.

"Grant must have been trying to plant evidence for some scheme he's concocted to clear himself," Hunter declared when Bender finished speaking. "He'd better not succeed."

Again, he listened.

"You listen to me, Bender," he interrupted. His voice had a deceptive calm. "You say Bailey Grant can't be arrested with what we have now. Then you'd better find some evidence so he can. You say Grant is nosing around Anne Peabody's office, trying to interfere with a murder investigation. Figure out what he's up to, and you'll have the motive for Frederickson's murder. I won't have you undermining my administration because of your lack of focus on the facts. Think, Bender! And remember who you're talking to. If you don't, I'll find someone who will."

He slammed down the receiver and sank back into his chair. He had much to do if he hoped to salvage the mess Bender was making. He couldn't trust anyone else to make the right decisions. Too much was at stake. As always, his hands would be the ones holding the reins.

Cynthia had given Grant the name of the officer in charge of the Peabody murder investigation, and after a tortuous detour to lose his tail, Grant went to the appropriate precinct station. He was kept waiting for almost half an hour before being escorted to Sergeant Alvarez's desk.

Alvarez ignored Grant's introduction and his outstretched hand, and instead doodled on a scratch pad.

"I know who you are," he finally said, throwing down the pencil. His tone left no doubt how little he liked what he'd heard. "If you expect me to spill my guts about Peabody, you're wasting your time. Muggings are a dime a dozen."

"What makes you think I'm here about Miss Peabody?" Grant asked, matching Alvarez's cool with his own.

The sergeant looked momentarily nonplussed. "Well, why don't you enlighten me, Senator Grant?" He emphasized the *Senator*. "Why *are* you here?"

"Anne Peabody," Grant said with a self-mocking smile.

Alvarez just stared at him, his brown eyes stony in his swarthy face.

"Was there anything about the mugging that seemed unusual?" Grant asked after a prolonged silence. "Anything that pointed to a deliberate murder?"

"Senator, we're talking mugging here. You think we don't have enough random violence not to recognize it? Mugging, Senator. *Comprende?* This was a mugging. That's all."

"Any witnesses?"

"Witnesses, Senator? You think New Yorkers stand around a stiff waiting to sign a statement, maybe?"

"So no witness?" Grant persisted.

To answer, Alvarez stood and looked toward the door. "I got my hands full working on solvable cases," he told Grant. He leaned on the stack of files on his desk. "Why don't you leave this alone, Senator? We'd both be a lot happier."

Grant left but not before he recognized the doodles on the sergeant's pad. *NIIA*. And Alvarez had carefully avoided answering his question about a witness.

After a quick but unproductive stop at Andrew's apartment, Bailey and Sherrill drove to Cynthia's, where they gave Bailey's mother the papers from Reggie Dixon's apartment. She was going through them now. Advertisements, some months old, scribbled notes, and bills, lots of bills, all unpaid, comprised the lot. A telephone bill, last month's, as well as jotted telephone numbers, looked the most promising. Bailey would do a computer search for those Rachel couldn't identify with a cross-reference directory.

First though, Sherrill and he were paying a visit on Frances Sandborne. Sandborne was the professor who had recruited Sherrill to set up Bailey. "Beard the lion in its den," Bailey had said, only half in jest. Radical feminists unnerved him. They bridled at common courtesy, labeling it demeaning, and treated equality as insufficient. He would rather face twenty Reggie Dixons than one Frances Sandborne any day.

"You should let me talk to her alone," Sherrill told him when they got in the car. "She'll never let anything slip if you're there. She doesn't like men and hates you."

"You're not going alone," Bailey said with finality.

No one answered Sherrill's knock, but they could hear music filtering through the door. She gave Bailey a questioning look, then knocked again. A brief but agonizing wait was followed by the slow opening of the door.

A petite brunette in a shocking pink leotard stood framed in the opening. Sweat glistened on the finely contoured muscles of her body as she leaned with studied grace against the door.

"Oh, it's you," the diminutive woman said. She started to close the door, shrugged, and threw it open. Her ponytail in its shocking pink fastener bounced as she turned. "Frannie!" she yelled over the sound of the exercise tape. "Sherrill Holmes is here."

They heard footsteps, and then Frances Sandborne stood before them. Cora Snyder seemed to gain pleasure from Sandborne's start of surprise at the sight of Bailey.

Frances Sandborne was big, almost six feet, Bailey supposed, and what his grandmother had called rawboned. Despite her aggressive physique, she obviously deferred to the other woman.

"Hello, Dr. Sandborne," Sherrill said. She stepped inside, and Bailey followed close behind. "I'd like for you to meet Bailey, Bailey Grant."

No one spoke. Bailey reached behind and closed the door. The click of the lock resounded loudly, even above the sound of the tape.

"I've been wanting to meet you," he said when no one spoke. "I understand you've been taking an active interest in my life."

Sandborne was suddenly galvanized into life. She poked her finger threateningly toward Bailey's chest. "Get out! You don't belong here! Get out! Out! Out! Out!"

"I don't belong here?" Bailey asked, his tone tempered with the tightness of anger. His eyes flashed. "You've tried to destroy my life, and now you say I don't belong here? Think again. I'm not leaving until I know who had you set me up."

"Ignore him, Frannie," her friend cautioned. "I don't believe we've been introduced, Mr. Grant." She sneered the *Mr.* "I'm Cora Snyder, Frannie's lifemate. Dr. Snyder to you, Mr. Grant." Again the sneer. She picked up a towel and began wiping herself, holding Bailey's eyes as she extravagantly massaged the tops of her voluptuous white breasts. Sandborne watched her as well. The tension mounted. Bailey sensed his advantage slipping from him.

"Cut it out, Cora." Sherrill's voice snapped the tension.

Cora grinned at her.

"Nobody's interested in your body," Sherrill said tartly.

Cora gave a throaty laugh. "You're wrong there." She continued drying herself, but the provocation had left her movements. Only Frances Sandborne continued to watch the progress of her hands.

"Dr. Sandborne," Sherrill said, moving slightly to the side in an attempt to draw the woman's eyes toward her, "I have a right to know what's going on. You've been using me. You, too, Cora."

"That's life," Sandborne said, her eyes still on Cora. "Besides, nobody was hurt who didn't deserve it."

"My father and I are nobodies?" Bailey demanded.

"You deserved it!" Sandborne's eyes left their hungry devouring of Cora's body and glared at him defiantly. "You're both male predators, preying on the weak and helpless. The world will be better without you!"

"How can you say that, Dr. Sandborne?" Sherrill asked. Her voice was pleading, a bid for some answer that would help diminish her own feelings of guilt and betrayal. "You don't even know them."

"But I know their kind," Sandborne said bitterly. "I know them only too well. Get out," she repeated, but her voice lacked its former anger. "You both make me sick."

Sherrill stepped toward her and put a hand on her arm. "Help me, Dr. Sandborne, Cora. Please help me. I deserve that much, don't I?"

Sandborne made no effort to answer or even to rid herself of Sherrill's entreating hand. The sound of the exercise tape filled the silence.

"She can't help you," Cora finally said. "Can't you see? She can't even help herself." The sneer was back in her voice. She looked at Bailey. "If you expect *me* to help you, buddy, forget it!"

The big woman's head snapped up. "Get out of here!" she screamed, throwing off Sherrill's arm and pushing her off balance. Bailey reached out and steadied her before she could fall. "Leave us alone! Leave! Now!"

"Who told you about me?" he demanded above the rapidly more incoherent screams. "Who told you to try to frame me?"

Sandborne ignored him. Instead she grabbed Sherrill and shoved her toward the door.

Cora tapped Bailey on the arm. "You heard the lady," she said, laughing with seemingly genuine enjoyment. "You're not wanted here."

He regarded her assessingly, then did as she bid.

Sherrill turned back. "Won't you tell me? Please."

Sandborne just glared at her, then slammed the door.

I can't stand it, Cora!" she wailed as soon as the door shut out Bailey and Sherrill. "I just can't!" She bent her head and sobbed into her hands. Cora Snyder patted her shoulder and murmured endearments until the torrent subsided.

"We're so close to ridding the Senate of that monster Grant!" Sandborne said plaintively. Like Cora, she tended to speak in clichés. But unlike her friend, she was unaware of the tendency. Sandborne wiped ineffectually at her nose with the back of her hand. Her jerky movements were as unattractive as her soft, blotchy face.

Cora regarded her with distaste. The townhouse was comfortable, and Fran liked to lavish her with gifts, gratifyingly expensive ones, but Cora wasn't sure how much more of sniveling Fran she could endure. Time to find another friend? she wondered. If she could find one as generous as Fran—too bad Fran had been getting on her nerves lately!—and if she could come up with another deal as remunerative as this last one of Bonfire's, she would have enough saved to move to the French Riviera, long before she'd ever imagined possible.

Bonfire had a reputation, true, a far from pleasant one, but she could handle him. There was no man alive she couldn't handle, Cora thought grimly, the mysterious Bonfire included. The shiver that coursed down her body was from the cold, she assured herself, grabbing her robe from the back of the couch.

"How could that mewling Holmes girl have betrayed us and our cause?" Sandborne wailed.

To Frances Sandborne, a convert of only two years, since soon after she'd met Cora, the feminist movement was a miraculous revelation, bringing her the friends and the love she'd long despaired of having. The power inherent in the movement worked on her like an aphrodisiac. She was a crusader, and for her the crusade was holy.

She felt imperiled by Sherrill and Bailey. Not only were they threatening to destroy FOW's plan to better the world, but they were forcing needles of doubt to penetrate the haze of idealistic nonsense she'd created around herself. She desperately needed to destroy her two enemies before they destroyed her illusions.

"What should we do, Cora?" The pleading in her voice was pitiful.

Cora just looked at her, enjoying watching her pain.

"Tell me what to do," Sandborne repeated, tears again welling in her eyes. "We have to do something."

Eventually Cora relented. Then she left to send a message which would ultimately make its way to Bonfire. She'd spoken to Bonfire himself only once, but that once had been enough. Even she, who deferred to no one, had, since that conversation, found her dreams overlaid with the rasping menace of his dead-alive voice.

Reporters and their equipment hid the brick of the half-circle drive in front of Jonathan Hunter's elegant Kalorama home. Mobile news trucks, many with satellite dishes on top, made the narrow street impassable. Several big-name anchors waited impatiently for their promised interviews with Jonathan Hunter and his grieving wife. The story was heartrending: a handsome young man, the only child of a famous and powerful father, cut down in his prime by a condition he'd battled bravely all his life.

Rebecca Hunter stood looking out the living-room window, but she saw none of the present chaos. Instead, she saw Joey: Joey tumbling in the grass and grinning as he tottered to his feet, Joey riding his two-wheeler triumphantly around the drive, Joey stretched out in the air to catch a football. She saw him and she heard his beloved voice. She listened for him to come to the door, but he didn't. He stayed in the yard, playing through the years in the eyes of her memory.

She didn't feel her husband's hand on her arm. She didn't hear his voice, but she must have felt his presence because she began talking.

"Joey wants to come in, but he can't." Her voice was matter-of-fact, but her eyes were unfocused.

"Joey is dead, Rebecca," Hunter said bluntly.

She looked at him, then really saw him. "You needn't worry, Jonathan," she told him. "I'm not going to disgrace you by going mad with grief. I know my son is dead, but for me he is everywhere. For me he always will be."

Hunter turned from her. "We're meeting with the press outside," he said, his voice cold. "Just stand beside me. I'll do the talking."

She walked behind him docilely, willing to abide by his demands. She heard his words to the reporters, but only at the mention of heart disease did her eyes come alight. So that was his story, she thought. She might have known he couldn't be honest, even to his own son's memory. Even now when grief should have made such nonsense impossible, he was playing his power games.

Hunter, on the other hand, was pleased with his performance, especially with his pathos in explaining the heart condition. No one could doubt that such a problem was beyond even his control.

Bonfire stopped at a bank of pay phones at the Metro stop. Shirley Spade had left a message at one of his relay posts, saying she needed to talk to him. He deftly placed the voice distorter and number scrambler on the handpiece.

"I'm to report to Sheriff Jenks again this morning," Spade told him. She kept her voice carefully normal. She wasn't about to be intimidated by a faceless voice! She was Shirley Spade! "Sergek is seeing him, too. I called her like you said and refreshed her memory. She went right along. The fool really thinks it all happened."

"She's taking the lawyer, isn't she?" Bonfire asked. He would check to make sure regardless of what Spade said.

"I reminded her," Spade said defensively. Despite her resolve, the metallic quality of Bonfire's voice always made her edgy. Like talking to Darth Vader. Spade shivered in spite of herself. "Sergek just laughed and said she was smarter than any sheriff. I warned you about her."

"I haven't forgotten you're the one who couldn't find anyone better," Bonfire said softly. "Don't you forget who'll suffer if her story collapses."

"Don't throw a hissy fit." Spade's voice held bluster but an underlying quaver as well. She bit her lip, wishing devoutly she could call back the words. She'd just told Bonfire—Bonfire!—not to have a hissy fit! "No one has ever gotten the better of Shirley Spade," she hurried on, hoping he wouldn't notice the words. "It won't happen now, especially not with that jerk of a sheriff. I can right things no matter what Sergek says or does. Of course, things aren't the picnic you promised."

"You feel you deserve more? I only pay for production, Spade. I thought you understood." The metallic distortion filled each carefully enunciated word with menace. "I'm disappointed in you, Spade."

Shirley Spade tried to form words with her suddenly dry lips but couldn't. Her mother'd always warned that her big mouth would get her into trouble, and trouble sat on Bonfire's shoulder like a beady-eyed parrot.

"You'll be paid according to the amount of media coverage you generate," Bonfire continued emotionlessly, "just as I promised. But, Spade, remember that any failure on your part will be paid in full as well. That's a promise, too. You'll find I always keep my promises."

Shirley Spade stood with the dead phone at her ear for more than a minute before she found the strength to return it to its cradle. Everyone who'd ever worked for Bonfire knew about his promises. None knew better than those rotting in their graves.

Sheriff Jenks looked from the brassy beauty of Gayla Sergek to the buttoned-down shrewdness of her lawyer and felt tired. He was running out of time. If he couldn't break down Gayla's story today and then get a lead to its source, he feared he wouldn't have time to try again. The election was too soon, and after the election the pressure of time would no longer affect the faceless enemy he was tracking.

He looked at Hank Farrar off to the side, saw he was ready to take notes, and began the questioning.

Gayla's answers to his initial questions were bored and predictably uninformative. Her lawyer was losing patience and making sure the sheriff knew it. Jenks brought out Maribeth Pariss's diary, just returned from the Atlanta lab.

"In here," he said, tapping the shiny red volume, "Maribeth wrote down everything that caught her fancy. Why, she even thought the weather worth a mention."

Gayla leaned forward with interest.

The lawyer looked skeptical.

"She wrote every word herself," Jenks continued, tapping the book. "We know that for a fact. And you know what, Miss Sergek?"

Gayla shook you head, looking even more curious.

"Your friend Maribeth never said one word about spending time with the Senator, let alone having an affair with him."

"Maybe the diary ends before it happened," Gayla suggested. She popped her gum, apparently unconcerned that her story about Grant might be falling apart.

"Hardly likely seeing as how the last time she wrote was right before her death, Miss Sergek." Jenks's voice held the patience gained through years of questioning witnesses, many much less bright than Gayla Sergek. "Any other ideas?"

"You don't need to answer," her lawyer interposed.

"Will the paper and TV people want their money back if things don't turn out exactly like they expected?" she asked, turning to face him. Her gum was stilled.

"They paid for what we gave them, no more. The contracts they signed guarantee that. If they misinterpreted what they bought . . ." His shrug was eloquent.

"So the money is mine, no matter," Gayla persisted. Her mascaraed eyes bored into him. For her, money didn't talk; it sang.

"The money is yours," the lawyer agreed.

"Okay, then, Sheriff," she said, once again bouncing the gum around in her mouth, "ask away. Maybe we can come up with another angle someone will pay for."

"I strongly advise you to remain silent," the lawyer cautioned, angry red splotches coloring his cheeks. "The sheriff can't force you to say anything."

"That right, Sheriff?"

Jenks nodded. He sat motionless, his slouched body as nonthreatening as he could make it.

"Miss Sergek," the lawyer began, his voice raised threateningly, "I strongly advise—"

She ignored him and turned to Jenks. "If I answer all your questions, and, say, I remember some things I'd forgotten, are you going to arrest me?"

"Have you lied?"

"No."

"Done anything criminal, including helping to forge the letter?"

"Forge the letter! Of course not! Where would I learn about something like that?"

"Then you have nothing to worry about," Jenks drawled reassuringly.

"Miss Sergek," the lawyer said again, rising to his feet angrily.

"Be quiet now," she interrupted, but mildly. Her attention was focused on Jenks. "If I need your advice, I'll let you know."

The lawyer slowly subsided into his chair. He remained alert, however.

"Miss Sergek," Jenks interposed quickly before she could change her mind, "why do you reckon the diary doesn't mention what was in your letter?"

By the time Jenks finished his questioning, he knew everything about the night that had begun so innocently—Gayla's word—at the Cottonball Bar. Further, she agreed to having her apartment fingerprinted, admitting that she wasn't much for cleaning so "the guy's" prints might still be there. A forensic team was dispatched. A waste of time, no doubt, Jenks thought. "The guy's" fingerprints were the one thing they wouldn't find.

Gayla was now with Sally, hoping to capture a likeness of "the guy." Sally would make two computer sketches, one with the beard, one without. Jenks doubted Gayla had looked beyond her own self-absorption to really study "the guy," so he wasn't expecting much more from the sketches than he was expecting from the fingerprinting. Nonetheless, one of Grant's faceless enemies would be faceless no more.

Gayla Sergek left the interrogation room momentarily dejected. She could see no way of wringing more money out of this new information. Her lawyer, however, offered hope. He would call the *Herald* and propose an exclusive about the man and the letter. Sounded to him like something Grant might have concocted to hide his real motive. Confusing the issue, Jenks heard him murmur to Gayla as they left. Jenks wondered if Gayla's disappointment hadn't been premature.

Still frowning at thoughts of the *Herald*, not to mention the lawyer, Jenks walked to his office. He jotted down his impressions of the interview, then reviewed his notes on Shirley Spade, who was waiting for him in a windowless anteroom down the hall.

He had planned to let her stew there for a short while, but a confrontation with an NIIA underling extended that wait into well over an hour.

He had to decide how to handle the NIIA—and decide soon, before he riled them too much, Jenks thought as he walked toward the anteroom, Farrar trailing behind. The feds would bypass him completely if he weren't careful.

"What do you mean keeping me holed up like this?" Shirley Spade demanded when they finally walked into the room. "My lawyer is going to hear about it."

"Sit down," Jenks commanded. Smarting from the NIIA's high-handed arrogance, he was in no mood for her petty tyranny. "Where is your lawyer?"

"Who needs a lawyer?" Spade's voice remained belligerent. She'd been told to bring a lawyer. She knew she didn't need him. Remembering Bonfire's words, she suppressed a shiver and fervently hoped she was right. She'd never worked for Bonfire before—normally she worked alone—but the last few days she'd heard stories about him, none of them guaranteed to improve her disposition. "I'm an innocent citizen, trying to do my civic duty," she declared defiantly.

"I hope so, Ms. Spade," Jenks said, allowing his expression to convey his doubt. "I certainly do hope so."

When she left almost an hour later, he had to admit she'd been right about one thing—the lawyer hadn't been necessary. Spade had done just fine on her own. Her story had been unshakable. According to her, Senator Robert Grant had sexually harassed Maribeth Pariss. Spade had witnessed said harassment on several occasions. Jenks could bully her all he wanted, but that was the truth. Period.

Five minutes after her triumphant departure, Hank Farrar joined the sheriff in his office.

"That old lady is a real piece of work," Farrar said with something akin to awe. "Looks like my sweet granny, but Cujo lives in her soul. You should see them reporters buzzin' round her like flies to a carcass. Your boy's not goin' to like what she's sayin'." He grinned maliciously.

"You think she's telling the truth?"

"Why not?" Farrar demanded, but he looked uncomfortable. At Jenks's continued silence, he broke into speech. "All right. All right," he conceded, "so that adultery story has more holes than my mam's undies, but so what? Grant still done the murder. Stands to reason. There's no one else."

"You never give up, do you, Hank?"

Farrar looked sheepish. "Leastways not till you come up with somethin' more tasty than this hogwash you're swillin' around. Cain't figure why you're so sweet on Grant. What's he to you?"

"I don't know what to say, Hank," Jenks said slowly, concerned that the nuances weren't as obvious to his deputy as they were to him. Hank shouldn't have had to ask, not if he counted on being sheriff someday. "My gut tells me Grant's not our murderer, and now that we know someone planted that letter . . ."

"If Sergek was telling the truth and didn't write it herself," Farrar reminded him. "A pretty face don't mean diddly except beware."

Jenks nodded. "But that still leaves Anne Peabody as well as that drug bust Tuesday night."

Farrar snorted. "A lot of smoke by Grant if you ask me."

"Maybe, but I'm not about to quit digging till I'm sure I've found the truth."

"Cain't say I much like those NIIA boys horning in on our case," Farrar said slowly. "Sticks in my craw. Anyhow, that's not what I come in for." He tossed a paper in front of the sheriff. "These folks figure they may have seen somethin' at Crazy Sam's. 'Bout the right time, too."

Jenks looked at the names—a husband, his wife, and their three young children.

"Good work, Hank. Probably be best to see them when they're all home together," he told Farrar. "Tonight if possible."

"Already done, boss. Six o'clock. Anything else?"

"Get the media together," Jenks told him. He sounded resigned. "Tell them I'm going to make a statement in fifteen minutes."

"Sure, boss." Farrar's face broke into a grin. "Cain't wait to see tonight's news." He walked out, punching the buttons of an imaginary TV remote control and laughing.

Eugene Corforth had come to love the White House during the almost two years he'd been Chief of Staff to the President. Of all the historic rooms in the stately building, the Roosevelt Room was his favorite. True, the Cabinet Room was more impressive, as much for its tradition as the center of world power as for its accoutrements. However, the Roosevelt Room, with its windowless snugness, exuded a warmth and familiarity the Cabinet Room could never attain.

During the last few months, Corforth had found himself spending more and more time in the room to the point that his staff now looked for him there first whenever they needed him. He used the room as an escape, he realized, wondering if he should find that realization disturbing. An escape, but from what?

He slowly surveyed the room, searching for something to take him out of his blue funk. Teddy storming San Juan Hill, Teddy carrying "a big stick," a portrait of Teddy looking dour but with a twinkle lurking in the shadows of his eyes: Corforth often studied those paintings. In them he found temporary surcease from the disturbing thoughts that filled his days and buffeted his sleep.

He was surprised that he didn't draw the same strength from the paintings of FDR that also decorated the walls. He studied the portrait of the World War II President that hung above the fireplace, its place of honor during any Democratic administration. FDR had been Corforth's idol throughout college, as he'd been for most of Corforth's friends and for most of those now in the White House. But somehow, Teddy's brash honesty and demonstrable love for family were more what Corforth needed now.

Honesty and faithfulness. Could an individual, much less a nation, survive without them? Absentmindedly, Corforth reached into his pocket, extracted an antacid, and popped it into his mouth.

The President with his insatiable sexual appetite and the ensuing lies necessary to keep it secret, Hunter with his equally insatiable need for unquestioned power in all things: These had become the focus of the White House. Affairs of state, both foreign and domestic, were considered only after the first two needs had been met.

Things had been different during their first year. The President had been keen to make his mark on history. However, as his sexual liaisons had grown in frequency, his interest in affairs of state had diminished to the point that Jonathan Hunter now made almost all decisions, important and otherwise. The President merely okayed them. Corforth sometimes wondered if Hunter, to further his own power, didn't encourage the President's distractions. The thought was sobering and not conducive to improving Corforth's already disturbed slumber. Hunter lacked any pretensions to honor. Personal power was his god.

Corforth loved his work, but he hated the deceit and the power games. For whatever reason, what he'd once viewed as political necessity now seemed base and close to treasonous.

Even though he knew his duties that day should be routine, Corforth felt that all-too-frequent leadening of spirit as he left his sanctuary in the Roosevelt Room, crossed the hall, and entered the Oval Office.

"Now that you've met him, what is your read on Caruso?" the President asked. In Washington for a briefing with White House staff, Tobias Caruso was to fly to Georgia on Air Force One. He would arrive at the rally with the President, alighting from the presidential limousine. The imagery would be perfect. Voters would be impressed by his proximity to the power and influence of the Oval Office.

"Caruso looks good," Corforth answered readily, coming to stand before the desk, "and should come across well on TV. That could be the winning factor this late in the campaign. How mentally agile he is, especially under pressure, who knows? He's virtually untried."

"Grant is a sly one," POTUS said thoughtfully. He gave no indication for Corforth to be seated. "Even if Caruso were the Devil incarnate, we can't trust him to handle Grant on his own. We need someone good to prep him for the debate."

"Edmund Miller has been working with him."

"Good. Miller understands."

Other staff members came into the room. Only then did the President give the signal, an inclination of his head, that they should take their seats. Within fifteen minutes a run-through of the Atlanta rally had been completed. POTUS asked Corforth to remain behind for a moment.

"I didn't want to bother Hunt," he said, coming up beside Corforth and putting a hand on his shoulder. Charm oozed from his voice, from every bit of body language. "I know I'll need some distraction tomorrow night, maybe before the dinner and then again at midnight. The rally will be an infernal bore." At Corforth's poorly concealed look of distaste, all charm evaporated. "Forget the sermon, Eugene. I don't understand you. You never used to be like this."

"I don't understand it myself," Corforth admitted. He paused, unsure how much of himself to reveal. "I suppose I worry about you."

"Why is it," the President interrupted sarcastically, "those words don't fill me with confidence?" He walked behind the desk and sat, his displeasure evident in every movement.

"But it's true. I want what's best for you, and I can't help thinking that you're throwing away something precious when you ignore your wife and allow your, well, appetite to grow."

"You wouldn't say that if anyone but Amy had ever found you attractive," the President retorted. He shifted some papers on his desk.

"Doesn't commitment count for something? And mutual respect?"

"Believe me, these girls respect me. You needn't concern yourself about tomorrow. Hunt will take care of it."

He took the gold presidential pen from its mottled marble base and began writing.

Corforth understood he was being dismissed. He stopped in the doorway and surveyed the room, the site of so much of dubious as well as genuinely majestic history. He had a feeling he wouldn't have the privilege of seeing it much longer. That knowledge filled him with desolation.

So you're back, are you, Mr. High and Mighty Reporter?" Hal Olexey sneered as he strutted into the visitors' room.

Vinton clenched his fists. He wanted nothing better than to smash the taunting sneer off the punk's face. He didn't trust himself to speak.

"You're back for the picture, aren't you?" Olexey asked as he hooked a foot around the leg of one of the gray metal chairs facing the wire grid. In one practiced motion he turned the chair around and sat down. "Knew you would be."

He undid the cellophane on a pack of cigarettes and shook one out. He put the pack in his pocket and the cigarette in his mouth. He struck a match. Every movement was deliberately slow.

"The price has just gone up," he said, appearing to watch the smoke curling from his cigarette. However, his eyes never left Vinton's face.

"The price isn't negotiable," Vinton told him.

"Guard!" Olexey yelled. "Take me back."

The guard pushed himself away from the wall.

Olexey stood, grinding out the cigarette. "Thanks for nothing," he told Vinton with a sneer.

"Okay, okay," Vinton said grudgingly. Yesterday, he'd thought Olexey might back down, but not today. Today, Olexey acted as if he knew he was safe in giving his ultimatum. Vinton couldn't take a chance. His story depended on the picture. This was one front page he intended to have. Pulitzer was written all over it. "Ten thousand, but that's the limit."

"My mistake," Olexey told the guard, handing him a cigarette for his trouble. "Looks like I need more time."

Shaking his head, the guard returned to his spot against the wall out of earshot. He lit the cigarette and went back to ignoring them.

"So how do I get this picture?" Vinton asked.

Olexey repeated Bonfire's instructions verbatim.

I appreciate your willingness to see me," Grant told Craig C. Flannery, Anne Peabody's startled lawyer, who couldn't believe that the beleaguered Senator Grant was actually in *his* office in New York City. But, as Grant had figured, the mention of that "beleaguered Senator's" name had gotten him immediate entrance into the lawyer's inner sanctum.

"Anne Peabody was a friend as well as a client," Flannery said. He stared at the gold Monte Blanc pen he held in his hand. Then he seemed to come to a decision. He looked Grant in the eye for the first time since the Senator had confirmed his identity. "You ought to know that I don't agree with your political philosophy and feel confident our country would be better served by someone else."

"I think we can safely say you're not alone," Grant replied with the trace of a smile. "Candidly, if you help me find Miss Peabody's murderer, you may also be helping my chances for reelection."

"Finding a mugger will help you get reelected?" Flannery looked skeptical.

"I don't think Miss Peabody was mugged," Grant said, not surprised at the skepticism. "I think she was deliberately murdered," he continued, "and that her scheduled interview with Russell Frederickson in some way precipitated her murder."

"Because Frederickson was murdered, too?" the lawyer asked. His tone was still skeptical, but he inclined his head as if to encourage Grant to elucidate.

"Certainly that was the clincher, but the whole chain of events is highly suggestive as well." Grant hoped telling Flannery wasn't tantamount to telling the enemy, a paranoid idea, maybe, but given the last few days, far from impossible. Nobody could say Flannery hadn't warned him. "Miss Peabody got a call from Russell Frederickson. She was visibly upset and indicated that her statement against the former President was the cause of her agitation. Then she telephoned Attorney General Hunter. Afterward, she telephoned you, and she telephoned Frederickson. She told several people"—an exaggeration, but one necessary to protect Julie—"that she would be meeting with both of you the next morning. Late that evening she was killed while taking her nightly run through Central Park."

"You think she was killed to keep her from talking to Frederickson?" Flannery asked. His tone was as noncommittal as only a lawyer's could be.

"And Frederickson was killed to keep it all secret," Grant agreed with a slight nod. "The two murders are too coincidental not to be related."

"Since you're the prime suspect," Flannery said, "diverting suspicion from yourself seems logical, ergo this story. Whether the story's logical as well and you're some kind of scapegoat . . ." His voice trailed off, inviting Grant to divulge more.

"I have the advantage of knowing I'm innocent," Grant told him. Then he told Flannery about the forged letter, the odd circumstances surrounding Gayla Sergek's accusations, and the efforts to embarrass him through Bailey.

"You mean your son was set up?" Flannery asked. He seemed genuinely disturbed. "You know for a fact it wasn't a coincidence? Sometimes parents are the last to know about their own children." His voice held the bitterness of experience.

"One of the two people co-opted to set Bailey up has explained how she was duped. No, Mr. Flannery, there can be no doubt. My son was compromised with the avowed purpose of compromising me. Given the preponderance of evidence, do you wonder at my questions about the events surrounding Miss Peabody's death?"

"Interesting, Senator," Flannery said. "While I'm not convinced of the reasoning of all your assertions, I'm willing to concede you've presented a viable argument. Given the proviso that I can conclude our discussion at any time, I'm willing to answer at least some of your questions. If you're right, Miss Peabody was as much a pawn as anyone. She was an accomplished woman. She deserved better."

Grant relaxed into the chair. He'd cleared the biggest hurdle: He'd gotten the lawyer interested. Now if he could prime Flannery so he would give some useful information, maybe even be coaxed into action, all the better.

The line of people coming to pay their respects to Joey Hunter seemed endless, so many people in fact that the wake was being held in the Departmental Auditorium on Constitution Avenue. The large ornate room was fittingly gloomy, Rebecca Hunter thought, as dark and vast as death. She was sure she didn't know any of those standing patiently in line. Not quite "any" maybe—a few seemed vaguely familiar. Friends of her husband? He wasn't there to tell her. The President had called an emergency which needed her husband's deft touch. In the last months he'd acted as if he and only he could properly handle any situation involving the nation, or even affecting the world.

Her black dress hanging loosely on her lean body, Rebecca turned back toward the line, ready to put a tight smile on her face. Tonight, even her lips were devoid of color. The incipient tightening of her mouth dissolved into a look of genuine pleasure.

"Janet!"

Rebecca felt Janet Loomis's arms embrace her. They stood holding each other, oblivious to the subdued murmurs and curious stares of those waiting.

Rebecca started to speak, but her eyes filled with tears, and the words wouldn't come.

Janet gently brushed away the tears. "I understand," she said, and Rebecca knew she did. Only months before Janet had been the one standing at the head of a similar line, waiting to hear words of condolence. That time, however, it had been a husband who had died, but he hadn't just died. He'd committed suicide. Even immersed in her own grief, Rebecca could remember the embarrassment she'd felt. What could she say to a woman whose husband had preferred death over life with her, especially when the wife had obviously loved him?

"Thank you for coming," she told her friend. She could only imagine the wounds this visit had reopened.

"I'm so sorry about Joey," Janet said, her eyes shiny with tears. "I had no idea about his heart condition."

Rebecca said nothing. She had yet to give voice to the lie. Her small attempt to be true to her son, she supposed. A rather pathetic tribute.

"I wanted you to know that the pain does get bearable," Janet said, looking back at some inner memory and unaware of the flicker of additional pain her mention of the heart condition had caused. "You'll doubt that. For a long time you'll doubt it, but it does. Something or someone, maybe just time, will be there to help pull you through. Rachel Grant was there for me."

Janet closed her eyes and swallowed against the trembling that assailed her. Rachel. She had to decide what to do about Rachel, about Rachel and Bob. They were in trouble, and time was so short. But her sons—how could she chance hurting them when they'd barely recovered from the devastating blow of their father's suicide? They, too, had felt cruelly abandoned. Might a disastrous revelation about their father be too much for their battered emotions to withstand? Oh, God, she prayed, forgetting where she was, forgetting everything but her misery. God, please tell me what to do! Help me to know what's right!

Misinterpreting Janet's distress, Rebecca was pulled from her own grief. She wanted to comfort her. She tried to think. Who was Rachel Grant?

"Isn't she Bob Grant's wife?" she asked.

With obvious effort Janet returned from the black despair blanketing her mind. She nodded and took Rebecca's hands in her own. Rebecca appreciated the warmth but was mildly surprised at their trembling. "Rachel wanted to come," Janet said, hesitating only slightly over the name, "but she was afraid she might cause a disruption."

Again, Rebecca nodded. She could remember reading of the accusations against Bob Grant. Could that have been only the day before? Her heart caught. Joey! She squeezed her eyes shut. One of her hands stole up to clutch a hunk of already tousled hair. Feeling Janet's hand on her arm, she loosened her grip and slowly brought her hand back to her side. She forced her mind back . . . What had they been discussing? Oh, yes, Bob Grant. Murder, wasn't it? She felt a surprising flicker of amusement somewhere deep inside. A visit by the wife of an accused murderer might indeed cause a distraction. This was Washington, after all.

Suddenly, Rebecca was overwhelmed with exhaustion. "I understand," she said mechanically. She wished Janet would leave, that they all would leave.

Janet squeezed her hands. When she spoke, she was talking as much to herself as to Rebecca. "Rachel has so much faith. She can help you find the strength you'll need."

"Faith? Help?" Rebecca repeated the words listlessly. She could think of nothing else to say.

Janet recognized her weariness. She wanted to give Rebecca the comfort she so obviously needed, but at that moment her own desolation consumed her. Comfort was beyond her. She could do no more than squeeze her friend's hands and leave, each to wrestle her demons alone.

When Vinton finished his piece, a half-page exposé containing every gram in Grant's drug history, he went to Peter Evans's office, where he handed Evans the Olexey picture, just delivered by a messenger.

"No doubt about that being Grant," Evans said with satisfaction, tapping the picture. It showed two men, both dressed casually, both faces fully revealed. Several indistinguishable figures mingled in the background. The location could have been anywhere. "That Olexey?"

"Sure is," Vinton confirmed. "Couldn't be clearer."

Evans flung the picture down on his desk. "We print the picture. We print the story. We let the reader draw his own conclusion. Good work, Vinton. Looks like you'll get your headline."

"Thank you, sir," Vinton said, putting the picture back into the envelope. "Couldn't have done it without your tip," he added.

"We met earlier today with Tobias Caruso," Evans continued, sitting down and tilting back in his chair. The "we" referred to the editorial board of the paper. "Caruso should go far. He looks good, he expresses himself well, and his ideas are right on target. We'll come out with a full endorsement in Sunday's paper."

"That'll make a lot of people happy," Vinton said. "Did you hear about the press conference that Sheriff Jenks held?"

"You mean where he said the Pariss story can't be true?" Evans asked, his eyes bright with derision. "He ignores the statement of the Spade woman, who is obviously reliable—look at her background!—and believes some married guy afraid to show his face. That sheriff is a simpleton, willing to do anything for his fifteen minutes of fame. Soon as he finds that his little games to get media attention won't work, he'll fall in line."

"No doubt about Grant's influence over him, is there?"

"None. That's why we're not running anything he puts out. His credibility is shot with everyone. In fact, we're demanding that the NIIA take over the entire investigation." Evans tapped his pencil thoughtfully. "Why don't you get some quotes from Spade?"

"A separate article?"

The pencil stilled while Evans considered. "Sure, why not? Emphasize all her work with charities," he said, dropping the pencil in its marble holder. "Be sure to keep in touch with Derek Bender, the NIIA official in charge down there. He'll be square with you."

Vinton nodded, dropped the Olexey piece on top of the envelope with the picture, and left to begin pulling together the Spade story.

Sheriff Jenks felt like a carcass ravaged by scavengers. The NIIA didn't want just a piece of him; they wanted it all. The county Democratic party had decided if they couldn't have him unconditionally they'd get rid of him altogether. And now the media had joined the hunt. They'd attended his press conference and heard about Maribeth Pariss and her noninvolvement with Grant. They'd seen the letters and the diary. They'd seen the memo detailing the lab's findings. Then they'd turned around and interviewed Shirley Spade—logical enough. But they were treating her allegations as gospel, and his verifiable proofs as the planted evidence of a police official beholden to a corrupt political system.

To add to his own problems, the Grant affair was one mess of maggots, self-perpetuating and disgusting. Smash one, and others burst forth. First a dead Russell Frederickson and the puzzling files in his computer; then the two-year-old death of Maribeth Pariss resurrected with the addition of Spade, Sergek, and the mystery man at the Cottonball Bar; add Bailey Grant, the two kids who had been recruited to betray him, the professors doing the recruiting, and a dead kid, the attorney general's son, no less; finally, a dead Anne Peabody and her apparent connection with Frederickson. On top of everything was the uncanny ability of the enemy to predict their every move and then make hay out of it.

Bob Grant was right in deciding to forget his campaign and hone in on the attack itself. Too bad about the campaign, though, Jenks thought. He was more and more convinced that Grant was a man of honor. Was Grant's honor the root of everything? he wondered. Did Grant need to be removed because he wouldn't turn a blind eye to shadings of right and wrong?

Grant was right about something else: Too often politics was not the profession of honorable gentlemen. The power stakes were too high, and love of power too often led to a corruption of values. Anything was acceptable as long as the goal was perceived as worthwhile. At least that was one problem he wasn't responsible for, Jenks thought, wondering at the same time who was.

He was straightening the papers on his desk when Farrar entered.

"I guess you've heard that Bender and his NIIA buddies are taking over the investigation," Jenks said.

The deputy nodded, his eyes on the floor. Then he lifted them. They were blazing. "Idiots!" he hissed through clenched teeth. "They're behavin' like we're Junior Birdmen, not experienced lawmen." He glanced at the paper Jenks handed him.

THE WALLS MAY HAVE EARS.

Farrar's eyelids went to half-mast, concealing his thoughts. He'd heard Judge Jackson had called the sheriff. Rumor was the judge was fair-to-boiling when he hung up. Mad enough to okay a bug, maybe even a wire tap? Farrar nodded to Jenks and smiled slyly.

"Like I was sayin'," he drawled, "we'd better get bustin' if we aim to show 'em we ain't got no flies on us."

"Good work finding the Patterson family," Jenks told him. They'd interviewed the family that had been at Crazy Sam's at the same time as Russell Frederickson on the night of his murder.

"Yeah, but that kid won't cut butter 'gainst no clever lawyer," Farrar said, "even if he's sharper than Mabel Eskew's tongue." Only Scott Patterson, age seven, remembered seeing a stranger at Crazy Sam's. As the family had been leaving, a man with a beard had rushed past them, knocking Scott down. Scott had seen the man clearly and was to come in the next day to work with Sally on a computer-generated composite drawing. Sally had a way with kids. Maybe she could coax him into remembering something useful.

"Bring him by my office when he's finished," Jenks continued. "I want to show him Gayla Sergek's sketch, see if it brings anything to mind.

Even if we can't use Scott in court, he might give us an idea. Right now, we sure could use one."

"A seven-year-old kid?"

"I know," Jenks said wearily. "A real long shot. Did you dig up any more on Spade?"

"That ol' biddy with salt in her veins? Course not. Sly one, old Spade. She's flusher than she's been since she first rubbed two Indian heads together, but we'll never reckon where she came by it."

"Don't stop digging, though." He handed Farrar another note. *MEET ME AT GUS'S TOMORROW MORNING AT 9.*

Farrar looked at him, then stuffed the note in his pocket when he heard footsteps in the hall.

"Course I'll keep sniffin'," Farrar said as if there had been no break in the conversation. "Cain't think of much that would pleasure me more than knockin' that sassy grin off her face."

"Let me know if anything comes in," Jenks said.

"That won't be necessary, now will it, Sheriff?"

Farrar and Jenks turned toward the voice. Derek Bender, his eyes expressionless above his charcoal-tinged square jaw, leaned against the door frame.

"I'm in charge now," Bender said. "Anything that needs to be reported, Deputy, you report it to me. You received the court order?" he asked, turning his gaze on Jenks. Though no smirk marred his lips, one lurked undisguised in his eyes. "As a matter of fact," he continued, his face softening into self-satisfaction, "I think the sheriff was about to leave. Am I right, Sheriff?"

"Believe you may be." As he'd done early that day, Jenks straightened to his full height and gave the NIIA agent one of his steeliest stares. "And that's probably a first."

The addition of Anne Peabody to the equation had pushed it into another dimension, Grant thought as he left Craig Flannery's office and looked for a phone booth away from prying eyes and curious ears. Peabody's murder and the introduction of the White House as somehow involved: He wondered what he would need to win against such power. Certainly more than he had now, dauntingly more.

He found a phone and got out a pile of change. He wasn't chancing a credit card or collect call. One of Yao's operatives had put a scrambler on Cynthia's phone. Even so, Rachel, when he reached her, kept her end of the conversation as uninformative as possible.

"Everyone all right?" Grant asked. He hadn't realized how tense he was until he received her reassurances. Too many murders and the attempt to incriminate Bailey—they hadn't affected his faith, but they'd given him a healthy dose of caution.

"Your friends have kept all of us in sight, regardless of where we've gone," Rachel told him.

"Bailey?" Grant asked, knowing his older son was the most likely to rebel.

"He's getting on famously with Ramon and Tommy. The same crazy sense of humor. Sorry about the loud music," she said, raising her voice to be heard above it. "They swept the house for bugs and didn't find any, but apparently the latest surveillance equipment can hear through walls from hundreds of yards. The music's supposed to make it more difficult. You're all right, aren't you?"

"Yes," Grant said, turning to look at the deceptively slight figure lounging against a far wall. Stephen Yao was one tough former Seal. His karate black belt was reassuring as well. "Stephen's following the guys who've been following me."

"Oh, no!"

"No need to worry. They're NIIA."

"And that's supposed to reassure me?"

Grant smiled at the familiar affectionate chiding in her voice.

"Good point." He toyed with the chain that should have had a phone directory attached to it. "They haven't caught on to Stephen, so that's a help. At the moment I've managed to lose them, hopefully without their realizing it was deliberate. Have you heard from our Cuban friend?" As before Grant was careful not to mention Benjamin Dashev by name.

"Yes. He said he would meet you. He didn't say why or where, just that you should keep to your present schedule and lose anyone following you."

"That sounds encouraging." Grant gave the chain a final flick. "He must know something, or he wouldn't go to so much trouble. I'll meet him and then fly to Washington later this evening. I'll need to get back to

Atlanta for a meeting with Ginger and the others early tomorrow. Cynthia can work out times with Mike."

"They've already taken care of it, but Mike told her he's having trouble lining up people willing to meet."

Grant was quiet for a moment. "Interesting," he finally said. "I thought I'd picked the real diehards, and with Ginger weighing in for me ... Tell Mike to do what he can. Have Cynthia make a few calls if she has time."

"He also says Caruso refuses to debate unless Kirk Vinton is the moderator."

"Caruso refuses?"

"You heard right."

"I can't believe I'm agreeing to a debate, much less letting Caruso set the ground rules," Grant said resignedly. "Vinton of all people. He's Evans's man." He turned and leaned his back against the phone ledge. The sidewalk was far from empty, but no one seemed to pay him any interest. Then he saw the heavyset woman hurrying purposefully toward him, a coin clutched in her hand. Uh, oh, he thought. He would have to wind this up while his end of the conversation was still private.

"So you refuse to agree to Vinton?" Rachel asked. "Mike didn't think you had any choice. If you refuse, Caruso will declare you're guilty."

"Mike's right," Grant said with stoic calm. The woman, a frown on her face now that she'd seen the phone was in use, was zooming in like a kamikaze on a search-and-destroy mission. Grant continued hurriedly. "Tell him to use his own judgment about their demands. Just make sure the only audience is family." He had a hazy plan in mind, hazy being the operative word. "I'd love to know who's giving Caruso his advice. Vinton's a clever choice; his Pulitzer makes him seem unbiased. Have Cynthia see if she can find out who's pulling Caruso's chain. Someone in Washington, I'd guess. Knowing might give us a handle on who's behind everything."

"I'll tell her. Another potential problem—Cynthia got a call just a few minutes ago from a friend at the *Herald*. Apparently, they're planning a huge exposé tomorrow. Details are sketchy, but the friend was disturbed enough to call. Cynthia's working on learning more."

"I can't imagine what more they could say, but a week ago ... You were right about Anne Peabody," he added quickly. The woman had almost reached him, and displeasure vibrated from every pound of her body. "I don't have proof, but Peabody's death and Frederickson's have to be connected. I'll fill you in this evening."

He hung up and smiled as he edged past the broad body swathed in its navy wool coat and red plaid cap. She scowled, but by then Grant had forgotten her.

A huge exposé? he wondered as he wove his way through the throng of New Yorkers clogging the sidewalks, even more body-intensive than rush hour in Washington. What could the *Herald* be planning now?

The mood in the Oval Office was tense. The President had called an emergency meeting. Hunter wasn't there, and no one had a clue to its purpose.

When everyone had arrived, a Secret Service agent opened the door to the inner office, and the President stormed in.

"Some bloody reporter said he'd heard I was a great one for snacks," he seethed. Veins in his temple throbbed visibly under his flushed skin. His hands were clenched into tight fists. "Snacks! He wondered just what kind I preferred."

"You told him popcorn and lemonade, I assume," Corforth said laconically. Hunter had finally left for his son's wake. Out of courtesy, Corforth had refused to have him beeped and therefore was the most senior person present.

"The nerve of the man!" the President bellowed. "We are a house of mourning! The son of my dearest friend has just died, and he's wasting my time on food! I can assure you I've never been more outraged." He stopped and looked at each man in turn as he spoke the next words. "Loyalty to me from the White House staff is paramount. I hope I make myself understood." Abruptly, he turned to Corforth. "Where's Hunt?"

Corforth explained.

"*You* decided he shouldn't be here?" the President demanded angrily. "You get him here, Corforth! Now! I need him! Get out!" he shouted, pointing to the door. "All of you! Get out! And there'd better be no more questions from the media!"

They left.

Against his better judgment, Corforth called Hunter, who was still in his car. Hunter's voice sounded disembodied over the cellular connection. He couched his words in discreet shorthand.

Hunter's only suggestions were that Estelle travel to Georgia with the President the next day and that the President limit his schedule for a while, at least until things had settled down and they had another protocol for procurement in place.

The President agreed to the first. He would tell Estelle. The second, he would consider. He knew exactly which schedule had come into question, and he wasn't sure he wanted it changed. He wasn't even convinced it needed to be changed.

The site was again the Mayflower Hotel. This time, the event was a fund-raiser for Tobias Caruso, the political neophyte from Georgia who'd sky-rocketed to celebrity status in a matter of days.

Caruso basked in the attention generated by this, his first Washington fund-raiser. The White House had organized two such events for him that evening, this one with the National Education Association (NEA) as sponsor and the next with a panoply of other labor unions.

"I've just been told that over one million dollars will have been raised by the end of the evening," Edmund Miller told him, leaning close so as not to be overheard. "Our friends from all over the country are pouring money into this race."

At Caruso's look, Miller added pointedly, "No one likes Grant. You'd be wise to remember who your friends are."

One million dollars! The thought made Caruso flush with breath-stopping disbelief. These powerful and influential people admired him, and they obviously thought he would soon be in a position to affect their wants and grievances.

Miller nudged him on the elbow and moved him on to the next group. The White House was committed to him, Caruso thought, ignoring Miller but well aware of the impact of his presence. Tomorrow's campaign visit to Georgia by the President would help cement the national stature the campaign was developing. Interviews on the networks had begun the process that morning. His views had been sought by the biggest names in television journalism, celebrities he'd never expected to meet, much less have seek his views. How glad he was that he'd defied conventional wisdom and agreed to run against Grant!

Caruso made appropriate comments to every supporter. He might not have previous political experience, but Miller had coached him well.

He was a super-salesman selling himself, and no one could do that better. Now that Grant had agreed to the debate on Sunday, all Caruso had to do was look the part of a Senator and that part would be his. He really was going to be the new Senator from Georgia, just as he'd been promised!

With practiced ease, Miller led Caruso to the final group, one near the microphone and stage. Smiling, Caruso listened to a glowing introduction by the president of NEA. Then taking the microphone himself, he began his speech. His nerves were quickly allayed by the audience's rapt attention. His natural charm and humor blossomed under their loud approval.

Miller heard more than one listener comment that Caruso was bound to go far. The White House would be pleased. So was Miller.

Grant, followed unobtrusively by Stephen Yao, arrived at Teeterboro Airport in New Jersey, as scheduled. He knew he'd shaken all surveillance, but in doing so he'd failed to make contact with Benjamin Dashev. What had happened? he wondered. Had his attempts to lose his followers been too inept or too late for Dashev's needs? Whatever the reason, Grant had missed him and that failure could be serious. Another opportunity for a meeting might not materialize. He needed Dashev's resources and expertise, and he needed them now.

At least Matt Goldie's plane was poised on the tarmac as scheduled. Grant glanced at Yao, standing in the shadows of a nearby building and conversing with one of his men. Receiving Yao's nod, he moved at a brisk but unremarkable pace toward the plane, then hurried into the dark interior, welcoming its safety but still preoccupied with his failure to meet Dashev.

"So you have finally arrived," a voice said softly.

"Dashev!" Grant shook his friend's hand, probably more vigorously than necessary. "You old devil, you! And to think I was worried."

An almost imperceptible smile played at Dashev's mouth, the only kind of smile he allowed himself.

"Mr. Goldie was kind enough to keep me company," he said. "We have spent a most informative hour. You are wise in your friends."

Goldie grinned at Grant.

Yao entered and pulled the door shut. With a wave to Dashev, he went to the front and sat in the copilot seat by Goldie.

"Ready to roll?" Goldie asked. He appeared to be enjoying himself immensely. A good friend, as Dashev had noted.

Grant looked at the Israeli, who nodded.

"I hope your warning that I might be followed means you've come up with something," Grant said as the plane raced down the runway.

"Several items of interest," Dashev assured him. "By the way, my men report you were, indeed, followed."

Grant looked warily out the window. Dashev looked amused. "You needn't fear. You have become quite adept at subterfuge, my friend. You lost them long before you arrived here."

"NIIA?"

"So we believe, though one of the men was unknown to us."

Grant regarded Dashev thoughtfully.

"But back to your problem," Dashev continued. "I can give no guarantees, but you know how I value my instinct, Bob, and that instinct tells me that what I've discovered is in some way part of this most complex campaign being waged against you."

Grant nodded. He did indeed know his friend's instinct, one that, through years of experience, was seldom faulty.

"I have determined three separate possibilities that may have some bearing on your situation." Dashev pulled notes from his inside coat pocket, but Grant knew from past encounters that those notes wouldn't be consulted. "The first has international overtones. You above all Americans understand the implications behind the restructuring of world power that was precipitated by the collapse of the Soviet Union. When the United States mistakenly decided this collapse meant the end of any threat and relaxed their vigilance, they created an even more volatile situation."

"And precipitated a rush for nuclear capability by every two-bit terrorist nation in the world," Grant said, nodding, "and unfortunately some not-so-negligible nations."

"Yes," Dashev agreed, "and whetted their appetites with thoughts of dominating their once-indomitable enemy, the United States of America. While Middle East nations, particularly Iran and Iraq, were the first powers to emerge and the ones of most interest to my country obviously, the latest to reach a level of positive threat to the free world are China and North Korea. The unimpeded transfer of advanced computer technology in particular which this administration has promoted so precipitously has pushed both China and North Korea to the brink of nuclear success. Since you, my friend, have warned of disaster while others have rushed to embrace the technology transfer, China and North Korea may well consider you the main obstacle to their acquisition of nuclear dominance. I've heard rumors that they've made a move to insure their continued favorable treatment by this administration, though the exact meaning of those rumors is as yet unclear."

"But you think it may refer to destroying my credibility?" Grant asked. He relaxed into his seat. Even this talk of nuclear blackmail didn't seem so threatening here in the sky with only clouds to attack them. "Fewer problems than eliminating me altogether?"

"They eschew creating martyrs," Dashev agreed. "How much better to discredit you personally so that your ideas are discredited as well. Now that you are being mentioned as a serious presidential contender—and I for one salute those who have the wisdom to do so," he added with a congratulatory tilt of his head to Grant, "your warnings are receiving even wider coverage and even greater credibility."

Grant looked at his friend thoughtfully. A small tidy man with a ring of black hair above tiny sculpted ears and below a shiny dome of pinkish scalp, Dashev hid his sharp black eyes behind round tortoise-rimmed spectacles and his prodigious intellect behind finicky mannerisms. Asked to describe him after a meeting, few could. He'd mastered the art of hiding his personality, that which gives definition to each individual.

"You've fastened on China and North Korea," Grant said thoughtfully, "rather than the Middle East or Russia. Why?"

"Drugs."

"Drugs?" Grant asked. "Oh." Understanding filled his eyes. "The money to purchase high-tech systems for nuclear weapons is coming through the drug trade, and lately the center of drug activity has shifted to the Far East."

"Just so." Dashev's eyes glinted approvingly behind his glasses. "These two nations have formulated new drugs, which are bringing high prices, especially on American markets. Again, you are the lone voice condemning the administration's policy on diminished drug interdiction."

"Technology transfer and drug interdiction," Grant said, correlating this information with what he'd learned that afternoon about the administration's involvement with Anne Peabody. A double incentive? Eliminate Frederickson, who for some reason had become a threat, and pin the murder on Grant, the main thorn in their side politically, both at home and internationally? Neat if it were true. "The President's pet policies."

"A connection I also had noted," Dashev said. He picked up a glass resting in the holder beside him. Grant knew it would contain water. Dashev drank nothing else. Rumor had it alcohol had once threatened to control his life; however, in the seventeen years Grant had known him, Dashev had never touched anything stronger than his omnipresent water.

"Much can happen in the two years before your misguided leader is up for reelection," Dashev continued, watching the play of light on the surface of the water. "He has gambled that he can fool the people long enough to gain his second term, but as with the Chinese-North Korean alliance, you, my friend, stand as the most vocal opponent to his drug policies." Dashev put the glass down and looked at Grant. "When the inevitable downside to his actions begins to be felt, how much nicer if you are no longer around to point it out, especially now that he is so assiduously cultivating a more conservative image. I feel confident he doesn't appreciate having his credibility and motivations questioned. You must seem a most tenacious and vocal questioner to him, as well as a legitimate political threat."

"The administration involved in this . . ." Grant said reluctantly. Though he'd reached the same conclusion already, giving voice to the possibility was sobering.

"Of that I can only surmise," Dashev admitted, "but the NIIA is dangerously powerful and answerable only to the President and his closest friend, the attorney general." He leaned across the aisle, laying his hand on Grant's arm for emphasis. "Several of my contacts suggest that the NIIA is taking a somewhat, shall we say, peculiar interest in your activities, and Jonathan Hunter . . ." He paused, choosing his words with care. "Many are concerned with the power Hunter is amassing, a power unanswerable to anyone but the President. Even more alarming to some is Hunter's hubris. He is Jonathan Hunter; therefore, he is right. Be careful, Bob. When a man gains godlike powers, too often he behaves like the Devil." Dashev leaned back. "I hope to have specific information for you soon, but you understand the difficulties. I have no agents in your country, of course, and must rely on other sources for my information."

"Of course," Grant said. "What you've told me only confirms my own feeling that much is at stake. I'm not convinced of this international connection, though, at least not as the primary motivation. These attacks feel more personal, as if someone hates me—not what I stand for, but me."

"An interesting observation," Dashev said. His eyes turned inward as he considered Grant's impression in light of his own information. "Possibly as an added impetus to the international connection? I'll look into it, also into the source of the funds being used to finance the operation. Financial trails can be so very informative."

"Regardless of who's bankrolling it," Grant said, "someone has to be masterminding it, someone who knows too much about me."

"Do the names Bonfire or John Smythe have meaning for you?"

Grant shook his head, but his face became guarded. He'd detected the change in timbre in Dashev's voice at the mention of the two names. His friend was seldom discomfited. That he was now was significant.

"Bonfire is the premier agent-for-hire in the world today," Dashev said, confirming Grant's premonition. "Some say he's a former Soviet mole who for fifteen years at least has been working within your government. Is that true? We do not know, just as we know little else about him. He is a clever man, who prides himself on the invulnerability of his cover and the impenetrability of his disguises. He is known for seeking and completing even the most difficult assignments. I mention his name because your situation has the convoluted brilliance that has become his trademark."

"The name Bonfire," Grant asked, "does it have significance?"

"For us, no, but for him . . ." Dashev shrugged. "That I cannot tell you. To whisper that name is to be contacted in some untraceable manner. If you have enough money, your wish is fulfilled. If you are trying to trap him," he said, his eyes darkening with remembered pain, "you are dead. He has spies everywhere, but they know as little as we do. They pass on their information, they do his bidding, and they are well paid—all without any link to Bonfire himself. They are uninformed pawns only, doing as they are told, that and nothing more. Those who have deviated from his orders have suffered, usually fatally.

"These paid pawns come from all levels of society, from the most depraved to the most respected. How many others have unknowingly advanced his evil plans is impossible to calculate. As I say, he is the master. He understands human motivation and uses it to his advantage."

"You believe Bonfire's an American?" Grant asked.

"That is so. An American of some considerable influence within your government. That is my belief," Dashev said, taking a long drink of water, perhaps to allow time to steady his thoughts. Bonfire seemed to have a strange power over him, as if too much dark rumination about his foe had diffused the Israeli's normally focused intellect. "Several of my colleagues disagree. Granted, he works for anyone willing to pay, but I see his imprint most dramatically on the inner workings of your country. Too many fine Americans have been ruined by unsubstantiated rumors. Too many behind-the-scene compromises have been made—all to your country's detriment."

Grant said nothing. His mind was cataloguing too many situations that fit into Dashev's scenario. Bonfire. Why had he never heard the name? It should have been well reported and documented in Senate intelligence reports.

"And John Smythe?" he asked. After Dashev's reaction to Bonfire, he was afraid he knew.

"Smythe appeared on the international scene two years ago," Dashev said, reflectively. Something in his tone made Grant wonder if Dashev had been personally involved in that first encounter. "He is as cunning as Bonfire but with a pronounced ruthlessness. Both men—I say men for convenience only; they could as easily be women—are said to be presently involved in something major. If for either of them that something is the destruction of you, then the stakes are, indeed, high. Bonfire and John Smythe are the best. They command the highest remuneration."

"You termed John Smythe ruthless. Does that mean he's more likely to be involved in the Frederickson and Peabody murders?"

"Possibly, though Bonfire is not averse to such expedients. Unlike Bonfire, however, Smythe seems obsessed by the use of disguise. I've heard a strange rumor, unsubstantiated as yet, that he has taken to using the same disguise throughout an assignment, changing only when the assignment has been fulfilled."

"But that doesn't make sense," Grant protested, "not for a professional."

"Only if he feels invulnerable and enjoys the added danger which he alone has demanded of himself." Dashev neatly stacked his notes and replaced them in his inside suit pocket. They were written in some shorthand Grant imagined only he could interpret. As Grant had expected, Dashev hadn't glanced at them. "As I said, such talk is speculation only. John Smythe is disturbingly similar to his mentor Bonfire—and as elusive. Yes," he said at Grant's look of inquiry, "Smythe has been trained by the master. Both are meticulous planners who leave nothing to chance."

The plane began losing altitude as they approached Leesburg Airport outside Washington, D.C.

"I'll continue pursuing all lines of investigation, my friend," Dashev said, "not just the two villains I mentioned." He stretched his legs out, as if to announce his exposition was almost complete. "I must admit that from a personal viewpoint," he continued with a deprecating lift of his hand, "I do hope that either Bonfire or Smythe is involved. I would be pleased to have the opportunity to rid the world of their presence. Too many revere those who will stop at nothing to succeed, as if success can be measured by getting one's way. The veneration they command frightens me."

"From a personal viewpoint," Grant said with a hint of dry amusement, "I certainly hope you succeed in their extermination."

Dashev allowed himself a small smile. "Yes," he said, "I can quite appreciate your hope. Regardless of your enemy's identity," he continued, his voice becoming decisive, "he appears to have given himself a deadline, next Tuesday, the day of the election. Maybe he will become careless in trying to meet that deadline. We must do what we can to guarantee such is the case."

"We must indeed," Grant agreed.

When her husband walked into her bedroom, Estelle tried to mask her surprise. Bitterness assailed her. Surprise? Because her husband sought her in the bedroom? Reality replaced the bitterness. What did he want? The answer, preceded by his usual pretensions at solicitude, wasn't long in coming.

"You look lovely as always, Estelle," he told her, his voice redolent with natural charm.

She stared at him silently, willing her face to remain impassive.

"I'm hoping you'll be able to come to Atlanta with me tomorrow," he continued, taking her silence as appreciation. "We'll go to Joey's funeral first, then come back here and take Marine One to Andrews."

"Have your other plans fallen through?" she asked. Immediately, she wished she could bite back the words. She wasn't ready for a confrontation. At times, she wasn't sure she ever would be.

His reply reassured her. "Fallen through?" he asked pleasantly, either unaware of her allusion to his "snacks" or pretending to be so. "No, Tobias Caruso's still coming, but I hope you'll come, too, Estelle, if it's not too hard on you." His voice became, if possible, even more solicitous. "You've not looked well lately. I don't like you overtaxing yourself, but I think this trip would do you good."

He sat down on the bed beside her and picked up one of her hands. She left it there but turned her head to look out the window.

"I can't go with you." Her voice was muffled. "You're right. I haven't been feeling well. I must attend the funeral, of course, but the Georgia trip will be too much."

He squeezed her hand, almost jerking her toward him. "Look at me, Estelle. Look at me!"

After a moment's hesitation, she did so. His face looking down at her was red with anger. She was elated. For once she'd been able to inspire some sort of emotion in him. How right that it should be anger! Suddenly, she too was suffused with it.

"Look at you? Look at you?" she snapped, unable to restrain herself any longer. "Finish what you have to say and leave." His mouth fell open to protest. She continued before he could speak. "You heard what I said. Leave. Now."

It had been years since she'd spoken to him with such anger, contempt naked in her voice and face. Not since she'd confronted him with his first two affairs years before, certainly not since he'd made her First Lady.

"Estelle," he whispered. His voice broke and he cleared it. "I don't understand your attitude. You're obviously overwrought. The trip will do you good. We never have time together. It would be nice."

"I'm not going."

"But—"

"Leave. Now. You can't change my mind."

The finality in her voice was unmistakable. He closed his mouth on the words he'd prepared and left the room, but not before he'd kissed her cheek and whispered a word of endearment.

Estelle picked up her notepad of illustrations and hurled it at the closed door.

After dropping Grant and Dashev at the Leesburg Airport, Goldie and Yao flew on to Georgia, where they would work on plans for the debate. Lining up dependable Georgians, especially to scope the sites, would be essential.

Robby was waiting outside the airport terminal to drive Grant to Cynthia's house. Yao's substitute protector would be following, but Grant made no effort to identify him. Yao had said he would be nearby, and Yao could be trusted.

Feeling like a returning hero after his lively welcome from Rachel and the kids, Grant called Jenks.

"What did the sheriff have to say?" Rachel asked when he'd hung up. "Why didn't he hold the press conference about Maribeth and the boyfriend?"

"He did," Grant replied. "Everyone was there, TV and print. Jenks read them the sections in Maribeth's diary that prove my innocence. Then he explained that Gayla Sergek's letter was a forgery. He even passed out copies of the lab report."

"So why wasn't any of it on the news?"

Grant looked at her wearily. "The NIIA issued a statement that Jenks was being removed from the investigation and they would be taking over. They didn't say outright that he's incompetent, but the inference certainly was there."

Rachel frowned and handed Grant a cup of coffee. "And now the *Herald*'s up to something." She looked at the clock. Cynthia had been gone for over two hours. Waiting was almost worse than knowing. Almost.

"Here's her car." Grant went over to the counter, poured a cup of coffee, and was just putting it on the table when the door opened. One look at her face was enough. His stomach knotted.

"They're linking you with a convicted drug dealer, Senator."

"A drug dealer!" Rachel exclaimed.

Cynthia nodded. "According to the *Herald*, this picture proves your involvement." She threw a grainy photocopy of a photograph on the table, then draped her coat over the back of a Windsor kitchen chair, picked up the cup of coffee, and cradled it in her hands, coveting its warmth.

Rachel and Grant looked at the picture, their faces registering the same confusion. It showed Grant handing something to or receiving something from a surprisingly ordinary-looking man.

"This guy is a drug dealer?" Grant asked, pointing.

"Hal Olexey, convicted of drug dealing about six weeks ago, now serving time at Lorton," Cynthia said, taking a sip.

"Brother!" Grant studied the picture more closely. "Even I have trouble not believing something must have been going down. Convicted six weeks ago . . ."

Cynthia nodded. Her mussed hair, shiny nose, colorless lips, and wrinkled dress—everything about her spoke of a long and exhausting day.

"A picture of me with him, obviously taken during the summer—look at our clothes—and then he's convicted of drug dealing," Grant said, his eyes focused in thought. "Either we have the mother of all coincidences, or this attack against me goes back at least that far."

"And Olexey allowed himself to be imprisoned to make his story credible?" Rachel asked doubtfully.

"What's the big deal about a prison sentence?" Grant asked. "He would know he'd be out in a matter of months. Even murderers aren't in for more than a few years. The drug implications are what I find interesting. First Bailey, now this."

"Sherrill said they wanted to discredit your drug stance."

"Looks like she was right," Grant said. "Dashev suggested the same thing. But why drugs? Did you learn any specifics, Cynthia?"

"Nothing much," she admitted. "My friend was conscience-stricken enough just giving me a copy of the picture. She felt disloyal to the *Herald* but was concerned they'd overstepped the bounds of decency in using a circumstantial picture to condemn you of a criminal act. That's what they're planning to suggest. Honestly. That you're a drug dealer yourself."

"A dealer?" Grant's dark brows met in a formidable scowl.

"Apparently, this Olexey said you bought so much you couldn't have used it all yourself." Cynthia gave a short laugh and ran a hand through her hair, completing the mussing that a hard day had begun. "No doubt they'll hint I was one of the nasty partakers."

"And from there it's only a short step to suggesting I provided the drugs for Bailey and his friends," Grant surmised. "Is this picture their only proof?"

"I don't know. She gave me the picture and told me the guy is Hal Olexey. I got the information about the arrest from a computer search."

"A convicted drug dealer?" Rachel asked. Her voice was puzzled.

"What is it, Rachel?" Grant asked.

"Look at your shirt, Bob."

Grant studied the picture. "That's the one India gave me for my birthday. I recognize the anchor design." India had given it to him as a remembrance of his years as a naval officer. He had been touched by her thoughtfulness. Those memories *were* special.

"Exactly," Rachel said, tapping the picture for emphasis. "Remember the barbecue sauce you spilled on it at our Fourth of July cookout?"

"Sure. A real mess."

"And one I could never get completely out. I ended up giving the shirt to the church for their clothes closet. You only got to wear it once before it was ruined, that fund-raiser on the Potomac, the one for all Republicans up for reelection."

"I remember." Grant studied the background of the picture. It had seemed uninformative until he'd had an event to connect to it. "I believe you're right. That could be the edge of the boat we sailed on that day." His long finger, slightly bent from breaking it in a high-school basketball game, tapped a dark shape at the edge of the picture.

"And I'll bet," Rachel said, her voice excited, "that's Carlos Van Tassel." She pointed to a blurred figure in the background. "See the cigar and the pattern on his shirt? I'm almost sure it's Carlos. Who else has a stomach like that?"

"Call your friend," Grant told Cynthia. "Tell her that picture was taken at a public fund-raiser."

"I don't know, Senator," Cynthia said slowly. "She can't really do anything without revealing she gave it to me. I hate to put her in that position."

"You're right, of course," Grant said, rising. "This is obviously Peter Evans's work."

Evans wasn't at the *Herald*, but Grant left his name and number. Within minutes, Evans returned the call.

"I hear you've been looking for me, Senator. What can I do for you?"

"Withdraw the picture you plan to run tomorrow."

Grant could hear Evans's sharp intake of breath. "Picture, Senator?" Evans finally asked. "What picture?"

"Being coy doesn't suit you, Evans. Does the name Hal Olexey jog your memory?"

"I do believe I may have heard that name," Evans said cautiously.

"I do believe so, too," Grant shot back, "and if I were you, I would rethink any plan to publish that picture and those allegations. I can prove it was taken at a Republican fund-raiser."

"So you admit you met with Hal Olexey?" Evans asked, satisfaction entering his voice.

"Didn't you hear me, Evans?" Grant demanded. "That picture was a setup. There was nothing private or underhanded about it at all. If you try to link me to a drug dealer, I'll take you to court."

"Senator, I have no idea how you know what picture we plan to use tomorrow," Evans said, biting off each word, "but I intend to find out, and your threats only reinforce my feeling that the story is there. Why else would you bother me? Can you prove the picture was taken when you say it was?"

"Prove it!" Grant's voice rose belligerently. "All you have to do is get the donor list for the fund-raiser." Even as he said it, Grant knew Olexey's name wouldn't be there. His enemy wouldn't have neglected such a fundamental mistake. Evans would look and be more convinced than ever that he was lying. "You know good and well I can't control who comes to those events," he continued doggedly. "You can check all my FEC filings. Hal Olexey has never given a dime to any of my campaigns. In the name of fair journalism, I ask you to withdraw the story. It is without foundation. It's pure fabrication. Can't you understand that, Evans?"

"I resent your tone, Grant," Evans said. His own tone was icy. "I'll publish the truth, regardless of any threats. You picked the wrong man if you think you can strong-arm me. I won't have it!"

"You're going ahead with the story?"

"You'd better believe it, Senator! You admit you met him, and you admit you accepted a campaign contribution from him."

"You're a disgrace to your profession, you self-righteous scoundrel!"

"I'll be glad to quote you on that, Grant." Evans slammed down the phone.

Grant looked at Rachel and Cynthia and shook his head.

"I just violated one of my cardinal rules," he said wearily. "I made a call when I was at the height of anger. We all need some sleep. We can't afford mistakes now."

They'd been in bed for more than an hour, but Grant wasn't asleep. He was watching the play of slivers of moonlight on the ceiling as he sorted through the implications of all he knew. Time was growing short, but the dangers and the intricacies of the attack seemed to be multiplying.

The bed creaked as Grant turned toward Rachel. Though it was late and they hadn't slept much the last few nights, he thought she was still awake. He was right. Her hand reached out and slid into his.

"I'll be going back to Atlanta in the morning," he said, wishing he could see her face. He reached out and traced its outline with his fingertips, trying not to think this might be the last time. "I want you to know how much I love you," he said, feeling the softness of her lips under his fingers. "I'm sorry you and the children have been brought into this, but you have my solemn promise, I will be vindicated, and our family will be made whole again."

He wanted to tell her so much more, about how her love sustained him, about the joy he felt just being near her, about his respect for her and the confidence he had that the kids would be all right because she'd nurtured them so . . .

He felt tears on her cheek and pulled her into his arms.

Friday, October 30:

Four Days Before the Election

Dad!" Bailey yelled as he bounded up the steps. "Dad!"

Grant jerked upright in bed, his heart racing. Rachel scooted onto her elbows, her body tense as if to ward off a blow.

The bedroom door banged open, and with one last stride, Bailey stood by the side of the bed. He shook a newspaper under Grant's nose.

Slowly, Grant's heart steadied. The paper, he realized with relief. Only the paper. He looked at the clock. Five thirty. The alarm was about to go off. He jabbed the off button. At least they'd slept a little, he thought, his body protesting for more.

"Look at this!" Bailey continued, unaware of the anxious moment he'd caused his parents. "You won't believe it! They practically say you're a drug dealer!"

Grant took the paper and moved so that Rachel, plumping up their pillows and stifling a yawn, could read it, too.

"Rather an eye-catching headline," Grant said. His voice sounded matter-of-fact. Alarming Bailey would serve no purpose, might even push him to do something rash.

"'SENATOR GRANT A DRUG DEALER?'" Bailey read, out-raged. The accusation was bad enough, but his father's cavalier attitude was almost too much to bear. "This is even worse," he said pointing to an easy-to-read typed page with DEA stamped across it. "Supposedly a page from your NIIA/DEA file. See? It says DEA's been monitoring your drug activities for years. How can you stand it?"

"Partly because we were warned to expect it," Grant said, his eyes racing down the page. It was just as outrageous as Bailey indicated. "And partly, I suppose, because it's so completely unbelievable."

"This is the *Herald*, Dad, not some rag at the supermarket checkout. And a DEA file!" He sat down on the side of the bed, just as he had as a child when he needed answers. "Everyone will read it, and probably most will believe it."

"A lie is a lie," Grant told him, fatigue edging his voice, "no matter who says it, no matter how much proof is offered, and no matter how many believe it."

"Nice, Dad, but so what?"

"Believe me, Bailey, your dad doesn't like this any better than you," Rachel said, patting her son's hand. She glanced at her husband, her look

278

full of understanding and compassion. "But he's right. We can't do anything until we find a way to refute it."

"You have to admit Peter Evans knows how to spin a lie." Grant indicated the picture they'd seen the night before, now appearing in bold relief above the fold on the front page. "Look at the caption."

"'Senator Robert H. Grant with convicted drug dealer Hal Olexey,'" Bailey read aloud. "'In an exclusive interview last night, Senator Grant admitted he had met with Olexey, who is now serving time for his latest drug conviction. Olexey has been arrested several times on suspicion of murder.'"

Rachel glanced sharply at Grant. Arrested for murder! Evans implied that Grant knew Olexey, a potential hit man, not just Olexey, a drug dealer. Evans was a vicious enemy made more frightening by his veneer of intellectual superiority, but even for Evans, this last innuendo was monstrous.

"Interesting interpretation of your comments last night," Rachel said after a barely perceptible pause.

Grant's jaw clenched. Somehow, someday, Evans was going to be held accountable.

"How'd they fake the picture?" Bailey asked, unaware of the undercurrent. He leaned forward to examine the photograph more closely.

"I don't think they did."

Bailey looked up, startled. Grant explained about the fund-raiser.

"But how could a character like Olexey get in?"

"They don't check the pedigree of people attending a fund-raiser," Grant said. "If you pay the money, you get to come—though I may reconsider that policy when this is all over," he added dryly.

"Okay," Bailey said slowly, thinking it through, "so Olexey could have gotten into the fund-raiser, no questions asked. But the *Herald* . . . if the *Herald* knows that's true . . ."

Grant nodded.

". . . I can't believe they'd go ahead and run it."

"Believe me, I wish you were right," Grant said, his eyes involuntarily straying to the picture. "Life would be much easier if everyone in the media were honorable. Sometimes I wonder what they wouldn't do for a story. You remember the exploding truck a network rigged to prove their story against a car company?"

Bailey nodded thoughtfully.

"False numbers and skewed studies to validate their stands on AIDS, the homeless, abortion, global warming, even alar on apples," Rachel added. "Any pet cause. And they ignore anything contradictory, even when the proof is overwhelming."

Bailey still looked unconvinced. "Sure, they do it all the time," he said, "but this isn't the same."

Grant thought a moment. "Okay. Here's the perfect example, almost exactly what's happened here. You're too young to remember, but when Rosalyn Carter was First Lady, she had her picture taken—at a public event—with cult leader Jim Jones."

Bailey looked blank. "Who's he?"

"Was," Grant corrected, "and not a nice man. Jones was an American who founded a cult, which he moved to Guyana. Subsequently, he convinced his followers, fellow Americans, to drink cyanide-laced Kool Aid."

"They knew they would die?" Bailey asked, horror mixed with astonishment. "And they still drank it?"

"Hard to believe, but, yes, several hundred of them. Children, even babies, were given it. A congressman down there checking on the cult for constituents was murdered when he tried to prevent it. Jones died there, too."

"And the picture of Mrs. Carter with him was published after he killed all those people and after he was dead?"

"That's right," Grant said. "I'm sure it sold lots of papers. The White House was livid, justifiably so."

"Okay, so maybe you're right," Bailey admitted. He picked up the paper and frowned at it. In that moment he looked exactly like his father, Rachel thought, and was pleased. "But that means someone sent this Olexey character to the fund-raiser just so they could get the picture, right?"

Grant nodded.

"That means this has been planned for a long time, even longer than my setup."

Grant nodded again. So much planning.

"By the paper?" Bailey asked, still examining the picture.

"Could be, but I doubt it. Not their style."

"Then who?"

Grant shrugged. "If we knew that, we'd know everything."

"Well, I know one thing," Bailey said, throwing the paper on the bed. "Today, I'm going to find Reggie Dixon and make him talk."

"Be careful, Bailey," Grant cautioned. Had he been wrong in not showing Bailey the depth of his concern? "I know you want to help, and, believe me, I appreciate it; but these people are dangerous."

"Don't I know it! Still can't believe I let them sucker me. I'm sorry about that, Dad."

"Don't be," Grant said. His heart swelled with love for his dejected son, who still retained traces of the carefree youngster he'd been such a few years before. Bailey had matured into a fine young man, but he was too untried to have developed the skills he needed against an amoral enemy. Grant wasn't sure he wanted any child of his to develop them—cynicism was an all-too-frequent by-product, and cynicism was an uncomfortable view of life. Much better to continue as he was, aware that problems would always be part of his life, but with the faith to face them. "No one could have anticipated such depraved behavior," Grant reassured his son. "That's what I'm trying to say. These people don't play by any rules. It's like getting into what you assume is a friendly pickup basketball game and discovering one of the balls has been loaded with an impact explosive. That's one discovery you want to make before you dribble the ball. You need backup, Bailey, someone trained to spot the booby traps. All of us do. That's why Stephen Yao goes with me everywhere, and that's why I expect you to stick close to your protection."

Bailey scowled. "Baby-sitters!"

"No!" Grant's naval subordinates would have recognized his tone. It allowed no argument. "Protectors, and don't you forget it. It's bad enough that Sherrill refuses to leave town, but I won't have you running around on your own, worrying all of us. We can't afford to have something else happen. Do you understand?"

"Okay, okay." Bailey's frown dissolved into a grin. "I'll be a good boy. But I can still go after Reggie, can't I? Sherrill and I?"

Grant looked at his son's face, so eager now. He wished he could say no, but Bailey and Sherrill were the only ones who could recognize Reggie on sight, and they were both over twenty-one, as they'd already reminded him several times. Even so, Grant knew Bailey would do whatever he asked. So hard to remember that his son was a man. So hard to let go. "You won't go anywhere without protection?"

"I understand."

"Then, thank you," Grant said, squeezing his shoulder affectionately. "I hope you find him, but don't forget, your computer hacking is important, too."

Even today, Jonathan Hunter attended the meeting in the War Room. He had to. His house was both too empty and too full: empty of the only one who could carry on his name, and full of the pseudo-pity of the person who called herself his wife. He couldn't bear the screaming silence. His son's funeral! The thought kept assailing him unawares, firing his anger. So much better to forget it completely and concentrate on affairs of state.

Corforth and the Vice President were already in the War Room. The President wouldn't be attending. He created the brush fires. Others put them out.

"Why is the press so interested in snacks?" Hunter demanded.

"Who knows," Corforth retorted, rubbing his eyes wearily. "By now most of the West Wing knows. Anyone could have let it slip."

"Stonewall," the Veep said. His face looked intelligent even as he uttered this inanity. He possessed a trait other politicians would have dearly loved: the ability to be perceived as intelligent regardless of his vacuous pronouncements. "That's what we have to do. Avoid the real issue. Keep answering innocent questions with innocent answers."

"Don't waste my time," Hunter said bitingly. "Any idiot knows that."

The Veep flushed angrily and turned away.

"Have POTUS keep treating any questions of snacks as literal," Hunter continued, ignoring the Veep and addressing Corforth. "No one will press him, not unless they have everything and not unless they think it's more than a minor indiscretion. They've had their own flings, that's for sure. He'll have to control himself for a while, that's all, until it dies down."

"I suggested that yesterday," Corforth said. "You know POTUS. He wasn't pleased. He's so single-minded about it, sometimes I wonder if it's become an addiction."

"Addiction!" Hunter snorted. "Pleased or not, he has no choice." His body suddenly still, Hunter stared over his half glasses at Corforth. "You can leave now, Eugene."

Corforth's involuntary start of surprise was instantly suppressed. Never before had he been dismissed from a meeting of the inner circle. He looked from Hunter to the Veep, who had turned back around and was regarding him with malicious satisfaction. Corforth returned the look, turned abruptly, and left.

Hunter picked up that morning's *Herald*. "A fine article," he said. "Tell Evans we're pleased, especially with the Olexey-as-hired-killer innuendo, but not pleased enough. Be sure he understands."

"Several evening news shows are planning follow-ups," the Veep said smugly. His rosy round cheeks under twinkling blue eyes gave the impression of bonhomie. Only those who looked beyond the twinkle recognized the cunning arrogance that had inexorably edged him to his present position, poised to grab the gold ring. Hunter alone understood the Veep's manipulative strengths and mental weaknesses. Hunter, in typical Hunter style, used them to his own advantage. Each man waited for the other to falter. Hunter was the more patient and adroit, not to mention the more intelligent, and the Veep knew it. The gold ring would come through natural eight-year attrition, not through a mistake, not if Hunter had anything to say about it—and he did.

"We're funneling information out on deep background," the Veep continued. He was especially tight with several major news figures. Information went both ways, the most sophisticated and possibly most effective information highway in D.C. "Anything you have that should be passed on—get it to me."

"Good." After a glance at his notes to be sure he'd covered everything, Hunter closed the folder. "I'll be monitoring this closely," he said. His eyes regarded some inner vision, one he obviously found gratifying. "Grant's about to learn a lesson in power politics, one he'll never forget."

Within a mile of leaving Cynthia's house, Grant knew he was being followed. Whether his followers wanted him aware of their presence, he couldn't decide, nor did he know if they were NIIA. He did know that he had to lose them before he called Benjamin Dashev and before he led them to Matt Goldie, waiting for him at the airstrip.

Remembering Yao's advice, Grant timed his speed so he went through three lights just as they turned red, then turned down side streets to avoid giving his followers, stopped by reds, time to catch him. After twenty minutes of such maneuvering, he decided he could safely drive to his prearranged meeting with Yao.

"Looks like you're clean," Yao told him. Then Yao grinned. "Not bad for an admiral." He turned to point down an alleyway. "If you'll just pull through there, the last door on the left will be unlocked. Use the phone on the desk. I'll keep watch."

Dashev, when Grant reached him, had learned disappointingly little since the previous evening. He asked if Grant could get a copy of the forged letter that had been planted on Gayla Sergek.

"The original would be even better," Dashev said. "Master forgers are artists in their own way, and as with every artist, each has his own imperceptible but distinctive style. Learn the identity of the forger, and we'll have an idea who hired him.

"And, Senator, I'm more convinced than ever that either Bonfire or John Smythe is behind this. Maybe both."

Bonfire or John Smythe. Maybe both. Grant's jaw clenched. Again, he'd heard the disquieting undertone in Dashev's voice. "You're right about Bonfire," Grant said. He related Reggie's overheard phone conversation.

"So the plot thickens, as you Americans say. I'll intensify inquiries in that direction."

"Motive would help."

"Certainly. I'll do what I can."

Grant heard Dashev softly humming "Whatever Lola Wants, Lola Gets" as he replaced the receiver.

When Grant left the back room, Yao had switched the previous car for a different one.

Bailey and Sherrill were confident they knew where to look for Reggie Dixon, an address they'd gotten from a phone number scribbled on the back of a long-overdue bill. Angel was the name written by the number. Sherrill had called the number, pretending to be a long-distance company wanting Angel to change carriers. Sherrill thought she'd recognized Reggie's voice when he'd answered the phone.

"We'll find him, Mom," Bailey said, giving her an unexpected kiss on the cheek. "Promise."

"Just be careful," Rachel told their retreating backs. She sighed. They looked so young, and they acted as if they were crusaders, out to right the wrongs of the world. She tore her eyes from the back door and reached for the ringing phone. If only she could be sure they wouldn't do anything foolish . . .

"I was trying to reach Senator Grant," the caller said. "Senator Robert Grant."

The voice was young and breathless, somewhat hesitant, with a pronounced Brooklyn accent. Was it Julie from Anne Peabody's office? Rachel wondered. Her heart began racing. Be Julie, she prayed. Please be Julie. Only Julie could tell them the questions Frederickson had thought important enough to ask the day he died. They needed to know. They were running into too many dead ends and too many new lies. Frederickson had found the truth. So could they, but they needed Julie's cooperation.

"I'm sorry, but Bob's not here right now," Rachel said. Whatever she did, she mustn't frighten the young woman. "This is Mrs. Grant. Rachel Grant. Is this Julie?"

"Oh, Mrs. Grant, you knew!"

"Bob told me you might call. I'm so pleased you did." She took a calming breath and adopted the tone she used with her patients, competence liberally laced with compassion. "I know he'll be disappointed to have missed you. It may be hours now before he can get to a phone. He's on his way back to Georgia."

The young woman didn't respond.

"You can talk to me, though," Rachel finally said, her heart thudding painfully. Don't hang up! Don't hang up! "You can trust me. I'm a doctor and used to keeping confidences."

Again, no response. The silent seconds dragged on. "Please, Julie. Bob needs your help. We all do." Unconsciously, she held her breath.

"It may be hours before I can speak to him?"

"I'm afraid so."

"Then maybe we'd better talk."

Rachel began breathing again.

When Eugene Corforth entered the Oval Office, the President was standing with his back to the door. He was motionless, staring at the barren Rose Garden. He spoke, but without turning.

"Estelle refuses to go with me to Georgia." His hands were clasped behind his back, and Corforth watched them clench and unclench. "You're going to have to convince her."

"Me, sir?" Corforth asked, trying to keep the surprise from his voice. "I'm sure she'd listen to you long before she'd listen to me."

"You're the one who's going to take care of it," the President said with finality as he turned and looked Corforth full in the face. "I'm leaving at one, and Estelle had better be at my side, just where I need her. You can do that, can't you, Eugene? Surely, Hunt doesn't have to do everything." He wheeled around and resumed his regard of the windswept walkway and garden. "Why did Joey have to die now?" he murmured. "Why now?"

Corforth wasn't sure the words were intended for his ears, but he heard and felt sick.

Half an hour later, he found Estelle waiting for him in the gallery at the top of the grand staircase. The area, actually a wide hallway, was decorated in shades of blue and yellow with green accents, and served as a semiformal seating area for the First Family. Sofas and chairs, their cushions plump with down, formed a square around a large glass-topped coffee table. Books about the White House rested on top. Bookcases lined the walls and were filled with Boehm porcelain birds, bronze sculptures—several of them Remingtons—books pertaining to former Presidents, and framed photographs, most of which showed the President with various heads of state. Three informal snaps of the children were on the table at Estelle's side. Large fanlight windows at opposite ends of the long, expansive hallway bathed everything in the mellow glow of late autumn sunlight.

Corforth had to say her name several times before Estelle looked up. Even then she seemed preoccupied.

"I appreciate your seeing me, Estelle."

She smiled then, affection warming her face. "Poor Eugene. He's put you right in the middle, hasn't he?"

"I don't know—"

"You needn't try to protect him," she interrupted. The sympathy in her eyes tore at him. He felt like a heel. POTUS was a fool! "We both know why he sent you. Atlanta. Right?"

Corforth struggled for words to soften the truth, but all he could do was nod.

"Poor Eugene." He started to speak, but she wouldn't let him. "I'd planned to defy him, to stay home regardless of his blandishments, but I won't do that, not since it's you he's sent. He's so clever, isn't he? He's always been good at getting his way, maybe too good. Tell him I'll be ready."

They stared at each other in knowing silence.

"I'm sorry, Estelle."

"I know you are. Thank you. Amy is a fortunate woman." Her smile broke, and she looked fixedly down at the sketchbook in her hands.

Corforth hesitated, wanting to give comfort. He had none to give.

Though Grant had tried to keep his arrival secret, a crowd was waiting when he entered the Atlanta airport's general aviation terminal. At least they hadn't seen Matt Goldie, he thought as he fought his way through them. He started to tell the media no comment, but bit back the words. He had their attention, so why not take advantage of it? Maybe he could make public what Jenks had been unable to the day before. If his enemy had alerted the media, this could be a way to turn his plan against him.

Grant walked to the cameras and stopped, facing them squarely. He stood quietly, ignoring all taunts, even ignoring the reporters' questions. Eventually, an uneasy silence settled on the crowd. Even the omnipresent protesters stopped heckling.

"I've listened to more than enough accusations and innuendoes in the last few days," Grant began. His cool gaze was as arresting as his calm assurance. "I'm in public office and have been for twelve years. I'm running for reelection and plan on winning."

Several protesters booed loudly. Grant just looked at them, a look he'd perfected during his years of command in the military, the same look that had quieted angry students when he was president of Landsdowne College.

"I expect to have my past examined minutely," he said finally. "I expect to have my political positions attacked by those who disagree with me. However, the attacks this time have gone beyond decency. They have impugned my honor both as a Senator and as a Christian. *That* I can neither condone nor tolerate. I am innocent, totally innocent, of all accusations that have been leveled at me."

The protesters resumed their catcalls, only to be shushed by others in the crowd. He'd enlisted their attention, Grant noted. He felt no elation. He knew the vagaries of public opinion too well.

"However," he continued into the now expectant hush, "while I might not have anticipated the viciousness of the attack, I was prepared for a battle. I knew elections could turn ugly when I made the choice to run for reelection. Maribeth Pariss made no such choice. She has no forum on which to protest. She has been given no rights or dignity. The truth of her life has been ignored by the media, ignored, I have to believe, because the truth doesn't support the evil caricature they're trying to draw of me.

"Probe into my past. I welcome it. Investigate Russell Frederickson's murder. No one has more at stake in finding that murderer than I do. But allow Maribeth Pariss the dignity she deserves. Don't link her good name in any way with the slime that's being thrown around in this campaign. Maribeth Pariss deserves better. She never had an affair with me. She was a hard-working employee doing her best to serve the people of Georgia. Sheriff Jenks has overwhelming proof of her innocence. If the media had any decency, they would report that truth and let Miss Pariss rest in peace.

"I'm sick of the lies," Grant continued. His deep voice was low and hard. His eyes were hard as well. "I intend to bring this campaign out of the gutter and back to a level that the office of Senator demands."

A single shouted epithet was immediately silenced. By now the crowd around him was huge, almost filling the small building. Grant hoped every one of these people would go home, fired with conviction about his innocence, but he had no illusions. Honesty, hard work, innocence didn't titillate, and they didn't sell newspapers or create rating bonanzas. That was the reality he was facing.

"While my political philosophies are totally different from Tobias Caruso's," Grant continued, "we do agree on one thing." His eyes moved slowly from face to face as he delivered each word with slow precision. This time none of the eyes he met slid away in embarrassed confusion. "It is time to give light to the truth and bury forever the lies and innuendoes that have defiled this campaign. I *will* debate Tobias Caruso. On Sunday, if I'm allowed an unbiased forum, you, the citizens of Georgia, will hear both sides of every issue, personal as well as political. I look forward to placing all facts before you with no part ignored or distorted so that you can judge the truth for yourselves.

"On Tuesday at the voting booth, you can make your decision known. I'm confident that by Tuesday you will know the truth behind this campaign to discredit me. I'm confident that you will reelect me Senator. Free and honest elections are the strength of America, and the foundation on which I willingly place my future."

Grant stared unsmiling at the cameras a moment longer. He was an imposing figure, fiercely confident in himself and the truth.

The crowd parted silently to let him pass. A few people touched him tentatively and whispered words of support, but the rest were held in silence.

Suddenly, the pack of reporters surged forward, clamoring for more, and the spell was broken.

"Quite a speech," Masterson whispered as he caught up with Grant.

"I meant every word," Grant said, his eyes still hard. "I wonder how the media knew I would be here."

They hurried toward the car Robby had pulled up in front of the main entrance. Reporters continued to dog them. Grant's face left no doubt of his low opinion of them. Silently, he and Masterson got into the car.

"Who knows?" Masterson said, continuing their conversation. "Maybe one of the people I called about the meeting?" He shrugged, then hurried on. "I'm afraid you're going to be disappointed with the turnout. I couldn't get everyone, and of those I did, not all could come."

"Could or would?"

"A few of both."

Thirteen people were waiting for Grant. Though the overall mood was grim, all seemed pleased to see him.

"I know I wasn't invited," Brandon Bascham, Oconee County Chairman, said, "but when Ginger told me about it, I wanted to be here. Hope you don't mind."

"I'm just sorry Mike wasn't able to reach you," Grant said with a thoughtful glance at Masterson, who shrugged his shoulders. "I'm glad you would come. I'm glad all of you would. I don't need to tell you this campaign is a mess." At their looks, he laughed ruefully. "I know. That's the understatement of the year."

"You're withdrawing, aren't you?" Ginger Wright asked. Her plump, unlined face was as worried as Grant could ever remember seeing it.

"No," he said emphatically, "certainly not with my integrity under attack. Actually, I'm planning to win."

Ginger didn't look any less worried. If anything, she merely added pity to her emotions. Skeptical pity. They all looked skeptical.

Grant smiled wearily in acknowledgment of their right to be skeptical. Then he proceeded to explain. He'd never had a more attentive audience.

He sounded confident as he outlined his plan because he *was* confident. Even so, these people had years of experience working on political campaigns. They were realists. The charges against the Senator were serious and many. The refutation would have to be unassailable, and even if he were able to prove his innocence to every charge, normal lines of communication—TV commercials, brochures, newspaper, and radio blitzes—would be impossible. Time was too short. The election was too soon.

The people in this room were the ones Grant would have to depend on to find atypical ways to disseminate his message. They knew the voters in their districts. They knew how best to reach them and convince them.

Hopefully, he would have the proof in time for the debate on Sunday when he could present the facts publicly himself. If not, if he were still struggling to find the truth even that late, they needed to be prepared for a literally last-minute, last-ditch effort.

They left the meeting committed to Grant and determined to do whatever was necessary. But one thought was uppermost in their minds: Would anything they did, no matter how brilliantly executed, convince enough voters soon enough to make a difference? In their own minds, Grant's friends were determined—no one was going to destroy a Senator of Grant's courage and conviction if there was anything, anything at all, that could be done to prevent it.

There's Reggie! I saw him, Bailey! There!" Sherrill grabbed Bailey's arm and started pulling him from the car. "He was going inside. I'm sure it was Reggie."

They raced up the steps, then paused for a moment before Bailey cautiously opened the door. The dingy vestibule was empty.

"Where'd he go?" Bailey whispered even as he took the stairs two at a time. Sherrill raced after him.

"You look down here," he said, pointing toward the gloomy second-floor corridor. "Come get me if you find him." He was already halfway up the next flight.

As he reached the top, he saw someone disappear into a door down the hall. Fourth door on the left, Bailey decided, counting quickly.

Pausing only long enough for whoever it was to get inside, he tiptoed down the hall and pressed his ear against the door. He could hear voices, a woman's and a man's, but could distinguish no words.

Silently, he ran down to the second floor, grabbed Sherrill by the arm, and explained his plan as they raced back up the steps. Below, the door to the outside opened, but they paid no attention.

They hurried to the fourth door on the left. Sherrill took a deep breath, then knocked.

"Who's there?" Reggie's voice! He'd been right! Bailey exulted, his adrenaline roaring.

He gave Sherrill a thumb's up.

"Federal Express," Sherrill said. "A letter for Reggie Dixon in care of Angel Soesbe."

"What!" They could hear whispers behind the door. Sherrill took another steadying breath. Reggie finally spoke. "Slide it under the door."

She looked at Bailey. He mimed using a pen. "I'm sorry, sir, but I have to get a signature," she said, unconsciously reaching out to grasp his hand.

They stood hand in hand, straining toward the door.

The door chain jangled. Bailey grinned at Sherrill triumphantly, then moved her back out of the way.

The door opened a crack, and Reggie stuck out his hand. "Give it to—"

Bailey kicked the door open, knocking Reggie to the floor. As Reggie scrambled to his feet, the girl in the room with him began screaming. Sherrill ran over and slapped her. The girl's stringy brown hair whipped around her face. The red imprint of Sherrill's hand stood out starkly against the white pallor of her cheeks. The screams stopped.

In the ensuing silence, Sherrill's agonized apologies mixed with the girl's sobs and the grunts of the struggling men.

After a brief tussle, Bailey grabbed Reggie by the shoulders, dragged him to his feet, and when he tried to run, slugged him hard in the stomach. With an *oomph* of released air, Reggie crumpled to the floor. The girl ran to him and cradled his head in her lap.

"What do you think you're doing?" she screamed. "Get out of here! Get out before I call the cops!"

"Not until Reggie tells us who paid him to frame me," Bailey said, rubbing his knuckles. He looked down at Reggie, almost sorry to see him getting his breath back. Reggie was scum. Too bad he needed to be able to talk.

"So you're Bailey Grant," the girl said, glaring at him. Her holey jeans were grimy. Her tight white top was stained and worn.

"Yes," Bailey said, taking a step toward her. "And we might as well start with you."

She scooted back, her eyes darting toward the door.

"What do you know about Reggie's scheme?" Bailey demanded.

"It worked, didn't it?" she asked, her face distorted with malicious triumph. "Served you right. A drug bust!"

"Who hired Reggie?"

She laughed. Bailey's anger flared. He reached out to grab her.

The door to the room banged open.

"We'll take over now," Ramon said, as he and Tommy walked into the room.

Reggie was fully recovered now. "You guys saw him." He pointed toward Bailey. "He tried to kill me. I want him arrested."

"You're talking to the wrong people, *amigo*," Ramon told him. "We don't make arrests. We give choices. You two can either come stay with us for a few days, or we'll call your boss. Take it or leave it."

"My boss?" Reggie stood and brushed off his jeans, faking nonchalance. With their arrival, he'd regained most of his swagger. "You're bluffing." He started for the door. "Come on, Angel."

"Bonfire will be glad to know where to find you, won't he?" Bailey asked softly. His father had told him about Dashev's suggestion. That combined with Bear's overheard mention of Bonfire by Reggie made the question less than wild.

The shot hit home. Reggie blanched and staggered over to lean against the wall. "Bonfire?" His voice was hoarse. "What do you know about Bonfire?"

No one answered.

"What do you know about Bonfire?" He screamed the first words, but the name Bonfire came out as a desperate whisper. Still they remained silent. He pushed himself wearily away from the wall. "We'll go with you."

"Reggie!" the girl wailed. "I can't—"

"Shut up! We'll go with you," he continued, unsuccessfully working to suppress a shiver, "but you've got to promise to protect us, and I mean real protection." The shiver subsided only to be replaced by an odd tic over his left eye.

The service for Joey Hunter was held in a small chapel overwhelmed by the cloying scent of funeral flowers. Sunlight streamed through the stained-glass window behind the gleaming mahogany coffin, throwing bright shards of color on his parents sitting in the front row and on the President and First Lady sitting beside them.

Rebecca Hunter watched the play of the colored fragments of light on her dress and on her hands clutched tightly in her lap. She tried to keep her mind on the words of the minister. She wanted to feel "the peace that passeth all understanding." She wanted to feel something besides emptiness. She couldn't look at the casket.

She gave no thought to her husband sitting beside her any more than he did to her. When their son died, the last link between them had died as well.

Jonathan Hunter didn't hear any of the minister's words of comfort. He was a captive of his thoughts. He'd failed his son—not in the drug use. That was Grant's fault alone. No, his failure, Hunter knew, was in not recognizing Grant's evil and crushing it before his son could be hurt. For the only time in his life, he'd had the power and failed to use it. Never again, he promised himself. Never again.

Surrounded by hundreds of friends and colleagues, Hunter made a solemn if silent vow to avenge his son's death. Robert Grant would suffer as he deserved. That would be the final tribute from father to son. He had the power. This time he would use it as it was meant to be used.

Immediately following the service, Hunter stood on the steps of the chapel, facing a vista of nothing but television cameras and reporters. The same stained-glass window that had illuminated him during the service formed a shield around him now. He'd never appeared wiser or more indomitable.

"My wife and I are eternally grateful to all Americans who have prayed for us in our time of sorrow," Hunter said in hushed but vibrant tones. "Your support has given us the courage to face the future."

His voice devoid of emotion, its emptiness enhancing his eminence, he continued. "No one has been more compassionate and caring than our great President. I am indeed honored to have him as a treasured friend as well as respected leader. I've asked that he not curtail his schedule because of our tragedy. His trip to Georgia today is essential."

Hunter paused for emphasis, determined to make his meaning clear. This was the first step in exerting his power.

"Essential," he repeated. "Again, I thank you, the good people of America, for your outpouring of kindness and support. My wife and I are deeply indebted."

The announcer appeared on the screen.

"We will carry the President's Georgia trip in its entirety, during special live coverage later today. In a related story . . ."

Reggie Dixon and Angel Soesbe were taken by Ramon and Tommy to a safe house. Every precaution was used to elude pursuers, including the two following cars they positively identified as no-goodniks, Tommy's term, pronounced with only a trace of humor. Despite Reggie's complaint that they were wasting too much time, they stopped at one point to change cars, a precaution that may have saved more than one life, Reggie's for sure.

Not one but two homing devices were found on the original car, the second device so cleverly concealed only Yao thought to look for it. He immediately increased precautions for every facet of their operation. "Know thine enemy" was gaining added importance with each sinister clue they uncovered.

Reggie and Angel were to be questioned, then held in safety until Bonfire was no longer a threat. Their information, for the most part confirmation of what Grant and his allies already had surmised, would make its way to Cynthia, Yao, Goldie, and Dashev as well as to Grant himself. It would be examined minutely from all angles with the ultimate goal being to find some weakness, some chink in his armor, that could be used against Bonfire himself.

Now, Bailey and Sherrill were back at Cynthia's, eating turkey sandwiches and chips while they watched the noon news. Additional bodyguards were posted around the house.

"Did you hear that idiot Hunter?" Bailey asked, the sandwich forgotten in his hand. "And at his son's funeral! How could . . ."

He stopped speaking. Footage of his college campus was on the screen.

"Isn't that the guy who screamed at you yesterday?" Sherrill asked, pointing to the young man being interviewed. His empty black eyes and bristly, almost bald head were disturbingly familiar.

Bailey moved to the edge of his chair but said nothing.

". . . and we students demand that the administration stop their craven pandering to Senator Grant and his son. Bailey Grant should be allowed no special leniency. He should not be allowed to return to this prestigious institution. Were the administration not cowardly slaves of the elite rich, action would already have been taken. We'll not leave this building until justice is served!"

Bailey stared at the screen open-mouthed as the cameras panned a crowd carrying placards denouncing the school administration in explicit terms and asking for Bailey's expulsion as well as the arrest of his father.

"There's Cora Snyder!" Sherrill exclaimed, pointing to one of the pickets. "And Dr. Sandborne!"

"Well, so much for graduating," Bailey said as the news continued to the next story and Sherrill turned off the TV. Bailey tried to fill his voice with bravado but failed miserably. He'd studied hard and done well. He was about to lose it all.

"I can't believe this is happening!" Sherrill cried out. Her eyes were haunted. The last two days had seen the exposure of one brutal truth after another. "Was this staged, too?" she asked miserably.

"You saw Sandborne and her 'lifemate,'" Bailey retorted, throwing his half-eaten sandwich on the plate. "You tell me."

When Estelle entered Air Force One, she chose a seat as far from her husband as possible. The presidential quarters on the plane were spacious, so her husband was oblivious to her snub.

At the funeral, outside the White House, at Andrews Air Force Base, she'd played her role of doting wife to perfection. She'd smiled wanly at the photographers. She'd even held her husband's hand. No one had reason to suppose they were anything but devoted to each other. Frequent practice had made them Oscar-worthy actors, fooling the world if not themselves.

Now that they were alone, she could drop the pretense. Not that they were truly alone—Eugene Corforth and other staffers were there doing one more walk-through of the rally. Hunter had wanted to come—imagine!—but her husband had refused. At least he still showed some sense.

Sometimes she wondered what bond united him to his attorney general. She doubted friendship, though that had certainly been there in the beginning. Power lust maybe? A need to win, to be in control? In spite of her husband's superior position and his belief to the contrary, Hunt was definitely the more powerful of the two and clever at promoting the President's illusion.

Estelle became aware of increased commotion nearing the presidential cabin. The man challenging Bob Grant for his Senate seat was being brought forward for the presidential interview. Odd how much he looked the part of a Senator, Estelle thought, though at the moment he was somewhat nervous and blustery. People unused to being around the President frequently were, especially in this setting. The pale, overstuffed furniture, the built-in home theater, the mahogany tables—an ambiance much like a Malibu living room—were so unexpected on a plane that they often overwhelmed first-time visitors.

Caruso didn't stay long. Corforth had been given his orders. But the purpose had been served. Now the media traveling in the back of the plane would be well aware of the courtesy shown this virtual unknown by the President of the United States. Mention would be made in many taped broadcasts and articles as well as on live national coverage. Quite a change for the former salesman with his string of appliance stores!

What did Bob Grant think of it all? Estelle wondered. She couldn't help liking him, admiring him, too. She remembered his calm courage in Cuba. He'd willingly risked his future for what he'd believed was right. She looked at her husband. Even he'd shown moments of courage then. Somehow she knew he couldn't find that same courage now. Not now, she thought with a sigh. He'd changed too much this past year. He'd abandoned too much of his integrity to feed his own craven desires. He'd abandoned too much of his responsibility to feed Hunter's lust for power.

She wouldn't let that happen to her, Estelle decided, feeling the first glimmer of spirit in weeks. As First Lady she still had influence. She would be a fool not to use it while she still could. Her causes were worth fighting for!

Her face thoughtful, Estelle turned her back on her husband and stared sightlessly out the window, trying to bring some order and meaning to a life rapidly careening beyond control.

Sheriff Jenks waited at Gus's for over an hour, but Hank Farrar never showed. Had he been delayed by Bender? Or had his antipathy for Grant caused him to join their lynching voluntarily? Maybe Hank just wanted to tack "Sheriff" in front of his name. Jenks knew the party machine had been after his deputy, dangling the sheriff's badge in front of his eyes.

Jenks reached for the phone. Dadburn NIIA! He'd just have to go around them.

Later that morning Jenks returned to his office. Sally brought in his mail along with a mug of coffee. A smaller stack of mail than usual, Jenks noted, sipping the coffee but too engrossed to appreciate it. Was the NIIA holding some of it back? He rustled through the stack and smiled for the first time that day. A note was buried in the middle. Good ol' Bubba! Coffee and support all in one trip.

PHONE CALL IN USUAL PLACE.
ONE HOUR. UNLOCK BACK DOOR.

Jenks reread the note, tore it into small pieces, and burned it in his ashtray. Then he finished his coffee, leaning back and enjoying it.

He'd barely seated himself at Gus's desk an hour later when the phone rang. It was Bob Grant.

"Is it safe to talk?" Grant asked.

"Yes, safe but less than satisfactory. The NIIA has officially commandeered the case."

"So I heard. I'm just surprised they waited so long."

"Figured they could wear me down, I suppose," Jenks said, "then discovered I'm too ornery. Them city slickers reckon to cut me out of everything. Guess they've never heard of the Bubba factor."

"Bubba factor?"

"You Washington folks aren't the only ones with a good-ol'-boy network."

"You've picked up something?"

"Shirley Spade is flush with cash," Jenks said. "Florida dog races, she claims. We can't prove different."

"But interesting." Grant glanced around, checking to be sure he was still unobserved. Yao, leaning under the hood of a car on the other side of the filling station from the pay phone, gave him a surreptitious nod.

"This might interest you more," Jenks said, leaning back, the better to relish his role as the bearer of good news. Grant was due for a spot of that. "Sheriff friend of mine knows Olexey's mother. She's no better than her no-good son. White trash, both of them. She's a mite richer these days, though.

My friend thinks he knows the right screws to turn to get her to talk. May take time, but maybe we can blow the whole Olexey story."

"That *is* good news," Grant said. "My debate with Caruso is Sunday at 3:00. Be nice to have it pinned down by then. That's the last time I'll be certain of having media coverage."

"Two days," Jenks murmured reflectively. "I'll tell him, but no guarantee. Another friend of mine—"

"Thank goodness for the Bubbas of this world!" Grant interrupted with feeling.

"Ain't that the truth," Jenks agreed, chuckling. He propped his boots on the desk, careful not to disturb Gus's papers. "Anyway, this Bubba's getting a copy of the report on the drug bust. Should come any time now."

"I'm most interested in who reported the party and why Joey Hunter wasn't mentioned," Grant told him. "Any arm twisting that occurred, too. Any irregularities."

"Arm twisting, hmm? Well, don't know they would want to admit to that, but I'll see what I can do."

"Your Bubba network doesn't extend to New York, does it?" Grant asked, making another survey of the area around the phone booth. Yao was holding a dip stick in his hand while he covertly examined everything but it. "As I told you, the officer in charge of the Anne Peabody murder," Grant continued, "Sergeant Alvarez, was less than helpful—I think the NIIA had gotten to him—but I got the impression that someone may have witnessed the murder. Be nice to know."

"I'll work on it," Jenks said. He leaned forward to jot down Alvarez's name, then leaned back in the chair, easing his back to get more comfortable. "Maybe this Alvarez has a composite. I've got two already, one from li'l Gayla—her bar-hopping sweetheart—and one from a kid who saw a strange man—his words—leaving Crazy Sam's about the right time."

"Any similarities?"

"Enough to be interesting. Mainly a more-than-manly beard."

"A disguise?" Grant asked, thinking of John Smythe and his apparent penchant for using the same disguise throughout a case. A chill edged its way up Grant's spine. First, Bailey had confirmed Bonfire's involvement through Reggie's phone conversation. Now John Smythe, too?

"A mighty fine disguise, I'd have to say," Jenks told him. "Covers most everything. A third composite, though? Who knows. We might just hit pay dirt."

Grant told Jenks about Dashev's request for the forged letter found by Gayla Sergek, keeping the details of the Israeli's identity vague, saying only that he was an expert on international forgeries.

"I'll get it," Jenks said. In his mind's eye he pictured the sack in the storage room. "Have to be a copy though."

Jenks heard the back door open. "Gotta go," he said, slamming his feet onto the floor and starting to rise.

"Thanks for everything."

"Sure thing, Bubba." Chuckling, Jenks hung up.

Rachel Grant tried to pay attention to Janet Loomis, but it was difficult enough to concentrate on driving when every thought told her time was running out. There was so much she and Bob didn't know and only four days left to find it. She wouldn't have gone to see Rebecca Hunter except that Janet had been so insistent. Rachel harbored the hope of finding a connection between Joey's death and Bob's persecution. Additionally, Cynthia had told her of Janet's thinness, and Rachel wanted to reassure herself of her friend's continued good health.

"I'm so glad you could see Rebecca," Janet Loomis told her. "She's lost without Joey."

"Poor thing," Rachel said sympathetically, even as her mind roamed around her own problems. The trip had been a washout from that standpoint. Rebecca Hunter was exactly as she appeared, a mother immersed in grief. Still, it was interesting that she'd avoided talking about the cause of Joey's death, about either a heart condition or drugs. "If she can see beyond her own pain," Rachel continued, "to Joey's perfect peace . . ."

"I think she does," Janet replied, wrestling her own problems and unaware of Rachel's preoccupation, "or at least she wants to. She'll have to reach that point. Nothing else helps, not kind words or keeping busy, not even understanding friends." Her voice broke on the last word.

Rachel glanced at her sharply, feeling ashamed that she'd neglected Janet for the last weeks when her friend was obviously suffering.

Neither spoke for several miles.

"Poor Jonathan," Janet said, breaking the silence. She sounded as if she were voicing a conversation she'd been having with herself. "I'm afraid God doesn't enter into his thoughts, except as a point of mockery. Power, that's what consumes him. Joey didn't stand a chance against the pull of the White House, and Rebecca certainly doesn't. Phillip loved being a Senator, but he loved me more." Janet said the last defiantly. "I know what people think, that he wouldn't have killed himself if that was true. Oh, Rachel," she said, looking beseechingly at her friend, "I know he loved me, but sometimes, sometimes I can't help wondering . . ." She broke down, sobbing into her hands.

Rachel looked for an empty parking place, pulled into it, and turned off the engine. She embraced Janet, comforting her. "You mustn't torture yourself," she said when Janet finally leaned her head against the seat and brushed the tears from her cheeks. "Everyone who ever saw the two of you together knew how much Phillip loved you. Believe me. It was obvious."

Janet looked at her, then turned to look out the window. A cool autumn wind whipped the few leaves remaining on the branches, sending them tumbling to the already leaf-studded ground. Rachel had to lean forward to hear Janet's next words. "I want to believe. I want to so much. I go over and over those last few days, wondering, trying to figure out . . . I finally made myself look through his things. I hoped I could find something to explain. Rachel?" She regarded Rachel with troubled eyes.

Rachel nodded, unable to force words through the lump in her throat.

"If you had to choose between helping a friend or protecting your children, which would you do?"

"Helping a friend or protecting my children?" Rachel asked, puzzled.

"Yes."

"I'm not sure I understand," Rachel said slowly, "but I would think that the welfare of the children would have to come first."

"Even if helping the friend is the right thing to do?"

Rachel's face filled with concern. "Why don't you tell me what's wrong, Janet? Maybe I can help."

Janet didn't answer immediately. Instead she sat motionless, staring at her tightly clasped hands. "You and Bob," she finally said. "Everything's going to be all right, isn't it?"

"With us?" Again, Rachel's face registered confusion.

"Bob's not with you now," Janet said.

"No, he's . . ." Rachel paused. "You're worried because of that business about Maribeth Pariss?"

"And you aren't?" Janet retorted. At Rachel's look, she hurried on. "I don't mean I believe it, but I know how much it hurts to know everyone's talking about you, pitying you . . ."

Rachel shrugged. "I wish the story hadn't made the news, because it's not true. But I can't change that."

Still, Janet looked worried. Rachel touched her hand. "I love Bob and he loves me. We'll be just fine." She started the car and looked back to find a break in traffic. She had to get home and get to work. She felt the urgency both of lost time and of too little time. Next week would be time enough to help Janet. "Whether we'll win this election, who knows? I'm not sure I really care, to be honest." She pulled out and joined the flow of traffic. "But I do care about Bob's good name. Whatever happens I'm determined people know the truth."

"The truth," Janet repeated. "But how can you be sure what *is* the truth? I can't decide . . ." She paused, then said with conviction, "Phillip was a good man, Rachel, a really good man."

"Of course he was!" Rachel exclaimed, concerned by this further evidence of her friend's fragile mental state. "You're all right, aren't you, Janet? You're not feeling any new symptoms?" Janet's color was good, Rachel thought. She didn't have that indefinable aura of a body under siege from cancer, but . . . "I want you to call my office and have them make an appointment for a checkup next week," Rachel said. "I'm serious," she emphasized. "Next week for sure."

Janet nodded, but her strange anxiety didn't seem at all diminished. "If things get too bad, you'll call me, won't you?" she asked instead, her voice burdened with a disquieting urgency.

"Why, thank you," Rachel replied, unsure—as had been true so often in this puzzling conversation—just what Janet meant. She seemed strangely troubled, just as Cynthia had suggested after the White House luncheon. Because Joey's death brought back the pain of her husband's suicide?

Rachel reached over and squeezed Janet's hand. "I'll remember. You're a dear to think of it."

Janet gave her a wavery smile. Her eyes remained haunted by some shadowy demon.

The President, a contented smile on his face, sat on the stage and surveyed the huge arena, packed with cheering supporters. People had been bused in from all over Georgia, not to mention nearby states. They carried their own homemade placards mixed with the thousands printed by the campaign. Those supportive of Caruso jockeyed for position with almost as many urging four more years for the President. Those blasting Grant—and there were plenty!—were being carried by hundreds outside the building. The media had been given full access to the more articulate of those Grant-bashers before the rally and would be given equally good access afterward.

Patriotic anthems played by high school bands; pom-poms waved by cheerleaders; red-white-and-blue streamers, bunting, and balloons; ministers from five different denominations; a military color guard: Nothing had been neglected. Everything proclaimed that Caruso was the choice of every God-fearing, country-loving American. All in all, it was a most well-orchestrated affair, especially on such short notice. But then most campaign events by necessity were put together at the last minute.

Edmund Miller had done well, the President thought, watching his subordinate still hard at work, presently playing up to the many media representatives ranged on scaffolding around the room. Coverage would be excellent, national as well as local. A good man, Miller. The President would remember.

Noticing cameras moving to focus on him, he turned to Estelle, smiled, reached for her hand, and squeezed it. She didn't return the squeeze, but she smiled. Last night must have been her time of the month, he thought, remembering her uncharacteristic—and unexpected—anger. Assuming she wasn't a dried-out old lady already! He'd been wrong to read something into her voice. He'd been careful. Besides, she had no cause to feel anything but gratitude toward him. She was First Lady, wasn't she, and he'd made it possible!

He supposed he'd better pay more attention to her until things quieted down, just to be sure she didn't become overly suspicious. With a smile to hide his sigh, he turned back to the crowd. After he was reelected, it wouldn't matter so much if anyone, including Estelle, knew.

Women: couldn't live with them; couldn't live without them. He grinned and waved.

Saturday, October 31:

Three Days Before the Election

Bob Grant spent the night at Ginger Wright's brother's farmhouse outside Atlanta. Her brother had no political connections. He was no more than an acquaintance of Grant's. No one would think to look for him there.

When Ginger walked into her brother's kitchen early Saturday morning, the sun wasn't up, but Grant was already sitting at the kitchen table, drinking a glass of orange juice and reading a faxed copy of that morning's bombshell in the *Herald*.

"Oh, no!" Ginger groaned, seeing the anger in his face. "What's that sorry excuse for a paper saying now?"

"Suspicion has arisen that I was behind the closing of the military bases here in Georgia, something about my making a financial killing. They wonder, quite politely, of course, if Frederickson learned about my devilish plan and if that knowledge contributed to my need to silence him."

"Financial killing? How on earth?"

"That's the clever part," Grant told her. "The details are vague. 'Sources high in the military and in government.' They have to know their story can be easily refuted, but by Tuesday?"

"You as the rich, money-grubbing Republican—figures. But using it as a motive for murder?"

"A lot of Georgians lost jobs when those bases closed," Grant said. "If I'd pushed to get the bases closed and been paid off by a business profiting because the base in another state stayed open—as this article insinuates—I sure wouldn't want anyone to know, especially not right before an election."

Ginger poured herself a glass of juice. "Want to bet the story refuting this—when it finally does come—will be buried on a back page?" She seated herself across from Grant.

Grant just looked at her.

"Okay, so it's a sucker's bet," she said. Her face got serious. "Does this change our plans?"

"No, it changes nothing. It's rather like the bite of a mosquito during an elephant stampede: annoying, but easy to ignore."

"Maybe," Ginger said slowly, "but we're going to look into it. We have to have answers for everything."

Everything, Grant thought. And the list grew daily, sometimes hourly. He pushed his chair back from the table.

"Time to do some digging myself."

Grant felt certain the phone in the den couldn't have been tapped, and he was reasonably certain no one could know where he was, but remembering Rachel's warning about long-range listening devices, he turned up the radio, then turned on the TV as well. Only then did he dial Sheriff Jenks at his new place of business, Gus's Hardware Store. Jenks was continuing his precautions, using a digital phone scrambler borrowed from his office.

"You better think about lying low," Jenks said. "I overheard talk about closing in on you. I'm guessing they plan to arrest you for Frederickson's murder after the debate. No warrant yet, but that's just a formality."

"They'll wait until after?" Grant asked, running possible hideouts through his mind. He would remain in Georgia until after the debate. If he were able to get away safely afterwards, someplace near Washington might make better sense. All lines of inquiry seemed to be converging on that city.

"That's my read," Jenks told him. "Give you a chance to hang yourself during it answering some pointed questions."

Kirk Vinton? Grant wondered. Or just Caruso, well primed. "They've decided I'm guilty?"

"They decided that before they saw the evidence. Arrogant jerks!"

"So you're out of the investigation?"

"They think so." Jenks's disgust was dispelled in a grunt. "As if I'd let them stop me. I got copies of the case files on both the Peabody murder and your son's drug bust if you're interested."

"If I'm interested!"

"Don't get too excited now," Jenks cautioned. "Never seen such empty reports in my life. No details to speak of and darn little for a bloodhound to sniff."

"Maybe not on the surface," Grant suggested, "but from a different perspective, in light of what we're learning?"

"That's what I'm hoping. Never can tell what little thing may spark a whole fire." Jenks leaned back and got comfortable. "I didn't strike out completely. I was told, confidential-like, that someone with the Peabody case just might be willing to talk. He's skittish though. Wouldn't even give a name. Said he would talk, but only to you and only face-to-face. Skittish, like I said. Probably wants to see if you'll play him straight. He'd be bucking the big boys. If you come yourself, he'll most likely figure it's worth his skin."

"Most likely? He may not show?"

"No guarantee."

"Sometime today?"

"Yep."

"What are the chances of a setup?"

"In your case," Jenks said, laughing mirthlessly, "about twenty to one, I'd reckon."

"Of course," Grant agreed with a dry chuckle of his own. "I'll be there. I really have no choice, do I? We've got to have more than we have now if we hope to break this open."

"We all have choices, Senator. You made the choice to run for office. Someone else decided he didn't much like that. Now I'm making a choice myself. I figure you and I better join forces—not like we have been, mind you, but an all-out assault on the vermin out to get you."

"Join forces?" Grant repeated, seeking to determine the extent of Jenks's commitment. "You know what you're saying? Especially since we're no closer to figuring out who's behind this than we were in the beginning?"

"Never been surer in my life, Senator," Jenks said, a smile in his eyes. "Been tending that way from the beginning."

"Could have fooled me!"

Now Jenks smiled outright. "Glad to know I still can play a bluff. Don't go quoting me, but I figure we're right on target. Shake enough hornet nests, and you're bound to start hearin' buzzing."

Hunter walked into the War Room and threw a sheaf of papers down on the table.

"The Anne Peabody mugging may be reopened," he announced with thunder in his voice. "Her lawyer—Craig Flannery," he said, consulting his notes, "is starting to ask questions and talking about the possibility of its being a deliberate murder."

"You're kidding!" the Vice President exclaimed.

"What difference does that make?" Corforth asked at the same time.

Hunter gave him a scathing look. Corforth felt his stomach knot. "Don't be stupid, Eugene," Hunter said. "What if they start wondering about the convenient timing of her allegations, right before the last election?"

"She wasn't lying." Corforth looked from Hunter to the Veep. The pain in his stomach intensified. "Was she?"

"I thought we controlled all law enforcement now," the Veep said, turning toward Hunter. "Can't the NIIA stop this?"

"What's the use of having the power if I can't use it?" Hunter retorted. "Flannery's being discreet, so we should be all right, but we need to have suitable responses ready in case the questions continue. A mugging. That's all it was. Tragic, but all too common in New York. I'll brief the President." He started to leave.

"I'm not sure I understand, Hunt," Corforth said. He ignored the antacids in his pocket. They wouldn't help the searing pain he was experiencing now.

Hunter stopped with his hand on the door. "What's to understand?"

"Anne Peabody, of course!" Corforth yelled. "Why does the President need to be briefed? We didn't have anything to do with . . . well, with what happened to her, did we?"

"Don't be a fool," Hunter said. That was all he said. The door clicked shut behind him.

The Vice President looked at Corforth and laughed. Then he, too, left.

Hunter went straight from the War Room to the Oval Office. He knocked on the door but walked in before the President had a chance to respond.

The President looked up from his paperwork. "What is it?" he asked irritably.

"Anne Peabody's death." Hunter walked to the desk. Recurring nightmares combined with mere snatches of sleep had dug black holes around his eyes and hollows in his cheeks. His firm step betrayed no weakening, however. "We may have a problem."

The President put down his pen and regarded Hunter a trace warily. "I thought she was mugged."

"She was. At least . . ." Hunter stopped, gave the President an appraising look, then continued. "Remember I said I'd contacted John Smythe?"

The President nodded. Now the wariness was obvious.

"I contacted Smythe because Anne Peabody called me." Hunter seated himself in the chair nearest the desk. He crossed his legs with slow precision, watching the tension mount in the President's face as the implications sank in. Hunter enjoyed having the upper hand, especially now. "Russell Frederickson had called her."

The President surged to his feet, setting his chair rocking. Wordlessly, he made a circuit of the room, his mind congested with conflicting thoughts. Only when he was once again standing by the desk did Hunter continue. "Peabody was upset. Frederickson was threatening her with proof that the bribery charge was rigged."

With sardonic amusement, Hunter watched as the President clutched the desk, his knuckles turning white.

"She made an appointment to meet with Frederickson the next morning," Hunter continued, regarding the President dispassionately over his half glasses. "As soon as Peabody hung up, I contacted John Smythe and left a message explaining the situation."

Hunter paused again, the better to flex his power muscles. The silence stretched.

The President lost the battle of wills. "And?" he prodded, his voice tight.

"And now Peabody and Frederickson are both dead."

The President's reaction was everything Hunter could have wished: ashen face, clenched fists, erratic beat of the pulse at his temple.

"But . . . I don't . . ." The President's eyes darted around the room as he tried to understand. Hunter gave him no help.

"Was Frederickson right?" the President finally asked. "Was the bribery . . ."

Hunter shrugged. "I know what you know," he said. He recrossed his legs and straightened the crease of his trousers, keeping his eyes on the fine gabardine, as if memorizing the weave were somehow important. "The bribery was rather providential, I always thought."

The President took a step, but stopped, his hand motionless above the corner of the desk. "Two people are dead." He looked straight ahead, seeing nothing.

Hunter said nothing.

"Tell Smythe . . ."

"Yes . . ." Hunter was the one prodding this time, not because he was impatient, but because he knew where he wanted the President's words to take him.

"Tell Smythe," the President said, rubbing an unsteady hand over his mouth, "that his services are no longer necessary."

"It may be," Hunter rejoined softly, "that Smythe knows that better than anyone. And," he added, standing, "I'd feel better if Corforth were kept completely out of the loop. I'm no longer convinced of his loyalty."

The President lowered himself into his chair. He seemed hardly aware of Hunter's words. Finally, he looked up and straight into Hunter's eyes. Whatever inner struggle he'd been fighting was over. "We may need to make even more changes," he said, agreeing, "but let's wait until after Tuesday. No need to court speculation before the election."

The decision had been made, just as Hunter had known it would be.

Cynthia!" Mike Masterson practically screamed her name into the phone. "Where is Bob? I haven't seen him since yesterday afternoon. No messages. Nothing."

"I thought he was with you." Masterson could hear surprise in her voice. "He's not checking out the debate facility, is he?"

"Give me a break, Cynthia. Where do you think I've been? He was supposed to meet me there but never showed."

"Then I don't know where he is. Have you tried the hotel?"

"He's not there. No message there either. He's all right, isn't he?"

"I talked to him just a few minutes ago. He's fine. He didn't mention you, but I would assume he wants you to work on debate strategy."

"Debate strategy!" Masterson ran a nervous hand through his already rumpled hair. "We're essentially moribund, and you're talking strategy?"

Cynthia didn't reply.

"Okay, okay," Masterson finally said. "I'll work on it, but if you talk to Bob, tell him I can't help him if I can't get hold of him. If you get a number, let me know. This is a heck of a way to run a campaign—even this one."

Estelle returned from her symposium on teenage pregnancy with a raging headache. She'd hoped immersing herself in her duties, duties she truly enjoyed, would insulate her from thoughts of the other. She'd been wrong. Nothing could mask those thoughts.

She lowered herself fully clothed onto her bed. The longer she lay there, the worse she felt. Like President Taft before her, she found the White House "the loneliest place in the world."

The irony was poignant. She was the most admired woman in the world married to the most powerful man. She was on a first-name basis with the heads of state of every country in the world. And she was miserable. She more than anyone, she supposed, understood that happiness was a peace of mind and soul, in no way influenced by wealth or repute.

Others might say that her material state made her emotional state easier to bear. But did it? She had no privacy. The White House ushers, who treated her with unfailing kindness, knew the cause of her misery. Their pitying eyes confirmed it. Her husband's associates knew. They must. How else did he make plans and cover his lies?

If his appetites had increased to the point that even she noticed, she who found it easier to be blind, could public exposure with its inevitable public ridicule be far behind? Only ridicule could pierce the armor of his arrogance and reacquaint him with the realities of life. Of that she was convinced.

She had considered calling Cynthia Novitsky, her oldest friend, there for her since they'd been college roommates. The White House operator had even dialed Cynthia's number, but still Estelle had hesitated. The woman betrayed—how could she bear for anyone to see her as such, even Cynthia?

Estelle was realizing what others before her had learned to their sorrow. Pity magnifies misery. Burden enough to bear personal despair without adding the crushing weight of private, much less public, pity. In the last few weeks, Estelle had come to understand that pity for her might soon become all too public.

When she'd made her disastrous discovery, she'd moved into a separate but adjoining bedroom, citing his late-night meetings and her need to have undisturbed sleep. He'd commiserated with her, he'd even apologized, and he'd continued to come to her once a week.

At the thought, a tear seeped from under her tightly closed eyelids. She still cared. Inside her hard-fought-for shell of indifference, she still cared. How could life be so unfair!

She couldn't stand it a moment longer, she thought, this being prisoner to her husband's urges. She had to do something. What, she wasn't sure, but something.

She jumped from her bed, ran to the door, and threw it open. The arched windows at each end of the wide gallery flooded the area with sunlight. The bright light caused her eyes to water, Estelle told herself fiercely. Just the light.

She hurried toward the staircase. The iron of the railing was cold in her hand. The marble at the edge of the steps was cold on her bare feet. She paused, but she couldn't stop. Some inner need urged her on. She ran down the sweeping steps, staying now on the red runner in the center.

As the Cross Hall at the bottom opened before her, she again paused. The hall was empty, but her mind supplied the music of the Marine band that so often played there. She and her husband always entered to "Hail to the Chief." The majestic tune assailed her, momentarily overwhelming her tenuous hold on her emotions. She closed her eyes. The tune continued pounding through her, bringing with it a ribbon of memories.

They'd greeted hundreds of people in that very spot: Americans, foreigners, good people, and not so good. Even some who were actually interesting, she thought with a touch of her normal asperity. Had they experienced the same wave of emotion she was feeling now? Had they, too, been visited by the ghosts of past greatness, the legacy of brave Americans behaving honorably?

Moving to the center of the hall, Estelle turned around slowly, taking in the familiar, yet always awesome details. Her gaze returned to the Seal of the President incised in marble above the door to the Blue Room. Feeling as if she were suffocating, she rushed out of the hall and into the East Room, but its gold and white expanse, three immense cut-glass chandeliers the sole light, only fed her melancholy. The grand piano with its gilt legs, ornately carved in the shape of eagles, dwarfed her but appeared a lovely toy in the room's vast emptiness. Beside the white and gold mantel, George and Martha Washington, eerily alive in their full-length portraits, held her in their unwavering gaze.

Pulling away from their spell, she hurried into the Green Room, given its enduring color by James Monroe. So much tradition, so much courage, she thought, her eyes clouding. The portrait of George Washington remained through the years only because of the heroics of Dolley Madison. Had Dolley left somewhere in this rambling house with its 132 rooms another relic of that heroism, an invisible, amorphous one that could be imparted to those who sought it? Estelle's eyes strayed to the antique fire screen with its intricate embroidery of the symbolic figure of Hope surrounded by a border of flowers. Hope: Was that Dolley's legacy, the hope that our country, because of the courage of others like her, would endure and prosper?

Chiding herself for the fantasies that continued to ensnare her, Estelle slowly approached the white Italian marble fireplace. Her eyes lifted to the portrait of a seated and contemplative Benjamin Franklin hanging above it. It was considered one of the finest portraits in the White House, and she'd often stopped to admire it. The normally plain Quaker sported French silks and lace as well as a powdered wig. Now she noted the twinkle in Ben's eyes and felt a wrenching at her heart. He'd been a womanizer, if accounts were accurate, but he'd never allowed his weakness to interfere with his duty to his country. And he hadn't had a wife.

Her mind was inundated by images of the trip to Atlanta. She'd hated it all: her husband's nearness, his adoring smiles and patronizing squeezes of her hand, the blind cheering of the crowd, the fawning of the media, the vile demonstrations against Bob Grant.

Estelle leaned against the mantel for a moment, fighting the images, wanting to recapture the joy that had been hers when they'd first moved into the White House. That joy was as elusive as the inexplicable urge she was chasing now.

She walked into the Blue Room, paused in the center of the lovely oval, and felt a familiar stirring of awe at the vista unfolding before her. Framed by the long central window were the South Lawn, the Ellipse, and both the Washington and Jefferson Memorials. A tear slid down her cheek.

She was remembering the first time she'd visited Washington. She'd been a young girl, ten at the most. They'd been touring the Jefferson Memorial when she'd become separated from her family. She'd wandered outside, enjoying the unexpected freedom to explore on her own. She could still remember the first line of the first inscription she'd discovered. "God who gave us life gave us liberty." For some reason, maybe because she'd found them herself, those words had stirred her young imagination and had stayed with her since.

Walking down the steps outside the monument, thinking about the words, she'd looked up, and the White House had shimmered before her in the distance, revealed in all its splendor. Even without understanding the roots of her heritage, she'd felt awe. She'd understood, at least in small measure, the special responsibility that rested on those living in the lovely house. That feeling rushed back now, but overlaid this time with an intolerable sense of failure.

Estelle rushed from the room, away from the view, away from the memories, not pausing until she reached the State Dining Room. She stopped just inside the door, motionless, suddenly sure this room had been her destination all along and frightened by that surety. Her heart thudded. She had to force herself to move forward toward the fireplace. A portrait of Abraham Lincoln hung above it, but she gave it the barest of glances. Her eyes were inexorably drawn to the mantel itself, to the words carved into it.

Hesitantly, she touched the inscription. The sharp edges of incised marble pressed into her fingertips. It felt cool, cool and permanent. The words were John Adams's on his second night of residence in the White House. "I Pray Heaven," she read, though she knew Adams's prayer by heart, "to Bestow the Best of Blessings on THIS HOUSE and on all that shall hereafter Inhabit it." Her fingers stilled. She took a steadying breath. "May none but Honest and Wise Men ever rule under this Roof."

"Honest and Wise Men." The words throbbed through her, slowly becoming a mocking pulse beat. "Honest and Wise. Honest and Wise."

She ran from the room, her hands covering her face. They'd accepted the blessings of the house without remembering the rest of the admonition.

She had to talk to Cynthia, Estelle thought, tears streaming down her drawn cheeks. Cynthia, secure in the conviction of her beliefs, would give her wise counsel.

None but Honest and Wise: The words continued to pummel her even after she locked herself in her bedroom.

I just had the strangest call," Sherrill told Bailey. He'd dropped her by her apartment to get a change of clothes while he checked a reference at a nearby library. He'd just returned. "It was Cora Snyder," Sherrill continued. She'd changed from a knit jumper and turtleneck into jeans and a baggy green sweatshirt. "She says she wants to talk to us. Something important."

"Run that by me again," Bailey demanded. "Cora Snyder wants to talk to *us?* That does not compute!"

"Cynicism doesn't suit you."

"Suits better than Cora!" Bailey said, frowning. "I wonder what gives."

"We can find out in an hour. She wants us to meet her at 12th and H, S.E."

"Nice neighborhood," Bailey retorted sarcastically, picturing the squalor of an area he, and most others, avoided.

"That's what I told her," she assured him. She threw an address book and baseball cap into the bag she'd already filled with clothes. "Cora just laughed and said if she wasn't scared, then why should we be. She said we had to come alone. No tape recorder either. She'll deny every word, but she said she doesn't like being used. She thinks we've been given a rotten deal."

"Brother, Sherrill, I don't know. Cora having a change of heart?" He turned, took a few steps, then turned back. "The whole thing stinks."

"Please, Bailey," Sherrill said, raising a hand imploringly. She studied his eyes, wishing for the softening her presence had invariably occasioned in the past. As always now the shutters were up. She sighed. "What do we have to lose? She sure can't hurt us, and if there's a chance we might learn something . . ."

Bailey could hear the plea in her voice, but he remained undecided. As he'd said, the whole thing stunk, and the days when he would gladly do as she asked were over, long over. "You're sure about what she said?" he asked, suddenly remembering his past gullibility.

Sherrill saw the distrust slowly seeping into his face. She stalked over to her answering machine, rewound it, and punched the play button. Her eyes flashed. Cora's voice, slightly tinny but easily recognizable, spoke.

Bailey listened, his distrust of Cora now uppermost. He tried to hear nuances, underlying meanings, anything that might explain her sudden capitulation. The tape ended.

"Okay," he said, a puzzled but intrigued look on his face, "I think you're right. We go, but not alone."

"But—"

"I didn't say she'd know anyone was with us," he said, a hint of impatience in his voice, an impatience born of heightened nerves, "but I'll feel better knowing Dad's baby-sitters are close behind. Ramon's not a bad guy. Tommy, either. I'll fill them in," he said, heading for the door. "And I'm taking this." He got the tape out of the machine, yanked a tissue from the box next to it, wrapped the tape in the tissue, and put it all in his pocket.

Ramon and Tommy were waiting outside, trying to look inconspicuous. Surely close behind would be close enough, Bailey thought as

314

he explained about Cora's call. As Sherrill had said, little Cora couldn't hurt them. She was up to something, no doubt about that, but mental and emotional games were *her* style—not physical confrontation.

Matt Goldie was flying Grant from a private landing strip outside Atlanta to New York City, where Grant would meet Jenks's mysterious source about the Anne Peabody mugging.

"Did we get away clean?" Goldie asked as the plane lifted into the air.

"I don't see anyone," Grant said, staring intently out the airplane window. A cloud intervened, and he turned to Stephen Yao, who was using a sophisticated communication system to link them to his associates on the ground. "Anything?"

"No. So far nothing suspicious."

"Good." Goldie turned back to the controls.

"That won't hold, I'm afraid," Grant told them. "At least not much longer. I just got word the NIIA is planning to arrest me after the debate tomorrow."

"We'll just have to make sure they can't," Yao said easily. He stowed his equipment behind the seat.

"As long as I attend the debate."

"Matt and I have it well in hand. Just be sure you have plenty to say," Yao said good-naturedly.

"We've a long way to go before we can be sure of that. The debate will have a huge audience if the networks have anything to say about it, but I don't know, Stephen. Things aren't falling together fast enough. I'm thinking we may have to use the debate to stir things up."

"Force Bonfire into a misstep," Yao agreed.

"Bonfire or whoever hired him," Grant amended, wondering who inside the White House that might include. "The longer I'm missing, the more nervous they'll be getting. I might even find the real murderer." The heavy irony in his voice was laced with disgust. "If I can push the right buttons during the debate," Grant said, his restless eyes betraying the intensity of his thoughts, "I just might start something Bonfire can't finish."

He and Yao, with Goldie adding an occasional suggestion, spent the rest of the flight considering every angle. They had to decide which buttons were the right ones, then how to push them. The more they learned of Bonfire, the more costly they knew a miscalculation would be.

When they landed, Grant had just enough time to call Benjamin Dashev.

"The copy of the forged letter," Dashev said. "My experts recognized it immediately as the work of a famous artisan of the former Soviet Union, now reputedly in the employ of Bonfire. Another confirmation of our surmise."

"John Smythe may be involved as well," Grant told him. "A man with a full beard has been spotted on two occasions." He explained about Gayla Sergek and Scott Patterson.

"I don't like this, Bob," Dashev said when Grant finished. "Both Bonfire and Smythe? The stakes must be high indeed."

"We have to pin down a motive," Grant replied, agreeing. "I haven't come up with anything conclusive."

"Nor I," Dashev admitted. "I'll increase my circle of sources. The hourglass is losing sand too quickly. Guard your family, my friend. Bonfire is a barbarian, and if he has called in John Smythe, none that you love is safe. I'll do my best to meet with you this afternoon. If you do not hear from me, you will know I have failed to learn anything of importance."

On that dubious note, the phone went dead.

Grant got to Times Square five minutes early for his meeting with the Peabody informant. He scanned nearby faces, seeing no one familiar, no one who seemed interested in him. He glanced at Stephen Yao, lounging against a storefront nearby. Yao looked through him. No one had followed them. Dressed as roughly as he was, Grant doubted any casual observer would recognize him.

"So you did come."

Grant turned slowly toward the voice. "Alvarez!" He stared, unable to hide his surprise.

The corners of Alvarez's mouth turned in a mocking smile. "Yeah, me. Sorry about the other day, but I had orders."

"Orders?"

"I think you know what I mean. Let's just leave it at that, okay? Time we were moving." He crossed the street. Grant followed. They merged with a crowd going in the opposite direction, Yao never far behind. After several minutes and several direction switches, Alvarez spoke. "Now what is it you want?"

"First, why the change in attitude? You decide against the mugger?"

"Against the mugger? In this city?" Alvarez asked with a short laugh. He steered Grant toward a sidewalk vendor. "Hotdog?"

"Sure." They were silent as they ordered, dressed their dogs with spicy mustard and sauerkraut, and went to a nearby bench. "The mugger," Grant prodded when the silence had extended for several minutes.

"Yeah, the mugger." Alvarez patted his mouth with a napkin. "Highly convenient, a mugger, but that's the official word."

"And yours as well?"

"Certainly possible. Not many people you can trust these days."

"You're one talkative guy, aren't you?"

Alvarez shrugged.

"One question," Grant said. "I got the impression the other day that someone may have witnessed the mugging."

"Possibly."

"Any chance of getting a composite from this possible witness?"

"Possibly."

Grant laughed good-naturedly. "At least I don't have to worry that you'll talk about me to the wrong person."

"Possibly," Alvarez said again, then laughed. He regarded Grant through eyes tempered by experience. "Might even be able to rummage up a copy of the ballistics report. Never know." He wadded his hotdog wrapper and threw it into a nearby trash can. "Two points. Never have liked mixing politics with an investigation. Never have liked anyone— and that includes the feds!—telling me what to think. If I happen to run across a composite in the next day or two, any way I can get it to you?"

"The sheriff will keep in touch." They stood. "Thanks."

"Sure. And, Senator, watch your back."

From Alvarez's tone, Grant wasn't sure if the last was a serious admonition or not. A waste of words if not. Alvarez could never be accused of that.

Why had the sergeant wanted to see him personally? To warn him to watch whom he trusted? To decide if he could trust Grant with something important, something that might endanger his own career if the NIIA discovered he'd passed it along to Grant? Or had Alvarez lured him to New York to stall Grant's inquiries? Everything else about the day reeked of the NIIA.

317

Grant agreed to let you moderate the debate," a gloating Peter Evans told Kirk Vinton. "Can you imagine! What a coup for the *Herald*! You'll control everything. Here." He handed Vinton a sheet of paper. "Go over this list of questions."

Vinton took the list and scanned it. "Every story that broke first in the *Herald*," he said, raising an eyebrow.

"A subliminal reminder of who's the number-one source for news in this country. Can't hurt."

"You sure you want me to bring up Pariss? What about Jenks's press conference?"

"Nobody reported it, and Pariss is big news. If Grant tries to rebut, make sure everyone realizes he's protesting too much. Sex scandals are too believable. If he presses, mention that Jenks was removed from the investigation by the NIIA. You don't have to say why. Just the bare fact will be enough."

Evans felt more relaxed than he had in days. Grant was just about finished, and he'd brought it all on himself. The debate would seal it. "You control the debate, remember, Vinton. Not Grant."

"Sure."

"Good." Evans fiddled with his pencil. "When you introduce Grant, list all the evidence against him and I mean all: Frederickson's murder; Maribeth Pariss's pregnancy and suicide, her letters; the evidence of Gayla Sergek and Shirley Spade; Grant's son's drug arrest; Grant's own drug dealing and relationship to a convicted drug dealer who has been alleged to have committed murders." He wrote the name GRANT in the center of a blank white page. "Leave nothing out!" Evans crossed Grant's name out with sharp, satisfied strokes.

"You're prepared to control the debate?" he demanded. "Grant can't be allowed to use it as a forum for his specious arguments. Attack! Attack! Attack! Force him into a public confession if you can!"

"You can trust me," Vinton assured him. "I've considered all the angles. Grant won't be able to pull anything. He'll be exposed for what he is: a lying, murdering scumbag."

"We're counting on you." Evans dropped the pencil with finality into its holder.

"You won't be disappointed. The timeline still on for tomorrow?"

Evans nodded. "Front-page summary of every one of Grant's dirty little secrets. Drugs, murder, political graft, adultery—it'll all be there. You've done a good job, Vinton."

"You ain't seen nothing yet." Vinton gave a wolfish grin. "Tune in tomorrow afternoon for the debate."

"Write it up for Monday's edition."

"Front page? Byline?"

"Of course. Modem it immediately."

"It's almost finished," Vinton told him. "A few quotes from the debate, and I'll have it."

"End it by predicting Grant's defeat Tuesday in case anyone still has doubts."

"That's one concession speech I can't wait to cover."

"And I can't wait to run," Evans agreed with a tight cat-who-caught-the-canary smile. He wadded up the paper, Grant's name now obliterated, and tossed it into the wastebasket.

John Smythe had taken his position in a vacant apartment building at the corner of 12th and H, S.E. He cradled a scoped rifle in his arms. This was one way to bring Grant out of hiding, he thought with a sardonic grin.

A dark green sedan slowly pulled into the abandoned parking lot below. Cora Snyder, right on time.

Smythe watched as she got out, looked around, then walked to a nearby dumpster. He couldn't see what she picked up, but he knew without seeing—a plastic bag of cocaine. He'd put it there.

Snyder would plant the stash on Bailey, thinking she was further compromising his father. Greedy little Cora.

He'd assured her she would be far away by the time Bailey was found in possession. He hadn't told her that Bailey would be dead by then, along with the girl, two victims of a drug deal gone sour. In this area, no one would question a drug deal any more than they would question shots. The dealer, his fingerprints on the bag and in police files, would be found, but he would have an unshakable alibi. Grant might yell for justice, but what could he do? Not campaign, certainly.

Following the red dot of the laser through the magnification of the scope, Smythe watched Cora Snyder return to her car. As she opened the door, he pantomimed pulling the trigger. Then he laughed. Laser-enhanced scopes were almost foolproof. He lowered the gun and rested it on the window ledge. He couldn't wait to see Snyder's face when the Grant kid and the girl dropped dead at her feet.

He looked at his watch. Ten minutes at the most until it would all be over, then eighty minutes before the plane's departure. He'd be late for his meeting, but so what? He could handle any complaints.

That's Cora up there on the left, isn't it?" Bailey asked. He slowed and prepared to pull into the abandoned parking lot.

Sherrill turned in her seat to look out the rear window. "I don't see Ramon and Tommy."

"I lost them a couple of miles back. A red light maybe." At her worried look, he reached over and squeezed her hand. "They can't be far behind, and they know where we are."

"This place gives me the creeps." Sherrill looked at the decayed buildings, defaced by faded graffiti, and at the trash and glass strewn on the discolored concrete. She shuddered, wishing Bailey hadn't let go of her hand. She wished she could hide herself in his arms and felt angry for wanting something so impossible. "Where is everyone?" she said, her voice verging on hysteria. "I can't believe no one would be around."

"Maybe it's the storm." Ominous gray clouds rolled in from the east, blocking the sun and throwing elongated shadows.

He let the car roll slowly across the weed-defaced concrete, stopping it a short distance from Cora's car. He, too, was infected by the area's squalid pessimism, that and the dead stillness of the pre-storm air.

Barely able to suppress a shiver, he nodded toward Cora sitting motionless in her car. "I'll let her make the first move."

"Good," Sherrill said. She hadn't even unbuckled her seat belt.

Smythe watched as the second car inched its way into the parking lot and stopped.

Grant's kid! Good boy!

He raised the rifle and centered the car in its sight. The red light of the laser waited for its target.

More than a mile away, the car carrying Ramon and Tommy flew down the street and skidded around a corner.

"I hope Bailey'll wait for us," Ramon said, his normally laughing face creased with worry. The area they were driving through could have been a war zone. "This setup stinks."

"Including that truck that cut us off," Tommy agreed angrily.

They'd been lucky to get away with only a controlled skid, a J-turn, and four minutes lost to backtracking around the truck.

Ramon pressed the gas pedal to the floor.

Cora got out of her car and walked slowly toward Bailey's. She was nervous. That was stupid, she told herself. She was in control. All she had to do was get Bailey out of the car and close enough so she could plant the drugs on him without his suspecting.

She would leave, the police would come, and he'd be caught. No one would believe him if he said she'd been there. She was driving a student's car, the license plate was obscured by mud, and her alibi was perfect. She was a respected professor. He'd just been arrested on drug charges.

So why couldn't she relax?

Lightning struck close by. She jumped. Her eyes darted everywhere. Blasted storm!

Here she comes." Bailey cleared his throat nervously, wishing Ramon and Tommy would hurry up and get there.

Sherrill turned to look at Cora, then turned back to stare out the side window. "I don't like this, Bailey," she said, speaking barely above a whisper. "You were right. We shouldn't have come."

"But we're here." He watched in wary fascination as Cora walked toward them, then skirted the car to come around to his side. She was so small and looked so helpless. "Suppose she really can tell us something." He reached for the door handle.

Again lightning cracked. For a surreal moment, its brilliant zigzag seemed impaled in Cora's car.

Through the rifle's scope, John Smythe saw Cora reach the boy's car. The door opened. He saw the top of the boy's head, the red laser dot squarely centered on it.

Gently, his finger began squeezing the trigger.

There! On the left! That's Bailey's car!"

Ramon slammed on the brakes and went into a shrieking skid.

Bailey and Cora jerked around at the sound. At the same moment, Bailey felt a rush of air by his head. A shot? Was someone shooting at them?

"Down!" he yelled, not waiting to be sure. He tackled Cora and rolled with her across the gritty pavement.

"Rape!" Cora screamed, clawing at him. "Get your hands off me!" Her own hands were all over him. She kicked him, her tennis shoes thudding against his shins. He jerked in pain, and her knee missed its target, smashing into his thigh. He clutched her to him, her imprecations ringing in his ears even as they rolled. She bit his hand. With a curse he pushed her away and scrambled toward his car.

A spurt of dust burst between his feet. Yes, a shot! And another!

He dove behind the car. The rough pavement took a chunk from his palm.

He scrambled toward the driver's door. "Sherrill! Get down! Someone's shooting!" He couldn't see her, didn't know if she was all right.

"Sherrill!"

Cora whimpered and began scuttling away. She, too, had recognized the sound of gunfire.

Smythe cursed. The skidding car had distracted his concentration just a fraction. He'd missed! He resighted and shot again.

The kid disappeared behind the car, but the Holmes girl was still visible, struggling to unfasten her seat belt. He squeezed the trigger.

Someone's shooting! From up there!"

Ramon swung the car around, placing it between Bailey's car and the line of fire. A bullet slammed through the roof and exited out the window by his head.

"I'm going after Bailey," Ramon shouted, wrenching open the door. "Cover me."

More bullets ripped into both vehicles and the pavement around them.

Dispassionately, through the crosshairs, Smythe watched. He couldn't see either the Grant kid or the girl, but he knew the boy was still unhurt; the girl might be. She'd released the seat belt just as he'd shot.

The arrival of the bodyguards changed everything, Smythe thought, his eyes narrowing dangerously. The truck should have taken care of them. That was one failure that wouldn't be repeated.

He fingered the rifle thoughtfully, rubbing his thumb on the satiny stock. With professionals now involved, he couldn't wait for a clear shot of Grant's kid. They would see he didn't get one.

Lightning flashed, illuminating the vacant lot, illuminating Cora as she scrambled desperately for her car.

One dead body was as good as another, he thought, centering her in his sight. "Try to explain this one, Senator Grant," Smythe said emotionlessly as he again squeezed the trigger.

In a flash of white-hot lightning, Bailey saw Cora frantically grab for the door handle. Her hair had come loose from its band and stood out wildly around her head. Her face was mad with fear.

Bailey froze, horrified, as a dark red hole sprang up in the center of her pale forehead. Instantly, she folded onto the pavement, her arms and legs akimbo.

"No!" he screamed, stumbling to his feet. He took a step toward her but was tackled from behind. His face hit the pavement, momentarily stunning him. A heavy body pinned him to the ground.

"Keep down!" Ramon hissed in his ear. "You want to get yourself killed?"

"But Cora . . ."

Ramon gave his arm a sympathetic squeeze but didn't answer.

"Sherrill? Where's Sherrill?"

"Just relax, *amigo*."

John Smythe lowered the gun and looked at his watch. Time to go. In one practiced motion, he broke down his weapon and stuffed it into a battered carryall. Within minutes he was in his "borrowed" car, driving back toward civilization.

A siren sounded, far away but coming closer.

"Cora!" Bailey yelled, pulling himself into a crouch. She didn't answer. He yelled her name again, but the stone in his stomach told him she wouldn't answer. Never again would she answer. "We have to help Cora!" he cried, turning haunted eyes to Ramon.

"You get in the car." Ramon said, giving him a shove in that direction. His body in a crouch, Ramon zigzagged over to stoop behind Cora's grotesquely twisted form. He knew even before gently touching her throat that he would find no pulse.

The scream of fast-approaching sirens intensified.

"Let's get out of here!" Tommy yelled, his hand like a jackhammer between the boy's shoulder blades. Bailey sprawled across the front seat and landed against Sherrill. She didn't move.

Tommy slid into the driver's seat, thrusting Bailey's legs aside and turning the key in the ignition. With a jerk, the car lurched forward.

Bailey scrambled upright and pulled Sherrill to him. He braced her limp body against the sway of the car and with shaking hands cradled her head to his chest. His fingers touched a warm stickiness. Blood!

"Sherrill!" Her name escaped as a moan.

Behind them, tires screeched as the second car, Ramon at the wheel, skidded into the street.

Both cars were barely a block away when police cars screamed into the vacant lot, their lights whirling blue shadows onto the walls, the concrete, even Cora's still face.

With a resounding roar of thunder, the skies let loose their storm. Within seconds, Cora was washed clean of all signs of the encounter, all signs but the black hole between her eyes.

When Estelle phoned, Cynthia had instantly agreed to come to the White House. Now the First Lady couldn't decide where they should meet. The thought of the listening ears of ushers and Secret Service agents—they would keep her secret, but *they* would know—had finally made her settle on her own bedroom. There she'd be safe from an unannounced visit by her husband as well. Perfectly safe, she thought bitterly.

Cynthia, who'd been out chasing down leads and hadn't even taken time to call Rachel, was a few minutes late. By the time an usher escorted her into the bedroom, Estelle was vibrating with nerves. Weeks of sleepless nights, not to mention the additional shocks of the last few days: She was feeling them all. That, combined with a sense of guilt at bothering Cynthia when her own world with the Senator was crumbling, was almost too much to bear.

"Oh, Cynthia!" Estelle cried, hurrying across and throwing her arms around her friend. "You've come!" She wanted to say more, to apologize at the very least, but words were too difficult. All she could do was weep. The tears she'd been holding at bay for weeks welled over and threatened to make speech impossible.

Cynthia seemed to understand. Her embrace tightened as she murmured words of sympathy and affection.

"There. I think I'm done," Estelle finally said with a quavery laugh that ended in a hiccup. She reached for a tissue, thought better of it, and yanked out a handful. "Quite a display, I'm afraid. I don't know what came over me."

Cynthia arched an eyebrow.

"You're right," Estelle agreed, understanding Cynthia's unspoken comment. "Of course I know. Only too well. Oh, Cynthia, I'm so glad you're here!" She gave Cynthia another prolonged hug.

"I've been concerned about you, Stell," Cynthia told her. "You look awful, and I don't mean from crying."

"That bad, huh?" Estelle asked, then giggled. "Though why I find that funny . . . Maybe because I'm relieved someone's noticed. Pathetic, isn't it?"

"Pathetic? I don't know. But a lot of bother for a hug and a few kind words."

They walked slowly, arms linked, to a cozy seating group, overlooking an expanse of the White House lawn, now sodden with rain. A fierce pre-winter storm whipped the bare-limbed trees. Cynthia found the sound of the rain pelting the glass soothing. Even the reverberating booms of thunder and stark glare of lightning were reassuring. God was in heaven. All was right with the world.

"What's wrong?" she asked, turning her gaze from the window to her friend.

"What's wrong?" Estelle repeated. She tried to return Cynthia's gaze but couldn't, not yet. Instead, she looked toward the window. Her unfocused eyes saw none of the Lord's majestic show, though judging by her expression, her inner vision was equally stormy. "My husband has left me."

"But—"

"Oh, I know he still lives here, but that's all. He has—" She stopped, then hurried on, a crimson flush staining her pale cheeks. "Girlfriends, mistresses, whatever. I don't know how many. He calls them 'snacks.'" She whispered the last word, her face raw with pain.

"Snacks!" Cynthia repeated, outraged. "What a pompous jerk!"

Estelle laughed weakly and wiped tears from her cheeks. "He'd hate you if he heard that."

"Doesn't he already?"

"Hate you? Probably," Estelle agreed. "He's never had much use for anyone who disagrees with him, and having you work for Bob Grant! Cynthia, what's going on there? The President acts as if he has a personal stake in what's happening."

"We've wondered just how much the White House had to do with the setup and lies," Cynthia said slowly, her eyes troubled, "but—"

"You know they're lies?" Estelle interrupted.

"Yes, and not just lies." She explained about Russell Frederickson and Anne Peabody, about Maribeth Pariss, and finally about Bailey and the drugs.

"I had no idea," Estelle said when Cynthia finished. If possible, she looked more stricken than before. "The media hasn't reported any of this. Destroying his children . . . That's unconscionable! Does . . . does . . . my husband know anything about . . . about any of this?"

"We don't know," Cynthia admitted. She wanted to ask for any information, to beg even, but she couldn't. Estelle's husband might be a jerk, just as she'd said; he might be much worse, but he was still her husband and the President. "We just don't know."

This time Estelle seemed to read her mind. "I'm not sure," she said hesitantly, "but I think I would help you if I knew anything. But I don't.

I don't know anything anymore, Cyn." She looked into her lap, twisting the silken fabric of her blue designer dress. "I'm married to a stranger, one I'm not sure I even like."

Cynthia read the tragedy shadowing her eyes and realized that her friend still loved the husband she was unable to like.

"It's as if . . ." Estelle continued haltingly, unaware of how much of herself she'd revealed, "as if he's begun to believe he's above the silly rules of mere mortals. He and Hunt have decided they have, I don't know, but I guess you would call it some kind of divine right to decide what's best for everyone. They like controlling people." She looked up, her confusion and bewilderment hard for Cynthia to bear. "Tell Bob to be careful," she said wearily. "I heard Hunt say he wouldn't rest until Bob was destroyed, that Bob had caused his son Joey's death. It doesn't make sense, but . . ."

"I'm afraid it makes only too much sense." Cynthia described the night of the drug raid.

"And Hunt blames Bob because Joey decided to take drugs?"

"Apparently."

"That explains Rebecca Hunter's comment, something about fathers who deny their sons' deaths just as they denied their lives. She looked almost haunted when she said it."

"'What a tangled web we weave . . .'" Cynthia quoted, her gaze wandering absently toward the window. "Human nature never changes, does it, whether we're deceiving ourselves or others."

"Deceiving myself," Estelle whispered, once again twisting the fabric of her dress. "That's what I've been doing, and it's been eating away at me. That's what I've been seeing in my husband and in Hunt, the corrosive effect of self-deception. Sounds grandiose, I know," she said with a twisted half-smile, "but it's true. I've known it all along but didn't want to face it."

"What are you going to do?"

Estelle gazed blindly into the distance for more than a minute before answering.

"You tell me," Estelle finally said. A wave of relief washed over her as she latched onto her friend's faith and good sense. She wasn't alone, Estelle thought. She was no longer alone. "Should I leave him?" she asked, her long, normally graceful fingers clutching and unclutching a wad of her dress.

"Oh, Estelle!" Cynthia cried compassionately as she leaned forward and took her friend's hands in her own. "You know I can't tell you that. No one can."

Estelle made no reply. She looked her question, her eyes holding Cynthia's.

"I think you have to ask yourself," Cynthia said finally, "if you'd be happier if you left. And would the children be happier." At Estelle's continued silence, Cynthia went on, choosing her words with care. "You obviously have the moral right to ask for a divorce—how could he be so stupid!" The words burst from her in a spontaneous eruption of disgust. "He's a fool! A libidinous fool!"

"Libidinous?" Estelle giggled again, covering the sound with her hands. Almost immediately her eyes above them became desolate. "Then you think I should leave him?" she whispered.

"Have you talked to him?"

"Talked to him?" she asked scathingly, returning her gaze to the rain-smeared window. "When he spends all his time feeding his appetites? Why would he want to be in the same room with someone as unimportant and old as his wife, much less talk to her?"

"Make him. Tonight."

Estelle's eyes darted to Cynthia's, then away. "I . . . don't know," she said, her face drawn and haggard. "I don't think I can say the words, much less listen to him, to his excuses. You can't imagine how humiliating it is! Anything to look good to the public—that's all he cares about. His precious reputation is as much a sham as our marriage and everything else about him. His precious reputation!" Her face became stricken. "Oh, Cyn, I'm so sorry. I'd forgotten about you and Bob. I may feel miserable, but at least with us no one knows what's going on. But with you . . . Everyone . . . I really am sorry. I wish I could help."

"So do I." Cynthia's tone made plain her sincerity.

Estelle regarded her with thoughtful intensity, relieved for a moment's respite from her own battered emotions. "All I know is that Eugene Corforth isn't like the others." In her mind, she saw his pitying eyes and heard the compassion in his voice. Her face again lengthened in pain. "He seems to have changed. Maybe he . . . I don't know."

Cynthia left twenty minutes later. Her heart was filled with a prayer for guidance and strength for her friend as well as one of thanksgiving for her own love-filled life. She'd been a widow now for almost as long as she'd been married, but how blessed her marriage had been! Steve had loved her, deeply and faithfully.

Poor, dear Estelle! Integrity, the foundation of a loving marriage, was no longer part of hers.

Was integrity missing from this administration as well? she wondered. And did that have any bearing on what was happening to her Senator?

Where have you been, Miller?" Tobias Caruso growled. "I won't stand for such insubordination."

Caruso was not happy. His afternoon debate prep had been scheduled to begin half an hour earlier. Already, he was finding it unpleasant to have his will thwarted. That his rise to power had become manifest only two days before was impossible for him to remember. He only knew he was specially chosen.

Miller ignored Caruso, instead fiddling with the papers he'd brought. Only when the tension had stretched, becoming almost unbearable, did Miller speak. "You are questioning the administration's plan? Is that right, Toby?" He emphasized the diminutive of the name deliberately.

Caruso's eyes darted around the room. Indignation or remorse—which would get the better long-term result from this arrogant underling? Unsure, he said nothing.

"You seem to have forgotten who made your present position possible," Miller said, the blandness of his tone belying the coldness of his gaze.

Caruso's eyes froze on him. What meaning was hidden in those words? Miller's next words were reassuring.

"The President hasn't given his endorsement lightly," Miller continued. "He has personally overseen the final stages of your campaign. Trust me, Senator—and by Tuesday afternoon, that appellation will be legally yours."

Miller handed Caruso a closely typed sheet of paper. "These are the comments and questions you must insert at some point in the debate. They highlight Grant's weaknesses. Don't wait for an appropriate question. Make your own moments."

Caruso looked through the list. "There's a lot," he said dubiously. "Won't people think I'm kicking him when he's down?"

"Not if you use the phrasing I've given you. Voters want nothing more than to be told how to think. That's what you'll be doing, directing their thoughts."

Caruso still looked doubtful.

"Look, Caruso," Miller said, not as patiently as Caruso might have expected. "I've been at this a lot longer than you. Do what I say, and you'll come out of this wearing a white hat. People are tired of criminals and corrupt politicians. You'll be exposing Grant as both. They'll think you care about them, that you want justice for their sakes."

"Care about them," Caruso repeated, musingly. "What about this humor?" he said, pointing down at the paper. "You sure it's appropriate?"

"Down-home stories and deprecating humor always play well. But don't be cute. A decent person in an awkward situation—that's you." Miller picked up a stack of papers and straightened them. "Let's get going. Charles will stand in for Grant."

Charles Kendall, who'd come in with Miller, took his place at one of two lecterns on the improvised stage. "And I'll be Kirk Vinton," Miller continued. "Even if you mess up, Toby, Vinton will be there to bail you out."

What's Grant up to?" the President demanded of Jonathan Hunter.

"No one knows," Hunter answered. "He's disappeared. And so has his car, according to Bender. No reported sightings of either Grant or the car." The pulse in Hunter's temple throbbed with every mention of Grant.

"Grant's not lying low, that's for sure," the President said, his eyes thoughtful. "Grant doesn't lie low. Grant attacks. No, Hunt, Grant is out there planning something, and we'd better be ready."

"Something about Anne Peabody, I would guess, since he was nosing around her office."

The President nodded. "Did you tell John Smythe to back off?"

Hunter looked uncomfortable.

Startled, the President shifted in his chair. *Nothing* made Hunter uncomfortable. What was wrong? Joey's death? Until that moment, the President had forgotten about Joey. Even Hunter acted as if he'd forgotten. POTUS felt an instant stab of guilt, but it was gone with Hunter's next words.

"Smythe seems to have disappeared," Hunter told him. "I haven't been able to contact him through the usual channels."

"Disappeared!" POTUS walked to the fireplace and stared at the flames. "What do you suppose that means?"

"Maybe he feels his job is finished," Hunter suggested. He took off his glasses and began polishing them.

"Is that what you feel, Hunt?" the President asked, turning to face him. "That everything is under control?"

"Yes." Hunter's voice was emphatic. "Yes, I do."

"Nothing we can do?" the President persisted.

"Grant has taken care of it all." Hunter's face was drawn, but his eyes were alive with an unholy fire. "Grant will take the blame for everything—Frederickson, the drugs, even Anne Peabody—and deservedly so."

The President studied Hunter, seemed reassured by what he saw, and turned back to the fire. "Keep trying to contact Smythe," he said. "We can't afford any more problems. How could Smythe have made such a bollix of things? He came highly recommended. He'd better not have murdered those people!"

"As long as he can't be connected to the White House," Hunter said, replacing his glasses, "it doesn't matter."

As prearranged early that morning, Grant waited at a pay phone near the air strip for Rachel's call. The phone rang.

"Sherrill's been shot," Rachel said breathlessly.

"What!"

"Only a crease in her scalp," she reassured him quickly. "Nothing really serious."

"Thank God for that." Grant reined in his wild thoughts.

"She was unconscious for a few minutes," Rachel continued, glancing around to be sure she remained unobserved, "so she may have a headache for a few days and possibly a scar under her hair where I had to place a few stitches, but she's fine. Bob, someone tried to kill her, and they did kill Cora Snyder!" The strain in her voice mirrored her thoughts—it could as easily have been Bailey or Sherrill.

Rachel described the scene at the abandoned parking lot and the phone call that had precipitated it.

"Ramon doesn't think her death was an accident," Rachel finished, fiddling distractedly with a button on her coat. "He saw it happen. It was deliberate."

"You're not at Cynthia's, are you?" Grant asked urgently. "You've got to get away. It's not safe."

"We left as soon as I took care of Sherrill," Rachel assured him, remembering their frantic haste. "Ramon wants to know if you have a safe place already in mind."

Grant did. He, Stephen Yao, and Matt Goldie had discussed it, a place near Washington but also near a small abandoned airstrip in Virginia, in case they needed to leave quickly. "Go to . . ." He stopped. He couldn't risk telling her outright, not over the phone. Instead, he gave her a description only she could understand.

"The perfect place," Rachel agreed, remembering the rustic cabin owned by the parents of one of Grant's staffers. Near a main highway, it was nonetheless isolated, with acres of trees surrounding it. "No one will think of looking there."

"Send Sherrill to her parents first," Grant urged.

"I still haven't been able to contact them." Rachel sounded as if that blow was almost as crushing as the others.

"Poor kid," he said. And poor Rachel, he thought. So much to handle, and nothing disturbed her more than arrogant parents who placed their own needs before those of their children. "But she has to go somewhere safe until this is over."

"She refuses to leave," Rachel said wearily. "She's determined to help. A form of atonement, I'm sure."

Grant lowered his head. Sherrill had no business staying, but what could he do? "We'll deal with that later," he said. "Right now you need to get away."

"First, you need to know Bailey discovered a plastic bag of white powder in his coat pocket when they got back here." Rachel's voice was matter-of-fact. Drugs seemed unimportant when murder was involved. Murder! And their son the target. A coat button came off in her hand. She looked at it without seeing it and stuffed it into a pocket. "Ramon says it's cocaine. Cora had to have put it there."

"Send it to Jenks for analysis, for fingerprints, too. I'll alert him it's coming. They find any cartridges?"

"Imbedded in both cars," she told him. "From a high-powered rifle, according to Ramon. They went back to the vacant lot a few minutes ago but couldn't find anything helpful—nothing but a windowsill wiped clean of dust in a building across the street. A thunderstorm washed away anything outside."

"Doesn't surprise me, storm or no storm. Our enemy is nothing if not thorough. Send the slugs to Jenks, too. I'll see if he can get a copy of the police report without tipping our hand."

"Bob, Bailey doesn't think anyone knows about the meeting with Cora," Rachel said, feeling as if she'd stepped into quicksand and it was rapidly reaching her throat, "but what if the police find out? What if Cora's woman friend knew about the meeting and tells the police? Bailey might be charged with murder!"

"If the drug bust is any indication," Grant said grimly, "the police *will* be told. Bonfire doesn't leave anything to chance. Just be sure both Bailey and Sherrill stay out of sight until we clear this up. Completely out of sight. They shouldn't even go near a window, no matter what. Have Bailey try to access the financial records for Cora's FOW group, her phone records as well. Tell him to use his imagination. That'll keep him occupied and out of trouble for a while. Tell him the White House phone records are even more important now. If he can get those . . ." He didn't waste time finishing the thought. "Also, have Ramon hide the cars and see about getting some others."

"He already has."

"Good. I'll meet him as planned." He tried to think if anything else needed mentioning. He hoped not. They'd spent too much time as it was. "I'll be waiting for your call in two hours and every half hour after. Now get out of there!"

"Be careful, Bob." Rachel's voice was husky with urgency and love. "You're the one Bonfire's really after."

"He wants me alive, remember."

"That was before you started figuring out his plans. He won't like that."

"That's what I'm hoping. We have to make him expose himself."

And soon, Grant thought as he replaced the receiver. Before anyone else could be hurt.

She couldn't stand another sleepless night, Janet Loomis thought, reaching back to give her pillow an almost savage thumping. Her husband was dead. He'd killed himself, and now he was torturing her with his letter to Bob

Grant. How could he have done it to her! She beat the pillow, blow after despairing blow. Finally exhausted, she buried her face in it and sobbed.

When she had no more tears, she lay still, without thought. But that couldn't last, no matter how resolutely she pushed the thoughts back. Bailey Grant. She kept seeing his face. He was a friend of her son's—a good kid. And he was being destroyed along with his father. Drugs. She wanted to believe it could be true—he was a college student, after all—but she couldn't, not after reading Phillip's letter. Phillip had known Bob Grant would be in trouble. Now even Bailey was suffering. Around and around, the thoughts kept going.

If Bailey were her son . . . The thought of their being hurt by revelations about their father was the crux of her despair. How could she stand to watch them suffer because of their father, suffer again because of their father. Phillip had mentioned evil and a compromise of ethics in his letter to Bob Grant—even atonement! How could she not think that he'd done something shameful, something that would bring immeasurable pain to their sons were it to become public.

But if Phillip had known something that could help Bob Grant—a pain shot through her at the unimaginable implications behind that dreadful possibility—did she have the moral right to deny it to the Grants? Moral right versus harm to her sons. She felt as if the sword of Damocles, which had hung over her head for days, had now dropped against her forehead and was drawing blood.

Bob Grant was certainly in trouble now, she thought, feeling as always the pressure of time passing too quickly. Could the information her husband had obviously collected with great care help in some way to exonerate the Grants, two people to whom she owed so much, including her life? Rachel had been the one who'd learned of the new cancer protocol and secured a place for her in the clinical trial. If it hadn't been for Rachel, she would be dead right now, and her sons would be orphans.

They were with friends for the weekend, and she was glad. She couldn't bear facing them in the morning.

The boys. She shut her eyes, trying to ease the hurt. Should she take a chance of reopening old wounds, especially for the boys, when, in all probability, it would do the Grants no good?

If only Phillip had trusted her enough to share his burden. If only ...

Again Bailey Grant's face loomed before her. His usually laughing eyes were wide with anguish.

She reached for the phone. This time there weren't going to be any *if onlys*. She was going to do what she'd known she should do from the beginning. She dialed the number quickly before her tenuous resolve could shatter.

No one answered at either the Grants' or Cynthia's. She would keep trying until she reached them, she decided. Now that she'd made her decision, the need to reveal the letter consumed her.

At the last moment, India, Olivia, and Henry Grant left the car Ramon was driving, hurried across the tarmac of Leesburg Airport, and ran up the steps into Matt Goldie's plane. Bailey and Sherrill, her possible concussion making flying inadvisable, would remain in hiding near Washington. So would Rachel, who refused to leave Sherrill unattended. Too, she hoped she might yet uncover some pertinent information about Joey's death.

Bailey needed to be near the prodigious records stored in D.C. computers. "Have modem; will travel," he'd told his mother with a grin. His resilience was reassuring.

"Any sign of trouble?" Grant asked Stephen Yao as the plane started down the airstrip for takeoff.

"I'm not sure." Yao held up a finger for quiet and listened to his men on the ground. "Someone may have made us," he finally said, lowering the walkie-talkie. "My men will try to find out for sure before we land."

Grant accepted this unwelcome information thoughtfully. He'd formulated his overall plan to capitalize on his main—possibly his only—advantage, his ability to keep Bonfire off balance. In disappearing himself, in having his family and close associates disappear, Grant hoped he could make Bonfire edgy enough to make a mistake. Barring that, he hoped to force him into altering his plans for Grant's destruction. Such alterations might also lead to mistakes.

Grant and the children would use extra care in going to their safe house when they arrived in Georgia. Whether someone had seen them leave the airport or not was immaterial. Grant knew his enemy, and he knew his enemy's ruthlessness. His children must remain safe.

That night on the news, no mention was made of Cora Snyder's murder, so no mention was made of Bailey. Because she hadn't been identified yet, Grant wondered, or for some more sinister reason?

Sunday, November 1:
Two Days Before the Election

Cynthia spent a short but uneventful night at a safe location. She was tired and irritable—too little sleep in an unfamiliar bed, too much on her mind. At least Cora's murder hadn't made the news, she noted as she sifted through the reports her staff had prepared during the night. Even the *Herald* was quiet. Maybe Bailey's presence was still unknown. Or maybe the police—or the NIIA—were playing a more devious game, just biding their time before they pounced. Feeling the first sharp pains of a migraine, a doozy to judge by the early symptoms, she took two pills instead of the usual one and prayed for a clear head.

When Janet Loomis called for the second time—staff had already fobbed her off once—Cynthia was less than diplomatic.

"I understand that you want to see Rachel," she said, "and you're right that Rachel hasn't been home all night and won't be again until after the election. What you don't seem to understand is that this election has placed the whole family in danger. Now if—"

"Cynthia Novitsky," Janet interrupted, "you listen to me and you listen carefully."

Cynthia leaned back in her chair, surprise widening her eyes. Janet Loomis, normally the most even-tempered of people, sounded positively possessed. What on earth was going on?

"You think you're protecting them by holding me and everyone else at bay," Janet continued angrily. "You may be right about everyone else. That I don't know. But I'm telling you straight out that you've never made a bigger mistake if you don't arrange for me to meet with Rachel as soon as possible."

"Well, Janet," Cynthia temporized, "I understand your concern, but—"

Again, Janet interrupted. This time, however, her voice was weary. "I'm sorry, Cynthia. I must sound crazy, but this has been a hard decision for me. All I know for sure is that I have something that Phillip wanted Bob to have if he ever got in trouble. I may be wrong about its having anything to do with what's happening now—I admit it—but if it did . . . and I didn't help Rachel . . . I'd never forgive . . ." Her voice faltered to a stop for a moment. "Anyway," she continued with a perceptible catch in her voice, "I think it does, and I think it's urgent. If she'll just—"

Suddenly, the gravity in Janet's voice, the sheer desperation, penetrated Cynthia's defenses. Her heart began pounding. Something from Phillip? What if it really were important? And what if someone were listening in? Stephen Yao had sent an expert to sweep for bugs, but could he be sure? And what about Janet's phone?

"Don't say another word!" Cynthia was practically screaming. She took a breath to bring her racing thoughts in check. "You may not be safe."

"But—"

"Just listen to me, Janet. Please. You don't know some of the horrible things that have happened."

"I'm afraid neither of us do," Janet said so softly that Cynthia wasn't sure she'd heard correctly. But she had. She knew she had. Her concern coalesced into a burning ball of fear, scorching its way up her spine.

"Leave wherever you are," she said urgently. "Don't wait. Go somewhere no one would think of looking. Then call me. I'll think of something. Do you understand? You have to get out of there. Now! The phones may be tapped."

"I'll leave right now and call you back," Janet said quickly. "Thanks. Thanks for trusting me."

"Leave immediately, Janet. I'm serious. And don't tell anyone—anyone—where you're going."

"I understand."

Cynthia could only hope she really did.

After wasting precious minutes trying and failing to contact Grant before he left to meet with Jenks, Cynthia went down the hall and then down one floor, not stopping until she came to the third pay phone—a safe one, she hoped.

Rachel answered on the first ring. Quickly, Cynthia summarized Janet Loomis's call, emphasizing her own impression of its seriousness.

"Set up a meeting," Rachel said without hesitation. "I'll be there."

"No."

"No?"

"I'll meet her," Cynthia said. "Harming me won't accomplish anything."

"I suppose you're right," Rachel agreed reluctantly, "though I can't say I like it much. Be sure Tommy stays close." With Bailey safe at the hideout with Ramon, Tommy was keeping an eye on Cynthia. "Tell Janet thanks." Rachel's voice became infinitely sad. "And make sure you're both very, very careful."

The sky was just light when Grant arrived at the home of Martha Jenks, the sheriff's sister-in-law.

"Thank you for letting us meet here," Grant told her when she opened the back door.

She nodded, a trifle shyly. "Just make yourself right at home," she said, self-consciously patting her fluff of gray hair. "I'm sorry I have to be going, but Sunday's our busiest day, and I like to have time for church." The door closed softly behind her.

Jenks was seated at the kitchen table, digging into a plate piled high with eggs, country ham, and grits with red-eye gravy. A similar plate awaited Grant.

Hungry despite his tension and general weariness, Grant took a bite. "You find out who leaked our meetings?" he asked Jenks.

"Nope. Buncha lily-whites on my end, or so they assure me, but who knows. You?"

"I have an idea," Grant said. Jenks leaned forward, a bite of egg forgotten on his fork. "Only a suspicion," Grant told him. "I'll let you know if I get proof."

"You're being careful? Not showing your hand?"

"Very careful," Grant assured him.

Jenks studied his intent face, nodded, and brought the forgotten bite to his mouth.

"If I'm right about the leak . . ." Grant's voice was rough. "I hate betrayal! Someone who knows me personally, who smiles, slaps my back, and calls me friend, but who knowingly betrays me! The thought turns my stomach!" He stopped, then blew out a whole lungful of air. "I trusted him, Sheriff. Considered him a friend. At least the rest of the plot is impersonal, planned by someone I don't know who for some reason views me as dangerous."

"Maybe," Jenks said mildly, giving Grant time to cool down. "But don't be too quick to pass judgment, specially not when so much rides on it. You may have more than one snake in your garden. Too many folks aren't willing to claim responsibility for their actions. A frightening dumbing down of morals, to my mind. Cain't be sure who all's been tainted."

"Dumbing down of morality," Grant said tiredly. "Perfect description of the rot that's laying waste to our society. You're saying to not trust anyone, aren't you? That's what Alvarez said, too."

He looked at his almost-full plate, pushed it away, thought better of it, and took a bite. He pulled the plate back.

"Suppose I am," Jenks said, talking through a bite, "leastways not till you know their loyalty for sure. Too much is at stake. And don't let this 'betrayal' eat away at you. Even if you're right—you may be, but I've still got a few ideas of my own about that leak—if you let it lay hold of you, you'll lose sight of the 'big picture.' Isn't that what you Washington types call it?"

"Usually when we're trying to justify something." Grant put down his fork and leaned forward. "Speaking of the big picture, what do you have for me?" That was the reason for this meeting. Jenks had promised to bring Grant information he could use in the debate later that day.

Jenks pulled a sheaf of papers from his gym bag. "First," he said, handing Grant the top paper, "an affidavit from that Atlanta forensic expert swearing that Sergek's letter was a forgery and that the diary entry where Pariss moans 'cause she'd never even gotten to talk to you was in her hand." He ate a few more bites while Grant looked at the sheet.

"Next," Jenks continued, handing Grant another sheet, "a copy of the composite of li'l Gayla Sergek's playmate at the Cottonball Bar as well as"—with a flourish, he handed Grant a set of papers stapled together—"a copy of the transcripts of my interviews with her and with the lovable Shirley Spade."

"Nice of the NIIA to let you have this stuff."

"Yeah, real nice guys," Jenks said dryly. "I wouldn't go waving this around until the last moment, mind you. Let's see. Here's another composite, this one from a witness at Crazy Sam's. Might not want to mention he's only seven."

While Jenks buttered half a biscuit, slathered it with homemade elderberry preserves, and popped it into his mouth whole, Grant compared the two drawings. Both showed a man with a bushy beard that hid seemingly nondescript features. "I don't know that these help much," he said dubiously. "A fake beard, without doubt."

"My guess." Jenks wiped a speck of preserves from his chin.

"Maybe a comparison with the murderer of Anne Peabody will point to some similarities. Could your police artist do composites with a mustache and clean shaven?"

"Already have the beardless one, computer generated." He handed it to Grant. "I'll get on the other one. Should've thought of it already. A composite combining all the composites, too, leastways the two we have. Alvarez's can be mixed in the pot when it comes."

If it ever comes, they both amended silently. Alvarez wasn't an easy man to figure. The meeting in New York seemed to have led to nothing.

"This is a mite more interesting," Jenks said, handing Grant another stapled set of papers. "The report from Bailey's drug bust."

Grant scanned it while Jenks talked. "All began with some good citizen—who remains nameless—calling the NIIA, saying to watch out for bad-boy Bailey Grant. Even mentioned your name. The NIIA called the locals."

"NIIA?" Grant asked, giving the sheriff a questioning look.

"Interesting, yes," Jenks agreed. "But only that. Captain Fleming *did* call headquarters from the apartment, probably when he learned about Joey Hunter, though mention of Joey is right glaring in its absence. No mention of an ambulance call even."

"Bailey has witnesses if it comes to that, though what good that would do, I don't know."

"Rule one of investigating: Latch onto every scrap of information you can. Never know when it might come in handy."

"And this?" Grant asked, pointing to the next set of papers.

"Report on the Peabody mugging. Nada. Zip. Nothing but a mugging."

"Until—or if—Alvarez comes up with his witness. I can't help feeling Peabody and the bribe are the beginning of it all."

"Could be," Jenks agreed. "Frederickson seemed to think she was worth a look. I'll do some more digging through his computer files, the Pulitzer one especially. See if Sally has dug up anything else by now." He refilled his coffee mug, leaned back in the chair, and with the steam from the coffee partially clouding his face, watched Grant.

"Bailey couldn't get that last file of Frederickson's," Grant told him. "He suspects someone at the *Herald* deleted it from the computer after they caught him trying to get in. He smelled a trap and backed out." Grant thought of what Yao had told him—that given the right equipment Bailey could have been nabbed easily—and felt thankful to have averted that.

"Too bad about the file," Jenks said. "Might have proved interesting. The fingerprints on that bag of drugs planted on Bailey match those of a known pusher. You know someone who might like a word with him?"

"Could be that I do," Grant agreed. He would turn the name over to Ramon, who would get it to the guys taking care of Reggie Dixon and his girlfriend. "Though I doubt he knows anything. Whoever's orchestrating this would be too careful."

"But another scrap of information," Jenks reminded him. "Don't be too quick to kill the pig 'cause he doesn't squeal just right." Jenks leaned forward again, thumping the now-empty coffee cup down on the table. "Now, this report may be the most interesting of all." He handed the last sheets to Grant, who began scanning them immediately. "My counterpart in Olexey's hometown was able to get Ma Olexey to talk. Seems sonny boy likes to brag, a trait he learned at his mama's knee. She told plenty of folks, confidential-like, that her son had come into a wad of cash, that his drug conviction was a setup, and that he would be out before long."

"Whew!"

"Gets better. She hinted he made another deal while he was in prison."

Grant was chuckling. "That's some Bubba network you have. Mama have any idea who was paying?"

"Only that it was two different sources. Thinks both were from Washington, though sonny boy was just guessing about the first. He never met him personally. Got his instructions over the phone—a Darth Vader voice, his mother said. Whatever that means. He picked up his money where he was told. Fifty thousand dollars."

Grant lifted an eyebrow in surprise. "Enough for a man to sit in prison for six months, I'd say."

"Olexey did pretty well for himself, all right. I'd guess he got a bundle from the *Herald*, too. That picture caused a right-powerful ruckus!"

"How'd Olexey get the picture?"

"Mama'd never heard of it. Did mention that her son was a smart one, getting money from a big-time paper. The picture probably."

"Makes sense," Grant agreed. "So Olexey must have made some kind of contact with whoever had the picture to tell them the *Herald* had taken the bait."

"Sounds odd, but Mama mentioned something about Bonfire." Jenks leaned forward at the look on Grant's face. "Seems like I may have sparked a fire of my own."

"A real inferno," Grant agreed, then told him about both Bonfire and John Smythe.

"Sounds like we've moved right out of my league." Jenks looked a trifle shaken.

"I doubt that." Grant gestured to the information Jenks had amassed, most of it with little to go on but his own instincts. "You've done yourself proud. You might suggest Olexey's mother be put under protective custody, though."

Jenks nodded and reached for the phone. "Either completely out of circulation," he said, "or inconspicuous so this devil Bonfire won't realize she's blabbed."

Grant relaxed. Jenks, the professional, had immediately understood the implications of Bonfire and Smythe's involvement.

"Any chance of getting phone records from the prison?" Grant asked when Jenks finished the call.

"I'm working on it quiet-like. Don't want to heat up those NIIA boys. Have to be sure now that Bonfire doesn't get wind, either. Think he's got a pipeline into the NIIA?"

The intensity left Grant's face to be replaced by fatigue. "I don't know," he said wearily, "but enough has happened to make me suspicious. I still can't believe I'm not on the same side with the feds."

"Now, Senator," Jenks said mildly, "let's not get those Big Brother robots mixed up with the real police in this great country. A world of difference, let me tell you."

"I stand corrected," Grant agreed, looking Jenks straight in the eye. "No one is more appreciative of that difference than I am."

Jenks nodded his understanding. He, too, was feeling tired. He, too, carried some of Grant's burden, a burden mushrooming alarmingly with every passing hour. "Well, that's it."

"Nothing earthshaking," Grant summed up. "Certainly nothing that leads to Bonfire, John Smythe, or whoever's paying them."

"Nope, but remember what I said. Something here may be just what we need."

"Let's hope so. And thanks. I know how much this could hurt you if they win. I'll try to protect you as best I can."

"We're too far down that road to make a never-mind," Jenks said. "Let's just be sure we get the buzzards calling the shots. Bonfire and his sidekick Smythe, too. When justice takes a back seat to expediency, then maybe it's time for me to hang up my badge anyway."

"I think you're wrong there, Sheriff. That's exactly when men of virtue are most needed."

Grant stood and carefully stowed Jenks's papers in a large pocket he'd sewn inside his jacket that morning. The stitches would have made his Grandmama Grant weep—his mother, too. But the pocket kept the papers safe. Grant liked the feel of hard evidence against his body, not much hard evidence, maybe, but a sign of trust from a good man. Combined with what else they were finding, maybe it would be enough.

"Guess it's time to be going." Grant shook Jenks's hand. "When I was a boy," he said, "my daddy told me that during my lifetime I would meet a few great men, that they most likely wouldn't be famous or powerful. Instead they would be men of integrity who valued right above everything and who had the courage to fight for that right. I'm thankful the Lord led me to one of those men the day he led me to you. I would count it an honor if I could consider you a friend."

Jenks swallowed hard. "Shucks, Senator," he said, his voice thickly southern with emotion, "you better believe we're friends. I want to be there when this story gets its happy ending, don't I?"

He walked with Grant to the back door. "Keep in touch, hear? Ol' Gus is plumb set up being 'a secretary to the sheriff,' even if I may soon be an ex-." He paused before opening the door for Grant. The bantering tone was gone. "Don't wait too long between calls."

"I won't. And thanks. Thanks so much. Thank Martha for her kindness, too." Grant slipped out the door and down the back alley to where Yao was waiting.

"And take care, my friend," Jenks whispered to the closed door. "Take care, hear? Great men are hard to come by."

Cynthia was fifteen minutes late for her meeting with Janet Loomis, and every one of those minutes had been agonizing. She'd spotted her tail almost as soon as she'd driven out of the Senate parking garage. Try as she might, she couldn't shake him. Five minutes, eight, ten: The minutes had piled up, each more likely to break Janet's resolve and cause her to flee, taking her information with her.

Just when Cynthia had despaired of ever getting away at all, salvation had appeared in her rearview mirror. She'd watched with mingled relief and dread as Tommy had changed lanes, preventing her tail from making the next light.

Her gas pedal pressed almost to the floor, she had turned the next corner and the next and the next. Thankfully, she was now shadow-free, but had Tommy jeopardized his cover just when it would be needed most?

One problem at a time, she cautioned herself, and Janet Loomis was problem number one. Had she waited?

With a heartfelt sigh of relief, Cynthia spotted the car, glad Janet had understood her cryptic mention of the alma mater of both of their sons. She surveyed the parking area per Tommy's instructions. It was filled with the cars of early churchgoers, but she could see no lurking watchers, nothing suspicious at all. Satisfied, she pulled into an empty space and walked to Janet's car. After a final look over her shoulder, she slid into the front seat.

Startled by the sound, Janet jerked her gaze from the stained glass of St. Aloysius Church. "Cynthia!" she exclaimed, her hand at her throat. "Where's Rachel?" Her voice was high and anxious.

Over the phone, she had been adamant that she would give her information to Rachel and Rachel alone. Cynthia had agreed, feeling guilty at the deception, but recognizing the futility of argument. Now she had to hope Janet would see reason.

"She's all right, isn't she?" Janet asked, her voice rising and close to hysteria.

"She's fine," Cynthia assured her, touching her coat sleeve soothingly. "They all are. She wanted to come, believe me, she did, but she couldn't. It wasn't safe. I'm sorry."

"I don't know," Janet said, her brow creased with doubt. "I didn't want anyone else to see . . ." She stopped and looked at Cynthia, the worry in her eyes no less intense. "I have to trust you, don't I? There's no other way."

"I'm sorry. I wish things were different."

"Don't we all." Janet smiled fractionally, but her hazel eyes remained clouded. "I should be the one apologizing. It's just that I was counting on Rachel. She's been so strong for me through everything." She paused, then burst out, "Oh, Cynthia, I'm so afraid that Phillip . . ." She squeezed her eyes shut and struggled for control. "I wanted to destroy this," she finally whispered, staring at the manila envelope she held. "But Phillip said Bob should have it."

She reached into the envelope and pulled out a smaller white one.

Cynthia's heart raced at the sight of *Senator Bob Grant*, written boldly on it. Her hands itched to grab it all and take it away to safety. She would do just that, she decided, if Janet changed her mind. Now that she'd seen it, Cynthia was as convinced as Janet of its importance.

"Tell Bob I'm sorry I opened it." Janet sounded more weary than contrite. "I know Phillip asked me not to, but with everything that's been happening and with the boys . . ." She shrugged. "I'm so confused," she continued, "so tired and confused. Nothing makes sense anymore. I just couldn't take a chance, not if it might make a difference, especially for Bailey. Take it." She shoved the envelope forward.

Unconcerned with niceties, Cynthia grabbed it and put it safely into the leather bag she'd brought. She put the bag well out of Janet's reach. Janet seemed not to realize.

"Give it to Bob," she said. "Tell him to use it if it helps. If not, please beg him to destroy it. I don't want Chris and Brian hurt, and I'm so afraid Phillip . . ." She stopped abruptly and stared fixedly out the window, struggling to regain composure. "Tell Bob the decision is his." Her words bore the husky imprint of sleepless nights and nightmarish fears. "I'm too tired to know what's best. I just keep thinking Phillip must have expected something like this." She turned fear-drenched eyes to Cynthia. "How could he have known?" she whispered. "How?"

Cynthia had no answer. The same question burned in her mind. The conclusion seemed appallingly inevitable. Phillip Loomis, dead now for months, was somehow, unbelievably, tangled in the web of evil ensnaring Bob Grant.

"Where can Rachel reach you?" she asked quickly. Time was short. If all had gone well, Rachel would be waiting for her right now. "She wants to talk to you."

"I'll be at home. Where else?"

"Is it safe?"

"You have the envelope." Janet said apathetically. "If there's danger, you hold it in your hands."

"But what if you're wrong?" Cynthia persisted. "What if they come after you?"

"So be it."

"Janet, think of Chris and Brian," Cynthia begged. She touched her friend's shoulder, her touch gradually taking on the insistence of her fears. Janet looked at Cynthia's fingers, then at her face. The glaze partly lifted from her eyes. "You have to take care of yourself for their sakes," Cynthia told her. "I want you to go to the Amoco station down the street. Go into the rest room, and someone will meet you. You can trust her. Will you do what she says?"

Janet stared, then blinked. Finally, a weak smile curved her lips. "So this really is serious. I'd hoped things weren't as bad as I knew they must be." She nodded toward Cynthia's bag. "Thank goodness the boys are away and safe. I'll do what you say. And," she continued before Cynthia could speak, "thank you for taking care of everything. Tell Rachel . . . Tell Rachel that I'll be praying for her just as I know she's been praying for me. And here are the other envelopes you wanted."

She reached under the car seat and pulled out two manila envelopes, both similar in appearance to the one Cynthia already had. "I couldn't decide whether to give them to you, but I did what you asked. The one with the dot in the corner is the copy I made of Phillip's papers, and, no," she said reassuringly at Cynthia's worried look, "no one saw what I was doing. This envelope," she continued, handing Cynthia the other one, "is the bogus one. I put every kind of weird and cryptic information I could imagine in it. I almost had fun making it up," she said, a tear coming unbidden into her eye. Fun—not a word she would have associated with any of this.

Cynthia compared the three envelopes. They were enough alike to fool a casual observer. "I wish I knew how to thank you," she said.

"I wish I knew that what I'm doing is right," Janet answered bleakly.

Grant met his children just inside the door of the small country church he'd attended with his Grandmama Grant so many years before. The parishioners were friendly and offered words of encouragement, but Grant could sense their uneasiness.

Within minutes, Tucker Grant, Bob Grant's older brother, had arrived. His wife Melissa and their children came with him. The meeting between the brothers was emotional, neither man capable of speech. For them, the bond of family was strengthened by the bond of mutual respect, and for both, the last few days had been devastating. Such injustice! The enormity of the evil arrayed against his brother brought sparks to Tucker's eyes. He would do anything—anything!—to help. That was why he was here. That was why they all were.

Grant ushered his family inside where they sank gratefully onto the wooden pews, unchanged since his childhood except for increased signs of hard use and loving care. The hymnals might well be the same, too, Grant noted with a feeling of satisfaction. They held great hymns, praising the Father of all goodness, the Dispenser of greater grace. Grace above all he could ask or think, his grandmama had called it. Grant relaxed fully for the first time in a week.

The organ burst into wheezy song. "Faith of Our Fathers." Rachel's face filled Grant's mind. Her favorite hymn. Faith was the sustainer of their lives individually and as a married couple. Faith was the source of the inner peace sustaining them now. Hopefully, he thought, looking down the pew, their children had the spiritual strength they would need, especially now. His grandmama, his father and mother, they'd filled him with it, viewing him like a sponge, able to absorb as much as they were willing to give and he was willing to receive. He and Rachel had followed that same philosophy, but only time would prove their success.

One of Grandmama's sons had heard the same stories, had lived with her daily example, but had not absorbed the principles of integrity. Instead he'd turned to drink and had died a frightened and bitter young man. Grandmama had told his story as often as the others, always ending with the same message. "I loved that boy, maybe more than the rest 'cause he needed it so," she would say. Her eyes would soften with sorrow, and the squeak of the rocker would quicken. "Poor child. I can see him now, his face screwed up with his hurt and his mouth always loose with blame for others. He couldn't understand he was the one made himself unhappy, and he couldn't forget his pain long enough to put his trust in the only One who could help. Sometimes, I think he liked feeling bad." She would shake her grizzled gray head and run a loving hand over the head of the grandson drinking in the excitement of her stories and unwittingly absorbing her wisdom. "Poor soul just hung onto his unhappiness till he died of it. Don't you do that, boy," she would finish, giving him a hug. "Nobody can make you unhappy unless you let him."

Grant had listened and had found for himself the same peace that gave her such comfort and strength. In turn he'd given her legacy of faith and integrity to his children. Now, all he could do was pray they'd listened and understood. And be a good example, he thought, maybe the hardest to do of all.

Was that why so many children joined gangs and behaved without compunction? he wondered as the music faded and the pastor began reading from the Bible. Because they lacked the example of a father with his steady dependability and loving discipline?

What about his own children? Would they lose their way if he didn't succeed and was sent to prison or even killed? Would their souls be twisted by bitterness or a feeling of betrayal? Would they lash out blindly, destroying their own lives because they couldn't withstand the destruction of his?

"'Yea, though I walk through the valley of the shadow of death,'" the pastor read, "'I will fear no evil.'" The Twenty-third Psalm, written by David at the nadir of his life when his beloved son Absalom was pursuing him to kill him—another son who had been taught but had allowed bitterness and arrogance to rule his life. "'Surely goodness and mercy shall follow me all the days of my life.'" David had penned those words while suffering the depths of an anguish few people would ever know. Even so, he had felt blessed.

Grant's problems, insurmountable as they now seemed, paled beside the enormity, the horror of Absalom's betrayal. For Grant, the words of the Psalm carried with them the balm of comfort the Lord had intended.

He listened to the pastor's message, gaining strength and hoarding for himself the peace of the Lord. Slowly, the lies and betrayals, the murders and attempted murders, even the debate that would take place in such a short time receded from his mind. For these few precious minutes, the church became for him a sanctuary as of old, a place to gain the weapons he would need to face the world and its pressures.

Faith, inner peace, an understanding of grace: These components of spiritual integrity were his weapons and the weapons of his family. They had protected and sustained David, not obliterating the pain of Absalom's betrayal but healing it. Likewise, his own trials and those of his family would not disappear, but the strength gained would help them surmount further, maybe greater pressures and injustices.

What had happened hadn't been good—Anne Peabody, Russell Frederickson, Cora Snyder. No, definitely not good. And what was to come would not be without grief. Such was life. But the Lord could make good come from it—if Grant had the faith to put his problems in the Lord's hands.

Grandmama Grant had called it resting on the everlasting peace. She'd talked about peace often, saying she'd had as much as a slave as she'd had as a free woman. Grant had thought that the talk of an old woman idealizing the past. Years later in a moment of liberating brilliance, he'd understood her words. Inner peace wasn't dependent on outside circumstances but came from within and was his to accept or reject. Grant had been free and at peace ever since.

All too soon, the service ended. The world, filled with both good and evil, awaited them.

He walked with Tucker to the parking lot.

"Curtis should be arriving from St. Louis about now," Tucker said, referring to their youngest brother. "He's going straight to the hotel, but the rest of the family will be in the studio. Stephen Yao's made arrangements for everything. Yao's a good man, Bob."

"Yes," Grant agreed. He wanted to say more, but one thing this week had taught him was how valueless words could be. Friendship, courage, honor: In their truest forms, they were beyond words.

"You're ready for this afternoon?" he asked instead.

"Can't wait," Tucker replied, a grin playing at the corner of his mouth.

"Just like when we were young, isn't it?" Grant asked, seeing in his brother's middle-aged face the spirited, I-dare-you boy of years before. "You getting me out of some scrape."

"Except the stakes are a little different," Tucker agreed, opening his car door. "You sure we can pull this off?"

"No, but I think we have a chance." Grant looked off toward the horizon. "If it doesn't work, we'll try something else." He reached out to shake his brother's hand but pulled him into an embrace instead. They held each other a moment.

"I'm ready," Tucker said, his eyes misty. "More than ready. Don't you worry, little brother," he added, giving Grant a last affectionate punch on the arm before getting in the car, "just like Grandmama Grant always said, 'The good Lord willing, everything's going to be just fine.'"

Giving a wave, he drove around to the front of the church to pick up both his family and Grant's children. They would travel together to the debate later that afternoon.

Grant stood alone in the parking lot, watching the car until it disappeared from sight, then he walked to his car, where Yao waited.

After her meeting with Janet Loomis, Cynthia drove directly to Washington National Airport. Even in the safety of the car, she kept the leather bag pressed to her side, the straps over her shoulder. She was confident, as confident as she could be, that she hadn't been followed, but she knew that wouldn't last. If they knew about Janet Loomis, if there had been a phone tap, then they knew she would try to reach Grant. They were sure to have the airport covered. If only she could have found a safe way to fax it all to the Senator in time!

A Senate staffer was waiting outside with a ticket to Atlanta. Cynthia brushed against her and took the ticket. Neither spoke.

Her heart thumping, Cynthia continued walking through the airport terminal. Never had she felt so exposed. She hoped the dowdy brown wig she wore changed her appearance enough to fool someone who didn't know her, but she couldn't be sure. She forced herself to walk confidently, without looking to see if she were spotted. If they were any good, and she was sure they would be, she wouldn't be able to see them anyway. She wouldn't give them the satisfaction of looking scared.

Finally reaching the rest room nearest her gate, she hurried inside and into the first stall. Everything depended on finding Rachel already waiting in the second one. Her heart in her throat, Cynthia bent down and looked under the partition. Black old lady oxfords, the left one untied. Rachel! So she *had* reached the Senator and made arrangements for Atlanta, Cynthia thought, her head light with relief.

With a shaking hand, she opened the leather bag, checked to be certain she had the envelope containing the originals, and sneaked it under the partition. Rachel took it from her.

Clothes rustled as each woman concealed her copy of Phillip Loomis's message. Each hoped it would provide the key to clearing Grant and destroying Bonfire. Neither could be sure. They just knew they had to get at least one copy to the Senator before the debate.

Three hours and hundreds of miles, Cynthia thought as she heard Rachel leave her stall and wash her hands. Then she heard tired old feet shuffling out of the rest room. Still, Cynthia remained hidden in the first stall. With every opening of the door into the rest room, her heart raced uncontrollably. She stared at her watch, agonizing as the hands inched forward.

"Final boarding call for United Airlines Flight 4921 to Atlanta." The words blared over the loudspeaker. Cynthia's heart stopped, then thudded in her ears. Her migraine roared back, the pain intense. She fumbled in her purse, extracted two pills, placed them on her tongue and swallowed.

The flight announcement blared again. Time for her to leave. She took a deep, steadying breath and opened the door. No one in the rest room paid her any attention. After a quick glance in the mirror to be sure her wig was on straight, she opened the door into the airport terminal. Again, no one seemed interested.

Gathering her courage, she hurried toward the gate. The leather bag was pressed close to her side, as much for its comfort as to protect it. No line of passengers waited to present tickets. Good. She wouldn't have to stand exposed in the waiting area.

That was the moment she saw the two men. She wasn't sure why they caught her eye. Maybe because they stared at her so intently. As she watched, the burly, dark-haired one pointed at her. She froze, unable to think, much less to move. The plane was so close, and she wasn't going to make it!

With that totally unacceptable thought, her paralysis was broken. Desperately, she looked around, seeking some avenue of escape. The men were almost on her, their intent no longer in doubt. She moved. With an agility that astonished her, she dodged around a happily chatting group of Japanese tourists, broke into a run, tossed her boarding pass to a surprised airline agent, and raced down the boarding ramp.

Behind her, she could hear the men swearing at the picture-taking tourists, then at the agent impeding their entrance onto the boarding ramp. They weren't delayed long, only a matter of seconds, but long enough for her to safely board the plane. As she turned down the aisle, she heard them behind her, bullying a stewardess to let them enter. She refused and threatened to call security. Cynthia heard no more.

Her lungs heaving to pull in air, she dropped into her seat, but not before she'd seen Rachel seated several rows back.

Rachel was safe, Cynthia thought, shutting her eyes in relief and bringing her breathing under control. And she was safe, but even so she couldn't stop trembling. Her mind was concentrated on one alarming thought: If men had been sent to stop her boarding the plane, others would be waiting for her to land. She kept reminding herself that Stephen Yao and Matt Goldie would have taken care of all that, but still her hands trembled. She tightened her grip on the bag and closed her eyes in prayer.

After an interminable flight that still ended too quickly, the plane landed in Atlanta. As it made its slow taxi to the gate, Cynthia looked out the window and tried to quiet her racing heart. Then it was time. Impatient passengers awkwardly carried or pulled their carry-on luggage down the narrow aisle as they maneuvered toward the door. Cynthia was propelled along with them. Earlier, she'd taken the bogus envelope out of her bag; now she held it as if trying to conceal it.

A stewardess stopped her just as she was about to exit the plane. "I'm sorry, Mrs. Novitsky," she said, with an apologetic smile, "but I have to ask you to come with me."

"Come with you?" Cynthia asked, turning to see if Tommy had heard, and, more importantly, if he'd expected this summons. She'd spotted him earlier, sitting several rows behind her on the opposite side of the plane, but they hadn't spoken, not since they'd made their original plans in her Senate office so many hours before. Much could have changed since then, but she had no way of knowing what.

Now, Tommy was ten or twelve people back, trapped in the crowded aisle. He wasn't close enough for her to read his expression or receive a signal. An elderly bespectacled black woman, obviously poor but respectable, stood patiently several people behind him. Rachel.

Her heart pounding in dull rhythm with the footsteps of passengers edging around her, Cynthia turned back to the stewardess. As she did, two men, strangers, stepped out of a side doorway. "We'll take over now," the tallest one told the stewardess, who looked momentarily confused. They flashed badges. She nodded and stepped back.

Cynthia's pulse rate upped its beat a notch as she spotted Rachel shuffling near. Whatever happened, Rachel mustn't be noticed!

"Let go of me!" Cynthia demanded, drawing attention to herself. She spoke loud enough to cause a distraction, but not so loud as to be heard at the end of the walkway. If these two men were Bonfire's people, she needed to get away. If not, the worst thing she could do was expose them to hostile attention. She glimpsed a man watching indecisively from the walkway entrance. Whose side? she wondered. How could she know? Suddenly, he whipped around and disappeared from view.

"I said let go of me!" she hissed again.

She ignored the men restraining her, instead struggling to free her arms and looking imploringly at those passing by, those directly behind Rachel. "Help me! Please help me," she begged. "I'm being kidnapped!"

An elderly gentleman stopped. "What's the meaning of this!" he demanded.

"Federal agents, sir. NIIA." One of her abductors flashed a shield. "She murdered three children, one of them her own."

"My goodness!" The man scuttled away, his voice high with right-eous horror.

Cynthia glanced swiftly back up the walkway in time to see Rachel walking safely into the terminal with its protective crowds. Then she felt a compelling hand on her back. Before she could protest, she was forced through a door on the side of the walkway, the same door the men had used earlier. It slammed shut after them.

Her abductors, partly carrying her, raced across the long, empty room toward another door. They were moving too quickly for her to manage more than an incoherent protest.

"Someone was watching from the terminal," the tall one said without breaking stride.

"Looks like we've been made," the other replied.

"Stephen!" Cynthia blurted, recognizing the voice. "Stephen Yao!"

"At your service," Yao said, grinning through the lush mustache his upper lip now sported. However, his eyes, which had magically lost their Asian cast, were worried as they darted back in the direction they'd just come.

They'd barely raced through the second door when the first one, leading to the walkway and the plane, burst open behind them.

"There she goes!" someone yelled. "Cover all exits! She's getting away!"

Yao paused a moment to jam the second door while his companion hurried Cynthia across the room. "We have to get out of here," he said urgently. "Now!"

"I'd better get rid of this while I can," Cynthia said, dropping the bogus envelope where it couldn't be missed.

Yao ran to her side. "Nothing like a little diversion," he agreed, glancing behind at the jammed door, which was now being forcibly rattled. Wouldn't be long before they got through it.

"Stay close!" he told her, his hand on her elbow urging her to run faster. They dashed through yet another door and again jammed it. "We still have a chance," he said, his eyes never ceasing their restless scanning.

Suddenly, they were outside, the airport tarmac seeming to stretch before them endlessly.

"This way," the second man said, not pausing as they turned a corner. They ran until they were almost under the building. "I work airport security," he told Cynthia, his words coming in snatches. "Have since I knew Admiral Grant in the service. Good man, the admiral. We'll be all right if we can make it to the end of this building."

"And Rachel?"

"She'll have gotten away by now," Yao told her.

Cynthia said no more. She couldn't. She needed all her breath for running. In the distance, she heard shouts, a slamming door, and running feet. She didn't look. Her breath came out in agonized gasps, seeming to sear her struggling lungs. She forced herself to keep running but knew the end of her strength was near.

Another corner.

Two men were barring their way!

"No!" She thought she screamed the word, but it came out a breathless whisper. To have come so far . . .

"Ma'am! It's me!"

Tommy in an airport uniform! Tears of fatigue and relief filled Cynthia's eyes.

Without a word, Yao and his companion disappeared back the way they'd come. How could they escape going that way? Cynthia wondered, too tired to feel more than a vague concern. She had no more time for speculation before Tommy lifted her onto a waiting baggage cart. The tarp was pulled down, and she clutched the sides as the cart jerked into motion.

As the cart swayed and bounced under her, threatening to spill her out onto the tarmac, Cynthia thought she heard muffled shouts somewhere far behind. Then, all she could hear were plane engines.

Several minutes and many jarring bumps and lurching turns later, the baggage cart stopped in an empty alley area. Again, Tommy lifted her, this time into a waiting delivery truck. The truck sped away. Almost before she had time to catch her breath, the truck stopped, she was quickly lifted out, and the door in front of her was opening.

Grant, standing in the shadows, pulled her into the room, closed the door, and held her close. She was trembling. "We were afraid they would get to you before we could," he said, rubbing her back comfortingly. "You're all right, aren't you?"

"I've never felt better," she said truthfully. Nevertheless, she sank gratefully into the chair he pulled up. "These papers must be good," she said, pulling off the wig and running her fingers distractedly through her hair. "Someone sure wants them. Is Rachel here yet?" She tried to keep the anxiety from her voice.

"Not yet, but I got word she's on her way. No problems."

Cynthia bowed her head as relief swept through her. Then she looked up and gave him a tremulous smile. "If you'll just turn around for a moment . . ."

"Under your dress?"

She nodded, standing. "I dropped a fake set at the airport—the one Janet made up for us," she explained as she carefully unstrapped Janet's copy of the originals. "I don't know who picked it up—if anyone."

"Not us anyway."

"Good," Cynthia said, her voice muffled. "I hope they waste hours trying to figure out Janet's nonsense. You can turn around now." With an embarrassed smile, she handed the much-creased and rumpled envelope to Grant. "Sorry it's such a mess. These are copies. Rachel has the originals."

Grant gave her shoulders a grateful squeeze as he took the envelope. "You're a wonder, Cynthia!" he said, relieved to find the tension gone from her body. "Thank God you're safe."

He lifted the flap of the envelope but looked up expectantly at a soft but rhythmic knock on the door.

357

Not as relaxed as he liked to pretend, Cynthia thought affectionately. For a brief moment, her heart ached for her own husband—so long since anyone had held that love in his eyes for her.

Grant strode to the door and threw it open. He had Rachel in his arms and inside the room in one movement. The look on his face twisted between relief, love, and amusement. Rachel was still in her disguise. "I'll love you when you're that old," he told her, a bemused twinkle in his eyes. "But I'm willing to wait. Any problems?" he asked Stephen Yao, who had come in behind her, then secured the door and pulled a chair in front of it.

Rachel disappeared into the bathroom. She left the door cracked so she could hear.

"None," Yao said, sitting in the chair. "Couldn't have gone better. We counted nine men and one woman at the airport. Got pictures of three of them. If we hadn't gotten Cynthia out immediately as you suggested and if Rachel hadn't been so well-disguised, things might have been different."

"Professionals?" Grant asked.

"Looked that way. Having inside help gave us the edge."

"One of the men who served under me in Manila," Grant explained to Cynthia, "is with airport security now."

"We're pretty sure they picked up the dummy envelope," Yao continued with a nod to Cynthia, "but they didn't give Rachel more than a glance. Great acting, Dr. G.," he said as she walked back into the room.

"I hope these were worth all this trouble," she said, holding the envelope out to her husband.

"You have a chance to go through it?" he asked. Handing Yao the duplicate envelope that Cynthia had brought, he opened the one with the originals.

"No," she answered, smoothing her dress, minus its extra underpinnings. It hung on her shapelessly. "We barely had time to hide them."

"The letter from Phillip to you is on the bottom, Senator," Cynthia said. "Janet showed it to me, but just the envelope. I thinks she's right though. It looks important."

Grant thumbed through the papers and retrieved it. He saw his name, then read the cover note asking Janet to give it to Bob Grant unread if he seemed to be in any kind of trouble.

"Janet apologized for opening it," Cynthia said, touching the jagged edge. "But she was concerned for her boys' sakes. Now she's jumping with nerves."

Grant gave her a thoughtful look, then took out the single sheet of paper the envelope held.

"She begged you to please destroy everything if it doesn't help," Cynthia finished, leaning closer to read. Phillip Loomis's words, written in his distinctive, almost elegant hand, seemed to leap from the page.

> My friend Bob—
>
> If you are reading this letter, my suppositions, sadly, will have proven correct.
>
> In life I find that small compromises of one's ethics tend to grow until, before one is aware, compromise has led to duplicity, and duplicity has led to evil. I find I cannot be party to that evil. Hence, the need for this letter. Our friendship allows me some atonement.
>
> Remember the discussions we've had about our greatest President? Oddly enough, he holds the key to my dilemma, possibly to yours as well. We discussed the plans for his entombment in our Capitol and about his refutation of the wishes of others. Now more than ever, I admire his integrity.
>
> Wouldn't you agree the greatness of his character is felt most profoundly by those who kneel and pray? May your faith lead you under the sacrament.
>
> In thee, Senator Robert Hawkins Grant, I put my trust.
> Phillip Loomis

Grant felt for a chair and slowly lowered himself into it. "Atonement," he said musingly. "Atonement for duplicity? For breaches of ethics?" He sorted through the remaining contents of the envelope. "Only newspaper clippings," he said, leafing back to examine the top one. It told of a bill that Loomis had championed in Congress several years earlier. Grant turned the clipping over. Only part of an ad for a discount furniture store. Why had Loomis considered this clipping important? Grant wondered, reading the article more carefully. Nothing but a dry account of an eight-year-old Senate bill, successfully passed into law.

He picked up a second clipping, this one about Loomis's support of the bill which had created the NIIA. The puzzled frown between his eyes deepened.

"Why include these?" he asked. "Why even keep them? They have to mean something. But what?"

"Look at the date on the letter," Rachel said, pointing to it. "The day Phillip died. They *must* be important, or he wouldn't have bothered with them."

Grant nodded thoughtfully. "Loomis was afraid something might happen to him and that something might happen to me. He died more than five months ago. Five months! What on earth could he have known, and why did he include these clippings?"

They spent several minutes studying Loomis's information, trying to understand its significance. Grant kept returning to the letter, so cryptic and so unlike the Phillip Loomis he'd known for twelve years. If Loomis had hidden something—and Grant couldn't imagine what else the letter could mean, Janet Loomis had shown rare courage, indeed, in giving the envelope to them. *A breach of ethics, duplicity, evil,* Phillip had written. Grant couldn't imagine the circumstances that would have prompted such words, but beyond doubt they would not reflect well on Loomis. Janet had understood that and given Grant the package anyway. He owed her a debt he could never repay.

"Our greatest President?" Rachel queried.

"Has to have been Washington," Grant told her, remembering their impassioned discussions just as Loomis had known he would. Basically, it had come down to Washington versus Lincoln. Both men had served during perilous times. Washington, however, with his grasp of the future needs of the country, a rare foresight proven through the years, had been deemed the greater.

"Then 'entombment' must refer to the crypt built for Washington's tomb in the basement of the Capitol," Cynthia said excitedly. "Since Washington refused to allow it to be used, just as Phillip said, the room is seldom visited. A perfect hiding place!"

"That has to be right," Rachel agreed. "Someone on the staff can go see."

Cynthia reached for the phone.

"Just a minute," Grant said, stopping her. "Would Loomis have been so enigmatic in the rest of the letter if the tomb were his hiding place, not just one of several clues? What if something else holds the key, something he hopes will have meaning only for me? I have a feeling he's trying to keep his information from falling into the wrong hands."

"I think you're right," Rachel said slowly, like the others trying to piece it together. "His mention of the sacrament and of 'kneel and pray' is odd. Not at all like Phillip."

"'In thee, Senator Robert Hawkins Grant, I put my trust,'" Cynthia added, her voice as puzzled as theirs. "Strange way to talk, almost like a minister. Maybe it's from the Bible, part of Washington's funeral service."

"That's why I have to go myself," Grant said with finality. "Loomis gave his clues, thinking I would understand."

"Is getting whatever he left—if he left anything at all," Rachel asked, her eyes holding his, "important enough for you to risk . . . so much?"

"Phillip knew I might be in trouble months before it happened," Grant said gently. He walked behind her chair and began massaging her shoulders. She leaned back until her head touched his hands.

"I think you're right about needing to get it tonight," Yao agreed, moving over from his chair by the door. "But you shouldn't go yourself. Too dangerous. You wouldn't get your foot in the door before someone recognized you."

"Probably true," Grant agreed, "but Loomis was too cryptic. He could have meant several different parts of the Capitol. I'm the one who spent time with him. If it isn't in the crypt—and I doubt that it is, or why the odd phrasing and enigmatic references—maybe being there will jog my memory." He gave Rachel's shoulders a final squeeze and went back to his chair. "Besides," he continued, "only Senators are allowed in some of the obvious places."

"Then I guess we'd better figure out how it can be managed," Yao said, bringing over a chair and sitting next to Cynthia.

"I'll have the staff pull together a list of all possibilities," she said, again reaching for the phone. "Anything in the Capitol that might refer to Washington."

"Be careful," Grant cautioned. "We have at least one leak, and for all we know several of the staff may have been compromised."

A look of pain flitted through Cynthia's eyes.

"I know," Grant said. "I hate the idea, too, but remember how clever Bonfire is. The leak could be totally inadvertent, even a bug in someone's home. We can't take a chance, not at this point."

Slowly, Cynthia nodded. "I'll wait till I get back this afternoon and handle it myself."

"Much better," Yao agreed.

"Everything ready for the debate?" Cynthia asked, knowing Yao had masterminded Grant's escape plan. She needed to channel her thoughts away from the possible treachery of those she worked with every day and in whom she'd always placed her trust.

"All ready," Yao assured her. "Everything depends on getting Bob away before he can be arrested."

Rachel nodded, her heart suddenly racing. So much depended on timing, hers more than anyone's. But all that was well in hand, she reminded herself. "Let's concentrate on getting Bob into the Capitol," she said aloud. Time was so short, only hours!

"While you're working on that," Grant said, rising and moving across the room to an extension phone, "I think I'll shake a few hornets' nests."

With infinite care, Corforth replaced the phone and turned to his wife. They were alone in their living room. "That was Brent." Brent Purnell was a senior member of the White House staff and had been a close confederate of Corforth's for years. "I'm completely out of the loop now," he told her. "POTUS is having the inner circle over to watch the Grant debate. I wasn't included. I didn't want to alarm you, but I wasn't asked last Sunday, either. There's no doubt my exclusion this time was deliberate. Brent didn't say so, but I'll be asked to resign next week."

"Resign!" Amy exclaimed, her eyes wide with shock. She leaned over to hold his hand, appalled to find it shaking. "You're sure?"

"Sure?" He brought her cold fingers to his lips. The tremor in his hand subsided, and his voice steadied. "I haven't been told in so many words, but, yes, I'm sure. I've been on the delivery end of too many terminations myself not to recognize the signs."

"Why don't they just get it over with?" she demanded. "Why are they torturing you so?"

"Not torture, Amy. Political expediency." Corforth's voice was gentle. This would be as much a blow to her as it was to him. "They're not about to chance anything taking news-play from the Grant story. That's why I expect the announcement to come Wednesday. Grant will be gone, and I can be disposed of quietly."

"Don't they feel any loyalty, any compunction, after all your hard work?" Amy asked angrily. "After all you've done for them?"

Corforth shrugged. "Does it matter? I may be better off out of it." He looked down at his hands, now clasped tightly in his lap. His voice was ruminative as he tried to find words for the thoughts that had badgered his mind for the past few months. "Nothing's the same. The fire's gone. I'm not even convinced that everything I've worked for was worth the fight. Or even right."

He'd never revealed these thoughts to anyone, even Amy. It was like baring his soul and finding it empty. He couldn't summon the courage to look into her eyes.

"I've always told myself that anything was right as long as it furthered the President's political agenda. Now I'm not sure. The lying, the deals . . . Could so much dishonesty, sometimes even injustice and cruelty, be justified no matter the end good that was intended? For too long, I've ignored the signs of corruption around me. That's not quite right," he said, bowing his head even lower. "I think in some ways I've abetted it. I've kept hoping the change was in POTUS and Hunt and the others, not in the value of our cause. But I don't know anymore. I just don't know. Not that it matters now. I'm no longer a player. My time has come to an end."

Amy watched his inner struggle, unsure how to respond. He cared so much! He had always viewed his life as one of service to his fellow man. For him, his position as Chief of Staff had been the fulfillment of a lifetime of work and dedication. That his position would be snatched from him on a political whim seemed the height of injustice.

"At an end, nothing!" she finally said with quiet vehemence. "You're admired and respected. Your advice will still be sought, at least by anyone with sense."

"By political hacks and media toadies!" he retorted bitterly. Her heart twisted at the raw pain he betrayed. "And would I even know what to say? I honestly don't know what I believe anymore. Bob Grant may be losing his job, too, but he'll never have to question his beliefs. I don't know how I can be so sure, but I am."

"Bob Grant!" Her mouth was twisted with contempt. "I'm sick of hearing his name!"

The phone rang, the sound shocking them both. They stared at each other, hesitant to answer. Finally, Corforth reached out his hand.

It was Bob Grant. All expression instantly left Corforth's face.

"No, no, Bob," he said. His voice was strong and confident, betraying none of his angry despair or inner turmoil. "It's no bother."

He mouthed Grant's name to his wife. She stared at him in shock.

"I've been reading an interesting account of the last election," Grant said, "especially as it had to do with Anne Peabody. I was told you might be able to give me some insight into it."

"An account? Someone sent you something about Anne Peabody?" Corforth asked, stalling for time. He couldn't seem to get a grasp on the conversation. Bob Grant was calling him? About Anne Peabody? "Specifics would help. Especially the name of the person who mentioned me."

"A name is something I can't give," Grant replied. "I have reason to trust my source, but more than that I can't say."

"So *you* say." Corforth was quiet for so long that Grant had to wonder if he'd hung up. "Why do you think I can help?" Corforth finally asked. "And why would I want to?"

"Because you're a man of compassion and honor," Grant replied, "or so another source tells me. I've never had reason to doubt that."

Corforth felt a rush of gratitude at the accolade. Almost immediately, his eyes narrowed as the irony assailed him. The man he'd for years considered his philosophical enemy was now the one praising him and giving him hope. Caution returned.

"I can understand if you refuse to help me," Grant said, "but at this point, I had to ask."

"They're celebrating your defeat at the White House right now," Corforth told him—a benign comment, he thought, one that would tell Grant nothing he didn't already know. Grant, however, would hear the "they"—a most revealing choice of words. "Which reminds me," he continued, "shouldn't you be preparing for your debate?"

"With my life going up in flames, not to mention that of my family," Grant retorted, the undertone of sarcasm unmistakable, "the debate is the least of my concerns."

"I'm sorry about what's being done to you," Corforth replied, well aware of the meaning behind Grant's tone.

"'Being done,' you said." Again, Grant would know Corforth's choice of words had been deliberate. Corforth didn't make mistakes. "Care to elaborate on that?"

Corforth hesitated. POTUS had shown no loyalty to him. Did that mean he could abandon his own code of ethics as well? So tempting to do so. "I can't, Grant," he finally said. His honor was all that was left him. Tattered it might be, but he would hold on to it nonetheless. "You can understand that. But I *can* tell you to watch out for Jonathan Hunter. His power is absolute. He's never liked you, and with Joey's death, that dislike has become an unreasoning hatred."

"And the matter with Anne Peabody?"

"I've said all I can say, except . . ." Again Corforth paused, then plunged ahead. If Grant was innocent, he deserved help. If not, this hint wouldn't mean anything anyway, only that Corforth had read more into a few random bits of conversation than he should have. "John Smythe has been mentioned."

"John Smythe?" Grant repeated, his voice tight. "What about Bonfire?"

"Bonfire?" Corforth queried. "You're not making sense. I've probably said too much anyway. You haven't a chance. I'm sorry, but that's just the way it is."

With an unsteady hand, he replaced the receiver.

"Bob Grant!" Amy exclaimed. "That was Bob Grant?"

Corforth didn't answer, didn't even raise his head.

She tentatively touched his hand. "Who is this John Smythe?" she asked. "And why would you mention him to Bob Grant?"

Corforth clutched her hand. "That's one name you must forget, Amy. I wish you hadn't heard it."

When the police knocked on the townhouse's door, Frances Sandborne almost didn't open it. She'd seen them pull up in front. She'd felt certain she knew what they'd come to tell her, and she wasn't sure she could bear it.

The officers were already halfway back to their squad car when she finally found the courage to face them. They came back, knowing their news had been expected. Her eyes were huge and weepy in her drawn face. She led them into the living room, seeming with each stiff and clumsy step to mentally insulate herself from their presence as if by drawing in upon herself she could ignore the devastating news she so feared.

The officers were as gentle as possible, establishing first that Cora Snyder had indeed lived there and that she had been missing all night. The circumstances were odd, they told Frances. The car she'd apparently been driving had been stolen. It had no registration papers and a deliberately muddied license plate. Dr. Snyder herself was carrying no identification. She hadn't been reported missing, and they would still be trying to identify her if it hadn't been for an anonymous tip a short while before.

Only when they mentioned that Cora had been shot did Frances Sandborne come to life.

"Shot!" she gasped. In some hidden recess of her mind she'd wondered if Cora had left her. She'd almost prayed for an accident, the other had seemed so monstrous. Now she was flooded with relief. Just as suddenly, that relief was swallowed by a wave of intolerable desolation. The soft contours of her face sagged as her unseeing eyes regarded the horror of a life bereft of the only person who loved her.

"I'm sorry, ma'am," one of the officers—a woman—said, taking her by the arm and leading her to a chair.

"Can you think of any reason Dr. Snyder would have been at 12th and H, S.E.?" a second officer asked.

"12th and H?" Frances's face twisted with confusion. Why would Cora have gone to that dangerous part of town? "Bailey Grant," she whispered, horrified. Then she looked at the officers, her eyes mad with rage. "Bailey Grant killed her, I tell you! I knew he was trouble! I knew it!"

When she said no more but again became engrossed with some disturbing inner vision, the policewoman took her hand. Frances crushed it in her own. Slowly, her eyes focused.

"Dr. Sandborne," the policewoman said gently, with effort releasing her hand, "do you have reason to believe Bailey Grant is the one who shot Dr. Snyder?"

"Cora was meeting him." Frances leaned forward eagerly. She had to make them understand. "Cora told me before she left. Not where she was going or I never would have let her go." Again, she started to drift away. Again, the policewoman took her hand and gently prodded her back.

"You said Dr. Snyder was meeting Bailey Grant."

"Yes," Frances said. "Yes, yes, yes! Bailey Grant. He called her. She told me. He said he had to talk to her. He had her go there so he could murder her! He murdered her, I tell you! Bailey Grant murdered her!"

She lowered her head into her hands and began sobbing. Her broad shoulders heaved convulsively. It was ten minutes before they could question her further. In the meantime, an APB was put out for Bailey Grant, on suspicion of murder.

Estelle was sitting in the window alcove of her bedroom, staring out at the bare lawn, when she became aware of her husband's footsteps in the hall. He was stopping at her door! Her heart raced, whether in anticipation or dread she wasn't sure.

At his knock—more tentative than normal? she wondered—she bade him enter.

"I've invited several people here to watch the Grant/Caruso debate on TV," he told her. "I'd like for you to join us."

Estelle felt her face turning to stone. He must have noticed, for he hurried into speech before she could say no. "Hunt's coming and bringing Rebecca. Her first time out since Joey's death. I know she would feel more comfortable if you were there. Won't you come? I thought we would watch it here in the family quarters. We'll have a fire and serve cocktails."

Was he actually asking her? she wondered in amazement. She couldn't remember the last time he'd asked instead of ordering. She felt her resolve melting.

"They'll be here a little before three. Come if you can."

He kissed her cheek and left before she could answer. She could do no more than sit where he left her, staring at the door, wondering what had caused his unexpected softening.

What was he up to now? she asked herself resignedly before she rose and began dressing to meet her guests. And why, with all she knew, did she still respond to his charm? A tear spilled onto her cheek. Why, oh, why couldn't she stop loving him?

Grant, accompanied by Rachel, arrived at the debate with only minutes to spare. Cynthia was on a plane back to Washington, where she would begin implementing plans for Grant's foray into the Capitol late that afternoon.

Grant had hoped to use the debate as a forum for demonstrating his innocence. That hope had died when Loomis's envelope had come up empty. They had proof of his innocence to the adultery charge, yes, but short of producing Frederickson's murderer, that proof meant nothing.

Instead, the debate would have to be used to push his enemy into some rash action, a futile hope, Grant was convinced, given the dispassionate precision of everything that had occurred so far. That left only one option: rattling the man or men who had hired Bonfire and John Smythe. They might not be as emotionless as the professionals they employed.

Walking into the downtown Atlanta hotel room set aside for the debate, Grant saw India, Olivia, and Henry sitting in the front row of chairs. The tension in their faces tore at his heart. He wished he could go to them and provide comfort, but he knew he mustn't. Tucker sat partly concealed behind them. Other family members filled the remaining three rows. Good, Grant thought with a brief surge of satisfaction. So much could happen to prevent his escape, but at least everyone was in position.

Caruso's side was similarly filled with family. No other audience had been allowed. That had been one ground rule Grant had refused to abandon. He wasn't about to have his words trivialized by preprogrammed hecklers. More importantly, he couldn't chance any bright-eyed Caruso supporters interfering with his plan.

He had time to observe no more before he was swept away by an angry television producer and an even angrier Edmund Miller, both sure until that moment that he had been going to stay away. For very different reasons, each was relieved, a relief that made itself manifest in querulous voices and angry recriminations.

An equally angry Mike Masterson tried to take Grant aside to find out what on earth was going on and where on earth he'd been. Before Masterson could do more than get Grant's attention, the producer pushed him away and hurried Grant, who gave his press secretary a rueful look in passing, to a makeshift stage. Masterson, fuming, stalked to the control room. Even the Grant children had refused—politely, of course!—to answer his questions, and now Grant was ignoring him as well. For a panicked moment, Masterson wondered if he would be able to fulfill his contract.

Tobias Caruso, unsure whether to hope for Grant to be a no-show or not, was waiting, not too patiently either, at one of two lecterns. Facing them both was a table with four panelists, two from television and one each from the print media and radio. Kirk Vinton as moderator sat at the center of the four, a look of sardonic amusement in his eyes, hardly unusual since this reflected his normal view of the world. Satisfaction exuded from him like a barely seen fog. He was about to make his national TV debut, and talk about a dynamite way to do it! Would more such opportunities, maybe even a weekly syndicated show, soon be in the offing? He had as much at stake in this debate as Grant and Caruso. Maybe even more, he thought, hiding a triumphant smile.

The red light of the camera came on.

The debate had begun.

Estelle was glad she'd come down to watch the debate if only because Rebecca Hunter needed a buffer against her husband's callous disdain. Always arrogant, Jonathan Hunter now exuded a single-minded, barely concealed anger. Anger against Rebecca? Estelle wondered. She didn't think so. He seldom paid his wife more than perfunctory attention. Anger against Joey didn't seem right either, although when Estelle had expressed sorrow at Joey's death, Hunter had acted almost as if he'd forgotten who Joey was. For a dreadful moment, she had thought he was going to deny ever having had a son. The moment had passed, but her discomfort in his presence hadn't. Jonathan Hunter was not behaving like a man who had just suffered an incalculable personal loss.

An odd unrest permeated the room. She wanted to believe it was all due to Hunter's strange, jarringly too-normal behavior, but there was more to it than that, she was afraid.

Someone turned up the sound on the television, and Estelle went over to sit beside Rebecca. The screen filled with the computer-designed logos announcing the debate. This was one debate all networks were covering. As the lights dimmed, Estelle turned to Rebecca and smiled reassuringly. Rebecca tried to respond with a smile but failed. Before Estelle could speak, Rebecca's thoughts again consumed her. Estelle turned back to the television, where Kirk Vinton was introducing the two candidates.

"... Robert Grant, the incumbent, and his opponent, Tobias Caruso, the challenger. After I give a brief summation of his background, Mr. Caruso will make the first opening statement. I'll then introduce Senator Grant, whose statement will follow. Questions will be asked, alternating between each candidate. Each will have two minutes to respond. Any questions?" Vinton's cursory glance was proof he expected none. He began his first introduction.

"Tobias Stewart Caruso, an Atlanta native, graduated from Georgia Tech University, where he was quarterback of the football team. Upon graduation, he became a successful appliance salesman. In the true American spirit, he took his modest savings and opened his own appliance store. His hard work and vision helped create a chain of electronics and appliance stores that are the pride of the South. Mr. Caruso has been married to his beautiful wife, Sandra, for thirty-one years. They have two children, Jessica, an executive with IBM, who spent two years as a Peace Corps volunteer in Africa, and Brad, a physician presently completing his residency in cardiology at the Mayo Clinic.

"Mr. Caruso . . ."

Caruso was good, Edmund Miller thought from his position in the control room as he watched his candidate's opening statement. Caruso may have been an unknown, but that wouldn't be true much longer, not the way he was performing. He'd remembered his opening statement perfectly, and his tone and expression combined just the right degrees of humility, understated passion, and basic values. He was proving himself a good choice. Not only would Grant be gone, but Caruso would be a credible Senator. More important from Miller's point of view, he would be malleable.

Grant, too, thought Caruso was good. He wasn't sure just what his opponent was saying—he was too intent on reviewing his own plans to really listen—but he could feel the empathy Caruso was generating. For a political novice, Caruso was surprisingly astute and competent.

Fleetingly, Grant wondered again if his political opponent could have some part in the attacks against him. Had he dismissed such a possibility too quickly?

Caruso wound up his remarks.

Hunter slipped into the empty seat beside the President. "Everything's under control," he whispered. The President continued to stare at the screen. "I just called Bender in Atlanta. NIIA agents are ready to blanket the studio once the debate is well under way. They didn't want to scare

Grant away by being too much in evidence beforehand. He'll be arrested the moment he finishes his closing statement."

The President made no response.

Hunter turned to the television screen as Vinton, sardonic amusement positively exploding from his eyes, began his introduction of Grant.

"Robert Hawkins Grant, the twelve-year incumbent, is a graduate of the United States Naval Academy, a career military officer who rose to the rank of admiral, and former president of Landsdowne College in Atlanta. Of more immediate interest, Senator Grant has been implicated in the murder of *Washington Herald* reporter Russell Frederickson."

The camera focused on Grant. His jaw was clenched, and his eyes held a combative glint.

"As a possible motive for the murder, several members of Grant's staff allege that Grant impregnated one of his youngest employees and that his rejection of her and their baby led to her subsequent suicide, an allegation Grant knew could fatally harm his reelection chances."

Vinton paused, giving his words time to adhere. "Further," he continued gravely, "Grant has been tied to a man who is currently in prison for drug dealing and who twice has allegedly been associated with murders."

Again he paused, malignant anticipation quirking at his mouth. He'd received a phone call from Peter Evans only minutes before the debate, a bombshell with Grant's name written all over it and which Vinton was about to drop.

"Senator Grant's son is currently under investigation for alleged drug dealing," he said, the look of anticipation growing as the thought of a possible television career—of true national fame!—gave emotional fervor to his words. "A warrant has been issued for his arrest in connection with the shooting death of Dr. Cora Snyder, a distinguished professor at Georgetown University. Apparently, Dr. Snyder was murdered by Grant's son Bailey when she tried to prevent him from initiating another drug deal."

Vinton felt a surge of satisfaction as he watched tension vibrate through Grant's body.

"The cloud over Senator Grant is so dark that many hope he will use this forum to resign.

"Senator Grant . . ."

Grant stared, unsmiling, at the camera. Vinton's introduction had been his first intimation that Bailey was officially wanted for murder. Prepared as he'd been for just such an eventuality, he couldn't completely suppress the jolt of shock that shot through him.

Apparently, Vinton hoped to turn the debate into a lynching, Grant thought, making a surreptitious survey of the room. No law officers, NIIA or otherwise, were visible. None had been around when he'd entered the building either. He would be wise to move up the timetable, Grant decided, while he still had the advantage of surprise. Nothing would be gained by remaining here, not with Vinton in charge.

Seconds only had passed, but Grant had made his decision. He looked straight into the camera.

"Everything that has been 'alleged,'" he said bitingly, "is untrue. I'm close to having complete proof, not only of my innocence, but of the guilt of the real murderers. The motive rests in Washington, in the highest levels of government. Since the NIIA is controlled by the White House and is incapable of conducting an honest and comprehensive investigation, I have been forced to investigate these murders myself. Courageous friends who believe in justice are helping me. Tomorrow, we will have proof. Tomorrow, I will make that proof public."

"Senator!" Vinton shouted angrily, seeing his chance at national prominence being wrested from him. "We cannot tolerate such blatant manipulation of this forum!"

"This 'debate' is a sham!" Grant raised his voice to be heard above Vinton's. He began unclipping his mike. "Just as the so-called evidence against me is a sham. The people of Georgia and of this nation deserve better. I intend to expose the truth, and no one, certainly not you, can stop me."

Estelle sat rigidly in her chair, afraid of the unnatural tension Grant's words had precipitated. Even Rebecca had come out of her self-absorption and was looking around, a puzzled frown on her face.

Hunter was the first to speak. "We have to find his 'friends.'" He rose and stalked toward the door. "I'll make some calls. Evans," he said, turning to glare at the editor, "you'd better hope Vinton takes control and puts Grant's allegations in perspective. Dishonesty in the NIIA, indeed!"

Without thought, Evans, too, was standing and on his way to the door. He didn't know which worried him more, the icy anger in the attorney general's tone or the disturbing allegations Grant had made. One thing he knew for certain: Never again would he suffer the humiliation that had been his after the Cuban fiasco. Whatever happened, this time he would make sure his skin remained whole, his credibility intact.

The door closed behind the two men.

The others looked uneasily from the television screen to the President and back again.

What did these men fear? Estelle wondered, her heart pounding unbearably. For that was what it was. Fear. The President of the United States and his advisors were afraid.

Rebecca Hunter reached a hand toward Estelle. They stared at each other, thankful for the solace of the other's presence.

As Grant uttered the last sentence, a prearranged signal to Rachel, she glanced toward the curtain behind the stage. Stephen Yao, dressed in a jumpsuit bearing a TV station's call letters, gave her a barely perceptible nod.

She stood immediately and with the rest of Grant's family, all twenty-eight of them, rushed the stage. In the confusion, Grant slipped in with them, and Tucker assumed Grant's place behind the podium. Rachel threw her arms around Tucker, kissing him and thereby obscuring his features, so like Bob Grant's own but so different. India, Olivia, and Henry reached up for hugs as well, doing their best to divert attention both from their father and from the identity of their uncle.

As Tucker took his place Grant moved to his sister-in-law, Melissa's, side. She started moaning softly about the horrid treatment of her beloved brother-in-law. As Grant placed his face next to hers in commiseration, she begged to be taken to the nearest rest room.

"Oh, Tucker, I feel so sick," she said, moaning even more convincingly.

He put his arm around her. His face partially hidden in her plump shoulder, he led her toward the door.

"Oh my, oh my," she moaned. "I'm sure I'm going to be ill." She grabbed her mouth with her hand and hunched her shoulders. Anyone watching gave Grant no more than cursory attention. Their concern was all for Melissa.

She quickened her pace. Out of the corner of his eye, Grant saw NIIA agents converging en masse on the podium. How long before they recognized the deception? he wondered. He hastened her ever nearer the door.

"Hey, you! Stop!"

Grant heard the shouted command but ignored it. Instead, he pulled Melissa into the hall and closed the door behind them.

Stephen Yao was waiting. "This way," he said, running toward the back stairway.

Even before he and Grant had moved away, Melissa had turned back and stuck a small homemade device, prepared earlier by Yao to resemble a much-used comb, between the door and the jamb. She then waited, still clutching her stomach and her mouth. Once NIIA agents either forced their way through the jammed door or came around from the back, she hoped to retrieve the device and try to divert the agents' attention from the true escape route. No one expected this subterfuge to last, but the success of the escape depended on many such extra seconds.

As Grant entered the stairwell, he tore off his tie. As they raced down the steps, he yanked off his jacket and shirt to reveal a neon tie-dye T-shirt underneath.

Yao opened the door to the third floor. Seeing no one, he signaled Grant, and they sprinted to the left toward a door marked Employees Only. The door opened as they reached it. Grant's younger brother Curtis was waiting. Grant thrust his shirt, tie, and jacket into Curtis's waiting hands.

"Everything's set," Curtis said over his shoulder as he led them, running, into the open service elevator.

During the few seconds it took to reach the basement garage, visions of the pandemonium upstairs passed in slow motion through Grant's mind. Melissa, the children, and above all Rachel and Tucker would be doing everything possible to slow discovery and pursuit. Would they be harmed? Arrested? Would the cameras record the blatant abuse of power by the NIIA? Or would Grant appear a typical fugitive on the run? Regardless, he had to escape. Only through his freedom did they have a chance of finding the truth.

After what seemed an eternity the elevator reached the basement garage. Yao hurried them to a waiting Blue Racer Cab. An attractive young woman, one of Yao's operatives, was seated in the back. Grant jumped into the driver's seat. The woman thrust a dreadlock wig into his hand, then a smoking cigarette. Grant jammed the wig on his head and stuck the cigarette in his mouth.

"Go for it!" Yao called, giving the fender a good-luck pat.

Grant pressed the gas. The cab leapt forward. Cursing his stupidity, he tapped the brake, got the cab under control, and continued more sedately up the ramp and out of the garage.

He leaned forward as if fiddling with the meter. The wig was in place. The cigarette wreathed smoke around his face. Would that be enough to camouflage his identity?

Not waiting to watch Grant, Yao and Curtis raced toward another waiting car, one with a deceptively fast engine. "Ready for the masquerade?" Yao asked, thrusting the car into gear.

"Ready," Curtis replied. He'd already put on Grant's jacket and was finishing knotting the tie. "Think they'll fall for it?"

"You look enough like Bob," Yao said after a quick glance. Curtis, though considerably younger, was definitely from the same gene pool as Grant, right down to the determined set of his head on broad, equally determined shoulders.

The car gained speed as it came to ground level, then squealed around the last corner on two wheels. NIIA agents, rushing toward waiting cars, paused, their attention drawn to the caroming car and away from the Blue Racer Cab it was trying to pass.

"Hang on!" Yao yelled as he overtook Grant and raced out onto the street.

Curtis ducked his head as if trying to hide, but not before giving everyone a brief but good look. "Try not to get us caught, would you?" he said through muffling hands. "I don't think they'll take kindly to this little maneuver."

Yao chuckled. "Don't suppose they will." In his rearview mirror, he saw Grant's cab turn right at the first corner and disappear from sight. He also saw cars racing out of the parking lot, red lights whirling and sirens wailing. For a heart-stopping moment, he thought they were going to turn after the cab. Then with a whoop of relief, he hit the gas. "They took the bait! Now let's see what this baby can do!"

The chase was on, and Yao knew exactly where he was going.

From her position behind the podium, her arms locked around her brother-in-law's neck, Rachel Grant watched as the door began closing behind her husband. She had no time for even a moment's exultation, for as she turned she found herself looking into the startled eyes of the head NIIA agent, Derek Bender. For a split second their eyes locked. Then, as Rachel tried to cover Tucker's face with her own, Bender grabbed him by the arm and stared directly at him.

"This isn't Grant!" Bender shouted. "Block all exits!"

He turned toward the closing door. "Hey, you! Stop!" He ran toward it. The few other agents in the room fell in behind, scrambling to reach the door. It wouldn't open.

"Break it down!" Bender commanded. "Grant's getting away!" He turned. "You!" he ordered, pointing to several agents running toward him. "Go around back and try to cut him off! Then see what's holding this door." An agent, walkie-talkie in hand, was already alerting those below. "And don't let Grant's family get away. I want them all in custody! Now!"

Rachel smiled to herself as NIIA agents crowded around. Bob had gotten away! Pray he had! Now if they could just pull off the rest of it . . .

"Bender," she said sweetly but with enough force that the media who hadn't chased the agents out the back door immediately turned their attention her way. "You said 'in custody.' What on earth for? This was a debate, for heaven's sake!"

"You've aided and abetted a criminal to escape," Bender said through clenched teeth. He modulated his anger as he became aware of the television cameras focused on him.

"A criminal, sir?" Again Rachel's voice dripped with southern civility. "Whatever do you mean?"

"Your husband just escaped, as you well know." Arrogant superiority fought with anger in his voice.

"But, sir," Rachel said sweetly, her face registering confusion, "how can you call my husband a criminal? How can you say he has *escaped?* My husband left quickly to avoid the uncivil media. He certainly had no thought of escaping anything other than the most disrespected people in America."

Bender's mouth opened to refute her. Instead, he glared. She was right. Even worse, she was stalling him, deliberately he was sure. She knew he couldn't come down on her, not with cameras catching it all.

"We'll be leaving now," Rachel said, indicating the family members grouped tightly around her. Olivia was clutching one of her hands. Henry looked excited. Only India seemed to understand the full import of the exchange. Sensing this, Tucker put a reassuring arm around her shoulder. She smiled at him tremulously, but the tension didn't leave her body.

Caruso's entourage watched the byplay with open-eyed amazement, wanting to support Bender but afraid Rachel was somehow getting the better of him. She was so dignified, typifying every embattled family in America.

"Unless you care to press charges against us?" Rachel asked, more of a statement than a question. She wanted a definite answer while the cameras were there to record it.

Bender stared at her, anger making his eyes black. The tension escalated.

Suddenly, the door at the back of the room banged open.

"Grant's gone!" someone yelled from the hall. "He had a car waiting."

Rachel's heart sang. So far, so good.

After a glance at the door and several shouted commands, Bender turned his attention back to Rachel. His look was speculative now, devoid of all anger, a look infinitely more dangerous. The silence stretched between them, a no-man's zone both were reluctant to enter.

Was he going to arrest them? In front of the cameras?

"Leave an address and phone number where we can reach you," Bender finally said.

Rachel gave Olivia's hand a reassuring squeeze. Then she saw the hardness in Bender's eyes, an implacability echoed in his next words. "We'll know every move you make," he said softly. The cameras zoomed in on him, just as he'd known they would. "Your husband is a murderer. That is the truth. He won't remain free for long. I hate murderers, ma'am, and I'll make sure he pays. You can bank on that."

Rachel returned his look with one equally determined. "You're wrong, sir," she said, "and tomorrow we will prove it. Tomorrow, everyone will know what a sham you, this investigation, and the administration really are. The murderers of Russell Frederickson, Anne Peabody, and Cora Snyder will be brought to justice, something you refuse to do. The American people can bank on that."

Matt Goldie's plane was waiting at the end of a private airstrip, engines running, when the car bringing Grant screeched to a stop beside it. Grant had changed cars twice since escaping the debate. This last time, Tommy had been at the wheel of the new car.

Sheriff Jimmy Jenks was standing just inside the door of the plane. His face broke into a grin as his bearpaw of a hand enveloped Grant's and pulled him inside. "Had us a mite worried," he told Grant as he thumped him affectionately on the back. "These last fifteen minutes went slower than my Aunt Mary Alice out for a Sunday drive. Mighty fine hairdo, by the way."

Grinning, Grant took off the wig and flung it onto an empty seat. He waved to Goldie, who waved back. The plane then taxied down the tarmac.

"Any problems?" Jenks asked as they sat and fastened seat belts.

"Not really." Grant had to yell to be heard above the engine noises. Goldie was flying a smaller plane than usual, a concession to the shorter runway. "We got caught in a traffic holdup caused by our esteemed Second Lady's arrival for a Caruso rally. Seemed fitting somehow. Any word from Yao and Curtis or from Rachel?"

"Rachel called, and everything went as planned."

Grant nodded, the intensity in his eyes abating somewhat.

"She said to tell you," Jenks continued, "that Operation Integrity is now entering Phase Two and right on schedule. Yao we haven't heard from—just a minute." He pushed a button on his walkie-talkie and listened.

Then, grinning, he turned to Grant. "That was Yao. Mighty pleased he was. Said he hadn't had so much fun in years. Everyone got away clean. Curtis sent you a message, something about life never being dull when you're around. They've begun Phase Two and will meet up with us in Washington. Ramon is working with Cynthia."

Grant spent the next twenty minutes filling in Jenks on the details of Phase Two, their plan to search the Capitol for Loomis's information.

Then he leaned back in his seat and allowed the engine noises to wash over him. Within minutes he was asleep, the last rest he would have for twenty-four hours.

Bonfire saw Grant leaving the debate site. He wasn't fooled by either the cab ruse or the dreadlock wig. He tried to inform Derek Bender, but the NIIA chieftain was too busy chasing red herrings to follow it up immediately.

Bonfire hadn't expected more and was actually pleased. Grant was his target. Only fair that he be the one to give chase.

Bonfire, too, had a plane waiting. Unlike Grant, however, he was able to land directly at Washington National Airport. He wasn't a fugitive from the law.

Cynthia was in a car waiting when Goldie's plane touched down at a small private airstrip outside Washington. Grant and Jenks hurried across the runway and climbed in. Goldie immediately turned and prepared for takeoff. He would fly on to the original destination of his flight plan, hoping this touchdown would elicit no attention from traffic control or the NIIA, at least long enough for Grant to get safely away.

A mile from the airstrip, Cynthia pulled into a lay-by where a second car was waiting.

Jenks got out. "I'll meet up with Yao like we planned. I reckon he'll make one hellacious distraction for you. I'll be waiting when you come out." Giving Grant's arm a pat, he closed the door, got in the other car, and drove away toward Washington.

As Cynthia pulled back into traffic, Grant got down on the floor of the backseat and covered himself with the blanket she'd brought. Quietly and without turning her head, she summarized her research on the possible meanings of Loomis's letter as they pertained to the Capitol. By the time they reached Washington twenty minutes later, Grant had her information well in mind.

"We're almost there, Senator." Cynthia's voice was steady, but her hands squeezed the steering wheel until her knuckles were white.

The Russell Senate Office Building was on her left as she pulled into its underground parking garage across the street. Smiling as pleasantly as she could manage with tense lips, she waved to the guard in the booth at the top of the ramp. He smiled back and waved her through as usual. She pulled into a space the next level down and turned off the engine. The quiet was absolute.

"No problems so far," she whispered to Grant. "The place looks deserted. No people and only a few cars. Take care."

The driver's-side door slammed. Grant heard her shoes clicking on the concrete. The sound diminished, then faded completely. He waited the agreed-upon time—three minutes by his watch—then climbed from under the blanket. Cautiously, he looked around. The garage appeared to be empty.

Careful to make no noise, he opened the car door and picked up the files Cynthia had left for him, part of his disguise as a faceless staffer intent on congressional business. He eased the car door shut, the whole while visually sweeping the cavernous area for any sign of danger.

Seeing none, he walked quickly across the garage, smoothing his shirt and straightening the identification badge hanging from his neck. It belonged to one of his staffers. The picture showed a black male, younger than Grant but enough like him to pass a casual examination.

The tunnel that connected the Russell Building to the Capitol was long and open, a vast chamber of echoes with the now-idle subway track taking up half the space. His footsteps masked by rubber-soled shoes, he sprinted down the expansive walkway next to the track.

Ahead was the escalator into the Capitol proper. The guard there had to be fooled into accepting Grant as the staffer of his borrowed ID.

Grant slowed his pace. A group of chatting tourists advanced toward him from the left. Mentally blessing the architect of the Capitol for agreeing a few years earlier to open the building to tourists on Sundays, he moved in front of them and hurried forward, the files repositioned so his ID was readily visible. Distracted by the tourists, the guard barely glanced at the badge. Even better, he didn't bother looking at Grant's face.

"Forty minutes until closing," he told the excited group gathering around him. "You can take—"

Grant turned a corner, cutting off the rest of the sentence.

Few people remained in the building, and most of those were guards, any of whom might recognize him. As if personal acquaintance made a difference, Grant thought, his eyes firmly turned down to the intricate gold, black, and brown mosaic of the floor and his ears attuned to every sound. His picture had been plastered in papers all over the country. Even more pertinent was the almost continuous TV coverage of every aspect of his life.

Grant glanced at his watch. Seven minutes were gone already. He'd told the others he would be out in thirty minutes, forty at the outside. After that the Capitol would be closed, and they would be forced to improvise.

He turned a corner and, seeing a figure ahead, pulled quickly into a doorway. Heart pounding, he eased his head forward. His heart steadied, and he smiled ever so slightly.

The man, presumably a husband impatiently waiting for his wife, was pacing in front of a glass case outside the Capitol museum. Grant's shoes were soundless on the limestone, and he was almost even with the case before the man's circuit turned him in that direction. It was Ramon, as Grant had guessed. Now Ramon was the one suppressing a smile.

Neither spoke, but Grant felt a slight lessening of the prickles running up his spine. With Ramon protecting him, he wasn't so vulnerable to a surprise attack or a surprise arrest. Bonfire or the NIIA—either would destroy any hope of finding Loomis's message.

Passing Ramon, neither man giving any indication of recognition, Grant turned and ran down another of the Capitol's staircases, this one leading to the basement. The offices of the architect of the Capitol at the bottom were dark. Grant paused a moment, noting the narrow corridor on the left, leading under the staircase. Then he turned into an identical corridor on the right.

The low ceiling closed in on him, quickening his pulse and intensifying every sound. The dirty white of the painted cinderblock walls glowed eerily in the inadequate light. The concrete of the floor was gritty under his shoes.

The corridor widened where it met the corridor to the left of the staircase. Grant stopped, searching the shadows. Once he entered the next corridor, he was committed. There was no outlet. If anyone came after him, he would be trapped.

He plunged forward, running now. Ahead he could see the iron bars protecting Washington's tomb or what would have been his tomb had Washington not demanded he be buried at Mount Vernon. Surely, this was what Loomis had meant by entombment. Grant reached through the bars and strained toward the catafalque, which was stored there and used for the caskets of those lying in state in the Rotunda. His hand fell far short. He shook the bars soundlessly, but the gate was securely fastened.

Infused now with a sense of lost time, he searched the area outside the bars. Nothing. No place of concealment.

His mind raced. Entombment. If Loomis hadn't meant here, where . . . His letter had said something odd about kneeling and praying. What if Loomis had used entombment as his clue to which President, not to location? Then where—

Grant froze. Footsteps were pounding down the staircase above his head!

He whirled and ran soundlessly back the way he'd come. He had to get out before he was trapped! Even so, he paused under the staircase where the corridor divided. The racing feet sounded on the right. Grant ran down the left. He paused at the main hallway. It was empty. He heard a shout behind him, then another, this one a different voice. Two people? He glanced back but could see nothing in the gloom. Not waiting to learn more, he bounded lightly up the steps, his footsteps silent.

Kneel and pray. Kneel and pray. Loomis's words pounded through his mind with every step. George Washington. Kneel and pray.

The Senate Chapel with its stained-glass window of Washington praying at Valley Forge, was that what Loomis had meant? Grant paused on the first floor. If he were being pursued, he would have time for one more search—if he were lucky. The chapel was open only to members of Congress, he thought, trying to decide. Loomis would have had privacy there.

Grant glanced down the corridor toward the museum, but Ramon had vanished. Where was he? And where was Yao? He should have been visible by now, he and his diversion to draw attention from Grant. Wasting no time in useless speculation, Grant took the next set of steps two at a time, grabbing the brass railing to steady himself on the landing. He'd made his decision. The chapel was the first door on his right. He tried the handle. Locked!

Footsteps echoed up the stairwell. Grant paused. He heard the footsteps again, this time coming up the stairs fast.

Grant ran to the desk where a docent sat during visiting hours, yanked out the drawer, grabbed the key to the chapel, and silently pushed the drawer closed. The footsteps had paused at the first landing. One more landing and Grant would be exposed to whoever was following. The bird nests, squirrels, deer, and vines of Brumidi's magnificent stair railing afforded no concealment.

Grant jabbed the key into the chapel lock, turned it, felt immense relief when the door opened, threw himself into the room, shut the door and relocked it, all in one fluid movement. Whoever had been running was now paused at the top of the stairs. Over his own labored breathing, Grant heard his pursuer's cautious progress as he first tried the door across the hall, then walked to the chapel and slowly twisted that doorknob.

Muscles tensed for attack, Grant watched the knob turn.

Again his pursuer paused, this time mere feet from Grant with only a closed door separating them. Finally, the footsteps moved away down the hall, the sound gradually diminishing. Who was he? Grant wondered. Not the NIIA, surely. They would have filled the building with heavy-booted pursuit.

Bonfire! Grant thought, his heart racing with exultation. At last, Bonfire had been forced to make a move not of his own design.

Even before the echo of the steps was silent, Grant was moving to the front of the chapel.

Light from behind the stained-glass portrait of George Washington threw blocks of color onto the altar, the cushioned chairs, the carpet. The seven lights of the two tall brass candelabra flanking the stained glass cast a soft glow that extended little beyond the two prayer benches in front of the altar.

Kneel and pray, Loomis had said.

Grant went to one of the prayer benches and knelt on its needlepoint cushion. Was this what Loomis had wanted him to do? he wondered. His eyes were drawn to the Bible verse in the stained glass: "Preserve me, O God, for in Thee do I put my trust." *In thee do I put my trust!* Loomis's words! This had to be the right place.

Still kneeling, he rapidly scanned the area, seeking a place of concealment. Unlike the crypt in the basement, the chapel offered too many possibilities.

Think, he told himself even as he listened for returning footsteps. The stained glass offered no hiding place. His eyes moved down. The offering table. The pulpit. The . . .

His eyes went back to the table, enclosed on three sides. What was it he was trying to remember? Of course! Under the sacrament! That was what Loomis had said. Grant rose and pulled the table away from the wall. He knelt again, this time behind the table where he could look under it.

The table was used for the sacrament, he thought as his fingers skimmed the front panel, feeling for the letter. Surely, this was the answer to Loomis's riddle.

His hand stilled. Only his eyes moved. Someone was coming down the hall, slowly, almost silently. Grant pushed himself under the table, his knees forced up to his chest. He pulled the table as close to the wall as he could. He heard the lock to the door jiggling. He heard a soft curse, then the sound of the door opening.

He was trapped. Even worse, the table was almost a foot from the wall. Anyone who had spent time in the chapel would realize that. It was too late. All Grant could do was pray—and breathe as silently as possible.

The footsteps moved up the aisle, paused, then moved again, coming ever closer to the table. They stopped, surely almost on top of him.

Grant lay motionless, sweat dripping down his face. He had no way of knowing if he'd been spotted. He had no way of defending himself if he had. Ramon and Yao—where were they? What had happened to the diversion?

Grant waited. Every nerve in his body strained to hear and decipher each sound. Finally, his stalker moved, his steps soft on the carpet of the aisle. Again, the footsteps stopped. The silence was finally broken by the sound of the door opening and closing.

Still, Grant didn't move. The door had seemed to close but so easy to close it and remain inside, waiting, watching. The numerals on Grant's watch glowed eerily green in the gloom of his confinement beneath the sacrament. Five minutes. He would wait five minutes before he—

At that moment he spied a pale triangle above his head where the lip of the table formed a natural ledge. His breath caught. Loomis's message from the grave? Grant ached to reach out for it. He knew he didn't dare.

The silence was oppressive, each creak and sigh of the old building piercing his body with the suddenness of a knife. The pale triangle mocked him with its nearness.

Four minutes. Five minutes. As Grant tensed to move, he heard a small sound, an unrecognizable but chillingly alien sound. He wasn't alone!

He stared at the glowing face of his watch.

Two more minutes passed. No sound.

Three. Still none.

Had he been mistaken? Was he jeopardizing the mission by allowing precious seconds to ease away? One more minute, he decided, eyes on the second hand. Then he would have to move.

Twenty seconds.

Thirty.

Forty.

As he tensed to move, Grant heard the soft rustle of footsteps, followed by the equally soft opening and closing of the door. His body sagged against the floor. Twenty seconds more, and his enemy would have had him! Twenty seconds!

Not stopping to be sure he was really alone, he reached above his head. The triangle grew into a manila envelope. Even in the dim light, his name stood out. He slid the envelope back where it had been.

With infinite care, he moved from under the table, easing his legs to rid them of incipient cramps. Pulling himself up until his eyes were just above the table, he surveyed the room. No one. Leaving Loomis's letter in the repository that had served it so well, he rose and cautiously moved to his left. His back against the wall, his body prepared for attack, he circled the room. It was empty. He was alone.

Back at the table he leaned down, retrieved the envelope, and slipped it into the files he still carried. Thank God he'd resisted the impulse to put them on a chair while he searched, Grant thought, remembering the footsteps and the time spent looking for just such a mistake.

Pausing long enough for a quick prayer, the brass door handle cool and knobby under his hand, Grant eased the door open. Nothing happened. Cautiously, he looked out. The hall was clear. Turning right, he hurried down it, away from the Brumidi staircase he'd used earlier.

He was two minutes behind schedule already. Should he chance going directly to the garage where Cynthia would be waiting? Giving a mental flip of the coin and coming up yes, he turned and sprinted noiselessly down the back corridor leading to the Senate side of the building.

The corridor was empty. The Capitol was closing.

Turning a corner, Grant heard footsteps close behind him. Heart thudding, he pulled into a niche, only partly concealed by the white marble statue resting in it. The footsteps stopped when he stopped. Had they turned down another corridor or into one of the rooms opening onto the hall?

A minute crept by. Warily, Grant peered back down the hall. No one. He moved out and began walking, glancing back often. He had to get out before escape became impossible.

The Majority Leader's office was ahead. Busts of former Vice Presidents lined the hall, some resting on pedestals, some in niches. Their eyes were cold in their marble heads.

Grant turned left into the corridor of the Minority Leader. The tall narrow doors into the chamber were on his right, closed and formidable. The glass at the top was black. No tourists remained. The building was empty of all but the guards with their suspicious eyes and their APB for his arrest.

Grant's pace quickened. He reached the back staircase and stopped. Nothing sounded but footsteps in the far distance. He started down.

Two steps from the bottom, a Capitol Hill police officer emerged from an adjacent corridor. Grant froze. Momentarily, he considered racing back up the stairs, but it was too late. The officer reached the narrow staircase and brushed by, not even bothering to look at Grant's badge, much less his face. Thank goodness for the anonymity of staffers! Grant thought, his heart still racing.

Desperate now to escape, he descended the last two steps to the subbasement level that led to the Russell Building tunnel.

Suddenly, he stopped. Someone was running down the corridor at the top of the steps he'd just left! Grant began running, too. The stairs and escalators were just ahead. So was the guard station.

He bounded down the stairs, trying to imbue his movements with the insouciance of a self-important staffer. He held up the files so they partly covered his face, grimacing conspiratorially at the guard as he did. The guard gave him a knowing nod, one put-upon employee to another, and waved him on.

As soon as he reached the tunnel, Grant stopped and pressed himself against the far wall. He looked back. His heart leapt. The man following him was the man of the composites, the man with the beard! John Smythe, not Bonfire? Grant didn't wait to see more. He sprinted down the tunnel, praying the guard would cause enough of a delay for him to get away.

The garage was just ahead. Grant stopped at the entrance, searching the vast space for Cynthia and the car. There! To the right! With one last spurt, he raced to the car and yanked open the back door.

"Let's get out of here!"

The car was moving before he finished the sentence.

He looked back. John Smythe had just burst into the garage and was pulling out a cellular phone.

"We've been spotted," Grant told Cynthia, lowering himself onto the floor and scrambling under the blanket.

With a wave, Cynthia passed the guard booth and entered the street. She glanced in the rearview mirror. "No one back there yet."

After making two quick turns, she pulled into a parking spot. In seconds, both she and Grant were out of the car and in another. Jenks was in the driver's seat. Grant dropped onto the floor in back as Cynthia got in the front and Jenks merged into traffic.

The sheriff had wanted to be part of the "Capitol Gang" as he called them, but even he had agreed that driving the getaway car was essential. A man and a woman, both white, would help allay suspicion.

"What happened to Yao and Ramon?" Grant asked from under the smothering confines of yet another blanket. This one smelled faintly of autumn bonfires, he thought, momentarily distracted.

"I don't know where they are," Cynthia said, sounding worried. She kept her face directed toward Jenks, but watched unobtrusively for signs of pursuit. "Stephen was waiting for Ramon's signal. When it didn't come as scheduled, he left. He said they would meet you at the cabin."

"Haven't heard a word out of 'em." Jenks patted his cellular phone. "Course I wouldn't 'cept for an emergency."

"I was followed," Grant told them. He braced himself against the backseat as the car took a corner a little too fast. "The man with the beard."

"John Smythe," Cynthia whispered, the anxiety in her voice laced with awe. They'd been right! "Loomis's papers," she asked urgently. "You found them, didn't you?"

"Yes," Grant said. "In the chapel."

"Kneel and pray," Cynthia quoted.

Jenks turned right to avoid a red light.

"And 'under the sacrament,'" Grant told them. "Phillip hid an envelope under the altar."

They dropped Cynthia at a Metro station. She would double back, then go to a hotel where one of Yao's agents had reserved a room. There she would check the latest staff reports.

Half an hour later, Jenks and Grant were turning into the long gravel drive leading to the cabin hideout. Jenks didn't think they'd been followed.

Bailey and Sherrill were waiting, their faces lighting with relief at the sight of the two men. Neither Ramon nor Stephen had called. No one speculated on the reason. Wondering if the price had been too high, Grant took Loomis's envelope from its protective file. He lifted the flap and emptied the contents onto the table. No one spoke as he sorted through it. More newspaper clippings. He put them to one side to be read later. The next was a group of typed messages. Grant read the signature on the top one.

"It's from Bonfire!" He handed it to an incredulous Jenks and flipped rapidly through the others, careful to avoid smudging fingerprints.

"Twenty-one in all," Grant said, "and all signed 'Bonfire.'"

"This one's over ten years old," Jenks told him. "Mentions a bill Bonfire wanted passed." He turned it over to look at the back. "Nothin' else."

"Each of these suggests support for or specific attacks against pieces of legislation," Grant said, skimming them quickly, "except for these five which recommend a political appointment he should support." His eyes narrowed. All five recommendations had been supported by Loomis, and all had been appointed. Four of the five were judges, one on the Supreme Court!

"Leastways we got proof this Bonfire really exists." Jenks took out a plastic bag and had Grant drop Bonfire's messages into it. "I'll check them out later for fingerprints. Probably a waste of time though."

"Except to prove they were in Loomis's possession," Grant noted.

The next envelope contained a paint chip, a shard of red plastic, and two pictures of the same car, one with a dented fender and one without. Grant frowned and rechecked the envelope. Nothing else. He put it all into another of Jenks's plastic bags.

Grant looked back down at the table. His heart began pounding. Next in the pile was a bulging business-sized envelope. Loomis's typewritten name had been crossed out, and Grant's had been written in its place. Grant opened it and took out the sheets of paper it contained. They were interoffice memos. On the back of each Loomis had handwritten a letter to Grant. It was dated the day of his death.

Grant began reading, handing each page to Jenks as he finished. Jenks handed them to Bailey and Sherrill. No one touched anything but the corners.

Bob—

I didn't ever expect to reveal this to anyone. Even now I hope, maybe even I pray, that this letter will remain unread. That will mean I misjudged the enclosed information as it regards you. It will also mean that I misjudged the effect of my defection on Bonfire. Yes, that is his name, the only name I know. I always associate it with *The Bonfire of the Vanities*, appropriate considering vanity is the basis of my present dilemma.

Even as late as an hour ago, I hadn't expected to reveal my iniquity, but I hadn't expected to be in the chapel either. Strange how that happened, almost as if my feet knew my destination despite my better judgment. I'm writing this confession, for that is what it is, on the only paper I have at hand, the backs of memos. Rather fitting, I feel, that the worthless be given a chance to have worth.

I feel a compulsion to confess, but that compulsion takes me only so far. I have no desire for my sins to become public. In all honesty I rather relish a solemn send-off with my virtues extolled in proper tones of reverence and respect. Therefore, here in this chapel with The Most Honorable George Washington looking down on me, I make a pact with God. I will place the truth in all its unflattering detail in a place of concealment. If it must be found, then you will do so, Bob Grant. If not, it will remain inviolate through the centuries until my bones are mere dust. Either way, I will be beyond caring.

As they say, I'll begin at the beginning. Early in my Senate career, I attended a dinner party, not a very good one I'm sorry to report, considering the effect it had on my life and, I'm beginning to think, on the lives of others. I was driving home alone. I'd had some wine admittedly, but I don't think I was drunk, at least not by legal standards. The road was dark, and I was tired. I felt and heard a thud, but since I hadn't seen anything and nothing showed up in my rearview mirror, I assumed I'd hit an opossum or some similar animal that had subsequently scuttled off into the woods. When I reached home, I found that my right fender was slightly dented, and some paint chips were missing. The turn signal cover was cracked, and several pieces of it were missing also. There was a little blood, but not much. I was mad about the damage and cursed the miserable creature who'd caused it but gave it no more thought.

The next morning an article in the city pages of the *Herald* told of a man who'd been killed in a hit-and-run accident. He'd been found at the side of the road in the exact spot I'd felt the bump. I panicked, I admit it, and decided to say nothing. I'm not proud of myself—I wasn't even then—but I couldn't think what else to do. Vanity as I mentioned. I tricked myself into believing it was only coincidence, that I hadn't been going fast enough to have hurt anyone.

One month to the day later, I received the first packet from the aforementioned Bonfire. It contained a paint chip, a piece of plastic from the turn signal, and photographs of my car both before and after it was repaired. In other words, irrefutable proof I'd killed the man, and more importantly that Bonfire knew and could prove it.

Even then, it was six months before he began his demands. I found the first less than onerous. He wanted me to sponsor a piece of legislation, one which I supported more or less anyway. I acquiesced. Maybe I would have even if the legislation had been abhorrent. I like to think not, but now I'm not so sure. As I said earlier, evil creeps up on one unawares.

And so it continued, year after year, request after request, never too often, never too much of a strain on my conscience. Bonfire understood my limits all too well. Remember that, Bob, if he does, indeed, get you in his sights. That, I fear, is his intention, to keep you in his sights until he has orchestrated your destruction.

How I came to dread the arrival of those blasted manila envelopes! They seemed to materialize from out of nowhere with the knowledge of no one. The last one, which came today, demanded I initiate ethics proceedings against you. Included was proof, most comprehensive proof, of your ethical violations. I tried to convince myself that the sex and drug charges were possible, even probable. But even my credulity has limits it seems.

An hour ago, I called to warn you, but you'd left. Only afterwards did I consider that my phone might be tapped and the timing of my call viewed as suspicious.

Don't think me heroic. Yes, I'd planned to warn you. I'd also planned to do as I was told. A grand but empty gesture, you might say.

I'm ashamed to admit I betrayed you once before. If you've come to the point of needing this letter, I assume you've already come to suspect.

You're a clever and tenacious man, Bob Grant. I wonder if Bonfire has yet begun to realize just how clever and how tenacious. For purely spiteful reasons, I hope not.

Kneel and pray. That's what I suggested you do. Oddly enough, that's exactly what I've been doing and that's why this letter. If you find it, Someone greater than myself so decreed it. If not, my secret will die with me.

Yesterday, I would have called it a flip of the coin.

Today, I know it is atonement.

Use the enclosed information if you must, but spare Janet and the boys if you can. I love them so much. My regret is for them, the grief they have already endured and that which I may cause them yet.

Knowing Bonfire as I do, I fear that the time of reckoning may be nearer than I might wish.
Phillip Loomis

Grant handed Jenks the last page, then realized final instructions from Bonfire to Loomis were also included. He read the message, finding it essentially as Loomis had written, a partial outline of Bonfire's plan to destroy Grant, emphasizing a proposed Senate Ethics investigation. Maribeth Pariss was named as a victim of sexual harassment. Shirley Spade was suggested as a witness to that accusation; Hal Olexey, to the drug charges.

Grant rose slowly and walked over to stare into the fire. Poor Phillip. How right he'd been about the evil he feared.

"I reckon that clears up one thing," Jenks said. "Loomis didn't kill himself."

"He was murdered, wasn't he?" Bailey asked, still holding the last page by a corner. "By Bonfire."

"Reckon so, son," Jenks said, putting a hand on the boy's shoulder. "Lessen I'm mistaken," he added, "that'll be welcome news to that unhappy man's widow."

Grant walked back to the table and sat down. "You're right," he agreed. "Janet's having trouble not blaming herself for his death, but I'm afraid she's just trading one kind of sorrow for another."

"He betrayed his country," Bailey said slowly, "just so no one would know about the accident. How could he? And how can anyone, even his family, ever forgive him?"

"Don't be too rough in judging him," Grant said, picking up the clippings and beginning to examine them. "At first," he said, looking up at Bailey, "I'm sure Phillip didn't think he was doing anything wrong. By the time he did, he felt trapped."

Bailey didn't look convinced. "That's no excuse."

"Not a nice thing he did," Jenks agreed. He spoke to Bailey, but his eyes were on Sherrill. When Bailey had said he didn't understand how anyone could forgive Loomis, Jenks had been watching her. He'd seen all hope drain from her face. "But doing something that shames us, I'd guess we've all done our share. It's a mite hard to judge others when we consider our own failings."

"Thank you," Sherrill whispered.

Bailey must have heard her, but he continued to regard Jenks. Finally, he spoke, turning toward his father. "Is this enough proof?" he asked, indicating the papers on the table.

"As proof of a blackmailing Bonfire, yes," Grant said, carefully inserting the clippings into the bag Jenks held. "As proof of a conspiracy against me, maybe. More than that?" He shrugged. "By now, every one of Bonfire's suggested accusations has been backed by 'fact.' Even his instructions to Loomis, though specific, aren't worth much without proof that they're lies. He sounds like a conscientious citizen, wanting to remain anonymous."

The phone rang. All eyes were instantly drawn to it. Four rings, then silence. Seconds passed. Two more rings. Silence.

When it rang the third time, Grant grabbed it. His end of the conversation was uninformative, but no one missed the tightening of his hand on the receiver. No one missed the sagging of his shoulders.

He replaced the receiver carefully. "That was Yao," he said unnecessarily.

They braced for his next words.

"Ramon . . ." His voice broke. He looked up and became aware of their anxiety. He continued quickly. "Ramon was attacked at the Capitol. He's been taken to a hospital. They're not sure he'll live. He was trying to protect me.

"Blast John Smythe!" Grant swore, hitting the table with his fist.

The attorney general sent an urgent request for the President to meet him in the War Room. Immediately.

The President stormed into the room. "This had better be good," he told Hunter angrily. "I had other plans."

Instantly, Hunter was angry, too. "You're supposed to be zipping it!"

The President stared at him coldly.

"You're a fool," Hunter seethed, the words coming out in a hoarse whisper. "You'd risk everything for . . . for a quick lay? Everything? Because that's just what you're doing. We've kept the media happy so far, but if they have any reason to suspect—"

"Lighten up, Hunt," the President interrupted, frowning his displeasure. "It's not that big a deal. But that's not why you called me down here."

"No, it's not, but I wish—"

"Stop! Or I may just decide I'm tired of you and your constant whining."

"Fine! I'll go now!" Hunter's earlier anger looked mild compared to the rage that engorged his face now. He couldn't allow the President to veer out of control, not now, not when media scrutiny was intensifying.

"Now, now, Hunt," the President cajoled with a placatory smile. He filled his voice with affection. "You know I couldn't get along without you, but leave this other alone. I'm serious, Hunt."

Hunter made no immediate reply, but gradually his breathing steadied. "Just keep it zipped until after Tuesday's election. You'll give me that, won't you?"

"Sure, sure," the President agreed impatiently. They were back in their old form of give-and-take. He felt no more need to placate, just as he felt no need to acquiesce to the demands of anyone. "Till Tuesday, but no longer. Now can we get on with whatever is so important?"

"A man was attacked at the Capitol a short time ago."

"So what?"

"So Bob Grant was seen there. We're concentrating the manhunt around Washington."

"Can we say officially that he's armed and dangerous?" the President asked.

"I already did."

"I don't like this, Hunt. Why would Grant go to the Capitol?" He looked around the War Room, realized it was too small to pace, so he remained standing, hands clasped behind his back, eyes riveted on Hunter. "Why would he risk going to such a public building?"

Hunter returned the President's stare. He'd been grappling with the same question since he'd gotten the message. "He didn't enter with the injured man," Hunter told him. "We're sure of that. Did he meet him there? Did the injured man somehow interfere with his plans? We're trying to determine Grant's movements inside the Capitol. Hopefully, that will tell us what we need to know."

"I don't like this," the President repeated. "I don't trust Grant even when I can see him. And now that he's on the loose... He's up to no good, whatever he's doing. Make sure the manhunt has no holes."

"Believe me," Hunter said, "Grant won't remain loose for long. I added a 'shoot on sight' to the APB."

Grant called Benjamin Dashev from the cabin hideout. The scrambler was in place. That should be enough, Grant hoped, given Dashev's equal desire to remain undiscovered from his end. It would have to be. Time was short, too short to try to find a safe phone somewhere else.

"I'm glad you were able to phone," Dashev said. "I have news."

"The source behind everything?" Grant asked.

"Yes," Dashev agreed. "Just so. An agent of mine, one of my most reliable, has learned that our supposition about an informal North Korean/Chinese alliance was correct. According to my source, Bonfire has guaranteed the continuation of technological transfers to these two countries, including transfer of the formerly restricted computers and computer parts essential to their nuclear future. The White House has demanded assurances that the computers will be used for humanitarian purposes only. A promise those governments are only too happy to give, I might add," he said with a mirthless laugh. "Contracts for additional classified parts are even now being initiated with your President. This is the interesting part. Both countries seem secure in their demands, as if they know their wants will be met."

"Someone inside the White House is guaranteeing it?"

"So it has been suggested."

"Then we were right," Grant said thoughtfully. "Bonfire is one of the President's top aides or has one of them under his thumb." He ran the information through his mind, then picked up a pencil and began writing. "That makes sense. We'll put them all under surveillance." He handed Jenks the note. Jenks read it and went to the fax machine Yao had brought to the cabin.

"Further, I have learned from another source that this same Chinese/North Korean alliance hired Bonfire to discredit you. That in part explains the emphasis on your use of drugs. If you appear to be covering up your own drug problem, no one will take seriously your findings about the dangers of noninterdiction. Again, Bonfire has given a promise, actually a dual one: First, that the current policy of noninterference with drugs coming into the United States will continue. And second, that he will destroy Senator Bob Grant, the most respected—and the most vocal— supporter of that policy."

"So we were right again. They're gambling on having a much freer hand to bring drugs into the country. The monetary implications for them would be staggering."

"Yes," Dashev agreed. "Easily enough money to purchase the nuclear technology and material they so desperately desire. Oddly, I have received word that the White House has hired John Smythe for much the same purpose, to discredit you, though drugs and technology transfer seem in no way involved. I must admit I am confused. These sources are seldom wrong, but two contracts on you at once? Especially when I have always sensed that Bonfire and John Smythe work together?"

Grant exhaled loudly. "Both Bonfire and John Smythe."

"So I believe. Even more curious, you mentioned a personal animus when we spoke before."

"Yes."

"Rumor again, I am afraid, but you and Smythe may have crossed swords in the past."

"Cuba," Grant said decisively.

"Then you knew."

"Knew?" Grant repeated, thinking of the fragments of memory that had led him to this point. "No, only wondered. With what you just told me, I think I can give Smythe a name."

"If that is so," Dashev said gravely, "you will have made life more secure for many."

"I must ask you to reveal his name to no one until after tomorrow."

"I am to be your insurance," Dashev said, amusement tingeing his words. "Is that not so?"

"That's right," Grant agreed. "You, I know, will insure he is brought to justice."

"You have my word and my silence."

Grant gave him the name. Dashev rang off to make plans.

Grant remained on the sofa, sunk in thought. He knew he was right about the identity of John Smythe. He had no proof, just too much coincidence to ignore, coincidence dating back to Cuba. He thought of the man whose dark side included the malevolent John

Smythe. Smythe consorted with equal ease with the President of the United States and the likes of Hal Olexey and Shirley Spade. He murdered and destroyed without compunction at the same time that he helped formulate the policies of the nation. How was it possible that such a man had remained undetected? And how could they force him, a man of steel nerve, genius intellect, and no conscience, into making a mistake now? They couldn't, Grant decided. Barring a miracle, they couldn't. They would have to find the chink in his defenses elsewhere.

"I think it's time to put some pressure on our esteemed attorney general," he said, rising. "Want to come for a ride, Sheriff?"

"Looks like a mighty fine night for one." Jenks ambled over to the door and took his coat from a peg.

"Bailey," Grant said, putting a hand on his son's shoulder, "I'll call if I can. If you get those computer records . . ."

Bailey had been trying to access any and every network that could exist at the White House. No computer system was completely secure— by the front door or back. He was determined to get telephone records and gate sheets for the offices of the West Wing as well as those for personal phones. His dad needed to know who'd been away from Washington at the critical times.

"I think I'm close. I'll do my best."

"I know you will, son," Grant said, giving his shoulder a squeeze. "I've always known that."

Then they were gone.

Twenty minutes later, an aide walked into the War Room. Hunter looked up from the NIIA reports he was studying and inclined his head for the other to speak.

"Sir, Senator Robert Grant just called."

"What do you mean Bob Grant just called?" Hunter demanded. "Grant called me?"

"Yes, sir," the aide said, swallowing convulsively at the unbridled anger his words had provoked. "He said he would call you back at the same number in exactly an hour. Then he hung up. That was four minutes ago, sir."

"The arrogant devil!" Hunter stood and gathered together the reports. He had taken control of the War Room. "Inform the President that I'm on my way to see him."

"He's occupied, sir," the aide said, an embarrassed flush spreading over his face.

"Occupied! Tell him to get rid of the tramp now, or I'm coming in to do it myself!"

He stalked out and slammed the door.

The President finally walked into the Cabinet Room almost twenty-five minutes later.

"So what's the big deal?" he demanded of his attorney general. "This had better be good."

"You're a fool!"

"Now, just a minute—"

"Yes, a fool!" Hunter snarled. "Your administration is falling apart." He thrust out his palm when the President started to protest. "Falling apart! I'm warning you: If you don't act quickly, you'll be the one destroyed, not Grant. All I've ever worked for will be destroyed."

"You're serious, aren't you?" The President strode to the dark brown leather chair reserved for his use alone. It was taller than the others and positioned in the middle of a row of chairs flanking the long mahogany table.

"Grant's calling me in twenty-five minutes."

"Grant's calling *you*? What does he want?"

"How would I know?" Hunter demanded. "How could any sane man know?"

"But you have an idea," the President prodded, sure from the look in Hunter's eyes that was true.

Hunter's response was elliptical. "The Peabody thing is collapsing, and without her to testify, an investigation could be disastrous. Unless you want to lose your presidency, maybe even go to jail"—the President blanched—"we have to have someone to take the fall."

"Corforth?" the President asked. Corforth's criticisms still stung.

"We can't have anyone even remotely associated with you during the last campaign," Hunter said, frowning his disgust at the President's lack of focus. "I was considering Edmund Miller."

"Miller? He's still in Atlanta, isn't he?"

"He left right after the debate."

"Didn't I hear he's resigning, something about an illness in the family?" With each question, more color returned to the President's face.

"Exactly. Miller faxed his resignation this afternoon. Totally unexpected." Hunter began polishing his glasses. "That's one reason he's so perfect. We can make his resignation look like guilt. Everything else can be made to fit, too."

"Peabody's bribe?" the President asked dubiously.

"Miller was working for Senator Westlake then and was perfectly placed to create Peabody's bogus information. Under those circumstances, no one will think to question our involvement, and if they do, it will be his word against everyone in the administration."

"Call an emergency meeting of senior staff for first thing tomorrow," the President said decisively. "Explain that you've just uncovered Miller's duplicity. It's the only story they'll know so they'll be credible when they talk to the media. In front of a congressional hearing, for that matter."

"Since only you and the Veep know the truth about Smythe," Hunter agreed, nodding, "no matter how many congressional hearings, the staff will sail through unscathed. Besides, the evidence against Miller will be overwhelming. After all, he's the one who made the initial contacts with Smythe."

"Just be sure I'm covered."

"If we all stick together, we'll all be in good shape," Hunter said perfunctorily. He moved his hands as if brushing away an annoying insect. "But you'd better get yourself together. Any hint of another scandal, and our administration will be finished. Some red-hot reporter's sure to start digging, just as Frederickson did."

"Don't worry, Hunt. Sounds to me as if Grant's playing by our script. Trace his call, and before he knows what's happening, he'll be in handcuffs."

"It's all set. With luck we'll have him within the hour."

"Good." The President stood and started toward the door. "Take care of Grant and Miller. Then get back to me. I don't know what you're worrying about, Hunt. There's never been anything we couldn't handle."

Hunter stared at the retreating back, contempt written large on his face. He would preserve the presidency, of course. That was fundamental to his legacy. But he had a personal duty as well—to make sure that Bob

Grant was destroyed. No one was going to challenge *his* power or harm *him* in any way without paying dearly for it.

When Hunter reached the War Room, he called Edmund Miller and ordered him to come to the White House immediately.

Then he turned to the NIIA agents across the room setting up phone-monitoring equipment. Grant's call was to be shunted here. "Everything ready?" he demanded.

They assured him that it was.

Grant would guess about the phone surveillance, but Hunter felt sure he could lull him into staying on the phone those extra few seconds that would insure capture.

Grant's wife and children, his close associates, even some not so close, had been located and were being followed. Still, too many were unaccounted for: his son Bailey, that redneck sheriff down in Georgia, and Grant himself.

Hunter looked at his watch. Ten minutes late already. Why hadn't Grant called? Had the incompetent who'd taken the first call garbled the message? An agent assured him of its accuracy. Then this delay must be a cute game on Grant's part, Hunter thought, a childish attempt to make him nervous.

The phone rang. Hunter ignored it.

Grant stood in a wooded area several miles from the cabin hideout. Sheriff Jenks was just climbing down from a nearby telephone pole. Their car was parked behind them, partially concealed and facing the country road in front of them. The night was black, a spattering of stars doing little to lighten it. Deep shadows hid both the men and the car, but that protection was illusory. If their location became known, they would be revealed under even the weakest of lights.

"Think Hunter's had enough time to stew?" Grant asked. The psychology of this call was infinitely more important than the content.

"The more immediate question," Jenks said, looking up at the telephone pole from which a wire led down to the handset in Grant's hand, "is whether this setup will work."

"You're the expert. Will it?"

"Supposed to. 'Course I've never tried it. Always wanted to, though." Jenks attached a small metal disk to the handset and pursed his lips in satisfaction. "Now this is one mighty pretty piece of work. If it does its business, Hunter and his NIIA lackeys will figure you're calling from northern Georgia. Should throw a right healthy corncob up their britches."

"Very nice." Grant lifted his hand to dial but stopped. "Sure you want to stay?" Both of them knew the gadget might fail. Capture might be just over one of the rolling hills surrounding them.

Jenks merely smiled and turned to look down the road.

Grant finished dialing. The phone rang once, twice, finally nine times. Grant looked a question at Jenks.

"Cat and mouse," Jenks said matter-of-factly.

Grant hung up. "Two can play that game."

Jenks punched the device on the phone. "A phone number change," he said, using a number from the list he held, "just in case. This one's almost on the Florida line," he said, grinning.

"Wouldn't you say five minutes, no, let's make it six, should get Hunter's adrenaline pumping?"

Jenks's grin broadened, and he leaned back against a tree. He looked relaxed, but his eyes never stopped scanning the road in front of them. "Been meaning to ask you," he said without taking his eyes from the road. "You right about the leak in your office?"

"Yes," Grant said tersely.

"Figured as much, especially after what Loomis wrote."

Grant said nothing.

"You figuring to do anything?"

"What can I do?" Grant asked, all emotion wiped from his face. "I have no evidence."

What could he do, indeed? Grant wondered. As Jenks had said earlier, he had a serpent in his garden, one let loose by Bonfire, and serpents were notoriously slick creatures.

As the phone rang for the fifth time, the door to the War Room opened, and Edmund Miller entered.

Despite the late hour and unexpected summons, Miller was dressed as neatly as ever. For a brief moment, Hunter wondered what it would take to ruffle this almost-too-cool subordinate. Then the phone rang again, and all other thought left his mind.

"That's Grant calling," he told Miller, who stared from him to the ringing phone in open-mouthed amazement.

"Bob Grant? On the phone?" The phone rang again. "How can you be sure it's Grant?"

Hunter wanted to ignore the question. He never gave away his plans prematurely, but Miller would know that and would be flattered at his inclusion this time. He would be more amenable later when it mattered.

"Grant called earlier," Hunter said. "Demanded I wait for his call. We'll just see how *he* likes waiting."

The ringing stopped. The men stood motionless, but the phone remained silent.

Hunter finally spoke, addressing the NIIA agents. "You didn't get him." A statement, not a question.

The agents made no reply.

"How much longer did you need?" Hunter demanded.

"Thirty seconds," an agent answered after a momentary but all too obvious hesitation.

"A better chance if I answer?"

"Yes, sir."

Hunter, his face expressionless, his eyes intense, turned his attention back to Miller. "You're always ready with advice, Miller. Don't think I haven't noticed."

Miller's face registered no response to this telling remark.

"What do you think?" Hunter continued. "Should I answer or should I keep Grant hanging for a while longer?"

Miller's reply when it came was cautious. "Since our goal is to destroy Grant . . ." At the startled look of one of the agents, Miller began backtracking. "A murderer, a drug dealer, who knows what else, Grant is dangerous and has a criminal's dangerous mentality."

"Your solution?" Hunter interrupted. His face was filled with caustic amusement at the other's discomfort.

"Answer the phone," Miller said with more conviction than he felt. "Give Grant a chance to brag, and he'll grab it."

"To brag or to deny?" Hunter countered, turning the needle and enjoying the turning. He wasn't sure why Miller was so uncomfortable, but whatever the reason, Hunter was glad for it. A few more digs, and Miller would be ready to drop into his trap. By the time the man realized the extent of his betrayal, he would be in too deep to get out. And he wouldn't be able to point the finger without incriminating himself even more. "Well, Miller," Hunter prodded. He looked at his watch. Five minutes since the last ring. "Which will it be? To brag or to deny?"

"Grant's guilty as anything," Miller said decisively, "but he'll know you're recording the call. He'll deny everything, if that's even the reason he's calling."

Again, Hunter was struck by an undercurrent emanating from Miller. The man was deep. Everyone in Washington, he thought contemptuously, had a secret agenda!

The phone rang.

Four rings and Hunter lifted the receiver.

"Hunter?"

"Yes?" Hunter's voice was wary.

"I expect you to be at Union Station tomorrow morning at 7:30," a voice Hunter recognized as Grant's said. "No NIIA. No one but you."

"Why would I agree to that?" Hunter hadn't taken his eyes from the agents working to locate the call. One held up ten fingers, closed them, held them up again. Twenty seconds. Twenty more seconds.

"You have no choice," Grant said. "I know about Anne Peabody."

"Anne Peabody?" Hunter repeated, obviously delaying. "I don't know what you mean, but what you ask is impossible." Stall. Stall. "I'm too well known." Ten fingers. "I can't just stand around waiting for you, not at that hour of the morning. That's rush hour." Five fingers. "Security would never let me. You know that. Don't be a fool."

A triumphant "Got him!" exploded from the other side of the room. Hunter leaned back in his chair, a half-smile on his lips. Several agents rushed out the door.

"Why should I even *want* to meet with you, Grant?" Hunter continued, knowing Grant would hear the release of tension in his voice. "The only reason I can imagine would be to cuff you myself."

Hunter was enjoying himself. Grant couldn't get away this time, as he had after the debate. They'd underestimated him then but never again. Every NIIA agent in the country had been alerted. The ones in Washington and Georgia were prepared for instant mobilization.

The connection was cut.

They traced the number," Grant said with surety.

Jenks, once again using the phone scrambler to indicate another number—Derek Bender's private line—looked at him with a philosophical lifting of an eyebrow. "Then if I screwed up, we're fixing to have some company. Three minutes, I'd reckon. Five at the outside."

In silence they watched the road. Even within the canopy of sheltering trees, they felt exposed and vulnerable. Two minutes later the outline of a car was visible cresting a hill about half a mile away. The two men pulled even farther into the blackest of the shadows, their eyes never leaving the car. It disappeared in a dip in the road, then was again outlined against the night sky as it reached the top of the rise nearest them.

"A '79 Caddy," Grant said quietly.

"Yep," Jenks agreed, relaxing against the tree. "A yellow one. Not our friends."

Grant began dialing. "No need to prolong this."

Georgia!" Hunter scowled at the agent bringing the information about Grant's location. "What do you mean, he's still in Georgia! You told me he'd flown to Washington, that he'd attacked someone in the Capitol. Which is it?"

"I'm not sure, sir," the agent said, refusing to be rattled. "Our equipment says Georgia, a number about ninety miles south of Atlanta." He paused to listen to someone speaking through his earphone. "They just traced the phone to a laundromat. An outside pay phone."

"Don't tell me—he'd left before you got there."

"If he ever *was* there," the agent replied. "No one actually saw him."

"But he had to be calling from there, didn't he?"

"There are ways of accessing a number without actually being there, but only with sophisticated equipment."

"All of this is a waste, isn't it?" Hunter asked, making a sweeping gesture toward the equipment. "He could be anywhere."

No one contradicted him.

"He'll try contacting me again," Hunter said. "I'm sure of it. I want increased surveillance around my house. Around his house, too, and those of any associates."

"We're already—" the agent began.

"It's not enough." Hunter growled. "Grant has to be somewhere, and I want him found. Bring in the local authorities if you need additional men. I want every angle covered."

The phone rang.

Hunter stared at it, finally lifting the receiver on the fifth ring. "Grant?" he asked.

"Does the name John Smythe mean anything to you, Hunter?"

Hunter's eyes narrowed. "You're speaking in riddles, Grant."

"If you want the riddles answered, meet me tomorrow morning. 7:30. Union Station. I want my name cleared and the name of my son. Work it any way you want, but those are the conditions. Otherwise I go to the media. I don't want our country destroyed," Grant said. He gave a dry laugh. "Not that I care about you, Hunter, or that poor excuse for a President. I don't want you to have any misapprehensions about that, but I do love our country. I would prefer to avoid a national scandal, but if that's the only way to clear my name and to see justice done, I won't hesitate to bring you down."

"I'm not sure—"

The line was dead.

Get out!" Hunter ordered the NIIA agents. "Take your worthless junk with you!"

Hunter took off his glasses and began wiping them. The agents, working quickly, cast covert glances at his brooding visage, being careful to draw no attention to themselves. Miller, too, eyed Hunter but with a speculation absent from the others.

Hunter was oblivious. His mind seethed with images of Grant. Did Grant think he could strike a bargain, his own vindication and that of his miserable son in exchange for . . . what?

Hunter stopped wiping the lenses and stared down at his hands. John Smythe. Grant knew about John Smythe. He couldn't know more than the name or he would have said so, wouldn't he? Yes, Hunter decided, slowly resuming his rhythmic wiping. Gloating was Grant's style. He couldn't have resisted rubbing their noses in it.

Hunter's hand stopped again. He cocked his head in thought. Why Union Station? Grant had to know they would be waiting for him there. What was his game? Hunter kept coming back to that. Unless stress had clouded Grant's judgment, Hunter couldn't figure the angle.

The room was quiet. They were gone. He was alone with Miller.

"You heard what Grant said?" Hunter asked.

Miller indicated that he had. Their discussion progressed from this innocuous beginning through the many problems caused by Grant to the Anne Peabody story. Hunter knew he'd laid the groundwork well. He'd made numerous omissions, but Miller had no way of knowing. He wouldn't realize he was being set up, and by the time he did, he would be in too deep to wiggle loose.

By tomorrow, Miller would be under suspicion, and Grant would be in their grasp. Neither would be able to escape.

Hunter, however, would be free. His debt to Joey would be paid, and his hold on the reins of government would be secure. All would fall neatly into its prescribed place.

Miller left the War Room unsure whether to laugh or curse. Hunter had had the audacity to try to make him the fall guy for the administration's stupidity! That wasn't what Hunter had said, of course, but Miller was too much a student of Machiavelli to be fooled.

Hunter had tried to sucker the wrong man this time, Miller thought, his mouth tightening grimly.

He entered his office and began going through files. It was early morning before the paper shredder stopped humming.

In the cabin hideout near Washington, Sherrill sat in front of a glowing fire, going through the stack of printouts Bailey had produced during his various computer searches. She was trying to find a link between the man they suspected was John Smythe and the events they thought he had masterminded.

If only this were all over, she thought, looking at the clock. If only they were all safe. The Senator and the sheriff had been gone for over an hour. The minutes crept by. How she wished she could find something, anything, that would help!

She stole a glance at Bailey, who sat across the room, hunched in concentration over his computer. Her heart seemed to fill her body.

Was this love, she wondered, this desire to devour him with her eyes, to memorize every angle of his face, every line of his body, in so doing to make him part of herself? He wasn't handsome, not really. Though a little shorter, he had his father's broad shoulders and a hint of his ample build. She imagined that son would look very much like father in a few years. The eyes were his mother's, though. The kindness, the gentleness in them were hers as well.

Tears stung her own eyes. She could only remember that kindness. Since the dreadful night at Andrew's apartment, Bailey's eyes when he regarded her held only a painful neutrality, devoid of any feeling—not hatred or even contempt, certainly not affection. Occasionally, she thought she saw a flicker of the old feeling, but it was gone, if it ever existed, before she could be sure.

Oh, Bailey, she thought, unaware of the naked yearning in her face, how can I make you understand how ashamed I am? What must I do for you to give me another chance?

"Eureka!" Bailey shouted.

Sherrill stifled a startled scream, for a wild moment afraid she'd spoken aloud. Bailey's next words dispelled any such notion. Until that moment, he'd forgotten she was in the room.

"Sherrill," he said excitedly, jerking his eyes from the computer monitor to look at her, "you've got to see this."

She walked to his side, her melancholy forgotten in the glow of his excitement. "You've found something?" she asked, trying to make sense of the information on the screen.

"You'd better believe it!" He handed her a printout. "See this White House schedule? Out of D.C. on the night Frederickson was killed." He flipped a page, pointing again. "And on the day Peabody was, too. And look here." He flipped more pages. "He signed out of the White House an hour before Cora . . ."

"How can it be?" Sherrill protested hurriedly. "He's one of the President's closest advisors. Everyone trusts him."

"I know. Incredible, isn't it? But look here." Bailey rummaged through the stack of printouts and handed her another. "A copy of his phone bills."

Sherrill looked impressed. "How'd you get all that?"

"Secrets of a hacker friend," he said with a grin. "Too easy, if you ask me. But look at the days of the first two murders and the day Sergek met with her bearded friend."

"I don't see anything."

"That's just it," he told her triumphantly. "Every other day, he made at least one long-distance phone call, but not at those times. Not only was he not at the White House, but he wasn't in D.C."

"I guess you could be right," she said, still doubtful.

"Of course I'm right. He's the only one who fits. All the others on Dad's list had at least one thing that wouldn't work. But not him." He tapped the paper. "It's him. He's got to be John Smythe. Dad was right."

"But didn't your dad say he had legitimate duties those days?"

"Sure," Bailey agreed. "But he would, wouldn't he? Any criminal knows about alibis, and John Smythe's not just any criminal! Alibis or not, he could have done everything. These records prove it."

He jumped up and strode over to the wall where earlier he'd taped copies of the two composites—the man in Crazy Sam's the night Frederickson was killed and the man at the Cottonball Bar with Gayla Sergek. Beneath he'd taped a block-lettered title:

BONFIRE? This had been crossed out.

JOHN SMYTHE?

THE ENEMY?

Now, he took a thick black marker and with a flourish wrote the name.

Impulsively, Sherrill stood on her tiptoes and kissed his cheek. Bailey seemed not to notice but went back to the computer and picked up another printout.

He might not have felt her lips, but the feel of his skin, warm and soft, the slight prickle of shaved beard painfully exciting, caused Sherrill's breath to catch and heat to flush her face.

Flustered, she hurried to stand beside him. The enormity of his information suddenly overwhelmed her. "Oh, Bailey," she exclaimed, timidly touching his arm. "You've really done it, haven't you?"

"Hold on," Bailey cautioned, but with a smile. He finally looked at her. "Dad may look at this and blow it full of holes, but . . ."

He continued to regard her. The shuttered look she'd come to dread was gone. Instead, his eyes were warm with understanding.

"Sherrill," he said softly. His eyes still holding hers, he reached for her hand where it rested on his arm. A tremor of longing shook her. "Sherrill, I—"

The phone rang. Bailey grabbed it. It was Grant.

"I found it, Dad," Bailey told him excitedly. "I found what you needed. You were right. He has to be John Smythe. Everything points to it."

"Good work," Grant said. "Get word to Yao. See, too, if there's any news on Ramon."

"I will," Bailey promised, his euphoria gone in the reality of Ramon's fight for life.

"We've contacted the White House. Phase Three of Operation Integrity is committed. See what else you can find, especially about Hunter. There's no turning back now."

As soon as Bailey replaced the phone, the fax machine in the corner began whirring. Sherrill ran to it. "It's another composite," she said excitedly, leaning forward to grab it the moment it fell out.

Bailey looked over Sherrill's shoulder. "So Sergeant Alvarez did come through! Now let's see what we have." He studied it thoughtfully. "What do you think?"

"That you were dead on."

The fax machine kept spewing out pages.

Bailey held the new composite beside the other two, compared the three with a photograph Cynthia had sent, and nodded with satisfaction. John Smythe. Surely this was John Smythe.

He taped Alvarez's composite onto the wall by the first two. The other reports that Alvarez had sent, including a ballistic report, he saved for the sheriff.

Estelle was sitting in the dark. She had been since she'd come upstairs after the aborted debate. She'd spent the time in thought: her marriage, the odd undertones of the Grant problem, Cynthia's advice, the effect on her children of what she was contemplating. For the first time in months she'd not given way to the self-pity that had of late absorbed her.

Earlier, in the darkness, she'd heard her husband leave. She'd also heard the ushers talking in the hall about his summons from Hunter and had recognized in his immediate acquiescence to Hunter's ultimatum the extent of his peril. Then she'd heard him leave again, but not before he'd put on more cologne. The smell had filtered under the door and wafted into her room. Even that smell, such a poignant reminder of her husband's betrayal, failed this time to move her to self-pity.

Now one hour later, when she heard him return to his room, Estelle stood, straightened her dress, patted her hair, and walked over to the door connecting their rooms. She knew he would hear her turning the knob and opening the door. Her heart fluttered at the thought, but resolutely she did it.

The light blinded her for a moment. Then she could see him turned toward her, a look of surprise on his face. She also saw a smudge of lipstick glaringly bright on the shoulder of his white shirt. Her resolve hardened.

"I see you've been feeding your cravings," she said, indicating the smudge with a slight bending of her head. She was glad her voice held steady.

"'Cravings,' Estelle? Whatever do you mean?" His tone was as guiltless and charming as always, but he had the grace to look uncomfortable. He began slipping his arms back into his jacket.

"We need to talk, really talk." Estelle walked to a grouping of chairs on the other side of the room. As she turned to sit, she saw that he was still standing, irresolute, where he'd been. Then he shrugged his shoulders the rest of the way into the jacket, walked over to the chair opposite her, and dropped into it.

"I'm in no mood for any of your melodrama, Estelle," he said, his voice sounding resignedly weary. "I don't need this now. I have important work to do."

"I have been rather pitiful lately, haven't I?"

He looked surprised at this admission.

"But," she continued, "no more. I've realized this evening just what a cesspool I've been living in. Your 'snacks' are only part of it."

He started to protest, but she held up her hand and hurried on. "Just let me finish, would you? Believe me, your snacks are the least of my concern."

At these words, the President leaned back carefully in his chair where he could watch her through half-closed eyes. He waved her to continue.

"I know you framed Bob Grant."

His body stilled.

She didn't "know," but sensing his wariness, she felt vindicated in her choice of words.

"I know you must have had something to do with Anne Peabody," she continued inexorably, "and I'm afraid you had something to do with Russell Frederickson as well."

Slowly, he straightened himself until he was leaning toward her, the look he gave her a combination of bewilderment and outrage. "You're saying I was involved in the murder of two people? Really, Estelle, isn't that a bit much even for you?"

"Stop patronizing me," Estelle said sharply. "We both know you could never pull the trigger. Does hiring the murderer make you more or less culpable, I wonder?"

"You're wrong, Estelle," he said, leaning closer, his look of innocence perfectly done. "I had nothing to do with any murders. I swear I knew nothing about them." But he continued to watch her warily, like a cornered animal. Waiting. Waiting.

"I could put up with the snacks," Estelle said, "at least I think I could. Plenty of other wives have, but the other . . ." She shuddered and looked away. Then she raised her eyes to her husband's and continued emotionlessly. "I'm moving out tomorrow. My attorney will contact you. Or your attorney, if you prefer."

"If I prefer!" He stood angrily and walked over to tower above her. "If I prefer! I prefer you to stay here. Don't you know what this will do to me? Especially now?"

Sorrow filled Estelle's eyes and slowly seeped into every pore of her body. "What it will do to me," she whispered. The words echoed in her mind, a death knell to the remnants of hope she still harbored, to the years of happiness they'd shared, to the marriage itself. She stood wearily. He backed away to avoid touching her.

She wanted to walk out. He'd just betrayed his total lack of love for her, but she forced herself to stand before him and look him in the eye. "Our marriage is over," she said wearily. "I understand that. But I beg you, if you still have any shred of decency, please do what is right for Bob Grant! Just this once behave with honor."

They stared at each other, neither willing to break the moment. Finally, he spoke. His voice held no life. "You don't know what you ask."

"And you don't know what you've lost," she said softly as she turned and walked from the room.

W here have you been?" Hunter demanded of Derek Bender when at close to midnight the NIIA officer finally arrived.

"I had to—" Bender began.

"I won't have your excuses!" Hunter interrupted angrily. "When I order you to come, you'd better come. Immediately!

"I want you to concentrate your men at Union Station," Hunter continued. "Remind them of the shoot on sight order."

"Union Station? But—"

"Of course, Union Station," Hunter interrupted. "You heard what Grant said." He regarded Bender appraisingly, sensing the other's reluctance. "We can't ignore Grant's words just because they make no sense. Grant may well be trying a double bluff. That sounds like something he would do. He said Union Station for some reason, maybe just so we'd discount it. That's why you'll be there. If you don't get Grant, Bender, you'll be out of a job, and I'll see you never get another."

"But Grant may have—"

"Grant is clever," Hunter thundered, leaning out over the desk. "Can't you understand that? He picked Union Station for a reason. You figure out the reason, and you get Grant. He's a lying murderer. Get Grant before he destroys everything!"

Bender left. Hunter was concentrating his hopes in too small an area, he thought as he got into his car. Not a good idea in a manhunt. But Hunter was still head of the NIIA. The President, the only one who could rescind such an order, had willingly relinquished his power to Hunter.

Bender had no choice but to concentrate his men at Union Station, the one place they needn't be. This was no double bluff as Hunter had suggested. Grant was too smart to take that risk. And if Grant were smart enough to anticipate Hunter's response, he would have free rein of the rest of the city.

Monday, November 2:
One Day Before the Election

The first glow of dawn smudged the edges of night. Grant watched, unsure whether to rejoice in the new day or pray for more time. Unconcerned by his ambivalence, the day continued its inexorable advance. By the next dawn, the course of his future and of the futures of so many he loved would have been decided.

Grant hoped and prayed that Jonathan Hunter would unwittingly lead them to the administration's connection with John Smythe. Only Smythe and the shadowy Bonfire had access to proof of his and Bailey's innocence. So far Bonfire had proved too elusive to even consider, although Grant continued to have a niggling instinct, never far from conscious thought, that he was overlooking some fundamental truth about Bonfire, some frighteningly important fact that might influence the outcome of the day. He couldn't pin down the feeling, but it wouldn't leave him.

Obtaining proof of his innocence, Grant knew, would not be enough. He had to present it on national television. Only then, with the weight of guilt firmly and very publicly in place, would his own innocence be secure, unassailable even by the most powerful men in the land. Only then would his family be safe.

With military precision, he mentally checked off each step of what he hoped would prove the final phase of Operation Integrity. He tried to consider every contingency but knew anticipating them all, even anticipating most of them, was impossible. Too much was still unknown. Too much would surely change as the day unfurled.

In a few hours, they would know if Hunter had been rattled enough to act rashly. If so, the decisions made in the heat of today's battle were the ones that would ultimately count.

Grant continued working, and the nagging concern about Bonfire continued plaguing him.

When the phone rang, it was 5:45. Hunter was awake, not surprising since he hadn't yet fallen asleep. He couldn't remember his last night of real rest. Not since Joey—

Angrily, he pushed that thought from him. Until vengeance was secured later that morning, he would continue to keep all such distracting thoughts carefully put away. He hadn't the luxury either of sleep or grief. Grant remained elusive, and the presidency was tipping precariously over the abyss into oblivion. Too much demanded his attention. Too much would bow to his delicate touch alone.

Hunter was awake when the phone rang, but his mind didn't focus completely until he heard the name: John Smythe. With recognition came an avalanche of fury.

"What do you mean by calling me?" he demanded.

"A slight change in plans," Smythe said, his mechanically altered voice making even those prosaic words sinister. "We have to meet."

"Meet? Are you mad?"

"Believe me, I know the risks better than you," Smythe said. "Nevertheless, we must meet and as soon as possible."

Hunter considered the situation, trying to assess every angle. At the moment, one superseded all others. Grant must be silenced, and no one, certainly not John Smythe with his silly altered voice and pretensions of super-spydom, could be allowed to interfere. "The only time I can spare is this morning, 7:30, Rockville Cemetery." That at least would keep Smythe away from Union Station at the crucial time. "Don't reveal our meeting to anyone. Anyone! I'll not allow you or anyone else to destroy everything I've worked to create!"

He slammed down the receiver.

While Grant was being hunted down like the vicious animal he was, Hunter would be at his son's grave, his first visit since the funeral. He would share that moment of triumph against Grant with Joey, the victim of Grant's evil. Then Hunter could resume his duties without the distractions of either grief or Grant. He could fulfill his destiny and the intertwining destiny of the presidency.

The phone rang in the cabin.

"I have your man," Matt Goldie told Grant. "He didn't get much sleep. His light came on two minutes ago. Be prepared for him to leave."

"We're ready."

Goldie had been watching that apartment. Others, for the most part Yao's agents, were spread around the city watching other dwellings, in case their inhabitants, White House insiders and possible John Smythes, did something that disproved Grant's theory.

Grant felt confident he'd accurately identified his enemy, but he wasn't risking a mistake. The drawback was that it stretched their already depleted manpower to the limit. Only Bailey remained to help Jenks. Grant watched as his son and friend walked from the cabin. Their car's tires crunched down the gravel drive and faded into the silence of crickets and frogs and early-morning breezes.

Operation Integrity had just launched the most perilous and pivotal maneuver of the bloody campaign.

John Smythe picked up the semiautomatic lying next to the phone and fingered it almost lovingly. He wore rubber gloves. It was Grant's own gun, stolen from his unoccupied house by the skin-headed hooligans who'd driven Grant's family from it.

Smythe had been forced by unforseeable circumstances into shooting Frederickson before gaining possession of Grant's gun. As its logical substitute, he'd chosen a Colt .45 government model semiautomatic pistol for the murder, reasoning that as a retired military officer Grant was likely to have that particular make and model still in his possession. With no spent slug to match, the natural inference would be that Grant had used his own gun, especially when that gun was found missing. How well he'd understood the hapless Senator even on an issue as insignificant as a gun, Smythe thought, looking at the gun, an exact duplicate of the one used for the murder.

Now Grant's gun would complete its destiny, destroying both men who dared to threaten him—one murdered, the other condemned for that murder. A curve of gratification sat on Smythe's lips, falling short of his eyes. Caressing the gun one last time, he carefully wrapped it in a hand towel, also taken from Grant's house, and stowed the tight bundle in his coat pocket.

Years ago, when life had become ineffably boring, he'd devised his present modus operandi—the ultimate virtual-reality game, using real people playing for life-and-death stakes. Life and death were held in his hands, man's most basic destiny controlled entirely by him, entirely without anyone's knowledge.

He'd studied his art well.

He soon learned to analyze the abilities and predilections of each of his pawns as well as the outside stimuli that influenced their actions. He used his knowledge to predict, then manipulate them into the course of action he'd predetermined.

His network in Washington was as comprehensive as it was creative. Idealistic newcomers were the easiest to ensnare. Nurturing their careers, applauding their achievements, exhorting them to further promotions: He willingly catered to their egos and to the advancement of their careers, for in each advancement resided the seed of his own triumph.

Every agency in government—judicial, executive, legislative, or merely bureaucratic—many at the highest levels: He'd conquered them all. His unwitting pawns toiled in them, as much for him—though most didn't realize it—as for themselves. A law passed to benefit a government, a decision delayed to benefit a company, a nomination blocked, a reputation destroyed or built, his abilities and influence were limitless—if the price was right. The business community, political arena, and media: They were his, worldwide, all without a whisper of suspicion.

No one knew his face. Everyone felt his power.

His eyes took in the room. He wouldn't be returning. His work in Washington and his work as John Smythe were at an end. He was retiring. His need for greater stimulation had become impossible to assuage here.

True, the challenges of his dual life were profound; the tightrope was exhilarating; and the rewards, both financial and emotional, were beyond reckoning. If only he didn't feel the need for something more. More of what he wasn't sure. Revenge against Grant for Cuba, the one failure of his career, certainly. But what then? Surely his plans for the future, so carefully birthed and nurtured, would fill the unfathomable void that daily widened darkly before him.

Smythe shook his head to dispel that depressing image.

He was all-powerful, his omnipotence revered in every corridor of power, but lately that didn't seem enough. Even entrepreneurs of his undeniable skill and success suffered job burnout, it seemed.

He looked down at the bulge of the towel-swathed gun. The melancholy dissipated in anticipation of sweet retribution. The smile returned to his lips. Bob Grant destroyed, Jonathan Hunter destroyed, maybe even the presidency destroyed—enough satisfaction for the day.

What did he want to take with him? Not much, he knew, not when developing new amusements was the object of his move. To that end, more money than he could spend in a dozen lifetimes on a plethora of diversions awaited his pleasure in numbered bank accounts around the world.

His diaries—his golden parachute—he would take. Opening an ingeniously concealed safe, one he felt sure would remain undetected until the building was razed, he removed the pile of notebooks it contained. A worn brown briefcase, a *memento mori* from Russell Frederickson, waited open in front of him. Smythe stared at it for a moment. He wasn't sure why he'd kept it. Certainly, he'd never kept evidence from other murders. Perhaps it was for the added fillip of danger, the edge, like his repeated disguise, all of which enhanced his reputation and proclaimed his superiority. Perhaps it was for the high of taking it through airport security unnoticed, a last extravagant gesture before retiring. Whatever the reason, the thought of it clasped in his hand, a direct link to the sublime performances of his past, was pleasing and seemed somehow fitting.

Placing the diaries, his record of triumph, in the bottom of the briefcase, he added the other papers in the safe, a step-by-step documentation of his life's work.

Only a small black book remained in the safe. Again a smile quirked the ends of his lips. That innocent book, the first of his diaries, recorded his entry into the world of manipulation. He'd learned much since those days in college. Initially, his pandering of sources among both fellow students and faculty members had been merely a fortuitous combination of ambition and intelligence. He'd soon decided, however, that nothing fortuitous would ever again determine his future. He would control his own destiny, even if having his way meant directing from the background, his power unsuspected.

With a shrug, he threw the black book into the briefcase, a sentimental gesture only. It had long since lost its usefulness, the names it contained insignificant in the power strata he now traversed.

His notebook computer came next. By its side he placed the tape recorder that he'd converted into a repository for his Glock semiautomatic pistol. The gun's plastic body would pass through airport security undetected.

Anything else? John Smythe surveyed the room, his home for sixteen years. He felt no stirring of regret. Now that the safe was empty, there remained no imprint of his habitation. With a decisive snap, he closed the briefcase. It was time, time for him to leave.

Jenks and Bailey took up their surveillance of the apartment of the man they'd deduced was John Smythe. Goldie left to ready the plane.

Half an hour later, the apartment lights went off. Within minutes a black BMW roared out of the underground garage and onto the street. The man they presumed to be John Smythe was at the wheel.

Bailey pulled their nondescript rental car into traffic, being careful to place several cars between himself and their quarry.

"He's headed away from the White House," he said, knowing Jenks was unfamiliar with Washington. "And away from the Capitol. Away from Union Station, too." Horns blared as he hit the gas and flew through a red light. "Hope we don't lose him in traffic," he said nervously. Washington traffic, always heavy, was already building to its typical morning madness.

"You're doing just fine," Jenks reassured him, his drawl soothingly slow. "Just don't get too close. Don't want to spook him. But don't get too far back neither," he added with a chuckle. "Wouldn't do to lose him."

"No," Bailey agreed, relaxing only slightly his grip of the steering wheel. "Wouldn't do at all."

Several miles later, Jenks leaned forward. "Get in the right lane," he said. Even his slow drawl sounded tight. "Then right at the next light. Might want to speed up a tad."

Bailey turned the corner almost on two wheels.

The BMW had disappeared!

"Relax, boy!" Jenks said, urgently scanning the area. "Just keep your eyes open."

They raced down the street, trying to scope every opening.

"There he is!" Jenks shouted, pointing. "Left at the next corner. There! Slow a bit, there's a boy."

They turned the corner in time to see the BMW pulling into the crowded parking lot of an office building.

Bailey tapped the brakes. The car behind him braked loudly, then honked its displeasure.

"Advertise we're here, why don't you?" Bailey muttered under his breath. His eyes never left the back of the head in the car they were following, but John Smythe, if he heard the noise, gave no indication. He pulled into a parking space, got out of the car, and hurried inside the nearest building.

"There's a space around the corner," Jenks said, "where you can still see his car. I'll just get out and mosey on over to see if I can figure out what he's up to. You stay put and try to stay out of sight. No need to chance his recognizing you. Now's a good time to call your dad," he added in an undertone as he eased the door shut.

Bailey was left alone, crouched in the front seat, pretending to read a newspaper—the *Washington Herald* of all things!—that they'd picked up before their surveillance. He gripped the paper tighter, trying to stop its shaking. Under its cover, he reached for the phone.

Bob Grant raced down the twisting back roads near the cabin, pushing the car to enough above the speed limit that he would make good time, but not so fast that he would be stopped by the police. What a superb piece of irony that would be! Sought for murder but arrested for speeding!

Grant tugged at the dreadlock wig, then glanced down at the cellular phone, willing it to ring. The indicator kept roaming in and out of cell reception. Where were Bailey and the sheriff? Had they tried to reach him and failed? The dashboard clock showed it was already after seven.

He forced his foot off the accelerator. Eighty! If he weren't careful, he would blow it all.

Relax, he told himself. With conscious effort, he put on his battle face and with that one mental shift his body responded—alert, ready for action, but relaxed. He wished Yao were with him, but Yao was coordinating the rest of the plan, including round-the-clock guards for Ramon, who was alive, but barely. John Smythe had much to answer for.

Grant was late because Rachel had called with a problem about logistics for that afternoon, a complication but not insurmountable. Masterson was working on it, but so was she.

Grant's eyes were flinty. Everything, his personal freedom, the welfare of his family, the safety of his friends, hinged on his having gotten enough facts and then interpreted them correctly. Had he seen through the lies and subterfuges, through the personal and political maneuvering and prejudices to the face of John Smythe? Were they following the right man? And what about Bonfire? Where was he and how did he fit into the equation?

Something about both Smythe and Bonfire troubled Grant, like a rattlesnake in the woodpile that instinct identifies before eyes see. Safety demanded he correctly identify his own rattlesnake before tragedy struck.

What's going on, Jonathan?" Rebecca Hunter asked her husband. Even she was surprised to hear the words. She seldom gave him a thought and certainly was beyond caring what he did.

"Going on, Rebecca? How Victorian you sound."

"And how odd you're acting," she retorted.

"Not that you would understand," Hunter said as he opened the closet and reached for his coat, "but I'm about to avenge our son's death and insure the continuation of the presidency."

"Avenge Joey's death!" Rebecca gasped, looking both outraged and appalled. "How can you talk about avenging anything? Joey died of a drug overdose, Jonathan."

He stared at her coldly, then started to put on his coat. She grabbed his arm. "Why can't you understand that? A drug overdose. He did it to himself."

Hunter tried to shake off her hand, but she gripped tighter.

"I knew better than to expect you to understand," he said through gritted teeth. "You've never appreciated the subtle balance necessary to maintain the presidency. Bob Grant is determined to destroy that balance just as he destroyed Joey."

"So that's it, is it?" she released his arm and wiped her hand on her soft woolen robe. "You can't face the truth, and so you've placed the blame somewhere else. I might have known. Joey *chose* to take drugs, Jonathan. *He* made that decision. No one else. Maybe he was trying to get you to notice him. Maybe he was crying out against all the years of neglect. Maybe it had nothing to do with you at all. We'll never know. But one thing we do know: Bob Grant did not cause Joey's death."

"Not cause it!" Hunter regarded her with the implacability he reserved for those who thwarted his will. "Bob Grant bought the drugs! The proof is irrefutable! Just as he destroyed Joey, so now he's trying to destroy everything I've built."

Rebecca's body sagged with fatigue and grief. She raised her bowed head. Her voice was so soft that Hunter had to lean forward to hear. He didn't want to hear; he wanted to leave, but he couldn't. Somehow he couldn't. "I'm devastated that Joey is dead, Jonathan. No one could feel greater pain." She regarded him wearily. "You feel that same grief, I know. You and I. I've asked myself why he had to die, what I could have done differently, how I could move back the days and change time. But I can't.

We can't. Not even you, Jonathan, not even the all-powerful Jonathan Hunter can bring back Joey. What you've created has totally corrupted you. Bob Grant isn't the problem. You are."

Hunter once again threw off her hand. His eyes were murderous. At that moment, Rebecca knew that her husband was as irretrievably lost as her son.

The phone rang. Grant reached for it, his foot unconsciously pressing the accelerator. He eased back and punched the talk button.

"Dad."

Bailey! Grant eased back on the accelerator even more.

"I'm here, son. Everything okay?"

"I'm not sure. I can't figure out what he's up to. Right now I'm waiting in a parking lot off the Old Georgetown Road and Wilson Boulevard. He went into an office building, and Sheriff Jenks followed him. They've been gone about seven minutes."

Grant pictured the area, trying to second-guess his enemy. Away from D.C. proper, away from any of the places they had expected. Where was John Smythe headed? Or was he staying right where he was?

Over the phone, Grant heard papers rustling. "Hold on," Bailey said, his voice tense. "Someone's coming."

A minute passed. Two. Grant's hand was sweaty on the phone. He could hear nothing but an occasional rustle of paper. Then he heard the engine start. A car door slammed, and Jenks was speaking.

"I almost missed him," Jenks said. "He ch—"

He didn't finish the word. Grant waited tensely, afraid to speak.

"That's odd," the sheriff said finally. "He's driving a different car, leaving the BMW here. Hang on."

Indistinctly, Grant could hear Bailey's voice, excited. The car. Something about the car.

"What's the license number on your Olds?" Jenks asked urgently. Grant told him.

Jenks must have lowered the phone, for his voice became distant. "Up there, Bailey. Turning left. We've got him now." Relief was apparent to Grant even though the words were muffled.

"Sorry about that, Bob," Jenks said after a few more hurried words to Bailey, "but things were downright difficult there for a moment. Afraid we'd lost him."

"But you haven't," Grant said, wanting confirmation.

"Nope. He's heading north on Wisconsin, but no telling where he's bound. Right now not knowing is like spit in a hurricane. Pretty meaningless. He's driving your car, Senator. Bailey reckons the Little League baseball sticker about seals it. It's your car for sure."

"So we were right," Grant said, grim triumph in his words. "He *is* John Smythe."

"I'd reckon so," Jenks agreed, "especially since he's sporting a most bodacious beard."

"What!"

"Sure nuff. It's the composites come to life. He went into a building. Few minutes later, when he came out, I nearly let him go by. If I hadn't remembered those composites . . ."

"We've got him now!"

"Maybe," Jenks agreed, "but I don't much like this, Senator. Wonder what he's planning with your car?"

"Doesn't matter," Grant said, "as long as we catch him doing it. I'm closing in on your location. I should be able to intercept you in seven to ten minutes."

NIIA agents blanketed the area around Union Station, men and women trying to look anything but official. Occasionally, one would speak into a two-way transmitter concealed somewhere on his person. Every sighting of Grant proved a false alarm.

Seven-fifteen.

Seven-twenty.

"Think he'll show?" Derek Bender asked his lieutenant, a variation of the same question they'd been asking each other since Grant had first suggested the meeting.

"Grant's crazy, but not that crazy."

Bender didn't respond. He'd thought the same all along and had argued its logic with his superiors, who'd agreed but said they had no choice but to give Union Station priority coverage per Hunter's orders. Hunter might even be right; this might be a double bluff.

Bender checked with his operatives again. No sign of Grant at the station. No sign of Grant on the street.

Seven-twenty-five.

Grant wasn't going to show. Bender would have bet on it. Some double bluff! he snorted.

Smythe's turning into that cemetery up ahead," Bailey said, surprised. He eased back on the gas and swung through black wrought-iron gates hanging on stone columns. Smythe's car was just disappearing around the curve ahead.

Jenks dialed Grant.

"Rockville Cemetery?" Grant repeated thoughtfully. "I'm almost there. That's where Joey Hunter's buried, isn't it?"

"By gosh, I believe you're right!" Jenks exclaimed. "Hang on." The phone was silent for a moment as they edged around the curve, concern they would lose Smythe battling with the need to remain undetected. Smythe came back into view, slowing even more as he passed the first road on the right and disappeared around the next curve.

"I think he's going to stop," Bailey said, taking his foot completely off the gas.

"Looks mighty like it," Jenks agreed. "Park here, why don't you, and I'll mosey ahead and take a look-see.

"We'll hold up here out of sight," Jenks told Grant, speaking quietly into the phone, "and see what he's fixin' to do. Hang back a bit, Senator. Just outside the gate would be mighty fine."

Jenks left the car and hurried across the grass, using tall monuments to shield him from view as he reached the top of the rise.

When his Town Car pulled to a stop inside the cemetery grounds, Jonathan Hunter didn't get out immediately. He was savoring the moment. The time had come, he thought, the time of revenge and vindication. Vengeance is mine, saith Jonathan Hunter. He smiled at the conceit, pleased at this last gift he could give his son. Of all people, Joey, who'd been destined for personal greatness and groomed for his role since birth, would understand how important saving this presidency was.

A small knoll hid the grave from the car. Hunter had had his protective detail park on the far side for that reason. This was a moment to share with his son alone.

He left the car and ordered his agents to remain where they were. They did his bidding without demur. One demotion had been enough to teach them their place.

Seven-twenty-five. Hunter quickened his pace. He would have five minutes alone with his son before Smythe arrived, five minutes to share the joy of his vengeance.

He crested the knoll, and for a moment his step faltered. One grave stood out from the others, a grave of newly turned sod, protected not by a lush if now brown covering of grass but by the decayed remnants of withered funeral flowers.

Hunter's face hardened, and he walked to that grave. He stared down for a moment, then, slowly, knelt on the mound in front of the temporary marker. The raw dirt dug into his knees, dirtying his trousers. He welcomed this symbolic sharing with his son. Raw, red earth. The sight pained him almost as much as the empty body had.

He didn't hear John Smythe approaching with muffled steps through the grass. At that moment he was consumed with explaining his precious gift of vengeance to his son, explaining all that his son had lost when he'd abandoned his birthright.

You called it," Jenks told Grant over the phone, his voice breathless as much from suppressed excitement as from exertion. "Joey Hunter *was* laid to rest here. His daddy's up at the grave as we speak."

Grant let out a long pent-up sigh.

"Take the back road in," Jenks continued. "You shouldn't be noticed. The feds are parked at the bottom of a small hill farther in. Hunter left them there and is now on the side closest to you and plumb out of their view. Smythe's car—your car, blast him!—is parked on that same side, but where Hunter can't see it from the grave. Smythe was still in the car but looked like he was about to get out. I got a picture of him in it but not face on."

"I'm entering the cemetery now," Grant told him.

"When you come on the first side road on the right, pull in, and no one'll be the wiser. Better turn 'round so you can pull out fast if need be.

Both Hunter and Smythe are up your side of the hill a bit and to the right, I'd expect about five hundred yards. We'll park ourselves on the other side," Jenks continued, "and keep an eye on Hunter's car. Maybe we can tell something when he returns. We can snap some pictures anyway."

Two minutes passed, minutes pulsing with tension, while Grant followed the sheriff's directions. Would he get in position in time to record the meeting between Smythe and Hunter?

"I've reached the side road and parked," Grant said, grabbing his camera from the seat beside him. "I'm going up the hill."

"Watch yourself," Jenks cautioned. "Smythe's for sure up to no good, and Hunter's tangled up in it somehow."

He was speaking to the air. Grant was already halfway up the hill, his eyes scanning the horizon for signs of his quarry.

Hunter started violently at the touch on his arm. Smythe. Only Smythe. For a moment he'd thought . . . He wasn't sure what he'd thought.

He reached out and touched the soil, cold and clammy, almost as cold as his hand but not as cold as Joey, not as . . .

Again he felt a hand on his shoulder. He cleared his throat and tried to clear his mind.

"Smythe?" he asked hoarsely, turning his face toward the other. He cleared his throat again. "Smythe?"

The bearded man nodded.

Still preoccupied, Hunter rose to his feet and brushed ineffectually at his soiled knees. Smythe's shadow blackened Joey's grave. Hunter moved to the side. Smythe moved also. Hunter glanced at the grave. Pale sunlight warmed it again.

"Hunter!"

The word snapped Hunter's mind from its macabre thoughts, and he jerked toward the voice. The arrogant nobody was addressing him as Hunter! Fury seized him. He raised his head, an angry rebuke on his lips. The words died under Smythe's cold gaze.

Suddenly, Hunter was afraid.

Grant slowed as he reached the hilltop. He moved behind a tree and peered around it. A figure was revealed, dark against the opposite hillside.

But only one figure! For a breath-stopping moment, Grant thought he'd misunderstood Jenks and come to the wrong place. Then the second man stood from the grave where he'd been kneeling. Grant's breathing steadied. He hunched down and moved cautiously forward, using monuments and tall stones, trees, even shrubs to shield him from view.

Another minute of cautious, purposeful advance and he was as close as he dared. He crouched behind a sword-brandishing, spread-winged angel, warily leaned out, and felt a moment of grim satisfaction. Jonathan Hunter and John Smythe—together.

Hunter's pulse slowly stabilized, and he chided himself for succumbing to Smythe's queer menace. The man was his employee, after all! He watched Smythe closely, trying to understand the peculiar feeling he had. He'd never met Smythe, but the man seemed eerily familiar. The reason escaped him. "You said we needed to talk?" he asked. In spite of his resolve, his tone was uncharacteristically tentative.

Smythe chuckled. Hunter felt another stab of unreasoning fear. "Talk?" Smythe asked. "Did I say talk? Actually, what I have in mind is for you to listen."

The voice, Hunter thought, something about the voice. "Edmund Miller!" he blurted. "You're Edmund Miller. But I thought . . ." He stopped abruptly, realizing he was losing control. "I don't understand," he resumed peremptorily, desperately grasping for some means, any means to regain ascendancy. "This silly masquerade. You don't need to play games with me. I've thought only of you. You know that, Miller. Be a team player, and you'll find yourself handsomely rewarded."

Again, Miller chuckled. "You poor, dumb, arrogant fool."

Hunter stared at him in slack-mouthed shock. No one spoke to him like that. No one! He started to turn, to leave.

Miller grabbed his arm. "I wouldn't if I were you." The cutting edge in his voice, the steel in his grip, sent a fresh paroxysm of fear surging through Hunter. "I said listen, and that's what I expect."

Hunter's eyes widened at the gun that had materialized in Miller's gloved hand, a government model semiautomatic Colt .45. Was that a silencer on the end? Hunter wondered. He darted a glance in the direction of the unseen security detail.

427

Joey was forgotten. Grant was forgotten. Even the Oval Office was forgotten.

The gun stood between them like a tense exclamation mark. Hunter jerked his eyes from it when Miller began speaking.

From his sanctuary behind the winged angel, Grant witnessed the confrontation between Hunter and Smythe.

What was going on? he wondered, chafing at his impotence to learn. To be so close and still to know nothing! He could hear no more than meaningless snatches of words carried by the wind.

Miller's back was to him. Miller's raincoat flapped distractingly, obscuring much of Hunter's body, but Grant could see the attorney general's face. The normally arrogant Jonathan Hunter looked frightened— tense, powerless, and frightened. Why?

Grant scanned the area again for a closer vantage point, found none, and instead raised the camera and began snapping pictures. If only Miller would turn so he could get one of his face and beard. Gayla Sergek and the youngster at the fast-food place might be able to identify him.

You planned to throw me to the wolves," Miller said. His tone was conversational, making a parody of the gun held rock steady in his hand.

"Throw you to the wolves?" Hunter repeated with a nervous laugh. His eyes darted from tombstone to tombstone, as if searching for a spiritual solution to what was an obscenely unspiritual problem. "No, that was never our intention," he said, trying to smile. His mouth trembled instead into a ghastly rictus of fright.

Miller's eyes never left his. They never blinked.

Hunter licked his lips and resumed doggedly. "The President told me again just last evening how impressed he's been with your work. We were hoping to find a way to convince you to stay."

Miller continued to regard him, no expression on his face or in his eyes. "You picked the wrong man this time," he finally said. Then he chuckled.

Hunter's body shrunk upon itself at the hideous sound. For one awful moment, he thought he was going to lose control of his bladder. He was beyond speech. Miller would get his wish: He would listen.

"Maybe I should reintroduce myself," Miller said, cocking his head as if in thought. "John Smythe, at your service."

The chuckle poured over and became an amused laugh as Hunter's face blanched and his legs buckled, his knees sinking into his son's grave.

Miller really was John Smythe, Hunter thought in some reflexive corner of his numbed mind, a direct link to the White House.

"I see you're surprised," Miller continued. "Does the name Bonfire mean anything to you?"

Hunter, his hands folded on the earth in front of him as if in supplication, merely stared at him.

"Ah, well," Miller sighed. He seemed genuinely disappointed at Hunter's ignorance. The gun, however, didn't waver. "I wanted you to know the truth," he continued, ignoring Hunter's pleading eyes and the fingers which had begun a rhythmic clawing of the earth beneath them. "I wanted someone to appreciate the scope of my achievements. I took care of Anne Peabody and Russell Frederickson, just as you commissioned. I even included Cora Snyder free of charge," he added with a feral grin. "But enough." He raised the gun slightly.

Hunter's eyes widened, and a spittle of saliva began a slow slide out of the corner of his mouth and down his slack chin.

"You've made a great show of avenging your son against Bob Grant, who, by the way, had no part in his death." His tone remained conversational but became amused as well at the flicker of disbelief on the other's face.

"The only thing you've been right about is that Grant *is* a threat to you and your puppet President. I'm carrying out your orders," he added with another chuckle. "I'm destroying the good Senator. The catch is I'm destroying you as well."

Though Miller remained turned stubbornly away from him, Grant saw Hunter, his face drained of color, fall to his knees on his son's grave.

Grant captured the image with his camera.

Patience, he cautioned himself. The pictures he'd taken proved nothing, nothing at all. Without proof that Miller was John Smythe and that the administration had hired him to kill Peabody and Frederickson, he had nothing.

429

The ground was cold, so cold under Jonathan Hunter's knees, but not as cold as the evil he recognized in Edmund Miller's eyes, an evil he realized he shared. With more astonishment than fear, Hunter felt the searing entry of the bullet.

Slowly, his body crumpled until his arms embraced the newly turned soil. He was home. Joey . . .

Even before Hunter's body recognized death, Miller lowered the gun. With practiced skill he removed the silencer and stuck it deep into his coat pocket. After a sweeping glance to be sure he was still unobserved, he took a torn corner of paper from an inside pocket and stuck it in Hunter's unresponsive hand. At the same time, he picked up a few grains of dirt.

Then he began loping across the grass, skirting tombstones as he ran. About three hundred yards from the body, he tossed the gun into some shrubs. One hundred yards farther on, near the car, he tossed the towel away as well.

Little more than three minutes after his most recent murder, he was in Grant's car. As he drove through the cemetery gates and into the suburbs of D.C., he dropped the bit of grave dirt on the car's floor pad.

Through the lens of his camera, Grant watched as Jonathan Hunter slowly slumped onto the raw earth. He watched as Miller bent toward him, paused, then turned and began running down the hill. Grant snapped pictures of it all. Only in the last was Miller, beard fully revealed, facing the camera.

Still, Hunter didn't move.

His mouth suddenly dry, Grant rose to his feet and watched Miller's retreating back. Then he ran to the attorney general. Hunter's cheek was pressed into the soil. His eyes stared sightlessly at his son's grave marker. With trembling fingers, Grant felt for a pulse. Hunter was dead! Then Grant saw the small red circle in the center of Hunter's forehead, now partially hidden by a lock of hair, and understood. Miller's back had been to him, but Miller must have had a gun.

Grant glanced in the direction he knew hid Hunter's agents, wanting to call for help. He couldn't. They didn't know Miller had been there.

Grant turned. His only hope lay in following Miller. Even so, he hesitated. A torn piece of paper was partially visible under Hunter's hand. The image of Miller bent over the body flashed through Grant's mind.

Painfully aware that every second took John Smythe farther from him, he reached down and tugged gently on the paper.

"*...nd unless I hear from yo...*"

His own handwriting! He *was* being framed for Hunter's murder!

Infused with anger, he stuck the paper in his pocket and raced after Miller. The gun! Maybe it was the same one used to murder Russell Frederickson. Maybe Miller had dropped it as he ran. Even as the thought formed, Grant knew. With sickening insight, he knew. His gun! Miller had stolen his gun as well as his car. Grant looked around frantically, knowing the gun was his, knowing it held his fingerprints, knowing Miller had left it for the police.

He heard a car engine start. Miller! With a final futile look for the gun he knew must be there, Grant raced toward his own car.

Miller was out of sight by the time Grant pulled from the curb.

The car phone rang. Jenks and Bailey both lunged toward it.

Jenks grabbed it.

"Hunter's dead," Grant said. "Miller shot him. I'm in the car, trying to catch up with him now."

"We'll be right behind you," Jenks said. He turned to Bailey. "Back entrance and step on it. Hunter's dead."

Only a momentary increase of speed gave indication of Bailey's shock.

"I'm afraid my car isn't the only complication," Grant said. "I'm afraid my gun is somewhere near Joey's grave."

His gun, Jenks thought, squeezing his eyes shut as the possibility became certainty. Of course, Miller would use Grant's gun.

"We're probably about a mile behind you," Jenks said. "I reckon I'd better call 911."

Grant was silent. "The NIIA will be everywhere," he finally said.

"Reckon so, but I still got to do it."

"I know," Grant said. His voice faded in and out. "I'm calling Yao." The phone went dead.

As soon as he was well away from the cemetery, Miller relaxed against the car seat. Jonathan Hunter was dead, and Bob Grant would be convicted of that murder. It couldn't have gone more smoothly.

Miller's route took him away from the city, away from the Cabin John Bridge, I–270, and the Beltway, where roadblocks would undoubtedly be put in place first. Soon he was twisting down back roads, gradually making his way toward Dulles Airport, his ultimate goal.

He glanced in his rearview mirror. The same car had been behind him for several miles, he realized, far behind but closing fast. Probably coincidence since this road led to the bridge over the Potomac and into Virginia, but . . .

He turned right at the next side road, then studied his mirror intently. The car came into view.

Had someone witnessed the shooting at the cemetery? Was that someone now following him? Miller pressed the gas pedal to the floor and made two more random turns, always careful to stay somewhat on track to the airport. The other car dropped back but continued to follow.

Must not be the police, Miller decided. No other cars had joined the chase.

If he couldn't lose him, he would eliminate him. First, however, he'd better get into rural Virginia, where back roads would be virtually deserted and roadblocks would be unlikely. The most vulnerable spot would be crossing the Potomac on Route 15. He had to get across before they closed it.

One thing was certain: He was going to leave this car as planned at the airport and board his flight on schedule.

Attorney General Hunter's NIIA agents heard the wail of sirens entering the cemetery. For a moment they stared at each other. Then one agent broke away and ran up the rise over which Jonathan Hunter had disappeared. Others followed, their guns drawn and their trench coats flapping around their legs.

The lead agent spotted Hunter's crumpled body and, without breaking stride, yelled for medical help.

He reached Hunter, found no pulse, saw the thin line of blood and then the bullet hole.

"Call for backup! The attorney general's been shot! He's dead."

Within minutes the cemetery was sealed, the White House was informed, and the NIIA had mobilized all their units, enlisting those of the D.C. police as well. Road blocks were set up in all surrounding areas. The Cabin John Bridge, I–270, and the Beltway were among the first in place.

Miller is somewhere ahead of me," Grant told Jenks over the phone, silently praying that was true. Miller had vanished somewhere between the last turn and the undulating hills beyond it. "We've just crossed the Potomac and are heading south on Route 15. I'm guessing he's making for Dulles Airport."

A straight shot of road stretched ahead. Grant floored the gas pedal. Leafless trees flew by, the grazing cattle under them chewing their cuds in total disregard for the racing car and the patches of gravel staccatoing like machine-gun fire from under its tires. Time was running out, and the road ahead remained stubbornly empty. Hoping he'd guessed right about Dulles, Grant barely slowed at the next crossroad, instead jerking the wheel to the right and screeching into the turn.

"Gotcha!" he shouted a moment later as Miller materialized about half a mile ahead. The hard knot in Grant's stomach eased. Immediately, he tapped the brake. Miller mustn't realize he was being followed.

Too late! Miller's car spurted ahead and disappeared over a hill. Grant wedged the phone between the seats and grasped the steering wheel solidly in both hands. He, too, flew over the hill, airborne at the crest.

"Can you hear me?" he yelled, never taking his eyes from the speeding car, once again visible ahead.

He heard a weak "Yes" from Jenks.

Grant yelled the turns as he made them.

Bailey followed his directions, turning off Route 15 onto a series of semipaved country roads.

What is it now, Corforth?" the President demanded irritably when his chief of staff walked into the Oval Office unannounced. "You know we can't begin our briefing until Hunt's here."

Corforth shifted his feet uncomfortably. "This is about Jonathan."

The President looked up sharply at the odd note in Corforth's voice. At the sight of the pallor of his sunken cheeks, he felt a frisson of fear.

Corforth waited for permission to speak, then realized it wouldn't be forthcoming. "Sir, the news isn't good," he began, the words dropping slowly from stiff lips. "Jonathan was shot while visiting Joey's grave."

All color drained from the President's face.

"He's dead," Corforth finished none too gently.

Deep grooves etched their way around the President's mouth. Slowly, his head dropped in despair to the desk.

The phone, the direct line, rang. He made no sign of having heard. Corforth reached down and answered. He listened, then spoke.

"All NIIA activities will be handled directly through me. I want to be apprised of everything, developments, potential problems, everything."

He listened again.

"Get however many men you need," he said, "and comb that cemetery. Question everyone within a mile of it and as many as possible farther out."

Several minutes later, he replaced the receiver.

Still the President didn't move.

Corforth called Amy, then he called Estelle. Rebecca Hunter would have to be told.

Miller checked his rearview mirror. The car was still there, behind but narrowing the gap. He pounded the steering wheel angrily, cursing Grant and his old car. The BMW would have left everyone in the dust, but if he were driving the BMW, he reminded himself, Grant's car couldn't be abandoned at the airport, the fatal bits of dirt awaiting detection.

He reached toward the passenger's seat, lifted the jacket resting on it, and removed his gun from the pocket. The next corner would have to do, he thought. He would shoot the fool following him before he or anyone else realized what was happening. Not that he expected witnesses. This was as lonely a country road as he could have hoped for. Too bad there was no time to stage an accident. Accidents raised fewer questions, but he would be cutting it close to make it to the airport as it was.

This time when he glanced into the mirror, the face of his pursuer was caught in full relief. Miller, seldom nonplussed, was now. The driver was Bob Grant!

Slowly, Miller replaced the gun on the seat beside him. He looked preoccupied. He had to lose Grant, he thought. Much as he wanted to kill him, he couldn't, not and have Grant labeled Hunter's murderer. With Grant an accused murderer, Caruso would become Senator. What a sweet puppet Caruso would make! He would do whatever it took to remain in power. And he understood who his friends were.

Again, Miller checked the mirror. Grant was falling behind, but not by much, certainly not enough for a clean getaway. When they neared the airport, Miller thought, he would lose himself in traffic. He'd certainly done it often enough in the past.

Grant! Miller slammed his palm on the steering wheel. First, Grant had sabotaged Cuba the year before, and now here he was again, threatening to wreck these plans.

At the next crossroad, Miller took the right-hand road in a screeching swerve. The driver of an oncoming car stood on his brakes and fishtailed out of control onto the soft verge. Miller skinned by, ignoring him.

Not this time, dear Senator, Miller thought, pushing the gas to the floor and urging the car forward. This time you're the one facing certain disaster.

He glanced at the dashboard clock. His plane would leave in half an hour.

Some premonition of danger caused him to look up. His breath caught spasmodically. A hairpin turn! Too fast! He was going too fast!

The steering wheel jerked in his hands. He pumped the brake. The car swerved into the turn, skidding on loose gravel. No berm, ditches on each side, he thought. Sweat broke out on his forehead as he twisted the wheel again, overcompensating. The car swayed, tilted, started to upright itself, then slid sideways on the gravel. He tried yet another turn of the wheel. The car responded violently. He hit the brakes harder, but gravel prevented the tires from catching.

Trees, fence, ditch, even the road combined in a blur of beyond-control speed. Out of the corner of his eye, Miller saw a blur of yellow join the others as a dog bounded from the underbrush at the side of the road. Its huge form and bellow of outrage distracted Miller for one second too long. His car ripped into the dog, tossing it effortlessly onto the hood and then off again onto the side of the road.

The car skewed from the edge of the culvert and became airborne.

Estelle stood outside the massive teakwood door to the Hunters' house and braced herself. She dreaded her mission. How could she tell Rebecca her entire family was now destroyed?

She raised her hand, paused to take a steadying breath, then knocked. No one answered. After a minute she knocked again. Still no response. The NIIA agents guarding the house assured her that Mrs. Hunter was inside. She refused to allow them in, but she *was* there.

Estelle tried the handle. The door was locked.

Suddenly, the lock clicked, and the door slowly eased open. Rebecca, her hair sticking out like stiff cobwebs around her waxen pallor, stood in the barely open door, her glassy eyes blinking at the sunlight. After a pause, she wearily gestured Estelle inside. Estelle motioned the agents back, edged past Rebecca, and closed the door.

Still silent, Rebecca led her into the living room. The windows were shrouded with heavy brocade drapes. The lights were off. Estelle shivered in the gray gloom. The other woman stopped abruptly and turned toward her. Her face wore the imprint of abandoned hope.

"Oh, Rebecca," Estelle moaned, all her rehearsed words forgotten. She threw her arms around her friend, not sure which of them needed comforting more.

Gently, Rebecca pushed her away and went over to face the draped front window. "He's dead, I know," she said in a low voice. "Jonathan's dead."

Estelle couldn't respond. She could do no more than stare at Rebecca's back.

"I knew something was wrong when he left this morning, and when the agents descended on the house, demanding to search it . . ." She turned slowly. "Poor, sad Jonathan. He lost his way a long time ago. He loved power. He loved it more than life, certainly more than he ever loved me, more than he loved Joey even."

"Rebecca," Estelle said, the name burnished with pain, "what can I say? What can I do for you?"

"Do?" Rebecca asked with a ravaged smile. "Nothing. You've done more than I deserve just coming here. We both know Jonathan corrupted your husband along with himself."

"No!" The word exploded from Estelle. "No, Rebecca, no," she said more calmly. "Jonathan did nothing of the sort. My husband knew exactly what he was doing, knew and still delighted in doing it." Her eyes pleading for understanding, she gripped Rebecca's arm. "He would have found someone else if Jonathan hadn't been there."

Rebecca gave her words careful consideration. "Maybe," she said finally, "but I think you underestimate Jonathan's skills. He was a master manipulator, he once told me. Quite proud of it. Poor Jonathan. He was never truly happy, you know. He thought power would bring him happiness, and then when he had more power than any man should, he found he was just as empty as before. But he's with Joey now. The search has ended for them both. I hope they found whatever . . . whatever . . ."

Like a ribbon of sand slipping through an hourglass, Rebecca Hunter slowly sagged to the floor.

As sweat dripped down his back and attached his suddenly sodden shirt to his jacket, Grant watched Miller's car swerve, right itself, then take the corner on two wheels. His eyes widened in horror as, at the last possible moment, a huge dog bounded from the underbrush directly in front of Miller's car. In a spew of gravel, fur, and blood, the car disappeared around the curve.

Grant gripped the steering wheel of his own car, as tight as he'd gripped the wheel of his reconnaissance boat on the perilous waterways of Vietnam. His heart pounded just as thunderously now as then. He let up on the gas, tapped his brakes, and slid into the curve.

In front of him, painfully vivid in the streaming colors of excessive speed, he saw Miller's car, airborne and on target for a huge oak tree, as immovable as one hundred years could make it. For several heart-stopping seconds, the car hung suspended midair, between safety and inevitable destruction, its undercarriage caught in brilliant relief by the sun.

"No!" Grant screamed, slamming on his brakes and yanking the steering wheel hard to the left.

Even as the command left his lips, the shriek of metal tangling with wood ripped the still sky.

Grant fought the wheel of his own skidding car, praying for rubber to grip road. Feeling traction, he pumped the brakes. The rear end swung out, but the car steadied and finally slammed to a rocking stop. Wrenching open the door, Grant jumped out and raced back toward the mangled remains, fifty feet behind him.

Steam hissed, and still bending metal screeched its protest. Jenks's and Bailey's car, tires wailing, skidded into the turn. Grant ignored it all, focused only on reaching Miller. Miller alone knew all the answers. Miller alone could exonerate Grant and his son.

The crumpled front of the car, a Picassoesque accordion in metal, embraced the tree a foot above the ground. The front wheels eerily hummed their continuing rotation, mocking the car and the man who had presumed to tame it.

A shiver of dread thrummed down Grant's spine as the smell of gasoline became stronger. The car was going to explode! He had to get Miller out!

Using the fender to steady himself on the rutted ground, he skirted the car and ran to the driver's side. His stomach heaved. Miller, so evil in life, was in death nothing more than a bloody pulp smashed against the steering wheel. Surely not dead, Grant prayed.

He grabbed the door handle, struggling to wrench open the door. The tree again had conspired against him. The door was wedged shut. Grant tore off his jacket, wrapped his hand in it and completed the smashing of the window that the crash had begun. Sticking his hand through the shattered glass, he felt Miller's bloody neck for a pulse. There was none.

Behind Grant, car doors slammed. "Dad!" Bailey shouted.

Grant looked up and waved them back. "He's dead. The car's going to explode!"

Jenks ignored him, loping toward the rear of the car. "Bailey," he yelled as he ran, "see if anything flew out of the car."

Bailey moved away, scanning the area.

Leaning over Miller's body, Grant grabbed the jacket wadded beside it. A gun was under it! He leaned in farther. A shard of window glass pierced his clothes and jabbed into his belly, sending the warm stickiness of blood down his body. He felt neither the pain nor the blood.

The smell of gas inflamed his nostrils and choked his throat. He stepped back from the car, Miller's jacket and gun tightly clasped in his hand. He looked for the others. Bailey was near the road, but Jenks— Grant's heart stopped—Jenks was leaning into the trunk!

"We've got to get out of here!" Grant yelled. "It's about to blow!" He twisted and dove into the culvert that edged the road.

Jenks, his pulse beating its own urgency, yanked out Miller's briefcase, turned, and ran. He'd only taken two long strides before the car exploded, throwing him through the air and flinging him pitilessly to the ground.

Grant scrambled to his feet, slipping in the wet, dead weeds lining the ditch. "Stay back!" he yelled at Bailey as half stumbling, he reached Jenks, unmoving on the ground. Sweat rolling down his face, his eyes dry from the searing heat, Grant grabbed Jenks's arms and dragged him away. Flames licked at them, singeing their clothes.

Grant slapped out a greedy flame on Jenks's pant leg, then loosed Jenks's collar. The sheriff opened his eyes and managed a weak smile. "I can feel I'm alive," he wheezed, a hand straying to his ribs, "but the briefcase. Is it okay?"

"Still clutched in your hand." Grant felt Jenks's pulse. It was rapid but not alarmingly so. Thank God.

He looked toward the burning wreckage, his eyes bleak as he recognized Miller's head, dark in the midst of the inferno.

Jenks tried to sit up, groaned, but managed it.

"Get the car ready!" Grant yelled to Bailey.

Jenks staggered to his feet, the briefcase still in his hand. "Time to go," he said, breathless with pain and shock.

"You're sure you should move?" Grant asked, putting Jenks's arm over his shoulder.

"What I'm sure of," Jenks said slowly, leaning heavily on Grant, "is I'm not staying here." He seemed to gain strength the closer they got to the car. "I don't trust anyone near this town, and I sure don't want to spend time with the NIIA."

Bailey had already started the car. He leaned over and pushed open the passenger door.

Stifling a groan, Jenks hauled himself into the front seat. "Now, you get on back in your car," he told Grant. "Bailey and I'll do just fine. We'll meet you at the cabin."

Not waiting to argue, Grant ran to his car.

Behind them, Edmund Miller's funeral pyre continued pricking the sky with golden flames and dusky plumes of smoke.

Corforth walked into the Oval Office, hoping to find the President ready to take charge.

"What am I going to do without Hunt?" POTUS asked, leaning beseechingly toward Corforth. "What am I going to do?" When Corforth didn't respond, his face became thoughtful, almost calculating, a Jonathan Hunter look. "Maybe John Smythe can help. Yes, that's it. Call John Smythe, Eugene. He'll handle everything."

"I don't know who you mean," Corforth reminded him.

"Don't know . . ." His voice trailed off.

Corforth could see the fight going on in his mind as he tried to regain his focus. Hunter's death had proven an almost crushing blow, possibly one stress too many.

"They've found the gun that killed Jonathan," Corforth told him, working to jolt him into decisive action. "A government model Colt .45."

The President looked up. "They've found the gun," he repeated. His face took on some color as the meaning sunk in. "Have they traced it?"

"It's registered in D.C. to Robert Hawkins Grant." Even as he said the name, Corforth felt a tremor of disbelief. Nothing made sense anymore, especially his own reluctance to believe what was obviously true. Bob Grant was a murderer, several times a murderer.

"Bob Grant," the President whispered. "He murdered Hunt."

From that moment on, the NIIA investigation into the murder of Jonathan Hunter was under the control of the President. He was driven by a single obsession, to find Bob Grant and bring him in, preferably dead.

Corforth manned the private line, relaying messages.

"A car was seen in the cemetery around the time of the murder," he told the President. "A cemetery employee noticed it."

"A good description?"

"Even better. A license number. They're running it now."

"Good. Good."

Again, the phone rang.

"They traced the car," Corforth said. This time he was the one who walked over to look out the window. He spoke without turning. "It belongs to Bob Grant."

The President looked at Corforth's slumped shoulders. Slowly, his own back straightened. "Bob Grant!" He spat the name. "Send out an APB for him: armed and dangerous, shoot on sight. For his murdering son, too. Then set up a press conference. Five minutes."

Corforth left the room. The APBs were already in effect. The press conference was easily arranged.

The investigation into the assassination of the attorney general was being covered live on all networks. Seated behind his desk in the Oval Office, the President gave an impassioned plea in which he asked every American to help apprehend the villain who'd so brutally murdered the finest man ever to sacrifice his life for his country. At his urging, millions of Americans joined the Grant manhunt. All knew Grant was armed and dangerous. All knew to shoot on sight.

The sky was overcast and the air chilling, but Sherrill, huddled in a down coat, sat outside on the steps of the cabin. She had stayed inside after first Bailey and Jenks and then Senator Grant had left early that morning. She needed to be near the phone, but as the minutes extended to an hour, she had found herself outside gazing toward the end of the driveway more often than she had been inside. Finally, she'd gone outside to stay, leaving the door open for the ringing of the phone.

At the first sound of tires crunching on the gravel at the top of the drive, she jumped to her feet and raced down the steps. She was beside the car before it came to a stop.

"Bailey?" she asked in a whisper when Grant got out. Her eyes widened with dread as she took in Grant's bloody hands and singed clothes. The streak of dried blood running down the front of his jacket taunted her with its message of mortality.

Seeing the anxiety draining her face, Grant gave her shoulder a reassuring squeeze. "Bailey's fine," he told her. "He and the sheriff should be here soon."

"But what happened?" she asked, touching his bloodied hand gently.

Grant thought of his vigil at the cemetery, of the harrowing race away from it, of the two dead men, of his wrecked car, of Jenks's injury and the unopened briefcase. Ignoring her question, he steered her toward the house. "We need to pack things and be ready to leave shortly. Put the evidence, anything we might need this afternoon, in a separate box."

As she began working, he went into the bathroom, tore off his clothes, and cleansed his wounds. The scratches on his hands were superficial, but the gash on his stomach gaped, its edges jagged and raw but mercifully no longer bleeding. Gritting his teeth, he soaked it with peroxide. He found some tape in the medicine cabinet, formed several butterfly bandages, and used them to close the wound.

In less than five minutes and dressed in clean clothes, he joined Sherrill. She'd scattered boxes around the room. Some were now full. Grant began helping her. She turned to him several times to ask more but hesitated to break into his preoccupation.

The minutes mounted, and still no one arrived. Every glance by Grant at his watch heightened Sherrill's alarm. When car tires finally crunched on the gravel, she stood motionless, paralyzed by fear.

Grant moved to the front window and cracked the curtains. Bailey and Jenks! He threw open the door, then contented himself to wait on the porch while Sherrill raced down the steps and into Bailey's arms. Grant watched with amusement as his son's face changed from surprise to dawning enlightenment. Bailey bent his head to kiss her, and Grant turned back into the house behind Jenks.

"What happened?" Grant asked. His eyes went to the battered briefcase Jenks still held. It was similar to millions of others, but this one, resting just inches from him, could contain proof of his innocence and of the innocence of his son. Or it could hold nothing of value, he reminded himself, reminding himself also that Bonfire was still out there somewhere, waiting and watching and ever dangerous.

"We took a long way back," Jenks told him. "Figured one car at a time would be less obvious."

Before Grant could comment, the door flew open, and Stephen Yao hurried in. Bailey and Sherrill followed him.

"You've got to get out of here while you still can," Yao said. "And that means pronto. They have an APB—armed and dangerous, shoot on sight—out for you, Bob. You, too, Bailey."

"Ramon?" Grant asked. The room became still.

Yao managed a tired smile. "Over the worst. He should pull through."

"Thank God," Grant whispered, the lines in his face easing.

"Gather up what you need," Yao said, moving over to take the composites off the wall, "but get a move on it. We're meeting Goldie in forty-five minutes, and he figures he's only got a five minute window for touchdown before air traffic control gets suspicious."

They finished the work Grant and Sherrill had started, methodically piling papers into boxes. Bailey unplugged and closed his computer. Only Jenks didn't help. He sat, Miller's briefcase in his lap. Grant eyed him thoughtfully, knowing the sheriff would suffer almost any indignity before he would admit to being injured. Grant started toward him.

Again, a car sounded on the drive, its tires loud in the gravel. Everyone inside the house froze. Bailey, closest to the door, turned and edged back the curtain.

"Uncle Curtis," he announced, throwing open the door. The tremor in his voice betrayed his relief.

In moments Curtis Grant bounded up the steps and walked in. A grin split his face at the sight of Grant. "Brother, am I glad to see you!" He clapped Grant on the back. "Talk about a manhunt!"

Grant looked from his brother Curtis to Bailey, whose arm was around Sherrill. He looked at Jenks, still seated, but bent forward now to rest against the table. He looked at Yao, whose body sagged with exhaustion. "From now on," Grant said, "I'm going it alone." He picked up the box containing the essential information and moved to take the briefcase from Jenks.

"Wrong, Bob," Yao said, stepping in front of him. "You wouldn't get a mile down the road. The place is crazy with cops and vigilantes. If you want to get away, you'll do as I say."

Grant eyed him. The set of Yao's jaw proclaimed his implacability. Tension mounted as the others recognized the sense of Yao's comments but also the qualities of character that motivated Grant.

Suddenly, Grant chuckled. The sound began as a low rumble deep in his throat. By the time it reached his eyes everyone in the room had relaxed. "Never could leave a fight half finished, could you?" Grant asked Yao with an affectionate squeeze of his arm. "I'm glad you're on my side. Thanks."

Yao commenced outlining his plan, beginning with their imminent departure from the cabin in two different vehicles by two different routes and ending in little more than three hours with Grant delivering his speech of vindication in one of CNN's Atlanta studios. It was the bits in between, he told them, that might cause some trouble.

The President had been studying the photograph of himself standing with Jonathan Hunter. Now he was staring out the window, seeing nothing but problems.

Corforth cleared his throat. "Sir," he said. POTUS ignored him. "Mr. President," Corforth said more imperatively, "we have to talk." Recognizing the stubborn set of the President's broad shoulders, he added, "Now, sir. Now."

Reluctantly, the President turned.

"Questions are being raised about Anne Peabody," Corforth told him. "Apparently, Peabody's lawyer is creating another stir, saying Frederickson called Peabody, Peabody called Jonathan, and now all three are dead. What should—"

"No problem," POTUS interrupted. "Miller has disappeared. Right?" Corforth nodded. "Hunt found out Miller was behind the Peabody deal. I'm not sure of the details, but Hunt was certain of Miller's involvement and confronted him with it last night."

"But where's the proof?"

"Proof? I don't know. Hunt had it." The President threw himself into his wing-backed chair by the fire. "You need to find it and give it to Evans right away."

"Maybe," Corforth said slowly, "but don't you think we ought to distance ourselves from this? Too many people have died. Too many questions are left unanswered."

"When Grant is dead," the President countered with grim deliberation, "we'll have all the answers anyone could want. Between Miller and Grant, we'll have more than enough answers."

He stared at Corforth until the other gave a reluctant nod of acquiescence. Senior staff was summoned, and the situation was explained. All were shocked at Miller's perfidy, but none questioned his involvement. Hunter's hand reached out from the grave, involving Edmund Miller in the cover-up just as planned.

Yao inched the truck forward, drawing ever closer to the line of police forming the roadblock. Grant could feel sweat forming on his forehead and wiped it away with his sleeve. Jenks, dirty and exhausted, was wedged in the jump seat.

"No one will notice your height with you stuck back there, Sheriff," Yao told him. "Just kind of lounge on the tool kit."

Jenks did as he was told. Seeing him bite his lower lip at the effort, Grant reached back to help. Jenks shook his head, then closed his eyes momentarily. He opened them and gave Grant a weak smile.

Grant started to speak, recognized the grit in the sheriff's eyes, and turned back to the front. Jenks was hurt, but he wouldn't take kindly to sympathy. Since Grant could offer nothing more at the moment, he might as well let Jenks have his way. Once they were safely away, like it or not, Jenks was getting medical treatment.

Yao glanced at Grant, dressed in a faded tan workshirt with "Bubba" embroidered above the pocket, wondering again why the Senator and Jenks had found the name so amusing. They all wore disguises. Grant's long-haired wig was pulled back in a pony tail. A fake gold hoop glittered from his earlobe, and a washable tattoo was on the back of one hand. Yao had worked a little magic—pads in his cheeks, discoloration of his teeth—that further altered Grant's appearance. He'd done the same for the others. "Might try leaving your lower lip open a little," Yao told him. "I won't ask you to drool."

Grant couldn't help laughing. Jenks started to join in, but the sound stopped abruptly.

Yao turned up the rap song on the radio. "Just some laborers on lunch break. Think happy."

"Think free," Grant said quietly.

Jenks said nothing. His eyes were closed.

Curtis Grant, driving a beat-up clunker with a powerful engine, was taking a different route to their rendezvous with Goldie. As they edged closer to the policemen waiting to check out both them and their vehicle, Curtis draped his arm around Sherrill. On the passenger side, Bailey, his hair spray-painted orange, couldn't help wishing he could change places, but Curtis needed to be the one doing the talking. No APB for murder was out for him.

Sherrill, in a miniskirt and provocatively unbuttoned blouse, was doing her best to attract all attention to herself.

"Well, here goes nothing," Curtis said as they neared the roadblock. He took a steadying breath. "And don't forget that pop," he reminded Bailey, who already had the can in his hand. He would take a drink when scrutiny seemed most intense. Curtis would do the same. They were counting on that, the distraction of Sherrill, and their borrowed IDs to get them safely through.

Just three no-accounts, not too bright and not at all ambitious, out bumming.

Bailey glanced at his watch. Twenty-five minutes to get to the plane, then an hour and a half to get to Georgia.

Sherrill gave his hand a squeeze, then began pawing and kissing Curtis. Her skirt hiked up even higher, and she gave Bailey an impish grin that quavered only slightly.

Rachel Grant watched the TV in frozen horror. An APB—shoot on sight order on Bob and Bailey both! How could this have happened?

She knew Bob wouldn't call until he gave the final signal, but, oh, how she wished she could hear his voice!

Jonathan Hunter was dead. Bob was accused of his murder. What did it all mean? And how did it affect their plans?

The phone rang. She answered it, listened for a minute, hung up, and let out a shuddering sigh.

The others in the room stood motionless, their eyes never leaving her face.

She raised her eyes and met theirs. "That was Bob. He and Bailey are all right. So far they're all safe."

The silence lasted for a second or two, then Henry let out a whoop of joy. The others began talking excitedly. Cynthia and Rachel exchanged looks, knowing the danger was far from over.

"We're to go ahead with the plan?" Cynthia asked.

Suddenly, the room was quiet, filled with a nervous expectancy.

"Yes, beginning now."

Cynthia left the room.

"The video will arrive on schedule," Rachel continued. "We'll have it the moment they land."

Someone said a relieved, "Right on."

"I'll alert Brandon." John Wright moved toward a phone. Brandon Bascham was waiting to make copies of the tape and take them to stations around Georgia. Goldie, assuming he was still free, would fly other copies north to New York and Washington.

No one in the media would receive a video tape until Bob began his press conference. The surprise had to be absolute.

Rachel didn't let herself think of the alternative, that the tapes would be delivered because Bob was unable to hold the press conference.

Shoot on sight. The words haunted her.

I don't like this," Corforth said, even before the door to the Oval Office closed behind him.

The President, who was staring sightlessly out the mullioned window, spoke without turning. "What is it this time?" His voice was listless. The anger against Grant which had sustained him thus far was being replaced by reality. Hunt wasn't there to direct the operation, and Corforth wasn't nearly as clever. No one was. And Corforth didn't know half of the problem! Who else knew? Only the Veep. The Veep! The President felt even more depressed.

"A news conference," Corforth said. POTUS still didn't turn. "To be held by Bob Grant."

This time the President's reaction was as passionate as Corforth could have wished. He spun around and with two angry strides was confronting him. "What do you mean Grant's holding a press conference? He's a fugitive. The entire country is searching for him. Where *is* this press conference? And when? He has to be stopped."

"No one's been told," Corforth said, playing with the worry beads in his pocket. He'd found himself doing so much less lately. Not since the news about Hunter, he realized, unsure what to read into that. "That's the devil of it. Short of jamming all our satellites, we can't stop him from being heard."

"But surely we have an idea of where he'll be, or at least when."

"Presumably he'll hold it soon. But where?" Corforth shrugged. "Grant's emissary—and we don't know who she was, just that she was using a pay phone in Atlanta—called stations in Washington, New York, LA, and Chicago. Maybe others. We can't be sure. She told them to spread the word, said she'd be calling different stations with the next instructions. Clever plan."

The President began pacing. "Grant has to be stopped." He made two more circuits of the room, then turned with slow deliberation to face Corforth. "He can't know anything about Peabody, can he?"

Corforth returned the look through unwavering eyes. "You'll remember that I was left out of those discussions," he said. "You tell me. Is there anything to know?"

The President's eyes fell. "I don't know," he said, barely above a whisper. He turned back to face the window. "I want Stevenson and the Vice President here. Now. We have to decide on a response and a plan of action. We have to be sure everyone understands Miller's part in all this."

After the phone call to Rachel, Yao drove Grant and Jenks to a side road near the abandoned airstrip where they were to rendezvous with Matt Goldie. He pulled the truck into a copse of trees which he hoped would conceal it for at least three or four hours. The rustling of leaves, scurrying of small woodland animals, and barking of a distant dog were the only sounds as the noise of the truck engine faded.

"Okay, Sheriff," Grant said, turning to Jenks, "enough heroics. What is it? Ribs?"

Jenks tried for a smile but found it difficult. "Could be," he said, slowly sitting upright. "No real damage I'd reckon, but a tad uncomfortable."

Grant leaned over the back seat and gently pulled up Jenks's shirt. No bleeding, no awkward bulges.

Yao handed Grant a long strip of sheeting. "Always keep some handy," he said matter-of-factly. "Tools of the trade."

Together, they strapped Jenks's chest tightly. Even as they worked they watched the road, Yao for trouble, Grant for Bailey and the others. Four minutes remained until Goldie would touch down. Only four minutes.

"Better," Jenks said when they finished.

"Any other problems you haven't thought to mention?" Grant asked.

"Nothing that won't keep." Jenks closed his eyes. He leaned against the seat but held his back straight. He looked better, not much, but better.

Grant hadn't been concerned that Bailey and the others weren't waiting when they arrived, but as the minutes ticked by he had trouble thinking of anything else.

"A description of one of the rental cars and a report of the burning car," Yao said, describing the news bulletin he'd just heard. The radio was turned down now, but loud enough that they could hear any further developments. "No mention that Miller was driving your car. That it *was* your car even." As he talked, Yao rummaged through a case he'd brought with him, then handed Jenks two small pills and a bottle of water.

Grant regarded Jenks thoughtfully. They'd already decided it would be safer to wait until they were inside the plane to open Miller's briefcase. No chance then of unwanted interruptions. No chance of losing something. Their plan was for the sheriff to accompany Grant to the Atlanta TV studio. His presence in his uniform would give Grant's accusations and supporting evidence the stamp of official approval. Looking at his friend, Grant wasn't so sure Jenks had any business going anywhere but to a doctor.

"None of it's any good if we can't get it into the right hands," Yao said, understanding just what Grant was thinking. He, too, was looking at Jenks and the briefcase. "In the right hands and in front of enough people so it can't be conveniently forgotten."

Where was Bailey? Grant wondered even as he listened to Yao. Goldie should be arriving at any moment, then only five minutes until they had to be airborne. Goldie's plane would have disappeared from radar just before he touched down, but five minutes should be too innocuous a blackout to cause air traffic control at nearby Washington Dulles Airport to contact the NIIA.

"I'm powerful upset to think ol' John Smythe might get his way," Jenks said softly but with steel lacing his words, "even with him being dead. And Bonfire's got to be stopped." He shifted uncomfortably. "There's got to be some way to put a stop to that devil. By the way," he said laconically, looking around, "if Goldie doesn't touch down soon, we're sitting ducks out here."

"I know," Grant said. "There's no doubt we need a video in case I'm not around to tell the story myself."

"Goldie will have everything on board and ready to go," Yao assured him. Yao was beginning to get edgy himself. Bailey and the others should have arrived by now.

They heard a plane engine, the sound gradually obscuring the quiet. Grant looked at the nearby abandoned airstrip. Grass grew up through a multitude of cracks. There hadn't been time to check it to be sure it was safe for landing. He just hoped Goldie wasn't being overly optimistic, knowing they had no other option.

It was too late now for second thoughts. The plane loomed overhead. Its wheels skimmed, then hit the pavement, bounced up, hit, bounced. The three men watched tensely. Even Jenks was upright, his ribs forgotten.

The plane hit what must have been an especially uneven spot, for it slewed suddenly sideways. Grant gathered in a wavering lungful of air, imagining Goldie fighting for control. "'Yea, though I walk through the valley of the shadow of death, I will fear no evil,'" he whispered, his eyes fastened on the plane.

Finally under control, it slowed and came to a jolting stop. Its wheels were barely on what was left of the tarmac.

"Brother!" Yao said reverently.

The three men left the truck and hurried toward the plane, Yao helping Jenks, Grant carrying the box of evidence, the briefcase, and Yao's case with its precious pills, precious certainly to Jenks, who was already looking better.

Still, no car arrived.

Goldie was waiting at the top of the plane's steps. "Glad to see you guys," he said, giving them a lopsided grin. His eyes radiated satisfaction.

Behind him, Grant could see Ginger Wright. Judging by her glazed expression, he felt sure she would look green if her skin weren't so dark. He walked over and gave her shoulder a squeeze. "See Matt's been treating you to his special brand of flying."

She shook her head but managed a slight smile. Ginger was a photographer. She was on board to film Grant's video. Normally, she did video productions of weddings. Today, her filming wasn't once in a lifetime. It was life and death.

"Where are Bailey and the others?" Goldie asked. "We've only got four minutes by my estimate."

Grant's worry came flooding back. "We don't know," he said, walking to the still-open door and looking out. He stayed back in the shadows, however. "They left right before we did but went another way."

By now Jenks had lowered himself into a seat and stretched his legs out in front. "I wouldn't fret none if I was you," he said, closing his eyes for a moment as he eased his back. "That boy of yours will be just fine. Mark my word. He's like his ol' man, stubborn as all get-out. A survivor for sure."

No one else spoke. Three minutes.

Yao conferred with Goldie about arrangements for their arrival. Everything was under control, Grant heard them say, but all he could think about was Bailey—Bailey, who was wanted for murder, too.

Grant heard Goldie's footsteps as he walked to the front of the plane. He heard the creak of the seat as Goldie lowered himself into it. He heard the snap of the seat belt and the checking of instruments.

One minute.

Yao came over and put his hand on Grant's shoulder. "Better buckle up, Bob," he said. "They know where to go if they miss us."

Grant nodded and went to a seat. Ginger touched his hand reassuringly. Grant checked his watch. Time to go.

Still, Goldie didn't start the plane.

Another minute passed. This time the engines did start. Yao pulled the steps up, latched the door, and got into his seat. Goldie turned the plane and poised it at the end of the runway, ready for takeoff.

"Wait!" Ginger yelled. "Here they come!"

Both Grant and Yao were out of their seats and on her side of the plane before she finished speaking. Curtis, Sherrill, and Bailey were running out of the woods that lined the west side of the airstrip. They raced across the cracked tarmac and had barely clambered inside before the door was closed and the plane was under way.

"Hurry," Bailey gasped, buckling his seat belt. "They're right behind us." Goldie heard and revved the engines.

They all grabbed the arms of their seats as the plane bumped its way down the runway. Both Ginger and Jenks had their eyes closed. Grant wondered in some odd corner of his mind if the next few seconds wouldn't be the most dangerous he'd faced all week.

"There they are!" Bailey yelled, pointing out the window.

A pack of men led by several uniformed sheriff's deputies ran out of the woods and toward the runway. Several carried shotguns. One man, his coat barely meeting over his bulging belly, stopped and raised his 12-gauge. Grant saw a spurt of orange followed by a cloud of smoke.

"Get her off the ground, Goldie!" Grant yelled toward the cabin. "Company at nine o'clock!"

Goldie goosed the throttle. The bouncing increased to a teeth-jarring intensity.

Every shotgun, semiautomatic, and rifle was now aimed at the plane.

"They're shooting at us!" Sherrill screamed. She pressed her head against the seat as if hoping to become invisible.

This time when the plane bounced, it took a slight hitch toward the left. The end of the tarmac loomed ever closer.

"Can you get enough speed to get this thing airborne?" Yao yelled.

Goldie, his hands grappling the stick, his teeth biting into his lower lip, said nothing.

Grant saw a deputy lower his rifle slightly and take aim. The tires! At that moment the plane lifted off and soared toward the clouds. Goldie let loose a yell of triumph. At the sound, Ginger opened her eyes and looked out the window. With a shaking hand, she pulled a lacy handkerchief from her pocket and wiped her forehead.

Grant unbuckled his seat belt, walked to the front, and clapped Goldie on the shoulder. "Extraordinary flying, Matt," he said, raising his voice to be heard. "Any damage?"

"Too soon to know for sure, but everything seems fine." Goldie's eyes never left the gauges. "You'll be one of the first to know," he added with his irrepressible humor.

Even before Goldie reached a protective layer of clouds where he could change direction undetected, Grant opened Smythe's briefcase. Even now, knowing what he did, Smythe seemed more real—and more sinister—than Edmund Miller.

Jenks looked over. "See those initials?" He pointed to worn gold letters under the handle. "That's Frederickson's briefcase, just like ol' Evans described it."

"So it is!" Grant exclaimed, lowering the lid and touching the letters. "The arrogance of Smythe! He sure didn't expect to be caught, did he?"

Everyone gathered around as Grant once again lifted the briefcase lid and began examining the contents.

Despite its frantic beginning, the flight was uneventful but barely long enough for all that had to be done.

Brandon Bascham but not the NIIA was waiting when they landed at the private airstrip. Too many airports and airstrips to cover? Grant wondered. Regardless, he and his allies wasted no time. The precious video tape they'd made on board was sent with Ginger and Bailey for a massive copying effort. Goldie took the one duplicate they'd been able to make on the plane. He would make his own copies before delivering them to as many cities as possible on the eastern seaboard.

Watches were synchronized. Rendezvous were coordinated. Everyone left.

Yao drove Grant and Jenks into downtown Atlanta without incident. Jenks had refused to remain behind.

They made it into the CNN skyscraper without being recognized. Bascham's forged requisition form along with their elevator maintenance uniforms did the trick. Now all they had to do was stay out of sight until time to go to the studio. Yao had a solution for that, too. He took an "ELEVATOR UNDER REPAIR" sign from his toolbox, hung it by the elevator door, motioned them aboard, and stopped the elevator between floors.

"Safe enough?" he asked with a grin. He took Frederickson's briefcase out of the canvas satchel Bascham had prepared for him and handed it to Grant. Reaching into the satchel again, he brought out a bag of clothes. These, too, he gave to Grant. For Jenks he had a sherrif's uniform. Then he slid to the floor. "Let me know if you need anything," he said. He closed his eyes.

Grant looked at his watch. "Ten minutes."

"Yep," Jenks agreed, carefully easing his arms out of the elevator maintenance shirt. He looked at the pants to his sheriff's uniform and decided he wasn't up to fooling with them. The ones he had on would have to do. Wouldn't be much cause to film him below the waist anyway, he reckoned.

"I'll get you into the broadcast room," Yao said without opening his eyes. "The feed is set so you can be on any networks worldwide that choose to access it, but you're the ones who have to make your case. You've all but been hung, Bob. You'd better make it good." He opened his eyes and looked directly at Grant. "Remember, I can't guarantee you'll have much uninterrupted time."

Grant nodded and finished buttoning his shirt.

Where are Stevenson and the Veep?" the President demanded.

As he had the previous three times he'd been asked, Corforth replied that he didn't know. They'd received the summons; that was all he could say for sure.

This time, instead of acting as if his summonses were routinely ignored, the President stopped his pacing and faced Corforth. "Grant's still free? No word he's been captured? No news on this supposed press conference?"

Corforth shook his head. "If you ask me, he's fooled everyone. He'll show up on TV any moment now."

All life ebbed from the President's face. He moved with hesitant steps toward the door. "I'm going to the East Wing. Might as well. Nothing for me here." He paused, leaning heavily on a wing-backed chair. Corforth could hardly make himself meet his eyes. Dark rings circled them and lines sagged around his trembling mouth. In a matter of hours, POTUS had become an old man.

The President seemed to recognize Corforth's discomfort, though he misinterpreted its source. "You can abandon ship if you wish, Eugene. Obviously, you wouldn't be alone."

Not waiting for a response, he left.

The television in John Wright's living room was on, the sound muted. No one in the room spoke. If Operation Integrity had gone as expected, if Grant was still free to speak, then his press conference would begin in the next five minutes.

If he was alive to speak—that thought roamed the back of everyone's mind, though no one allowed himself to form it into words, even mentally.

Rachel was comforted by the presence of her family and friends, these precious people who had been so stalwart in their support despite the odds, despite the threats to themselves. Regardless of the outcome of this day or of tomorrow's election, she hoped she would never forget or even minimize the extent of the sacrifice and courage of all of their friends. She and Bob owed a debt impossible to repay. But wasn't that the definition of a patriot: someone who denied self in order to provide freedom and justice for others?

Two minutes left. Her heart thudded in her chest, every beat a prayer.

The picture on the TV changed to a live shot. India's fingers tightened painfully on her mother's hand. Rachel wanted to smile reassuringly, but she was unable to force her eyes from the television.

With Stephen Yao in the lead, Bob Grant, dressed in an only slightly mussed navy suit, white shirt, and red tie, walked out of the elevator on the studio level of the CNN building. Sheriff Jenks, officially attired in his tan uniform shirt, badge gleaming above the pocket, walked at his side. Only a slight hitch in his step gave indication of his pain.

One of Yao's agents was waiting for them. He handed Yao several thick manila envelopes.

"I labeled each one by the affidavit it contains," the operative said as he fell in step with them. "Mrs. Novitsky said you were aware of the contents of each." He addressed this last sentence to Grant, who nodded.

"And the pictures?" Grant asked.

"Clear shots. We blew them to 10 x 14."

Yao opened the door to the studio. One of Goldie's friends, an executive of CNN, was waiting for them.

Grant and Jenks were miked and escorted by an excited technician to a table and floor mike in front of three cameras. Grant placed Frederickson's briefcase under the table.

Only then were those in charge told of his presence. Only then were cameramen sent to the room. Almost immediately, other CNN personnel rushed in, all flushed with the media scoop which would be theirs.

As a hush descended, Grant closed his eyes in prayer. He had seconds only, but his needs were simple: wisdom to speak the truth and faith to accept the outcome, whatever it might be.

In moments, Senator Robert Hawkins Grant would begin the speech for his life.

The news of Grant's impending broadcast immediately reached NIIA headquarters in Washington.

"Grant's going to be on CNN!"

"Which studio?"

"We think Atlanta."

"Contact Bender. He arrived there fifteen minutes ago and is already headed in that direction. He can handle Grant. But get hold of Bender now!"

We interrupt CNN's regular programming for a CNN exclusive live broadcast of Senator Robert Hawkins Grant, the man accused by the President of the United States of earlier today assassinating Attorney General Jonathan Hunter. With Senator Grant in our studio is Jimmy Jenks, sheriff of Oconee County, Georgia. Sheriff Jenks has been investigating the murder of reporter Russell Frederickson. Senator Grant is accused of that murder as well."

Grant, with Jenks beside him, appeared on the screen. Then the camera angle tightened to show only Grant. Grant: formidable but at ease. Grant: confident in the truth.

Heeding Yao's warning that the door at the back of the studio might open at any moment—NIIA agents arriving to silence him—Grant had chosen his opening words for the greatest impact.

"It is with sorrow for our nation that I come before you today," he began gravely. "For the past two weeks my family and I have been subjected to an evil and unremitting persecution, a persecution planned and implemented by the President of the United States."

Grant never looked toward it but was acutely aware of the door behind the middle camera, the only door into the room.

"Unfortunately, to further his quest for personal power, our President has held himself above the law and has held human life as expendable. Tonight, as a sitting United States Senator, I demand the impeachment of the President of the United States of America."

The door flew open.

"Grant! There's Grant!" Derek Bender's voice.

Grant's face was obliterated from the TV screen by a huge gray-suited back. Another camera zoomed in. Televisions around the world pictured Grant being manhandled by four burly NIIA agents.

Estelle didn't know why she'd come to the library to watch. Maybe because Eugene Corforth was there, and she felt she owed him her support. Maybe because she felt sorry for her husband. Strange, if that was true, but Chadwick Stevenson as well as the Vice President, that infamous voyeur to power, had refused to come. Even Amy Corforth had become suddenly ill. Somehow, Estelle had been unable to add to her husband's abandonment.

No one spoke, even when Grant's face disappeared from the screen.

Estelle clutched the arms of her chair. She wanted Grant to be allowed to speak. She desperately thought he deserved that right. So much evil had been attributed to him and without any opportunity for him to refute it.

Just as desperately, she wanted him to be taken away, forever silent. She feared what he would say. She looked at her husband and shuddered to see that same fear written in his sunken eyes and drawn mouth. What horrors were enacted in your name that cause you to silently die before my eyes? she wondered despairingly.

Leave the Senator alone!" Jenks's disembodied voice boomed over the airwaves. "He's innocent, I tell you! Is this the American way, condemnation without justice?"

The agents, confused and wary, loosened their grip momentarily. Grant straightened his suit coat and spoke into the microphone. "I ask for a few minutes only. Then if you still demand it, I'll go with you."

"Arrest him!" Derek Bender barked. He strode purposefully toward the front. More agents hurried in behind him.

The cameras whirred, recording Bender's anger and the drawn 9mm semiautomatic pistol held steady in his fist. In stark contrast was the calm assurance of Grant even as his arm was twisted behind his back and his knees kicked from under him.

"Turn off those cameras!" Bender yelled.

Agents grabbed for them, putting their hands over the lenses while they tried to disconnect the power. The picture went black, but Jenks's words rang out all the more dramatically. "Senator Grant is innocent. I'm Sheriff Jimmy Jenks of Oconee County, Georgia. I know who killed Russell Frederickson." His voice faded as he twisted from an agent. He grunted in pain but continued speaking, his words carrying a breathless intensity. "The NIIA is afraid for the American people to learn the truth. They're afraid you'll learn of their gross abuse of power and obstruction of justice."

A camerawoman, her handheld camera steady on her shoulder and directed at Grant, stepped out from behind a backdrop where Stephen Yao had stationed her.

"Take that camera from her!" Bender shouted.

"Let Grant speak!" the camerawoman demanded, clinging to her camera and repeating what Yao had told her to say. "Or is the NIIA afraid of the truth!"

"Let Grant speak!" Yao yelled.

CNN personnel, seeing their advantage being taken from them, joined him.

"You can arrest Grant later!"

"What are you afraid of?"

"Let Grant speak!"

Bender looked from Grant to the handheld camera. Its red light glowed like a warning. His job was on the line. Bender knew it. Everyone viewing knew it. And in the new NIIA, he was unsure of his duty. Hunter was dead, Bender reminded himself, and this single-minded manhunt for Grant, spearheaded by Hunter, had been suspect from the beginning.

"All right, he can speak," Bender growled, moving away from the angry eye of the camera. "Stay right beside him," he told his agents, "but let him speak. Lock and guard all exits," he added to agents at the back of the room. He began holstering his gun.

"And the sheriff?" Grant asked, picking himself up and moving to the table.

"Uncuff him," Bender said resignedly. The agents holding Jenks hesitated. "Take them off!" Bender barked.

They complied. Jenks came to stand beside Grant. Agents followed him, staying just out of camera range.

Grant reached down and retrieved the briefcase, thankful that no one had bothered it during the brief tussle. As Grant opened it, Jenks suddenly leaned heavily on the table, his eyes squeezed tight. Grant watched his struggle. By now red lights glowed on every camera. Tension rose almost unbearably.

Grant was ready to call for a doctor when Jenks opened his eyes, slowly removed a huge white handkerchief from his back pocket, wiped the sweat from his forehead, and nodded to Grant.

"Thank you," Grant said, gently touching his shoulder. Then he turned back to the cameras. The air was expectant, like the heavy dull throb before a violent storm.

"I repeat," Grant said, his tone resonating with the fervor of innocence, "it is with regret that I, as a sitting United States Senator, must demand the impeachment of the President of the United States. I'll present my evidence. I ask you, the American people, to judge its worth.

"The trail of deceit began during the last presidential election. Finding himself far behind in the polls, our current President, the challenger, hired John Smythe, a nefarious underworld agent, to grasp victory from sure humiliation. Within weeks, the incumbent President was accused of accepting a bribe from a foreign government. That allegation was based on information fabricated by John Smythe. Our current President was subsequently elected, largely because of those lies. As the newly elected President, his first act was to pardon his predecessor, ostensibly a generous gesture to save the nation from the shame of a trial. Actually, he acted to prevent the thorough examination that a trial would have demanded.

"He conducted himself in a manner that was not only dishonorable but which also dishonored a man of unblemished reputation, our former President. He, as you know, died almost immediately, a broken man lacking the will to live, according to media reports. I have reason to believe his death was not natural, that, in fact, he was murdered—"

"Murdered!" someone in the studio gasped.

"Yes, murdered," Grant said. His eyes blazed with fierce passion, but his face remained expressionless. "Murdered by a mercenary known as John Smythe to prevent a private probe into the evidence of the bribery accusation. I ask for an immediate and comprehensive investigation into both the bribery charge and the subsequent murder, including an exhumation of the body for a comprehensive autopsy. That an American President could be framed, run from office, and then murdered is a black mark on our country's history, one that must be rectified immediately.

"Russell Frederickson, a reporter for the *Washington Herald,* was murdered while investigating that same bribery charge. On the surface the charge appeared irrefutable. On examination by Frederickson, the truth was revealed: No bribery could have taken place because no money had been involved. A bogus electronic trail camouflaged a transfer of money which never occurred. Frederickson called Anne Peabody, the broker who originally leveled the bribery accusation. He confronted her with an outline of his suspicions and made an appointment with her for the next day. Ms. Peabody immediately reviewed the appropriate files and pulled up some information on her computer. Then in great agitation, she placed a call to Attorney General Jonathan Hunter.

"Forty hours later, both Ms. Peabody and Mr. Frederickson had been brutally murdered.

"The phone call from Russell Frederickson to Anne Peabody as well as the one from Anne Peabody to Attorney General Hunter have been confirmed by Ms. Peabody's secretary and by phone records from the Department of Justice. The notes Frederickson made after his phone call with Ms. Peabody and his documentation of the bogus bribery evidence were retrieved from his computer at the *Washington Herald*. All this evidence has been sworn to under oath by Ms. Peabody's secretary and by representatives of every financial institution, both domestic and international, that was compromised by Smythe's operation."

Grant lifted two stacks of papers which Jenks had laid ready for him on the table. "These are those sworn statements," Grant said, turning them toward the camera.

He replaced them and picked up two single sheets of paper. "These composite drawings," he said as the camera zoomed in on them, "one of the murderer of Anne Peabody," he lifted the one sent by Alvarez, "and one of the murderer of Russell Frederickson," he lifted the other, "suggest that both murderers are, in truth, the same man.

"Russell Frederickson was murdered to prevent disclosure of the bogus bribery plot. Anne Peabody was murdered by the same man because she discovered she'd been deceived, thereby becoming a potential threat."

Grant returned the composites to the table.

"These questions remain: Who is this man John Smythe who so callously murdered Russell Frederickson and Anne Peabody, and why was I brought into the plot? Part of the answer lies with the late Senator from New York, Phillip Loomis, who discovered that someone using the code name Bonfire was mounting a campaign to destroy my reputation. Drug and adultery charges were to be the basis for the attack. Senator Loomis tried to warn me, and as a result he had to be eliminated.

"Yes, Phillip Loomis was murdered.

"Sheriff Jenks has reviewed the evidence found at the scene after Loomis's death and ignored by NIIA investigators. This evidence indicates that Loomis did not commit suicide as was alleged. No powder burns were found on his body; a left-handed man, he was shot in the right temple; and though he had lost much blood, little evidence of bleeding was found at the supposed death scene. I repeat—Senator Phillip Loomis was murdered. I ask that the investigation into his death be reopened.'"

Grant picked up the letter from Loomis which Jenks had laid ready for him.

"Phillip Loomis wrote this letter to me the night he was murdered," Grant said, holding the letter so nothing damaging to Loomis, or more importantly to Janet Loomis and her sons, would be revealed. "I received the letter only yesterday evening. In it, Senator Loomis described the plan to destroy me, attributing it to a shadowy figure he knew only as Bonfire. Loomis ended the letter by saying he feared for his life because of what he'd discovered. Were it not for Senator Loomis's courage in trying to expose the plot against me, the truth might never have been revealed.

"And so another question must be added to our list of questions. Who is this mysterious Bonfire who murdered Senator Loomis and plotted my destruction?"

Grant returned the letter to the table. Deep lines of fatigue were chiseled into his face. His eyes were bleak, those of a man saddened by what he'd learned, not of a man exulting in his vindication. He looked at Jenks, who gave him a slight nod. Grant faced the cameras once again.

"Senator Loomis was dead," he continued, "but Bonfire couldn't be sure Loomis hadn't gotten word to me or to someone else; therefore, Bonfire concocted another plan. I was to take the blame for the murder of Russell Frederickson, a murder that was necessary to silence his investigation into the bribery. Unfortunately for Bonfire, Sheriff Jenks all but ruled me out as a suspect in that murder, in part because telephone records indicated I was on the phone at the crucial time. However, Attorney General Hunter ordered the NIIA to take over the investigation. The NIIA had only one suspect: me. They considered only that evidence which implicated me.

"They alleged that Frederickson had discovered I'd had an affair and that I killed him to protect my secret. A letter was produced that seemed irrefutable proof of my infidelity. This is the composite drawing of the man who fabricated and planted that letter."

Grant held up the drawing. He remained silent, allowing time for every viewer to draw the obvious conclusion.

"Yes," he said, tapping the picture, "the same man who murdered Anne Peabody and Russell Frederickson also planted the forged evidence incriminating me. My innocence to this loathsome adultery charge is attested to in the diary of the unfortunate young woman implicated in the affair and in a sworn affidavit from the man whose child she was carrying."

Grant held up the plastic diary. It looked even more pathetic under the harsh glare of the studio lights. Then, careful to cover the signature, he held up George Beterman's statement.

"The attacks against me escalated, and—I find this unconscionable—my son Bailey was made the target. I have affidavits," he said, holding them up, "from two individuals, indicating they were part of a conspiracy to set up my son on drug charges. The ultimate purpose of that scheme was to embarrass and further discredit me. One of these individuals acted because she honestly believed the country would be better served were I no longer Senator. The other was paid. This second individual has sworn in his affidavit that the person who hired him used the code name Bonfire.

"At the same party where my son was 'set up' by these tools of Bonfire, Joey Hunter, son of the attorney general, inadvertently ingested a lethal combination of drugs and alcohol. All evidence of Joey Hunter's presence at the party, of the true nature of his drug-related medical emergency, and of his transport by ambulance from the party to the hospital where he subsequently died were omitted from the police report and his hospital records. I don't blame Attorney General Hunter for wanting to protect his son; however, I do fault him for using circumstantial evidence to try to destroy my son. A Breathalyzer test as well as urine and blood samples taken at the scene detected no trace of drugs in my son's body. At no time has my son bought, sold, or used drugs. His only crime was in trying to prevent friends from doing something stupid, taking drugs, and then in trying to prevent them from harming themselves when they wouldn't listen.

"Nonetheless, Bailey was transported to jail, and pictures of him in handcuffs were shown on television and run in newspapers throughout the country. As with the accusations of murder and infidelity against me, Bailey was immediately tried and convicted by the media of our country, tried and convicted on the basis of highly questionable 'evidence.'"

Grant stared out at the CNN personnel and NIIA agents who filled the room. Almost as one, they leaned forward expectantly, transfixed by his words. He could only hope that millions of others were equally interested and that they understood the implications. Such a tortuous trail of deceit and callous disregard for life was involved! One presentation couldn't begin to explain the intricacies. He consulted his notes, drawing out the suspense.

"Bonfire's next attempt to discredit me," he continued, "involved drugs as well. It had its roots in this past summer. You have no doubt heard or read the statement of convicted drug dealer Hal Olexey in which he swears I bought drugs from him. You have no doubt seen the photograph purporting to show me buying those drugs. Both are false. The picture was taken last summer at a national fund-raiser attended by more than a thousand people. Further, Olexey was paid to go to prison in order to implicate me. I have the sworn statements of five people who heard Olexey's mother say her son had been paid to frame 'someone big.' Her words. Since Olexey's imprisonment, she has bought a new home and a new car, paid for with cash."

Grant picked up another set of papers.

"This is a copy of the drug report supposedly gathered over a period of several years by the DEA arm of the NIIA. This report suggests that I have a history of suspected drug abuse. The entire report is false and was planted by Bonfire. Every word is a lie. Again, the media chose to trumpet it as the truth. Again, the media was unwilling to do the investigative work necessary to substantiate the claims.

"This"—he picked up another set of papers—"is the computer readout from the same DEA/NIIA computer that stored that false file. This readout of the computer's log shows that my drug file was input into that computer"—he smacked the report against his hand to emphasize each word—"only ... last ... week. I repeat: This report, which was supposed to have been gathered over a number of years, was first put into the DEA computer only one week ago. It is another clever fabrication. Had the NIIA not already decided on my guilt, had the media not already published it, this second bogus paper trail would have been uncovered. Only because of the conscientious work of Sheriff Jenks am I able to bring the truth to you now."

Jenks's face remained impassive as if such accolades were better left unsaid. In truth, the blot on law enforcement being revealed so methodically made this moment a sad one for him. No amount of personal acclaim could erase the stain.

"Now I must add a fourth murder to John Smythe's list. Cora Snyder. Dr. Snyder, another of Bonfire's paid operatives, used her influence in the university community to dupe unsuspecting idealists into doing

Bonfire's bidding. She did so for money. I have copies of her bank accounts, showing several deposits of large sums. Each deposit correlates with a period of campus unrest.

"Dr. Snyder is the one who recruited the student to set up Bailey on drug charges. When that plan failed to compromise my son completely, Dr. Snyder phoned my son, requesting a meeting. Sheriff Jenks has a tape recording of that conversation."

The sheriff held up a plastic bag containing the tape.

"At that meeting, instead of providing information about the plot against me as she'd promised, Dr. Snyder planted a bag of cocaine on Bailey. Apparently that meeting was also supposed to be a setup for his murder. When the former military intelligence officers who were acting as Bailey's bodyguards foiled the murder attempt, Dr. Snyder became the assassin's target. She was gunned down in cold blood by John Smythe. Bailey was accused of that murder just as Smythe planned.

"In sworn statements, the ex-military intelligence agents exonerate Bailey completely. In fact, the bullet that killed Cora Snyder was from a high-powered rifle fired from a vacant building across the street.

"No one witnessed the murderer of Cora Snyder; however, I am confident he was John Smythe, the same man who murdered Russell Frederickson, Anne Peabody, and our former President.

"I feel personally responsible for the sixth victim," Grant said. If his face had looked weary before, it looked haggard now. "My friend Ramon Guiterrez was critically wounded trying to protect me. Mr. Guiterrez, who remains in intensive care and is under guard to prevent a further attempt on his life, has identified John Smythe as his attacker. Only by the grace of God is Ramon Guiterrez still alive."

Grant stopped and looked steadily, unwaveringly, into the eye of the camera as if focused on the soul of the nation.

"Now we come to the attorney general of the United States, Jonathan Hunter," he said gravely. "His longtime friendship with our President is known to everyone. What may not be known is that for the past year, Mr. Hunter had made most decisions, domestic, international, and political, for the President and with the President's blessings. It was after a phone call to Attorney General Hunter that both Anne Peabody and Russell Frederickson were murdered.

"A high-level White House advisor has agreed to testify to the collusion with John Smythe by both the attorney general and the President. This source, who will remain anonymous until he can be provided proper protection, alleges that during the past presidential campaign, John Smythe was hired by Hunter with the knowledge of the President to secure the defeat of the former President. Several weeks later Anne Peabody made her damaging statement about the bribery. I repeat, Anne Peabody did so believing it to be the truth.

"This White House official will further testify that in July of this year, John Smythe was again mentioned, this time in connection with the upcoming presidential election. Because I was considered the strongest opponent the President could face in two years, Smythe was hired to insure I would be in no position to mount a challenge. A short time later, so close to my Senate election that I would have difficulty proving my innocence, I was accused of the murder of Russell Frederickson.

"John Smythe was initially recommended to Attorney General Hunter and the President by Edmund Miller, a senior White House staff member who died earlier today in a fiery crash in rural Virginia. Unknown to either Hunter or the President, Edmund Miller was in reality John Smythe."

Someone in the studio gave a startled exclamation.

"However," Grant continued, a tired sorrow in his eyes, "before I prove that an infamous international terrorist was a member of the inner circle of our own White House, an explanation of the NIIA is necessary.

"Because all federal law enforcement powers had been consolidated under the office of the attorney general and because the NIIA could grab control of any local investigation, Attorney General Hunter and through him Edmund Miller were able to monitor and control the local investigations into the murders of Russell Frederickson, Anne Peabody, and Cora Snyder. They were able to alter DEA/NIIA files. They were able to control Bailey's arrest and detainment. The computer logs at the NIIA and at the various local agencies involved show that Miller's White House computer was the one used to input and remove, in other words to doctor, the 'evidence' used against me and against my son.

"Standardization of all law enforcement computer equipment and software was necessary for Miller's schemes to succeed. It was Edmund Miller who initially suggested such a standardization to the attorney general, and it was Edmund Miller who drafted the bill which Congress passed.

"We don't yet know in what other instances this abuse of power was used to alter documents and records, to impede investigations, and to stifle justice. The impact could be far-reaching."

As he spoke, Grant was watching Bender at the back of the studio. Bender, his face ashen, groped for a chair and sagged into it. Grant continued, sure now he would be allowed to finish. He felt no elation.

"With the help of Sheriff Jenks and other concerned Americans, I was coming close to finding the truth, not just about John Smythe but about the White House involvement as well. Ironically, unaware of his other persona as John Smythe, Attorney General Hunter and the President decided to make Edmund Miller the scapegoat for their problems. They recognized that Miller possessed all the necessary qualifications. During the Peabody bribery episode, Miller had been administrative assistant to a high-ranking Senator. As such he had access to the information necessary to make the bribery plot succeed. Further, Miller was away from the White House during the crucial time of each murder.

"I can't tell you why Edmund Miller, wearing the beard of John Smythe, was at the grave of Joey Hunter this morning. However, Sheriff Jenks, convinced that Miller was Russell Frederickson's murderer, was keeping him under surveillance. At 6 A.M. this morning, the sheriff followed Miller from his apartment to an office complex on the D.C./Maryland border. When Miller walked out of that building several minutes later, he had transformed himself into the bearded John Smythe. The composites of the murderer of Russell Frederickson and Anne Peabody had come to life.

"Miller left his car in the parking lot, where I presume it still remains, and drove away in my car, a car which, unknown to me, had been stolen from my Washington, D.C., garage several days earlier. Sheriff Jenks followed Miller to Rockville Cemetery, where Joey Hunter is buried. The sheriff contacted me, and I arrived soon after."

Grant picked up the 10 x 14 photos Yao had been given as they walked into the studio. The shots, remarkably clear, were the ones taken at the cemetery. Grant sorted through them and picked one showing Hunter, his face tight with fear. Miller's back was to the camera. The black-and-white film captured the eerie shadows of the early morning gloom and the overcast sky. Grant's breathing quickened as the horrors of that morning flashed through his mind, horrors he'd been unable to anticipate or prevent. He held the photograph steady for the camera.

"Hunter met with Miller," Grant said after a few tension-filled moments. "We'll never know what was said, but we do know that when Miller left, Hunter was dead. He was shot with a gun stolen from my home, presumably at the same time my car was stolen."

Grant put that photograph down and picked up the one showing Miller bending over Hunter's body. He let the camera focus on it long enough for the tension in the room to again mount. Then he put that photograph back on the table and replaced it with the one showing Miller full face. The well-defined shadow of the winged angel, like a phantom avenger, played across the grass at Miller's feet.

"Yes," Grant said. "The man with the beard. The man who not only murdered Jonathan Hunter, but the man who murdered Anne Peabody and Russell Frederickson and attempted to murder Ramon Guiterrez."

Jenks held up the composites from Gayla Sergek and Scott Patterson. With the photograph still in one hand, Grant held up the Alvarez composite. Again, he waited, wanting the truth to hit hard.

"While we don't have eyewitnesses," he finally said, "we can assume that Edmund Miller's bloody hand also killed Cora Snyder and our former President. We must add Phillip Loomis to that list of murders because as we were soon to learn, Edmund Miller went by another alias, one other than John Smythe. Edmund Miller was also Bonfire, the mastermind of the operation. Edmund Miller, Bonfire, and John Smythe were one and the same person."

They replaced the composites, but Grant continued to hold the dramatic photograph of John Smythe under the shadow of the angel.

"I followed Miller, who was still driving my car, from the cemetery. Sheriff Jenks was close behind. According to airline tickets found later, Miller planned to catch a flight out of the country. Instead, he lost control of his car, slammed into a tree, and was killed."

Grant replaced the photograph.

"Before the car exploded, Sheriff Jenks in an extraordinary act of bravery retrieved Edmund Miller's briefcase, the briefcase he planned to take with him on his flight from this country."

Grimacing slightly in pain, Jenks lifted the briefcase and spoke into the microphone. "Edmund Miller had this briefcase with him, but it wasn't his. It was Russell Frederickson's. That's right. For some reason we'll never understand that arrogant assassin took the briefcase from the dead man after he'd shot him. And he kept it." Looking grim, Jenks leaned on it. His skin was gray under his faded summer tan. "Hidden in it, I found four passports in different names and with different pictures, including a legitimate one for Edmund Miller and a bearded one for John Smythe. According to his notes, Miller used another code name as well, Bonfire. I know for a fact both Bonfire and John Smythe are wanted by most every major country in the world. Edmund Miller, using those code names, has been the mastermind and frequently the perpetrator of the most depraved assassinations and terrorist attacks our world has been forced to endure. The record's right here in this notebook in his own words and in his own writing."

Jenks held up a plastic bag containing Miller's record of infamy.

"Miller was proud of his work," he continued, his face never changing expression. "He wrote down everything he'd ever done, going back seventeen years—names, places, dates, methods." He paused. "And what he got paid. This Son of Satan made millions wreaking havoc on our world."

He put the bag containing the diary down directly in front of him, where it couldn't just happen to disappear.

"Miller's personal computer was also in the briefcase," Grant said, Jenks standing impassively at his side. "In it he recorded numerous White House meetings, the conversations presumably verbatim for the most part. Sheriff Jenks has left that computer in a secure place until such time as he can turn it over to the Senate Intelligence Committee or a Congressional Impeachment Panel.

"And so we are back to the White House," Grant said slowly, "the beginning chapter of a long and sordid story. As you've seen, the President subverted this nation's law enforcement agencies through his manipulation of the NIIA. Knowingly or not, he conspired in at least four murders. He obstructed justice, tampered with evidence, and interfered with the elections of both a United States President and a United States Senator. For these reasons, I ask that this President be removed from office."

Grant stopped. He wanted time to imbue his words with the benchmark of truth, certainly, but he paused for a more fundamental reason. He needed to refocus his mind. For the last forty-eight hours, he had thought of little but this moment. He must be certain he'd said everything. He might never have another chance, certainly not before an audience of this magnitude.

"If the people of Georgia," he continued, "see their way to reelect me their Senator, I promise to insure a full and fair investigation into this White

House. Further, I promise to insure the return of law enforcement power to local agencies, where it belongs. Never again will the federal government be allowed to amass so much power that a few are able to control the many. Never again will such abuse of individual rights be tolerated."

It was time for him to close. Grant wanted those listening to understand that this was America and that American principles of freedom allowed good to ultimately triumph. He wanted to fire their souls with the hope and thanksgiving he truly felt. He wanted them to love America as he loved her and to be willing to fight to preserve her unique freedoms.

"Yes, this is a dark time for our nation," he said, his words ringing with the conviction of his beliefs, "but tomorrow we hold an election. This election, like those that have come before, proclaims the enduring principles on which our greatness was founded and for which we must be willing to sacrifice: Freedom. Honor. Selflessness. Respect for privacy, individuality, property. Hard work. Courage. Integrity.

"Tomorrow, as has been true of every election since the founding of our great nation, we can vote freely, casting our ballots for those we feel will best preserve these principles. Tomorrow, we can once again show the world that we, the people of the United States of America, will not tolerate any abuse of power. In the words of our second President, John Adams, ours must be a nation of 'Honest and Wise' leaders, willing to stand firm in preserving its liberties. That is our American legacy, and that legacy will once again preserve us from the evil of our enemies. The United States of America, the greatest nation the world has ever known, will triumph in this black time because our trust is based, not on man, but on God. In God there is no failing."

Eugene Corforth turned off the television. The room was overwhelmed with silence.

Finally, with infinite care, the President stood. He turned and slowly lifted his head. Eugene and Estelle. Only they remained. No one else. Nothing else. Only Eugene and Estelle. A tortured shudder wracked his body. He clenched his teeth, controlling it. He ignored the pitying hand Estelle reached toward him. He ignored the tears that only partly masked the horror in both their eyes.

He sucked in a lungful of air, exhaled, then spoke, looking at neither, talking to both.

"Forgive me. Please forgive me. I didn't realize. It didn't seem . . ." His voice trailed off as if even he recognized the futility of denial. The microscope of truth had laid bare years of rationalization. His head hung between his shoulders under the weight of his own conviction.

With halting steps, he walked to the door, pausing with his hand on the knob. He started to say more, couldn't, and left.

Seemingly directionless, he stopped just outside the door, his hands hanging by his side. Slowly, head still bowed, he turned and walked down the corridor.

His security detail fell in behind.

Walking outside, he crossed the breezeway that paralleled the Rose Garden. He didn't feel the cold. He didn't feel the wind, carrying with it the first icy bites of sleet.

Finally, he reached the Oval Office, entered, and closed the door, shutting it to all others. He was alone, blessedly alone.

Feeling like a stranger transported to an alien land, he leaned against a chair and slowly surveyed the room. The tall, narrow windows, looking out over the Rose Garden, the stately mahogany desk, the Presidential Seal in the blue carpet, the portrait of Washington above the white marble mantel, even the blazing fire itself: None brought him the warmth of remembrance. None seemed to welcome him.

With halting step, he walked behind his desk, the desk of the President of the United States. Just as he was ready to sit, a picture of Estelle and the children, resting on the table in front of the window, caught his eye. He'd forgotten it was there. He picked it up, his eyes softening as he regarded it. Almost tenderly, he placed it on the desk. Only then did he sit, the presidential flag on his left and the flag of his country on his right.

How had he come to this? he wondered in numbed confusion. What road had he not taken? What siren song had he heeded gladly as it wailed his destruction?

The photograph of his family drew him now. How could he have forgotten? How could he have thought anything worth such an unbearable sacrifice? His finger trembled as he touched each precious face. Thoughts of all he wished to say to them flooded his mind. The trembling overwhelmed him as he realized that fulfilling such a wish was not in his power.

Clenching his fists to control the trembling, he tore his eyes from the photograph, then reached down and clumsily took paper from a drawer. The Presidential Seal embossed in gold at the top of the paper hit him like a condemnation. How had he allowed himself to forget his purpose? So easy to blame others. The image of Estelle, lovely and loving, filled his mind. Tears stung his eyes. Too easy.

The pristine page of vellum mocked him. How could he explain to others what he was unable to explain to himself? He couldn't. All he could do was apologize.

Picking up his pen, the one he'd used with such relish so often the last two years, he began writing. Finished, he looked up and saw Estelle's face in the photograph in front of him. Her eyes reminded him of Eugene somehow: Eugene, who had recognized the danger and tried to warn him.

He wrote two more sentences. No one must ever doubt Eugene's loyalty to his country. At least it was in his power to insure that.

He wrote a final sentence, thought for a moment, knew nothing more could be added, and signed it.

Carefully, he folded the page into three equal parts and inserted it into an envelope. He started to address the front but stopped, his pen poised above. Who did he leave it to when he'd wronged an entire people? He centered the blank envelope on the desk.

One more letter to write. Darling Estelle. He broke down then, putting his head in his hands and sobbing.

Finally, he straightened his back and again picked up the pen. Time had almost run out. "My darling Estelle." He wrote four lines, unsure she would even care, but he had to tell her.

Regret. He had everything he'd always thought he wanted, and all he could feel was regret.

He folded the page, put it in an envelope, wrote her name on it, and put it with the other.

Again, he looked around the room, hoping to find comfort. None was there. He was an intruder.

This was as it should be, he thought, opening the bottom drawer. He'd failed Estelle and his family. He'd failed his country. He'd grabbed the power and forgotten the responsibility that went with it. He, and only he, had failed.

The gun was cold in his hand as he raised it to his head.

His last sight was of the Presidential Seal sculpted in plaster in the ceiling. Odd, he thought as he squeezed the trigger. He'd forgotten it was there.

The room was empty; the television screen black. Yet Estelle remained, motionless in the gathering shadows.

She heard running footsteps and muffled shouts. She knew what they meant, what they must mean. She had thought the sorrow she'd felt earlier that day and the night before and the day before that was as hurtful as she could endure, but now her heart was a ball of ice, its pointed shards ripping deep into her being. She would never be warm again. Never.

The door opened, spilling light from the hallway into the room. She looked into Eugene's eyes. Her heart caught at the gleam of tears she saw there.

She'd been right. Dear God, she'd been right. She held up her hand when he started to speak. "He's dead, isn't he?" she whispered.

Unable to speak, Corforth crossed the room and handed her an envelope. Her name was written on the front, the handwriting unmistakable. Sobbing, she clutched it to her breast. Her hands were too clumsy to open it. Her eyes were too full of tears to read it.

Corforth started to speak, realized she'd forgotten he was there, and silently left the room, softly closing the door.

Minutes passed before her body stopped its uncontrollable shaking. Unsteadily, the envelope unopened but still held close, she walked to a window. She stared out at the bare branches, recently so familiar, and wondered how they could have changed so much in only a few hours, how they could have become so mocking in their unfamiliarity. Unable to wait any longer, even as fearful as she was of what she might read, she removed the single sheet of stationery and unfolded it.

"My darling Estelle," she read. Tears blinded her, and she fought for control. My darling Estelle, she thought, her heart aching. He'd called her his darling. Her eyes devoured the rest.

"You were right—I didn't know what I was losing. Though I failed you in life, know that my love is yours for eternity. The children—please explain if you can. I'm so ashamed."

Four sentences, but for Estelle they meant more than anything her husband had ever given her. Carefully refolding the page, she replaced it in its envelope and pressed both next to her heart.

Turning, she walked to the door and out into the corridor. Upstairs, she called the children. Then she began packing to leave the White House.

Tuesday, November 3:
Election Day

Senator Robert Hawkins Grant was interviewed on the morning news shows of all three networks. His appearances were brief. Attention was focused on the suicide of the President and the assumption of office by the Vice President. Grant had to hope voters in Georgia understood the correlation between those events and his own campaign.

His family, friends, and a legion of supporters were canvassing Georgia, trumpeting his innocence to any who would listen. They called radio and television talk shows and argued the issues with vehement if not always eloquent conviction. They stood outside grocery stores, schools, shopping centers, any place they thought voters might be. They called every registered Republican, then went to see those who were still skeptical. They enlisted the help of anyone who expressed the slightest interest. In short, they did everything possible to spread the truth about their Senator, Robert Hawkins Grant.

The voting polls would close at seven that evening. After that it would be too late.

The newly sworn-in President surveyed the Oval Office with obvious satisfaction. The walls were bare. His first act had been to have all signs of his predecessor removed. Giving that order had afforded him great pleasure. Now he was in control, holding the position he'd coveted for as long as he could remember.

The office door opened.

"Mr. Masterson, sir," an agent announced.

Mike Masterson, visibly nervous but working to cover it, walked in. The President motioned him to a chair.

"The transition to the new administration will be a difficult one," the President said.

Masterson nodded warily, unsure of the reason for his summons, knowing it could mean disaster. He could feel sweat beading on his forehead. Should he wipe it away or would that only draw attention to it? He fidgeted, debating, when the President's next words sunk in.

"I'd like for you to be my press secretary."

"Me?" Masterson asked incredulously. "Me?"

"Yes, you," the President said with a pleased smile. "My administration faces a severe testing."

Masterson leaned forward, absorbing each word eagerly.

"The country has been shocked, and rightly so," the President continued. "I'm determined to mend the wounds of the past. What better way than to have you, Senator Grant's most valued advisor, at my side, the most visible member of my administration. Could anyone then doubt my sincere desire for peace and justice?"

"I'm honored, sir," Masterson said, barely able to hide his jubilation.

"You see no problems in assuming your duties immediately? Grant won't object to losing you on such short notice?"

"No, I'm certain the Senator won't object to losing me," Masterson said, an exultant laugh threatening to erupt at any moment. With effort he kept his face properly serious. "He is as cognizant of the need for bipartisan solidarity as you are, sir."

Returns are just beginning to come in from what has to be the most bizarre Senate election in history," a television announcer intoned. Elaine Thomas, the spokesperson for the "Grant Affair," was not handling coverage of the election. It would be a long time, if ever, before her face would reappear, a too-obvious reminder of the media's fallibility. "Incumbent Georgia Senator Robert Hawkins Grant is in a virtual dead heat with his challenger, respected businessman Tobias Caruso. To comment on the far-reaching implications of this race, one that is certain to go down to the wire is . . ."

It's almost over," Rachel Grant said from her position inside her husband's protective arm.

Grant smiled at her. He was tired, never more tired in his life. His body ached with fatigue. A few restful days with his family would cure that, but he wasn't sure anything could cure the heaviness in his soul. He'd seen too much. "Man's inhumanity to man." Murder, of course, but murder seemed benign compared to the deceit and betrayal that lurked beneath, destroying just as surely but without the clean finality of death.

At least the former President would be exonerated, Grant thought. At least that intolerable injustice would be righted even if atonement for his electoral defeat and murder were beyond attainment.

Grant caught Janet Loomis's eye and smiled. She, too, had found a modicum of comfort in the truth he'd brought. Phillip Loomis had not committed suicide. Instead he'd been murdered by Miller, murdered for trying to warn him, Senator Robert Hawkins Grant. Another death to hang around his own neck. Dear Janet. Would she think that measure of comfort worth the notoriety she might well receive? "The authorities" had promised that Phillip's hit-and-run accident wouldn't be made public nor would his abuse of office, but these were the same faceless powers who'd spent the last two weeks hounding and defaming Grant and his family, sure their cause was just. Could they be trusted to use common sense now?

Bonfire had been one of them, his anonymity, his cloak of bureaucratic verbosity and heavy-handedness shielding him from detection as well as magnifying his power. As John Smythe he'd murdered the former President, Anne Peabody, Russell Frederickson, Cora Snyder, and Jonathan Hunter. As Bonfire, he'd murdered Phillip Loomis. He'd compromised at least two administrations, dealt traitorously with numerous foreign powers and terrorists, and gloried in defiling all he touched. A trail of blood and betrayal stretched behind him, going back seventeen long years.

Except for the accident of a large dog in the middle of a deserted country road, a similar trail had threatened to expand before him. This time, however, carefully chosen pawns, manipulated by him from a distance, would have continued to wreak his havoc. Grant thought of Mike Masterson, and his gut twisted.

Masterson: Bonfire's hand-chosen minion.

Masterson: the traitor.

And now Masterson was to be the mouthpiece for the new administration! Miller hadn't mentioned Masterson in his notebooks, not by name, but Grant knew.

Masterson: in Phillip Loomis's confidence, then transferred to Grant when Loomis had become expendable.

Masterson: reporting on Grant's conversations, his meetings, his plans.

Masterson: sabotaging Grant's every effort to clear himself.

How many other Mastersons, how many other Millers were buried in the basic fiber of the country, undermining and debasing the good of the majority of the people?

Bonfire had betrayed his country and gloated in that betrayal. Much of his evil work might never be made public, but his influence would be felt in all levels of government, business, even the media, for years to come. So many had been compromised. So many would be unwilling to accept their own culpability.

Grant's eyes clouded. The late President had taken full responsibility for his actions as well as for those made in his behalf. In a terse, unemotional letter, he had outlined his dealings with John Smythe. He had made no mention of Jonathan Hunter, even of Edmund Miller. He'd implicated no one else. His darkest hour had become his hour of greatest courage and dignity. The only other name he'd mentioned had been that of Eugene Corforth and that to exonerate him of any knowledge of wrongdoing. The Vice President—now the President!—had received no such commendation because his hands were as bloody as the rest.

The gunshot that had been the President's judgment on his own guilt had catapulted that same Vice President into the most powerful position in the world.

Grant felt Rachel's hand grasp his own. He looked down into her serene eyes, overflowing with love.

"Dad."

He turned to Henry.

"Dad, we want you to know," Henry said, indicating India, Olivia, and Bailey, "that even if you don't win, we think you're the best."

"No one could be prouder of their father than we are of you," Bailey said earnestly. "You *are* the best, Dad."

Grant regarded Bailey, his arm draped around Sherrill. Their eyes returned his look, almost pleading for him to understand. Grant felt a slight ease in the burden he carried in his heart.

"We hated everything they said about you," Bailey continued, "but we knew it wasn't true. You were right. Nothing can change the truth, not words, not proof, not having everyone believe it."

"Not even that stupid Peter Evans and his stupid paper," Henry added with a scowl. "Boy, is he a jerk!"

Suddenly, Grant felt free. He started chuckling, then laughing outright. The others watched for a moment uncertainly, then they, too, joined in.

Grant was surrounded by those he loved, laughing and exulting in their shared love and respect. Jenks's southern twang, out-twanged by that of his Deputy Hank Farrar, mixed with the Washingtonian accents of

Cynthia and Janet, the excited babble of Tucker and Melissa's children, the elation of his friends and family.

On the television, votes continued to be tabulated. Would he win? Grant wondered, or would Bonfire's hand be felt even now, nudging Caruso to victory? And what about Masterson and the newly sworn-in President? With another laugh, Grant turned his back on the television, glorying instead in the sight of his loved ones, safe and free.

Regardless of the outcome of the election, tomorrow he would begin digging into the evil that Bonfire had unleashed. Excising that evil cleanly from the heart and soul of the nation was to be his mission. Only then would Operation Integrity have succeeded.

But that was tomorrow. Tonight, he would celebrate the freedom which allowed him to be with his family and friends. If Bonfire had done any good, it was to remind him that nothing could be more precious or more worthy of celebration.

"Look, Dad," Henry said excitedly, pointing to the TV.

"With 99 percent of the precincts reporting and with a 52 percent to 48 percent margin, Senator Robert Hawkins Grant has been reelected to a third term in the United States Senate."

We want to hear from you. Please send your comments about this
book to us in care of the address below. Thank you.

ZondervanPublishingHouse
Grand Rapids, Michigan 49530
http://www.zondervan.com